Tempting Fate

A VOLUME IN THE SERIES

Cornell Studies in Security Affairs

Edited by Robert J. Art, Robert Jervis, and Stephen M. Walt

A list of titles in this series is available at cornellpress.cornell.edu.

Tempting Fate

*Why Nonnuclear States Confront
Nuclear Opponents*

PAUL C. AVEY

Cornell University Press

Ithaca and London

Copyright © 2019 by Cornell University

First published 2019 by Cornell University Press

Library of Congress Cataloging-in-Publication Data

Names: Avey, Paul C., author.
Title: Tempting fate : Why nonnuclear states confront nuclear
    opponents / Paul Avey.
Description: Ithaca, [New York] : Cornell University Press, 2019. |
    Series: Cornell studies in security affairs | Includes bibliographical
    references and index.
Identifiers: LCCN 2019019612 (print) | LCCN 2019020251 (ebook) |
    ISBN 9781501740404 (epub/mobi) | ISBN 9781501740398 (pdf) |
    ISBN 9781501740381 | ISBN 9781501740381 (cloth)
Subjects: LCSH: Asymmetric warfare—Case studies. | Nuclear
    weapons—Government policy—Case studies. | No first use
    (Nuclear strategy)—Case studies. | Security, International—
    Case studies.
Classification: LCC U163 (ebook) | LCC U163 .A983 2019 (print) |
    DDC 355.02—dc23
LC record available at https://lccn.loc.gov/2019019612

To Mom and Dad

Contents

Image

Acknowledgments

Nuclear weapons hold out the promise of peace through the prospect of devastation. That is a dangerous bargain. The number of wars that have occurred when only one side has nuclear weapons suggest that it is also a fragile one. Regardless of whether one views nuclear weapons as a benefit or danger to humanity, they are not likely to disappear anytime soon. Like many other students of nuclear politics, then, I believe that it is important to grapple with the nature and the limits of the nuclear shadow. This book represents one contribution to that effort.

It is common in acknowledgments to note that many individuals had a profound influence on the final product. I never fully appreciated just how true that was until I went through the process myself. This book is very different today from when it began. Its strengths are due to the patience of many friends and colleagues who took time to engage with this project. Its weaknesses remain those of its author.

My biggest intellectual debt is to Michael Desch. The idea for this book took hold while I was working with him on a separate project at Notre Dame. Mike is a model for how to be a scholar, and his support has been instrumental at every stage of this book and in my career. Keir Lieber, Dan Lindley, and Sebastian Rosato shaped much of my thinking on international relations. They have each read and offered incisive comments on multiple drafts, particularly during the critical early period, and continue to provide guidance today. Frank Gavin, Todd Sechser, Nicholas Miller, James Wilson, James Cameron, and Tim McDonnell all graciously read the entire manuscript and gave up a full day to meet to discuss it. Their insightful suggestions led to significant changes that made the book much stronger. Eric Jardine, Barry Posen, Robert Reardon, Joshua Shifrinson,

Rachel Whitlark, and Zachary Zwald all read multiple chapters, in many cases multiple times, and provided detailed feedback. At Cornell University Press I thank Roger Haydon, the anonymous referee, and the series editors for their direction and careful reading of the manuscript. Their suggestions helped me clarify many key claims.

Portions of this book draw on material previously published in Paul C. Avey, "Who's Afraid of the Bomb? The Role of Nuclear Non-use Norms in Confrontations between Nuclear and Non-nuclear Opponents," *Security Studies* 24 (2015), reprinted by permission of Taylor & Francis Ltd.

I benefited greatly from the diverse intellectual environments at several institutions that provided me space to work on this book. I am grateful to each one. The research began at the University of Notre Dame and expanded with the support of the Managing the Atom and International Security Program at the Belfer Center for Science and International Affairs at Harvard University. The Stanton Foundation provided generous funding to allow me to spend a year with MIT's Security Studies Program. I thank Chris Alkhoury for his excellent guidance through the Iraqi documents then held at the Conflict Records Research Center. The John G. Tower Center for Political Studies at SMU offered me the ability to refine my thinking at a key stage of the project. I owe special thanks to Joshua Rovner for his support and willingness to discuss a wide range of issues while I was there and since. I finished the book as a faculty member in the political science department at Virginia Tech, which offers a collegial and stimulating environment spurred on by a wide range of perspectives. It is a great place to call home.

For helpful conversations, feedback, and support, I thank Megan Becker, Mark Bell, Kirstin J. H. Brathwaite, Robert Brathwaite, Stephen Brooks, Matthew Bunn, Peter Campbell, Mauro Caraccioli, Fotini Christia, Owen Coté, Rebecca Davis-Gibbons, François Debrix, Priya Dixit, Melissa Emmert, Greg Endicott, Charles Fagan, Patrick Flavin, Gene Gerzhoy, Nicholas Goedert, Kim Hedge, James Hollifield, Karen Hult, Caitlin Jewitt, Jason Kelly, Karin Kitchens, Margarita Konaev, Alexander Lanoszka, Christine Leah, Chad Levinson, Timothy Luke, Susan Lynch, Sean Lynn-Jones, Richard Maass, Martin Malin, Jonathan Markowitz, Steven Miller, Vipin Narang, Scott Nelson, David Palkki, Soul Park, Abigail Post, Bruce Pencek, Dianne Pfundstein Chamberlain, Miranda Priebe, Besnik Pula, Ray Rafidi, Matthew Reitz, Joli Divon Saraf, Ji Hye Shin, Gregory Shufeldt, Ray Thomas, Edward Weisband, and William Wohlforth. My sincere apologies to anyone I have forgotten.

Most of all, I thank my family. I dedicate this book to my parents, Kathy and Donald. Their support at each stage of my life has been unwavering. I would not have been in a position to even begin this book without them. Their biggest influence, though they may not know it, has been through their own example of humility, fairness, and hard work. I have tried to bring these traits to my research and how I live my life. My sister, Laura, has offered her encouragement as long as I can remember. I could not ask for a better one. Finally, I thank my wife and best friend, Megan. Her grace and good humor while we moved from Indiana to Massachusetts to Texas to Virginia made completing this book possible. She is an unfailing source of love and support to a grateful husband.

Tempting Fate

Introduction

Surveying the devastation in Japan after World War II, the United States Strategic Bombing Survey concluded that "no more forceful arguments for peace and for the international machinery of peace than the sight of the devastation of Hiroshima and Nagasaki have ever been devised."[1] The world quickly sought to make sense of the "absolute weapon."[2] Yet the power of the two bombs unleashed in 1945 would pale compared to the thermonuclear variants that would follow. The sheer speed and destructiveness of nuclear arms seemed to constitute a "nuclear revolution," destined to upend international politics.[3] Any country that lacked a nuclear arsenal would find itself vulnerable, unable to prevent becoming the target of a nuclear strike by threatening retaliation on the same scale.

Despite these weapons' awesome power, though, countries without nuclear arms have not shied away from challenging and resisting nuclear-armed states. In 1948, less than three years after the United States had demonstrated its willingness to use nuclear weapons, the Soviet Union blockaded Berlin, directly challenging the American nuclear monopoly. The Soviets then stood firm for nearly a year against US efforts to undermine that blockade. Two years later, the young People's Republic of China attacked US troops in Korea. Egypt and Syria combined to launch a massive assault on Israeli forces in October 1973. Iraq ignored US threats in 1990, and Serbia did likewise in 1999. In 1979, nonnuclear Vietnam fought a war against nuclear-armed China. The list goes on. According to one widely used conflict list, there have been sixteen wars between nuclear weapon states and nonnuclear weapon states from 1945 to 2010 and hundreds of lower-level militarized disputes. During that same period there were nineteen wars between states with no nuclear weapons. In other words, wars in which one side holds a nuclear monopoly occur about as often as those between states where neither side has nuclear weapons. Moreover, the nonnuclear weapon state (NNWS) frequently starts the trouble. In other cases,

1

the NNWS could have ceded to the demands of the nuclear weapon state (NWS) without giving up its rule or territory. Instead, it resisted.[4]

Why has the "absolute weapon" so frequently failed to impress states without it? This type of conflict is puzzling for both deterrence and compellence explanations. Bernard Brodie, whose early writings served as the foundation for thinking about nuclear politics, and whom nuclear strategist and Nobel laureate Thomas C. Schelling called "the dean of us all," wrote that "certainly a monopoly of atomic bombs would be a sufficiently clear definition of superiority to dissuade the other side from accepting the gage of war unless directly attacked."[5] After the Cold War, Robert A. Pape argued that "when nuclear capabilities are completely one-sided . . . if the coercer's capability is relatively unlimited, coercive success is virtually assured."[6] Addressing the United States specifically, James J. Wirtz highlights that theory predicts without "the constraints of mutual assured destruction or in some cases the possibility of even weak retaliation in kind, the United States and its allies should enjoy great success in deterring weaker states or compelling them to comply with their wishes."[7]

In perhaps the most important statement on the nuclear revolution, Robert Jervis argued that mutual vulnerability induced restraint.[8] He recognized that if one party gained a nuclear first-strike capability—if one side could completely eliminate the opponent's arsenal—the situation would be vastly different. Yet his key insight that vulnerability induces caution can be applied to nuclear monopoly. The extreme vulnerability of an NNWS facing a nuclear opponent should encourage restraint. That danger should deter the NNWS from acting against the NWS. To be sure, the NWS might use nuclear weapons as a shield with which to conduct aggression against its hapless nonnuclear-armed opponents.[9] Yet even then states without nuclear weapons should give in to all but the most extreme demands rather than risk a conflict in an environment of intense vulnerability.

A number of studies support these theoretical expectations by showing that nuclear superiority has historically provided political benefits. These include both deterrence (preventing an adversary from acting) and compellence (causing an adversary to change its behavior).[10] Historian Marc Trachtenberg and political scientists Keir Lieber and Daryl Press have all found that US nuclear advantages relative to the Soviet Union in the early Cold War provided significant benefits during crises.[11] Beyond the American case, Kyle Beardsley and Victor Asal argue that states with nuclear weapons facing nonnuclear opponents tend to prevail—by which they mean "either gaining concessions or having an opponent back down from its demands"—and prevail quickly. As they conclude, "the immense damage from the possibility of [nuclear] escalation is enough to make an opponent eager to offer concessions. Asymmetric crises allow nuclear states to use their leverage to good effect."[12] Erik Gartzke and Dong-Joon Jo show that nuclear weapons provide broad bargaining advantages to their possessors.[13] And Matthew Kroenig finds that states with larger nuclear arsenals than their opponents tend to win crises. As he puts it, "States in a position of nuclear superiority are more likely to issue compellent threats and to achieve compellent success."[14] If correct, then complete asymmetry in nuclear capabilities should provide substantial benefits.

Even those that contend nuclear weapons are poor tools for compellence generally accept that nuclear weapons are nevertheless useful for deterrence. Thus, Matthew Furhmann and Todd Sechser argue that the "ability to destroy does not necessarily convey the ability to [compel]," but add that nuclear weapons are "useful for deterrence . . . as weapons of self-defense, they are irreplaceable."[15] Indeed, they find that simply having an alliance with a nuclear-armed state provides benefits against would-be challengers.[16] If an alliance with a nuclear state helps, one would expect that actual possession of a nuclear weapon would deter nonnuclear opponents.[17]

The coercive benefits of nuclear weapons are also at the center of strategic explanations for nuclear proliferation. According to these arguments, states facing large security threats will seek nuclear weapons. Such arguments therefore rest on the view that nuclear monopoly matters.[18] If a nonnuclear state faces a nonnuclear opponent with superior conventional capabilities, then building a nuclear arsenal to manufacture a condition of nuclear monopoly can offset that danger and provide bargaining leverage. Conversely, if a nonnuclear state faces a nuclear-armed opponent, then acquiring a nuclear arsenal is beneficial because it eliminates nuclear monopoly. That allows the formerly nonnuclear state to deter nuclear strikes and counter efforts at nuclear blackmail. As Mao Zedong noted in 1956, China needed a nuclear weapon because "in today's world, if we don't want to be bullied, then we cannot do without this thing."[19] In other words, nuclear monopoly provided a potential compellent advantage to China's nuclear-armed opponents that Mao sought to offset.

In sum, theory and evidence from a wide range of studies make NNWS belligerency toward nuclear rivals puzzling. Why, then, do states without nuclear weapons confront nuclear-armed opponents? A simple explanation would be that these conflicts occurred because no one believed nuclear weapons would be used. To begin with, I show that nonnuclear weapon states frequently did take their opponents' nuclear arsenal into consideration. Moreover, such an explanation is unsatisfying because it does not answer the more interesting questions: *why* would leaders believe that nuclear weapons would not be used in certain situations? What factors lead NNWS decision makers to discount the prospects for nuclear use and be willing to challenge or resist a nuclear-armed opponent?

The Argument

I argue that the nonnuclear weapon state is able to act because it can take advantage of various strategic and material inhibitions against the use of nuclear arms to minimize the likelihood of a nuclear strike. In essence, the NNWS identifies red lines and gambles that, by its not crossing those lines, the costs of nuclear weapon use for the nuclear-armed opponent will outweigh the benefits. The precise strategies available and pursued by the NNWS will vary across cases. In general, though, the more militarily capable the NNWS is relative to the NWS, the more difficult it will be for the NNWS to reduce the incentives for nuclear strikes. This forces a powerful NNWS to behave in a consistently constrained manner, and wars in nuclear monopoly will tend to occur only in the face of large power asymmetries favoring the NWS. My argument thus shows that nuclear weapons are neither irrelevant, as some argue, nor do they dictate state behavior. There are a variety of tools available to an NNWS to challenge, resist, and even win limited victories in a war against nuclear opponents.

States without nuclear weapons can focus on raising the costs or lowering the benefits of nuclear use for the NWS. There are real material and strategic costs to using nuclear weapons that constrain nuclear-armed states. These include the possibility that nuclear use destroys valuable objectives, harms friends or neutral states, generates diplomatic backlash from those not directly affected, expands a conflict to include new actors, or encourages nuclear proliferation. The NNWS can manipulate many of these factors in different situations to further raise the costs of nuclear use. For instance, the NNWS may seek out third parties to restrain the nuclear-armed opponent. The greater the danger to the NWS, the larger the benefits of using nuclear weapons, though. As benefits go up, a set of costs that were sufficient to dissuade nuclear use at one point may no longer do so. The NNWS can therefore also prosecute the conflict in a way that it believes will not create large dangers for the nuclear-armed opponent. This lowers the stakes for the NWS and reduces the likelihood of a nuclear strike. The key for the NNWS is to act so that some level of costs from using nuclear weapons sufficiently outweighs the benefits. I discuss these costs and benefits of nuclear use as well as NNWS strategies in much more detail in the next chapter.

The stronger the NNWS is, the more constrained it will have to be; the weaker the NNWS, the more options it can pursue, subject to its own conventional limitations. The claim that wars are more likely when the NNWS is conventionally weak is counterintuitive. Yet the basic logic is that the larger the conventional threat, the greater danger the NNWS poses and the fewer conventional options the NWS has to offset that danger.[20] This raises the benefits of nuclear strikes for the NWS. As such, a powerful

NNWS must sharply limit its behavior to signal restraint and reduce the incentives for nuclear strikes. This is not to claim that it is great to be weak. A weak NNWS faces its own challenges and must weigh the likelihood of success in a conventional confrontation. Numerous factors aside from nuclear weapons will influence whether a militarily weaker NNWS will act or escalate during a conflict. The point is rather that a conventionally weak NNWS can fight a war against a nuclear opponent if it believes it has a plausible pathway to a favorable settlement precisely because it poses a smaller overall danger to the NWS. Because the NNWS poses a smaller danger, the benefits to the NWS of using its nuclear weapons are lower. This in turn makes it more likely that the costs of nuclear weapons use will outweigh the benefits. In other words, a militarily powerful NNWS must behave very cautiously; a militarily weak NNWS has more room to maneuver.

My argument leads to four main predictions. First, wars involving a conventionally powerful NNWS relative to its nuclear-armed opponent should be rare. Those wars that do occur in nuclear monopoly will tend to be fought between states with large conventional military disparities in favor of the nuclear-armed state. Second, the NWS should not face major dangers to its territorial integrity, critical military assets, and regime survival during wars in nuclear monopoly. Third, during political disputes, the NNWS leadership will focus on strategic factors that it believes will result in the NWS deciding the costs of nuclear use outweigh the benefits. Finally, my argument predicts that the NNWS should then act in a consistent manner, confronting the nuclear opponent in a way that limits the incentives for the NWS to execute a nuclear strike.

My argument addresses the conduct of political disputes and wars rather than which side starts the conflict. First, as outlined above, a large amount of theory and evidence suggests that nuclear monopoly provides coercive—that is, both deterrence and compellence—benefits. Yet conflict in nuclear monopoly is fairly common. My argument seeks to address both aspects of this puzzle.

Second, the NNWS faces the prospect of nuclear strikes when it elects to challenge rather than accept an undesired status quo and when it refuses to make concessions necessary to avoid a fight.[21] This is not to claim there is no meaningful distinction between deterrence and compellence. It is likely more difficult to get an adversary to act rather than not act. As Kroenig points out, though, "it is one thing to argue . . . that compellence is more difficult than deterrence. It is quite another to claim . . . that nuclear weapons do not influence compellence at all."[22] The relationship between many of the costs of nuclear strikes for the NWS is contingent on the nature of the dispute and proposed consequences. For instance, both a deterrent and compellent threat that promise to overthrow a government and liberate its people for noncompliance with a demand generate the same costs to the NWS for nuclear use, namely that such a strike would harm the people to be liberated. To be sure, it would be unsurprising that an NNWS would, to borrow from Brodie, accept the gage of war if suddenly attacked. Yet in most cases there were clear opportunities for the NNWS to avoid a fight.

Third, many disputes contain elements of both compellence and deterrence, with different actors making the first move at different points in the dispute. Kelly Greenhill and Robert Art highlight that "compellent actions are often undertaken in a crisis by a coercer in order to shore up its deterrent posture."[23] Additionally, Trachtenberg points out that in "the real world . . . wars are often not simply 'started' by one side, and the distinction between defender and attacker can be very problematic."[24] For instance, Iraq invaded Kuwait knowing it would invite some form of US response and then resisted US demands. Focusing on the dispute, rather than its initiation, shows how the shadow of nuclear weapons influenced Iraqi decision making over the course of the conflict. In several cases examined in this book, NWS policies intentionally or unintentionally created intolerable situations for the NNWS, blurring the line between offensive and defensive action. Relatedly, different conflict lists apply different criteria for initiation, and the authors themselves identify reasons one could code a dispute multiple ways.[25] Defining the status quo is often problematic, particularly in disputes where it is in flux. The participants themselves will frequently disagree on what constitutes the status quo. "What one considers an innocent deterrent," writes Richard Betts, "the other may see as a pernicious compellent."[26]

I limit the scope of my study to situations where there is a political dispute between states. I avoid cases where an NNWS takes no action at all because it is so weak that it lacks any options to redress its grievances. In addition, if the NNWS has few interests at stake in an issue or no disagreement at all with a nuclear-armed state, then my argument does not apply. If the NNWS had little incentive to act in the first place, then it does not matter much if the NNWS possessed remarkably effective strategies to minimize the likelihood of a nuclear strike.

Previous studies suggest that in asymmetric conflict the weaker party will possess strong motivations to act.[27] In the cases that I examine, the nonnuclear weapon states were highly resolved. In many of the cases the underlying political trends or actions by the nuclear-armed state were directly or indirectly threatening to the NNWS, which led to that high resolve. For example, US policies toward Germany following World War II created major concerns in the Soviet Union. With those concerns came an intense interest in reversing those policies. Similarly, the status quo facing Egypt after the Six Day War proved intolerable to Egyptian leaders. As I show, though, high resolution alone was not sufficient to cause NNWS leaders to ignore nuclear weapons.

At the same time, the cases I examine in detail are ones in which the NWS had a demonstrated interest. Though in some cases the NNWS may believe the NWS will not act at all, and therefore discount nuclear weapons, in many it is clear that both sides have interests at stake. For instance, in 1950 the United States was already fighting in Korea when China intervened. One could doubt American commitment to the Korean Peninsula in the spring of 1950; one could not by the fall of the same year. In 1973 Israel had already fought to acquire (1967) and then hold on to (1969–1970) the Sinai Peninsula. The key is that the NNWS avoids posing a major danger to the NWS's survival or creating a situation that can lead to large additional losses beyond the immediate dispute.

This book focuses, then, on how the NNWS probes the limits of the nuclear shadow, and how conventional military forces influence the likelihood for escalation. In practical terms, this means that the universe of cases to which this argument applies is not all possible interstate interactions but rather existing disputes. In social science terminology, an NNWS has already "selected into" some form of confrontation with a nuclear-armed opponent by challenging or resisting the NWS. I do not seek to explain the underlying factors that cause an NNWS to oppose an NWS in the first place. As noted, existing research suggests that weak actors who select into conflicts are likely to be highly resolved and have some baseline ability to act. These expectations are borne out in the case studies discussed in this book, with the NWS pursuing policies that create large strategic and domestic problems for the NNWS that then contribute to NNWS determination to act. However, I do not examine cases where nothing at all happened to fully demonstrate that states without an intense interest and baseline ability to act do in fact not do so. My argument instead accounts for the planning and behavior during disputes, including those few that escalate to wars. Despite these limitations, this book nevertheless covers a large number of important cases.

Implications for Scholarship and Policy

Understanding confrontations in nuclear monopoly has important implications for scholars and policy makers. To begin with, it helps clarify the role that nuclear weapons play in international politics. How far does the nuclear shadow extend? Much of what we know about the role that nuclear weapons play in disputes is limited to when both sides have them. This is not surprising, given the reasonable focus on the US-Soviet nuclear standoff during the Cold War. Today a great deal of attention goes to the nuclear relationships between the United States and China and between India and Pakistan.[28] Even work that explicitly deals with nuclear asymmetry often focuses on cases when one country has a large qualitative or quantitative advantage over another nuclear-armed power.[29]

The core claims of the nuclear revolution build from situations when both sides possess nuclear weapons. According to these arguments, mutual nuclear vulnerability makes crises and war unlikely, favors the preservation of the status quo, and ameliorates the security dilemma.[30] In short, mutual vulnerability reduces many of the traditional external pressures in international politics. This situation is thought to be relatively durable because it is difficult for any state to gain a meaningful advantage against a nuclear-armed opponent. These claims were never universally accepted.[31] Some argued the political effects of nuclear weapons were oversold, others that nuclear advantages could be made meaningful, and still others that normative conditions generated discourses that led nuclear-armed opponents to internalize mutual deterrence as the appropriate behavior for their status.[32] Recent work by historians and political scientists using a variety of methods and armed with access to new archival and quantitative sources has further qualified and challenged several of these contentions.[33]

The nuclear revolution nevertheless offers a plausible account for some basic observations. Most notably, joint nuclear possession seems to deter nuclear strikes and reduces the chance for major war between two nuclear-armed states. Fortunately, there has yet to be a single instance of nuclear use by one nuclear power against another. There have also been, at most, two minor conventional wars directly between nuclear-armed states: China–Soviet Union in 1969 and India–Pakistan in 1999.

The stability-instability paradox can help explain why low-level conflict continues.[34] The basic argument is that two nuclear-armed states are mutually deterred from using their nuclear arsenal and thus freed to fight low-level conventional wars and stumble into crises. This potential limitation of the nuclear revolution depends completely (by definition) on joint nuclear possession, thereby excluding cases of nuclear monopoly.

Left unexplained in these formulations is conflict in nuclear monopoly. Yet, as noted above, this type of conflict poses a puzzle for many existing explanations of nuclear politics. This book contributes to the understanding of the role of nuclear weapons in international politics by focusing exclusively on the comparatively understudied dynamics of nuclear monopoly, joining a small number of works that deal directly or indirectly with conflict in that context. It builds on, extends, and challenges portions of these studies that address aspects of NNWS behavior. I do not claim to provide the only explanation for the dynamics of nuclear monopoly. My aim is more limited: to expand on existing treatments to provide a fuller explanation for conflict in nuclear monopoly. To that end, I turn now to the relation between my argument and some of the most prominent studies in this area.

Insights from normative arguments help explain conflict in nuclear monopoly. By themselves, however, they are at best incomplete. The basic normative claim is that states do not use nuclear weapons because there is a norm that arose over time proscribing nuclear use.[35] As a result, NNWS leaders do not take nuclear use seriously and feel free to confront a nuclear-armed opponent.[36] As a complete explanation for conflict in nuclear monopoly, what I term the "strong norms" claim, this argument is seriously flawed. Referencing the nuclear nonuse norm, T. V. Paul asks rhetorically: "If there existed neither an explicit legal ban nor a deterrent capability to prevent possible nuclear retaliation, what else could explain the belief among decision makers of nonnuclear states that nuclear weapons would not be used against them in their impending conflict?"[37] As I show, a great deal of other factors help explain decision making in nonnuclear states. To be fair, Paul recognizes that "other possible political and strategic constraints" may operate, though he does not develop these in any detail. Similarly, Michael Gerson writes that the reason states without nuclear weapons "are not intimidated by an opponent's nuclear capabilities" is "due in part to the perceived impact of the 'nuclear taboo.'"[38] Yet there is no effort to explore the other "parts" that influence NNWS decision makers. Paul Huth and Bruce Russett argue that, at least in extended deterrence situations, NNWS leaders do not think nuclear use is credible because "normative inhibitions associated with this disproportion [of nuclear destruction] made it absurd to consider nuclear use a real possibility."[39]

Others provide even fewer qualifications. In the most important book on the nuclear taboo, Nina Tannenwald concludes simply that "because of the taboo, a nuclear threat against a nonnuclear state is no longer credible."[40] The former US national security adviser McGeorge Bundy made a similar point when he noted that as a result of the tradition of nonuse, "no government without [nuclear] weapons needs to be easily coerced by nuclear threats from others, because both history and logic make it clear that no government will resort to nuclear weapons over less than a mortal question."[41] There is often little effort to demonstrate that NNWS leaders relied on normative factors; the mere fact of conflict is taken as evidence that the norm must be at work.

If the strong-norms claim is correct, NNWS leaders should simply identify nuclear nonuse norms as the reason that nuclear weapons would not be used and be willing to confront a nuclear-armed opponent. Leaders may not even discuss their opponent's nuclear status at all if they have internalized the belief that norms constrain nuclear use. The taboo should also operate regardless of relative conventional capabilities. The case studies and pattern of war in nuclear monopoly makes clear that these claims do not hold.

Yet normative factors are not irrelevant, even if they are not a comprehensive explanation for conflict. NNWS leaders may believe that international opinion might lead to negative consequences for the NWS in the form of diplomatic blowback, sanctions, or even active support for the

NNWS following nuclear use. This would particularly be the case if nuclear use resulted in large numbers of civilian deaths. Indeed, this is consistent with views that harming civilians—even by conventional means—should be avoided.[42] NNWS leaders at times highlight such considerations when deciding how to confront nuclear opponents. They may even attempt to manipulate international condemnation to minimize the risks of nuclear strikes. They do so in the belief that this type of negative blowback will create a strategic disincentive for nuclear use even if the NWS was willing to internally set aside normative considerations.[43] My argument incorporates this insight by highlighting how evolving norms can generate strategic consequences that the NNWS can leverage. In short, the NNWS can use norms instrumentally. The focus on normative factors occurs alongside consideration of material and strategic issues.

A number of studies highlight how various costs of nuclear use, force structures, and interests influence the effects of nuclear weapons. For instance, Sechser and Fuhrmann identify several similar costs to explain nuclear compellence failures.[44] Vipin Narang shows how nuclear-armed states facing conventionally powerful militaries are more likely to see the benefits of nuclear use as outweighing the costs and adopt corresponding force postures and doctrines. Moreover, wars in those situations are unlikely to occur.[45] Still others contend that states will confront a nuclear-armed opponent when they have a much larger stake than their opponent does in the issue.[46]

I go beyond these existing studies in several ways. First, I focus exclusively on these dynamics in nuclear monopoly. As such, I consider additional costs and benefits of nuclear use and show that many of the costs others identify have implications for both deterrence and compellence when only one side has nuclear weapons. Second, this book demonstrates that wars involving NNWS militaries with strong conventional capabilities relative to their nuclear opponents will be rare in nuclear monopoly, regardless of the specific force posture. Most importantly, I am able to demonstrate in a number of cases that NNWS decision makers explicitly considered various costs and benefits of nuclear use across discrete types of nuclear deployments. Finally, I show that even if the NNWS has a greater relative interest in the issue, that does not mean it ignores the possibility of nuclear use.

Beyond nuclear politics, some perspectives claim that power asymmetries dampen conflict by clarifying who will win. For example, Geoffrey Blainey argues that many wars start because both sides believe they could win.[47] That type of mutual optimism is more likely when both sides have similar capabilities, because each can entertain hopes of victory. This insight is at the center of the influential bargaining model of war, which, as Dan Reiter notes, predicts conflict when there is "disagreement over the balance of power."[48] War thus becomes less likely when power asymmetries increase, because the balance of power is clear. Numerous quantitative studies find support for the relationship that war is less likely as power imbalances increase.[49] The inverse prediction is also true, that states are unlikely to fight if they expect to lose. These dynamics still exist in nuclear monopoly, with many weak states seeking to avoid war because they would lose, but they are counterbalanced by the reluctance of militarily powerful nonnuclear states to fight against an NWS.

Turning to more practical considerations, the world is no longer dominated by the superpower standoff between the United States and the Soviet Union. Many actual and potential conflicts involve states without nuclear weapons in confrontations with states that have nuclear weapons. Since 2000 alone, the United States has used or threatened force against Iraq, Iran, Libya, North Korea (nonnuclear prior to 2006), and Syria. Russia has invaded the territory of two of its nonnuclear neighbors. Israel continues to have serious disputes with actors, all nonnuclear, along its border. Although nuclear use in any of these conflicts is unlikely, any time conflict occurs, the risks of nuclear use increases. Understanding the dynamics of these conflicts can help minimize the chances that the world witnesses its first nuclear detonation in combat since 1945. A better understanding of conflict in nuclear monopoly is thus hardly a trivial matter.

If states without nuclear weapons simply ignore such weapons, then nuclear-armed states face an uphill battle convincing such opponents that nuclear weapons might actually be used. This can create a space for NWS policy entrepreneurs who argue for potentially dangerous policies to demonstrate credibility, such as delegating launch authority, forward deploying nuclear assets, or investing in a new generation of more "usable" nuclear weapons. A nuclear force rendered virtually incredible might also cause adversaries to misinterpret red lines for actual nuclear use. Such miscalculation could result in catastrophe.

Finally, if nuclear weapons only deterred nuclear strikes, with few other political consequences, this would strengthen calls for global nuclear-zero arguments.[50] After all, what is the point of keeping a weapon that everyone knows no state will ever use? Ridding the world of nuclear weapons would achieve the same effect as mutual nuclear deterrence—preventing someone from striking you with a nuclear bomb—without the risks of nuclear accidents.

The rest of this book develops my argument and assesses the predictions against the historical record. I then return to broader implications for nuclear strategy and politics in the conclusion.

The Strategic Logic of Nuclear Monopoly

The crux of the argument is that there are costs and benefits to any use of nuclear weapons. A state without nuclear weapons contemplating confronting a nuclear-armed opponent can take advantage of this situation. As long as the nonnuclear weapon state believes that it can maintain a situation in which the costs of nuclear use for its opponent outweigh the benefits, it is able to take action. The NNWS essentially sets its own "red lines" and gambles that those lines are below the red lines for nuclear use by the nuclear weapon state. In many situations the NNWS will actively seek to manipulate the red-line threshold by pursuing strategies it believes will further reduce the benefits and/or increase the costs of nuclear use. In other situations, the preferred strategy of the NNWS will already exist below the red line, and it will not need to alter its behavior. The exact mix of strategies varies across cases. All else equal, though, the more conventionally capable the NNWS is militarily relative to the NWS, the more constrained the behavior of the NNWS will be. As such, conflicts are likely to escalate to war only when the NWS possesses a large conventional military advantage.

The opponent's nuclear arsenal is not the sole determinant of NNWS strategy or behavior. Similarly, my argument does not predict that a conventionally weak NNWS will rush into war. A state without nuclear weapons may avoid fighting because of the conventional military balance, the level of international support it enjoys, its domestic situation, cultural features, and even individual personalities. The argument is simply that the NNWS will act below the threshold it identifies, and that a conventionally powerful NNWS must behave more cautiously.

To construct this argument, I first identify the main benefits and costs of nuclear use. I initially focus solely on nuclear weapons, ignoring conventional capabilities and strategies. This provides a baseline treatment of the nuclear environment that both the NWS and the NNWS confront. Next, I use this baseline to outline NNWS strategies to reduce those benefits and/or raise the costs of nuclear use. I pay attention to both deliberate and inadvertent pathways to nuclear escalation. As long as the NNWS believes that the costs outweigh the benefits of nuclear use, it has a space to act. The third section incorporates the role that the conventional military balance plays in influencing the costs and benefits of nuclear use. Having built the argument in three stages—abstract nuclear monopoly, NNWS strategies in nuclear monopoly, and the role of the conventional military balance—I then present its main predictions. In the following section I discuss how I assess the argument. I conclude by summarizing the core claims of this chapter.

Costs and Benefits of Nuclear Use

Nuclear weapons promise nuclear-armed states various benefits in a dispute. I use the term "benefits" to refer to the military and political utility for the nuclear-armed state of a threatened or executed nuclear strike. The discussion on nuclear-weapon effects necessarily informs decision making prior to strikes because leaders can assess the likely consequences of nuclear use.[1] The relative efficacy of nuclear versus conventional strikes influences the scope of the benefits. At the same time, there are costs associated with nuclear use that go beyond the typical costs associated with using force. The rest of this section outlines both elements.

BENEFITS OF NUCLEAR USE IN MONOPOLY

The core benefit of threatening or using nuclear weapons for a nuclear-armed state is to improve the likelihood of attaining a favorable settlement. The benefits of a nuclear strike depend on the conventional alternatives and the military and political situation. Failure to appreciate this point might lead one to conclude that nuclear weapons would always be used in the absence of a strong legal or normative prohibition. There is no specific benefit from a nuclear strike if the mission can be performed equally well by a conventional alternative. Any costs associated with nuclear use would then be sufficient to dissuade such a strike. Additionally, the higher the danger to the state and the worse the military situation, the greater a state benefits by using nuclear weapons to attain a favorable outcome. Inhibitions on the use of force decrease as the likelihood and consequences of defeat increase.

The NWS can threaten or execute several types of nuclear strikes. The two most basic are punishment and denial.[2] In brief, punishment seeks to harm or threaten the opposing population. Depending on the situation, that hardship will cause the adversary to not undertake some action, cede to political demands, or stop fighting. The victim government may see the destruction visited on its society and accede to the desires of the NWS. Alternatively, the population may itself rise up to demand their government implement (or not implement, in the case of a deterrent threat) the policies the NWS seeks. Punishment was the primary logic behind the American decision to use nuclear weapons against Japan in 1945 in hopes of compelling Japan to surrender.[3] By contrast, denial strikes target the opponent's military capabilities to block the adversary's ability to successfully prosecute its campaign. Denial threats seek to deter any action or compel acquiescence by convincing the opponent its military strategy will not succeed. The two categories will sometimes blur, but they are important to keep analytically distinct. In addition, nuclear-armed states may contemplate using limited strikes to de-escalate a dispute or to catalyze third-party involvement. I discuss each option in turn.

Nuclear weapons offer an effective, if gruesome, tool for punishment strikes. Most basically, nuclear weapons are very destructive.[4] Accuracy is not particularly important when targeting a large urban area with a nuclear device. The overpressure generated by nuclear detonation is sufficient to destroy most civilian structures kilometers from the blast center. Individuals near the blast will also be exposed to lethal radiation. The heat from the blast, combined with high wind speeds and debris, create firestorms that cause even greater devastation. As Lynn Eden notes, depending on the conditions, the fire could "generate ground winds of hurricane force with average air temperatures well above the boiling point of water."[5] To be sure, a low-yield fission weapon would not completely destroy a large city. Hills and other geographic features can shield people otherwise near the blast. Yet even comparatively low nuclear yields can have devastating effects. The 15-kiloton blast at Hiroshima—current US intercontinental ballistic missiles have warhead yields of 300 to 335 kilotons—created a fire that "covered an area of roughly 4.4 square miles and burned with great intensity for more than six hours after the initial explosion. Between 70,000 and 130,000 people died immediately from the combined effects of the fire, blast, and nuclear radiation."[6] Faced with the prospect of such destruction, the pressure to cede to the adversary's political demands is intense.

Nuclear weapons are also useful at destroying vital civilian infrastructure. Dams, ports, large rail centers, and other critical components may withstand conventional attacks not powerful or accurate enough to do sufficient damage. For instance, Secretary of State Dean Rusk told President Lyndon Johnson in 1965 that Israeli officials believed that a nuclear weapon would provide Israel "a capability to bomb and release the waters behind the Aswan High Dam. Destruction of the Aswan Dam would require a nuclear warhead; bombing with high explosives could not be counted on to do the job."[7] An earlier State Department report in 1964 highlighted that "a single well-placed nuclear device would bring a sheet of water 400 feet high cascading down the narrow Nile valley where the entire Egyptian population is concentrated"[8]

States can carry out punishment campaigns with conventional weapons, of course. Naval blockades and scorched-earth land campaigns can devastate civilian populations. The advent of air power in the early twentieth century provided a powerful new punishment tool. For instance, on March 9, 1945, the United States launched a massive firebombing attack on Tokyo. The raid burned 15.8 square miles and killed an estimated 84,000 to 100,000 Japanese.[9] Advances in precision-guided munitions can cripple infrastructure to impose suffering. During the 1991 Gulf War, precision bombing avoided directly targeting civilians but destroyed electrical and water facilities. Nina Tannewald highlights that those strikes caused "vast numbers of civilian deaths due to infectious diseases, and lack of food, water, and medical care."[10] Conventional punishment campaigns have occasionally been successful, though they often require major fighting to first degrade the adversary's military capability and can take a long time to result in the desired effects.[11] Moreover, prior to hostilities target-state leaders frequently believe they can outlast limited air strikes.[12]

The key distinction with nuclear weapons is economy and speed. A single weapon is enough to do what can otherwise require a large number of strikes. A state need not outfit an aerial armada and command the skies to threaten or inflict severe punishment. Developing stealth and precision-guided technology and overcoming enemy air defenses is not necessary to impose widespread hardship.[13] In a conventional world, intercepting most of the adversary's aircraft or missiles allows the population to escape destruction. In a nuclear world, intercepting most of the adversary's aircraft or missiles still results in devastating destruction.[14] Moreover, nuclear strikes can occur in a matter of minutes and in many cases are on platforms that offer coverage of the entire enemy territory. As Christine Leah puts it, "It is the sheer destructive power, and the speed at which that power can be dealt, that make nuclear armed missiles unique."[15] In a conventional situation, then, leaders may be willing to roll the dice and press ahead or not give in to demands. "Wars start more easily" in a conventional world, Kenneth Waltz argued, "because the uncertainties of their outcomes make it easier for the leaders of states to entertain illusions of victory at supportable cost."[16] By contrast, faced with the prospect of immediate nuclear devastation on at least some part of their society, those same leaders and publics are more cautious.

Nuclear denial strikes possess many of the same advantages of speed and economy. They allow an outnumbered or outgunned actor to radically increase its units' firepower. Nuclear weapons would be particularly useful against massed enemy formations. Nuclear strikes in an operational role can interdict the adversary's ability to bring up reinforcements and supply frontline units. During World War II, various American leaders were already speculating along these lines. In 1943 General Leslie Groves, head of the Manhattan Project, and his advisers discussed using a nuclear weapon against "a Japanese fleet concentration" in harbor.[17] Following initial uses at Hiroshima and Nagasaki, Lieutenant General John Hull noted nuclear weapons might be useful at "neutralizing a division or a communication center or something so that it would facilitate the movement ashore of troops."[18] More recently, Pakistan is widely believed to have adopted a nuclear posture that envisions battlefield use of nuclear weapons against Indian conventional forces to offset Pakistani military inferiority. As Vipin Narang argues, Pakistan's status as the "conventionally weaker power" led it to integrate nuclear weapons into its military doctrine and adopt "an asymmetric escalation posture that attempts to credibly deter conventional attack by threatening the first use of nuclear weapons against a large-scale Indian conventional thrust through Pakistan's vulnerable desert and plains corridor in Sindh and Punjab."[19] Though in the latter example both sides possess nuclear weapons, the essential logic applies in nuclear monopoly.

States can also use nuclear weapons in a strategic denial role, such as targeting the adversary's industrial production so that it cannot sustain its military forces. American planning against the Soviet Union in the early postwar period called for targeting industry to degrade the Soviet ability to wage war.[20] Another target set is the staging areas for the adversary's military forces. For example, conventional cratering of runways may not do sufficient damage over large enough areas to make the runways inoperable. Nuclear strikes, by contrast, are more likely to successfully destroy runways and can be used against hardened aircraft shelters.[21]

Nuclear weapons are especially valuable in destroying hardened and buried targets.[22] This is particularly true if weapon accuracy is limited. In those cases, larger yields compensate for reduced accuracy. Strategic studies tend to focus on targeting an adversary's hardened nuclear forces.[23] In nuclear monopoly, the NNWS possesses no nuclear assets to attack. Yet conventional missiles, aircraft shelters, artillery units, communications and command centers, and other military targets that the adversary may harden, bury, or dig into mountains still pose difficulties for conventional weapons.[24] For instance, experts debated whether even the most powerful US conventional weapons could destroy the deeply buried Iranian nuclear facility at Fordow.[25] Particularly when speed is critical, nuclear weapons may offer an attractive alternative against such targets.

The increased destructive power and speed of nuclear-armed missiles offer advantages against mobile targets relative to conventional alternatives. During the 1991 Gulf War, the United States tasked approximately one thousand "Scud-patrol" sorties alongside fifteen hundred strikes against Iraqi ballistic-missile capabilities. There were no confirmed destructions of Iraqi Scud missiles.[26] As Charles L. Glaser and Steve Fetter note, though, "On many occasions U.S. forces located Scud launchers in Iraq, but without enough precision to allow a successful attack with the conventional weapons available. Nuclear weapons have a much larger radius of destruction against mobile missiles, which would make relatively unimportant any lack of precision."[27] Similarly, Austin Long and Brendan Green argue that "uncertainty about target location matters much less when using fast nuclear weapons rather than much slower fighter-bombers armed with conventional weapons."[28]

Limited nuclear use against a military target or isolated area may have little immediate effect but instead serve as a warning. In this sort of "escalate to de-escalate" scenario, the nuclear state derives benefit by signaling to the NNWS a willingness to use nuclear force. Such a signal conveys that now that the nuclear threshold has been breached, any additional action can result in more substantial denial or punishment strikes. As Caitlin Talmadge writes, "Nothing says 'you've crossed my red line' quite like a mushroom cloud."[29] Because this ultimately rests on the threat of additional denial or punishment strikes, it can be folded into the general denial and punishment discussion above.[30]

Nuclear-armed states might also believe that nuclear weapons can provide a catalytic benefit. In this scenario, the NWS threatens to or actually detonates a device, likely in a remote area, to spur third-party involvement.[31] The third party can support the NWS through direct engagement, furnishing of supplies, or pressuring the NNWS. There is some evidence that Israeli leaders performed various operational checks on their nuclear arsenal in the 1973 October War to spur greater US involvement.[32]

This is unlikely to be a major factor in NNWS decision making in nuclear monopoly, though. First, as Narang argues, since third-party intervention is only probabilistic, the NNWS may believe it can achieve limited objectives before any outside help occurs.[33] As I argue below, an NNWS is likely to pursue limited objectives in the case of nuclear monopoly; this would thus not harm its strategy. Second, a catalytic strike is unlikely to cause any immediate, direct harm to the NNWS, and therefore the NNWS will be less concerned by such a strike. Third, this strategy is an option only if the NWS has a capable third party willing to intervene on its behalf. When facing an NWS such as the United States, the Soviet Union/Russia, or today's China, any ally coming in on the side of the NWS will be unlikely to tip the scales, because any potential ally would be much weaker than the NWS. Finally, in some cases the NNWS will *prefer* third-party involvement, seeing it as likely to restrain any additional nuclear use by the NWS and allow the NNWS to continue to pursue its objectives at the conventional level. For instance, Egypt deliberately informed the United States of its planning during the October War both because it believed the United

States could exercise a restraining influence on Israel, and because Egyptian leaders understood US involvement was ultimately necessary to realize Egyptian goals.

COSTS OF NUCLEAR USE

There are real military and political costs to nuclear use. Not all costs discussed below are present in equal measure in every circumstance; some work at cross-purposes.[34] The key point is that some will always be present, and efforts to avoid one set of costs involve trade-offs that can lead to others.

First, the physical characteristics of nuclear weapons deployed by most states throughout history have made it difficult to limit collateral damage.[35] Nuclear strikes are likely to destroy or irradiate valuable territory, resources, and populations.[36] As Austin Long writes, "The vast power of all but the smallest nuclear weapons is likely to produce significant collateral damage if used against targets in any but the most remote and uninhabited locations."[37] As noted above, even yields in the low kilotons directed against urban centers can create devastating firestorms.[38] Ground bursts of nuclear weapons will cause radioactive material to mix with particulate matter, creating long-term health hazards. Inaccurate delivery platforms necessitate larger yields for nuclear devices to guarantee target destruction. Strikes against hardened military targets with such delivery platforms are therefore doubly destructive, requiring ground bursts and large yields. In cases of geographic proximity, the radiation may directly harm the NWS's own territory or that of its foreign bases and allies.[39] Battlefield use cannot avoid these complications. As John Mueller points out, "when one considers the impact of nuclear weapons in combat situations . . . of special concern would be the messy problems presented by fallout and radioactive contamination—particularly because many battlefield applications would require that the weapons be groundburst."[40] Terence Roehrig makes a similar point, noting that nuclear weapons, "including tactical nuclear weapons, contaminate the battlefield and greatly complicate the military's ability to conduct follow-on ground operations."[41]

Allies, adversaries, and neutral states not involved in the initial dispute that found themselves harmed or believed themselves likely to be harmed by nuclear use would oppose nuclear strikes.[42] This opposition can result exclusively from the material self-interest of these states. Depending on the nature of the nuclear strikes, terrain, and weather, nearby states could suffer the aftereffects of nuclear fallout. Nuclear strikes could also create large refugee flows that destabilize neighbors. As Matthew Fuhrmann notes, "The presence of refugees from neighboring states increases the likelihood that a country will experience political turmoil and armed conflict."[43] At the least, states forced to admit refugees are likely to blame the nuclear state for creating what many will perceive as an additional burden. Nuclear use that expanded the scope of fighting could endanger states. For instance, in 1950 some of America's European allies worried that nuclear use in the Korean War could expand the conflict to involve the Soviet Union and then spill over into Europe at a time when NATO defenses were very weak.[44]

Opposition from third parties can range in intensity. On the low-intensity end, states opposed to nuclear use can seek to oppose or isolate the NWS diplomatically, frustrate NWS goals in international institutions, reduce cultural and educational ties, or expel NWS citizens from within their borders. Allies of the NWS can exert intra-alliance pressure on the NWS, move toward a neutral stance, or deny territorial access for NWS military forces.[45] Moving to mid-intensity, states can sanction the NWS economically by limiting trade, freezing NWS financial assets, or undermining the NWS currency. At higher levels of opposition states may begin to support the threatened or actual target of the nuclear strikes with economic and military aid. At the extreme, states may decide they must intervene militarily against the NWS. For example, the Soviet Union proposed intervention in the October War to save the trapped Egyptian Third Army. It is likely, then, that the Soviet Union would have intervened had Israel resorted to nuclear weapons.

The destructive nature of nuclear weapons also means that they will almost always expand the level of violence in the conflict.[46] If the NNWS is not defeated, this could encourage it to expand the geographic scope of the conflict. Nuclear use might also cause the NNWS to use chemical or biological weapons. Any expansion in the geographic space or weapons used represents a potential cost to the NWS. In addition, strategic or tactical nuclear use that expanded the level of violence would necessarily introduce uncertainty on the battlefield. Leaders generally seek to avoid such uncertainty, preferring to fight with known, conventional capabilities if possible.[47]

Thus, paradoxically, one of the benefits of nuclear weapons—their destructive ability—can become one of their chief costs. To be sure, the destructiveness causes more harm to the victim. But that destructiveness also greatly complicates operations for the NWS. If the goal is regime change or to liberate a people, it makes little sense to irradiate those people. If the political dispute involves territory or resources, destroying the territory or resources is counterproductive. If the purpose is to safeguard one's own homeland or an ally's, nuclear use on that territory against enemy military forces will hardly be appealing. Likewise, a nuclear strike that poses as much danger to one's own troops as the opponent's is not a particularly attractive option. To be sure, if the danger to the NWS is great enough, the NNWS may fear that the NWS would use the weapons even knowing there would be significant destruction. In that case the benefits of eliminating a great danger would trump the costs. The point is that destructiveness can act as a brake on nuclear use in many situations; the NNWS can realize this and act accordingly.

These costs associated with destructiveness will not be present in every case, of course. Targeting military forces in isolated locations is less likely to harm civilians or neighbors. Recent advances in guidance and information processing allow states to substitute lower warhead yields without sacrificing effectiveness.[48] As I detail below, improvements in accuracy that allow conventional weapons to perform missions previously accomplishable only through nuclear-weapon use reduce the latter's benefits in the first place, allowing the other associated costs to loom larger. The key issue is that in most cases throughout history, and for most states today, nuclear use carries with it the prospect of destruction that can prove counterproductive to the interests of the NWS.

Limited strikes that minimize destructiveness may prove ineffective, diminishing benefits and allowing other costs to grow in import. For example, in 1990, Secretary of Defense Richard Cheney inquired about nuclear options against Iraqi military forces. A sizable number of tactical nuclear weapons—reportedly seventeen—was required to significantly damage an Iraqi military unit. As Colin Powell later noted, "If I had any doubts before about the practicality of nukes on the battlefield, this report clinched them."[49] One or two strikes against military targets, even when the NWS had a large technological advantage, were thought to be ineffective. If an adversary had few valuable military targets, or fought with guerrilla methods, then limited nuclear strikes might do nothing to impede its military effectiveness. Similarly, one or two very low yield weapons detonated against urban targets that did not destroy those targets could avoid some of the destructiveness costs but at the expense of failing to cause the adversary's collapse. The bottom line is that there are tradeoffs between various levels of destruction; a movement one way or the other can generate higher costs or lower benefits.

The second set of costs that NWS leaders must worry about concerns the long-term challenges nuclear weapon use may create. Nuclear weapon use might spur other states to develop nuclear capabilities. Those proliferating states may one day use their newfound nuclear capabilities to harm NWS interests. At the least, more nuclear actors reduce NWS freedom of action in global politics and increase the number of states that can inflict significant harm.[50] The United States, Great Britain, and the Soviet Union, among others, have all worked at times to constrain proliferation, particularly in areas where they could project conventional power.[51] "One effective nonproliferation strategy is to make the world think that nuclear weapons are utterly useless," writes Fuhrmann. Successful nuclear weapon use could "cultivate the opposite perception—that possessing the bomb allows one to get their way in international relations."[52] This would also undermine international efforts, such as the Nuclear Nonproliferation Treaty, to prevent proliferation. Nuclear use that encouraged more states to get the bomb would therefore be a major cost. This mechanism is similar to, but distinct from, arguments that nuclear use would set a negative precedent by violating a shared expectation for nonuse.[53] The argument here is simply one of emulation. States in an anarchic system that witness nuclear use providing major benefits will be more likely to believe nuclear weapons will offer them utility—if only to deter nuclear use—and seek to acquire their own nuclear arsenal.[54] Emulation might also make it more likely that other states use nuclear weapons in future disputes.

Alternatively, NWS leaders may fear that nuclear use would be ineffective. Ineffective nuclear strikes would demonstrate the weakness of a state's ultimate deterrent and potentially encourage more challenges. For instance, historian John Lewis Gaddis notes that during the Korean War one major US concern cautioning against nuclear use was that "the enemy might keep coming, and so obvious a demonstration of the bomb's ineffectiveness could impair its credibility elsewhere."[55]

Finally, nuclear use would violate norms against harming noncombatants and against using nuclear weapons specifically.[56] Though the strength of noncombatant norms and the nuclear taboo are sometimes overstated, they are not nonexistent.[57] States unharmed materially by a nuclear strike might impose various sanctions to punish an NWS for violating these norms.[58] This opposition would take many of the same forms discussed above, such as diplomatic maneuvering, economic retribution, and even support for the nuclear victim. Domestic public opinion in the NWS itself might mobilize against the state's leaders for using nuclear weapons. And public opinion in third parties could pressure their own leaders to take some action against the NWS.

PRECISION GUIDANCE AND THE LIMITS OF THE BENEFITS-COSTS CALCULUS

Have improvements in weapon accuracy and information processing fundamentally transformed the costs and benefits of nuclear use?[59] Is the discussion of nuclear benefits and costs hopelessly outdated, without relevance for today's world? On close examination, these dynamics of nuclear monopoly remain valid for three reasons. First, it is important to note that not all nuclear-armed states have developed and exploited this technology to the same degree. One should be cautious in generalizing to all nuclear monopoly situations as a result. Additionally, an effective conventional military technology at one point in time may be offset by future adversary adaptation or technological innovation.

Second, even the most sophisticated conventional weapons cannot yet perform all missions as effectively as nuclear weapons. Nuclear weapons can visit larger amounts of devastation in shorter periods of time. Precision strikes can disrupt water and power facilities, but if a state cannot maintain such strikes, then the target can repair those facilities or find substitutes to supply civilian needs. Civilians living near a precision strike's target will survive; those same civilians are likely to be killed if the target is destroyed with a nuclear weapon.

Nuclear strikes continue to offer benefits against hardened facilities or where intelligence limitations preclude precise knowledge of target locations. Conventional prompt global-strike missiles may be able to hit a target quickly but cause insufficient damage in a short enough period to lead to the desired outcome.[60] Moreover, such strikes require an intricate support network, including, Dennis Gormley writes, "highly accurate and swiftly gathered intelligence collection, analysis, and dissemination, rigorous mission planning, precise knowledge of the target's aim points (i.e., its vulnerabilities), post-attack damage assessment capabilities (to determine whether damage objectives have been achieved and whether additional strikes are necessary), and finally, an agile command-and-control system to manage these complex, interconnected tasks."[61] A breakdown in any one stage can leave the target intact. To be sure, nuclear weapons require support and can fail as well. The greater destructive power means that such failures are less likely to leave the target intact *relative* to conventional alternatives.

States that lack sufficient platforms to overcome enemy air or missile defenses will continue to see utility in a class of weapons that can inflict significant harm even if most such weapons are intercepted. Stealth is not a panacea, either, simply because stealth does not make aircraft invisible.[62] Against a capable adversary, even stealth platforms will suffer attrition. Faced with that prospect, nuclear strikes that increase the certainty of success despite losses remain attractive.

It is undeniable, though, that improvements in accuracy and information processing have increased the number of missions formerly reserved for nuclear forces that can now be accomplished by a conventional alternative. As former commander of the US Strategic Command General C. Robert Kehler notes, "While not practical as a large-scale replacement, the combat performance of conventional U.S. forces over the last two decades showed that precision strike capabilities could provide viable options in certain scenarios and against certain targets where nuclear weapons were once seen as the best (in some cases the only) choice for the president."[63] There remain some benefits of nuclear use, but those benefits have shrunk.

Third, to the extent the scope of nuclear benefits has declined, this has been offset by the reduction in costs of nuclear use. Increased accuracy and information-processing power allow states to reduce the nuclear warhead yield while still achieving the objective. This reduces the likelihood of collateral damage, removing a powerful cost that constrains nuclear use.

Indeed, many worry that increases in accuracy make nuclear use *more* likely as a result.[64] States can now contemplate "clean" nuclear strikes. The implications for the likelihood of nuclear use in monopoly are therefore mixed. To the extent that there exists a conventional platform that can promise the same mission performance, the benefits of nuclear strikes necessarily decrease. At the same time, technological advances reduce the potential costs associated with nuclear use. Since it is not clear which factor dominates—reduced benefits or reduced costs—the ultimate effects are indeterminate.

This is not to say the benefits and costs are fixed for all time. If technological advances allow conventional weapons to perform all missions as effectively as nuclear weapons, most of the benefits of nuclear weapons, at least in nuclear monopoly, drop out.[65] Similarly, if nuclear strikes could be conducted in a way that created no collateral damage, one of the most potent costs would no longer apply. Much of the analysis presented here, while still potentially an accurate description of the past, would be less useful. Yet as long as there remain benefits and costs with the use of nuclear weapons, nonnuclear states will be faced with assessing the likelihood that such weapons will indeed be used.

SUMMARY

There are benefits and costs to threatening or carrying out nuclear strikes. The benefits center on attaining a more favorable political settlement. The costs include destruction that frustrates the NWS's own goals and generates greater opposition, encourages proliferation, or proves ineffective. The NWS will be willing to endure those costs provided that the benefits are large enough. If the benefits shrink—if nuclear use does not shift the political outcome sufficiently in favor of the NWS from what the NWS could accomplish with conventional weapons—then the same level of costs will be enough to dissuade nuclear use. For an NNWS facing a nuclear-armed opponent, then, the critical issue will be whether it believes that its opposition will create a situation where the benefits of nuclear use outweigh those costs. The conventional military balance and NNWS strategies play an important role in such an assessment. I therefore turn to those issues next.

Nonnuclear Weapon State Strategies

The NNWS has a number of policy levers it can pull in an attempt to minimize the risks of a nuclear strike. The NNWS will not pursue each policy in every case. Indeed, if the NNWS has no capacity to harm the NWS—if it is very weak—it is unlikely to need to do anything to reduce the likelihood of nuclear use (of course, the NNWS is also very unlikely to attain its objective in such a situation). While the precise mix of policies will therefore vary from case to case, the NNWS is likely to pursue some combination that raises the costs or lowers the benefits of nuclear use. Doing so manipulates the political and military situation facing the NWS. In the rest of this section I first outline NNWS policies that can reduce benefits. I then discuss ways the NNWS can attempt to raise the costs. Not every factor is subject to manipulation, but enough are to provide a wide menu to an NNWS.

NONNUCLEAR WEAPON STATE STRATEGIES TO REDUCE BENEFITS

An NNWS can reduce the benefits of nuclear use against it via two key mechanisms. First, it can reduce the danger that it poses to the NWS. Second, it can seek to reduce the damage of limited punishment or denial strikes. I outline each in turn.

The level of danger the NNWS creates for the NWS looms large in governing the benefits of nuclear strikes. The lower the threat the NNWS poses, the lower the incentive of its foe to use nuclear strikes to remove that threat. As the danger the NNWS creates for the NWS increases, other strategies to reduce the benefits or raise the costs of nuclear use may no longer be sufficient to offset the immediate benefit of nuclear strikes. The NWS is likely to prioritize the immediate benefits of nuclear use when facing a massive threat and worry less about additional costs that might occur later. In essence, the NWS will discount the future and focus on the short-term necessity of reaching the future.

The NNWS can directly influence the amount of danger to the NWS by limiting its aims and the means by which it confronts the nuclear-armed opponent. In many cases, this will not require the NNWS to alter its behavior; the NNWS is simply unable to do more. At other times, the NNWS will need to deliberately alter its strategy to minimize the danger to the NWS. The NNWS leadership gambles that it will not create a military necessity for the NWS to use nuclear weapons or create a use-it-or-lose-it scenario for the nuclear opponent.

To begin with, the NNWS can direct its challenge to isolated areas, signaling limited intentions. Such challenges provide a natural stopping point that does not create further dangers for the NWS. These "thresholds" or focal points, to borrow from Thomas Schelling, represent "finite steps in the enlargement of a war or a change in participation. . . . Any kind of restrained conflict needs a distinctive restraint that can be recognized by both sides, conspicuous stopping places, conventions and precedents to indicate what is within bounds and what is out of bounds."[66] The NNWS can commit to pressure an area without automatically expanding demands. If the NWS makes the desired concession in that isolated area, it will not result in a major defeat, an untenable security situation for the NWS, or necessarily invite additional challenges—the presence of any of which make nuclear use more appealing. For example, geography provided the Soviet Union an ability to threaten Berlin, isolated deep within the Soviet zone, in order to pressure the United States without needing to challenge US forces in western Germany. The Soviets could credibly signal they had limited intentions by focusing on an area completely inside their occupation zone. In 1982, Argentina attacked islands thousands of miles from the British homeland. There was no danger Argentina would keep going to threaten other British territory.

The NNWS can also limit its aims and means in any fighting. The precise scope of the limitations will vary because war "may be limited in a great many ways and degrees."[67] There are nevertheless several specific actions the NNWS should be expected to avoid regardless of whether it behaves offensively or defensively. Most importantly, the NNWS will avoid threatening the very survival of the NWS, its ruling regime, or the destruction of the NWS's conventional military ability to protect itself. This reduces the benefits for early nuclear escalation because the NWS does not need to stave off destruction. By contrast, facing destruction or being unable to contest the NNWS effectively at the conventional level increases the benefits of using nuclear weapons to avoid defeat. The NNWS can inflict costs on the NWS and is likely to attempt to destroy a portion of the NWS's conventional forces to do so. Indeed, a key part of the strategies adopted by Egypt in 1969–1970 and 1973, China in 1950, and Iraq in 1990–1991 was to kill NWS soldiers. By imposing those costs, the NNWS hoped to cause the NWS to negotiate or quit the fight. The key for the NNWS, though, is to limit the destruction to fielded forces in a way that does not open the NWS homeland to conquest. This generates an interesting dynamic: the amount of damage the NNWS can inflict on the NWS increases as the danger it poses to the NWS's homeland decreases. Thus, in 1950 China could envision destroying entire American divisions, in part because doing so would not provide China with the ability to threaten the survival of the American state or its ruling regime. Egyptian leaders in 1973 expressly conveyed to the Israeli leadership, through the Americans, that they had no intention of advancing deep into the Sinai, let alone threatening pre-1967 Israeli territory.

The NNWS will also avoid operations to destroy its opponent's nuclear arsenal. The benefits of nuclear use increase if a state fears that it will be unable to rely on its nuclear arsenal in the future. In other words, if the NWS believes that it is in danger of losing its nuclear arsenal, it has an incentive to use the weapons now for fear that it will not be able to use them later. To be sure, the lack of a nuclear arsenal for the NNWS removes some of this dynamic for the NWS.[68] Conventional military campaigns that endanger the nuclear arsenal, command and control, or conventional military forces supporting the NWS's arsenal can nevertheless pose a significant danger to the ability of the NWS to execute a nuclear strike.[69]

Even if the NNWS does not deliberately target the nuclear forces of the NWS, it can inadvertently threaten their survival through certain types of military operations. In the face of "large-scale conventional attacks on nuclear forces or their supporting structure," Barry R. Posen argues, "the salience of nuclear forces for the conflict is raised inadvertently, before the imminent loss of the stakes that precipitated the conflict raises the nuclear specter."[70] Though this type of inadvertent escalation logic has been discussed primarily in situations of joint nuclear possession, aspects are relevant for nuclear monopoly. Talmadge argues that a state that found its nuclear arsenal under duress might use nuclear weapons "to halt the components of the opposing conventional campaign that posed the greatest threat to the target's nuclear forces. Nuclear weapons could achieve these effects more rapidly than conventional forces." In addition, "a state might engage in limited nuclear escalation to try to generate coercive leverage, signaling its resolve to make the opponent pay significant costs until the counterforce campaign was either suspended or completed."[71] In nuclear monopoly, the concern would be NNWS conventional counterforce capabilities.

The claim that the NNWS will avoid efforts to destroy its opponent's nuclear arsenal may seem counterintuitive. After all, if the NNWS can eliminate the opponent's nuclear arsenal, doesn't this guarantee that the NNWS will not suffer a nuclear strike? The problem is that in most cases the NNWS is unlikely to be able to quickly and completely destroy the opponent's nuclear arsenal. For example, Keir Lieber and Daryl G. Press modeled a conventional attack against twenty fixed missile silos by US B-2 bombers using GPS-guided bombs. "If GPS signals were not jammed, an attack would destroy most of the silos and have about a 50–50 chance of destroying them all. . . . If an enemy can jam GPS signals near the target, the odds of destroying all 20 silos with current bombs are essentially nil."[72] Such a scenario represents a best case for an attacker that possesses advanced technology that most countries—including the United States in the past—lack, against a small number of fixed targets, with minimal efforts to interdict the air strikes. To be sure, mobile platforms are more vulnerable to conventional strikes because mobility comes at the cost of hardening. Yet mobility and other forms of concealment increase the intelligence demands on the attacker attempting to eliminate the nuclear forces.[73] Unless the NNWS is able to completely eliminate the NWS's arsenal and ability to deliver nuclear weapons before the NWS can respond, which at least historically and in the near term is very unlikely, then posing a large conventional danger to the nuclear arsenal is dangerous. True, the NNWS will attempt, if it is able, to intercept any incoming nuclear strikes. The key distinction is that intercepting strikes means that the NWS has already acted, and the NNWS is attempting to minimize damage rather than launching a strike designed to destroy the adversary's nuclear arsenal.

Any fighting need not be limited for both sides. As Robert Osgood points out, "limited war is not only a matter of degree but also a matter of national perspective—a local war that is limited from the standpoint of external participants might be total from the standpoint of local belligerents, as in the Korean and Vietnam wars."[74] In nuclear monopoly, the critical distinction is the amount of stress placed on the NWS. The fighting may require significant effort for the NNWS.

The NNWS will frequently rely on defensive strategies. Ivan Arrequín-Toft identifies such a strategy as one that seeks "to damage an adversary's capability to attack by crippling its advancing or proximate armed forces."[75] The defensive strategy can rely on both mechanized and guerrilla operations.[76] Mechanized operations focus on using cohesive armed forces to degrade and destroy the enemy forces through a series of battles at a set line or through defense-in-depth. Guerrilla warfare centers on small units fighting over dispersed areas to undermine the adversary's control of the population; there is a lack of clearly defined battles and front lines.[77] In both cases, the NNWS limits its aims and reduces the danger to the NWS by not harming the nuclear opponent's nuclear arsenal, conventional reserves, or territory directly. With the NWS not facing major defeat, the benefits for nuclear use decrease. Guerrilla warfare also offers few military targets for the nuclear-armed state, further reducing the benefits of nuclear use.

The NNWS need not fight entirely defensively. It can also execute a limited offensive. In order to do so, the NNWS must manufacture a local superiority against the nuclear opponent, often relying on the element of surprise to offset the intrinsic advantages enjoyed by defenders.[78] The NNWS then launches an offensive with the purpose of taking some small objective and switching to a defensive posture. John Mearsheimer notes that once the original attacker switches to the defensive, the burden for starting a war "is transferred to the [original] defender. The assumption is that the [original] defender would not start such a war and that therefore the conflict will remain limited."[79] In essence, the NNWS hopes to present its nuclear-armed opponent with a fait accompli, signal limited aims, and thereby reduce the benefits of a nuclear strike. Thus, in 1973, Egypt planned to take only a few miles east of the Suez Canal and then seek negotiations with Israel. In 1982, Argentina quickly took the Falkland Islands and settled into a defensive posture while calling for new talks.

Limiting fighting reinforces a general tendency in international politics for inducing restraint by the opponent. Carl von Clausewitz recognized this propensity when he wrote that in real war, as opposed to war in the abstract where each side would quickly use all the force at its disposal, the "smaller the penalty you demand from your opponent, the less you can expect him to try and deny it to you; the smaller the effort he makes, the less you need make yourself." Moreover, "anything omitted out of weakness by one side becomes a real, *objective* reason for the other to reduce its efforts, and the tendency toward extremes is once again reduced."[80]

The second mechanism to reduce the benefits of a nuclear strike centers on NNWS efforts to minimize the effects of limited nuclear strikes through civil defense measures, the hardening of valuable civilian and military targets, or the dispersal of military forces. For example, before the 1991 Gulf War, Iraqi leaders explored evacuation procedures in the event of an American nuclear strike on Baghdad and believed dispersing their military forces would minimize the danger of a nuclear strike. Similarly, leaders in the Soviet Union, China, and the United States have examined and implemented civil-defense measures when facing potential nuclear strikes.[81] In a general sense, these efforts serve as a hedge for the NNWS. In an anarchic international environment, it makes some sense to prepare for the worst possible outcome. Even if the NNWS believes that nuclear use is unlikely given the cost-benefit ratio, it may nevertheless see prudence as the highest virtue.

In addition, the NNWS can hope this reduces the likelihood of a nuclear strike. If nuclear use is unlikely to inflict sufficient costs on the NNWS given adequate preparations, then the benefits of executing the strike for the NWS decrease. That is, if a nuclear strike cannot significantly harm the NNWS population or military forces, such a strike is unlikely to deter or compel the NNWS, because a strike benefits the NWS little. To be sure, the NWS may then threaten escalation or carry out more widespread punishment or denial strikes. In those cases, though, the NWS is likely to incur additional costs associated with widespread destruction. The NNWS is gambling that the NWS would only be willing to incur such costs if it gained significant other benefits.

NONNUCLEAR WEAPON STATE STRATEGIES TO RAISE COSTS

Leaders in nonnuclear weapon states can seek to raise the costs of nuclear use for their nuclear-armed opponent by expanding the conflict in response to nuclear use. As Fred Iklé argues, governments exhibit a natural tendency "to refrain from escalating a war if they expect that the military gains of increased violence would be canceled out by the enemy's counter-escalation or by the intervention of other powers on the side of the enemy."[82]

The NNWS can manipulate the level of violence by threatening to use its own unconventional weapons. The most commonly recognized way to raise the costs of nuclear use is to threaten nuclear use in retaliation. This type of nuclear deterrence is, by definition, not available to a state that does not possess nuclear weapons. However, NNWS may possess biological or chemical weapons, the so-called "poor man's" atomic bombs.[83] This logic says that faced with the threat of weapons that can do damage beyond an initial explosion, the nuclear-armed opponent will be reluctant to use nuclear weapons.

This type of action obviously comes with a risk: by inflicting greater damage on the NWS or its allies, the NNWS increases the military benefits of nuclear use. The distinction between first use and retaliation resolves this tension. The NNWS is threatening the latter, not the former. Unconventional weapons will be viewed as a last resort; indeed, most nonnuclear weapon states are likely to identify this as a red line not to cross first. For example, Iraqi leaders in 1990 recognized that using chemical weapons might invite American nuclear retaliation. They simultaneously hoped that the threat of an Iraqi chemical response to nuclear use would constrain the United States. In addition, the destructive power of chemical and biological weapons is not similar to that of nuclear weapons. Such weapons are largely ineffective against prepared military forces and are useless for counterforce operations targeting nuclear weapons. Thus, the incentive of an NWS to eliminate the chemical or biological weapons of an NNWS is smaller than the incentive it would have to eliminate the nuclear arsenal of another, opposing NWS if it believed war inevitable.[84] Nor does the NWS leadership face a use-it-or-lose-it dynamic for fear that if the NNWS used unconventional weapons, the NWS would then be unable to fall back on its own nuclear arsenal.

The NNWS can also deliberately court external actors to constrain the NWS. The logic is that the NWS will be less likely to use nuclear weapons if it believes other actors will either directly intervene in the conflict or otherwise sanction the NWS. At times, these may be formal or informal allies. For instance, Chinese leaders sought greater certainty of Soviet air support prior to making their final decision to intervene in the Korean War in 1950. At other times, though, the NNWS will rely on allies of the nuclear-armed state itself to restrain the latter. Egyptian leaders believed that the United States exercised a great deal of influence over Israeli actions and pointed to that relationship as a constraint on Israeli nuclear use.

The NNWS can also seek to leverage nuclear nonuse norms by diplomatic and media means to constrain the NWS. In doing so, it hopes to shift public opinion in the NWS or other states that will raise the prospects of some type of sanction in the event of nuclear use. That sanction can take the form of diplomatic isolation, economic retaliation, or even the legitimation of the use of force against the NWS. The constraint is direct when influencing the NWS's citizens. It is indirect when targeting other publics, hoping that they lobby their own leaders to pressure the NWS to exercise nuclear restraint. In other words, the NNWS is using normative factors instrumentally to impose additional costs on the NWS.

SUMMARY

Leaders in states without nuclear weapons confronting nuclear-armed opponents can recognize that nuclear monopoly provides incentives and disincentives for nuclear strikes. This creates a space within which the NNWS can challenge and resist its nuclear opponent. It also provides opportunities for the NNWS to further reduce the likelihood of a nuclear strike by increasing the costs and/or reducing the benefits of nuclear use. The NNWS can pursue policies to challenge and resist the NWS that it believes fall below the threshold for nuclear use where benefits begin to outweigh costs. At times, this will require the NNWS to do very little; the costs will simply outweigh the benefits, given NNWS capabilities and behavior. At other times, the NNWS leadership will believe it must actively seek to raise costs or reduce benefits. It can reduce benefits by taking steps to lower the danger of any action to the NWS and minimize the effects of nuclear strikes. It can raise costs by threatening to expand the scope of the conflict to include additional unconventional weapons or third parties. The nuclear balance alone does not determine precisely what actions the NNWS will select. The point is simply that the NNWS will act in a manner in which its behavior falls below the nuclear-use threshold.

The Conventional Military Balance

The conventional military balance looms larger in nuclear monopoly than it does when both sides have nuclear weapons. Analysts have argued that in situations of joint nuclear possession, which side has more conventional military forces does not matter because the nuclear shadow means that fighting simply invites mutual nuclear suicide.[85] In nuclear monopoly, though, the absence of a nuclear capability for the NNWS removes a major benefit of nuclear use: staving off a potential nuclear strike. There is no need for the NWS to use nuclear weapons early in any conflict in a counterforce strike to eliminate a nonexistent nuclear arsenal. By contrast, an NWS facing another NWS has incentives to strike early if it believes that escalation is inevitable, in order to eliminate the opponent's ability to strike with nuclear weapons. "Even if one cannot knock out all of the other side's weapons," Jeffrey Knopf argues, "the possibility of destroying some of them before launch might still look like the best option. Losing two or three cities is a terrible disaster, but it is not as bad as losing five or eight or ten cities."[86]

The NNWS's conventional strategy and military capabilities are therefore the main sources of danger to the NWS. I addressed the conventional aims and means in the previous section. Here I focus on the underlying military capabilities. All else equal, the greater the danger, the more likely the NWS is to use nuclear weapons, because the benefits of eliminating a large danger are greater than the benefits of eliminating a small danger. The greater the conventional capabilities of the NNWS relative to its nuclear-armed opponent, then, the more it must restrict its behavior. That is, the more it must limit its aims and means. In practice, this means avoiding actual combat. Conversely, the weaker the conventional capabilities of the NNWS relative to the NWS, the further the NNWS can push its opponent. A weak NNWS can challenge or resist to the point that a dispute escalates to war. For instance, the Soviet Union had to exercise greater restraint when confronting the United States in 1948 than China did in 1950.

THE RELATIONSHIP TO RESTRAINT

A militarily powerful NNWS must exercise greater restraint than a weaker NNWS for four reasons. No one reason by itself is decisive; taken together, though, they create a powerful inhibition against escalation for the NNWS. First, a powerful NNWS will create more difficulties for the NWS to execute military missions with conventional forces and, at the extreme, can defeat the NWS militarily. The NNWS will be in a position to deny the NWS's conventional platforms military success. For instance, a weak NWS may be unable to overcome NNWS air defenses to conduct militarily meaningful conventional air strikes. Knowing this, the NWS is likely to eschew conventional options and rely instead on nuclear weapons. More ominously, a powerful NNWS can threaten to quickly overwhelm or seriously degrade the nuclear-armed state's conventional forces. This confronts the NWS with the very real prospect of major military defeat. In this situation defeat occurs because the NWS loses its conventional forces, not because the benefits of continuing the struggle are low. For example, the United States saw little possibility of using conventional weapons alone to defeat the Soviet Union in 1948. As such, US planning explicitly incorporated nuclear weapons. By contrast, US planners knew that conventional military forces could defeat Iraqi forces in 1991; the debate centered on how costly such a victory would be.[87] In one case the choice was framed as victory or defeat in a critical region of the world, in the other it was how much victory would cost. Beyond the US case, Narang shows that states facing powerful conventional adversaries are likely to directly incorporate nuclear use into their military planning.[88] In sum, when the NNWS is powerful, the tradeoff between nuclear and conventional military efficacy leans toward nuclear, raising the benefits of a nuclear strike.

Second, it is difficult for a powerful NNWS to signal limited intentions. A weak NNWS can manufacture a local advantage to achieve some limited gain but still credibly commit not to expand the scope of the conflict to threaten the nuclear state's survival or nuclear forces. The reason is simple: the weak NNWS lacks the physical ability to do so. True, a powerful NNWS may be in a better position to execute a limited offensive than a weaker actor. The problem is that a powerful NNWS has an incentive to bluff, feigning limited intentions to avoid early nuclear retaliation before expanding the scope of the conflict to a point where nuclear strikes are ineffective or counterproductive.[89] Indeed, conventionally powerful states have incentives to make large demands.[90] Nuclear-armed states will therefore discount signals by a powerful NNWS to limit their aims and means. As a result, a powerful NNWS must engage in greater efforts at costly signaling than a weak NNWS.[91] One critical way to do this is for the NNWS to avoid military preparations that would put it in a position to seriously harm the nuclear-armed opponent. By not preparing for a major conflict, the NNWS reduces danger to the NWS and leaves itself vulnerable should the conflict escalate. A state planning to escalate would be unlikely to deliberately place itself at such a disadvantage. The nonpreparation thus serves as a credible signal.

Third, a powerful NNWS poses a significant danger to the NWS's arsenal. As noted above, threats to the NWS's nuclear arsenal increase incentives for nuclear use by creating a use-it-or-lose-it dynamic. NNWS conventional operations will tend to avoid the NWS's arsenal, support forces, and command and control as a result. Yet a powerful NNWS generates a danger simply by virtue of its superior military capabilities. Indeed, in many ways a powerful NNWS finds itself in the worst of all possible worlds. It is strong enough to pose a legitimate threat to the NWS's arsenal over a relatively short time. This creates a motive for the NWS to use nuclear weapons in the event of a war. At the same time, for reasons outlined in the previous section, the NNWS is unlikely to be able to completely eliminate its opponent's nuclear arsenal in a single or even series of rapid preemptive strikes before the NWS can retaliate in some manner. This provides an opportunity for the NWS to use nuclear weapons once fighting starts. The result is another nuclear brake on a strong NNWS's willingness to fight.

Fourth, a powerful NNWS is more likely to create situations that lead to unintentional or accidental nuclear use by an NWS opponent. This follows in part from the steps the NWS may take against a powerful NNWS as discussed above. For example, directly incorporating nuclear weapons into military planning or making them ready to use in the event of conventional hostilities requires several actions that make unauthorized and accidental nuclear use more likely. These include the peacetime or intra-crisis dispersal of nuclear weapons and the delegation of launch authority. This necessarily gives more individuals the ability to use nuclear weapons outside central direction.[92] To borrow from Harry Truman, "some dashing lieutenant colonel" may now be able to execute nuclear strikes.[93] A powerful NNWS is more likely to generate a false alarm that a nuclear arsenal is under attack. A weak NNWS is unlikely to possess the capability, given NWS military forces, to attack a nuclear arsenal even if it wanted to do so.

Reports of attacks on nuclear facilities would therefore be discounted or, even if believed, unlikely to generate concern that a counterforce attack capable of eliminating the nuclear arsenal was under way. The NWS is more likely to believe that a powerful NNWS is capable of executing such a strike and may be attempting to degrade the NWS's nuclear arsenal.

THE RELATIONSHIP TO ADDITIONAL STRATEGIES

The conventional balance has its most direct effect on limiting the NNWS's conventional aims and means for several reasons. To begin with, as noted earlier, an NWS that can perform a task equally well with a nuclear or conventional weapon will rely on the conventional weapon if there are any added costs with nuclear use. A weaker NNWS will pose fewer challenges for conventional tasks, reducing the benefits of nuclear strikes and allowing other costs to loom large. Additionally, as the immediate danger to the NWS increases, a particular level of costs may no longer be sufficient to offset the benefits. Limiting the scope of its actions is the most direct route to offset the danger created by an NNWS's conventional capabilities that can inflict major defeat, complicate signaling, and threaten the NWS's arsenal.

By contrast, the effect of the relationship between conventional capabilities and the other NNWS strategies to minimize the dangers of nuclear strikes is either smaller than the link to restraint or it reinforces the leverage of weak actors. This pushes the conventional balance's influence on the scope of NNWS aims and means to the fore. Dispersing forces and population is not very expensive, so neither strong nor weak states have much advantage. Iraq was able to devise a rudimentary command and control system for its mobile missiles during the Gulf War that frustrated the much more powerful United States. Even skilled non-state actors have been able (on a smaller scale) to make effective use of dispersion, cover, and concealment.[94] A powerful NNWS may be in a better position to harden targets, thereby reducing the benefits of nuclear strikes. At the same time, a weak NNWS is likely to have fewer targets that necessitate nuclear strikes, reducing the costs of securing those sites as well as the benefits to the NWS of nuclear use in the first place. Very poor and technologically deficient states are unlikely to develop unconventional weapons, but the barriers to such programs are modest. In a comprehensive analysis, Michael Horowitz and Neil Narang find only "weak evidence that GDP per capita and GDP per capita squared are positively associated with a greater risk of chemical weapons pursuit." According to their data, states such as Egypt, India, Syria, Yugoslavia, and Zimbabwe all acquired chemical weapons during periods when they were weak.[95]

A stronger NNWS has advantages and disadvantages in leveraging outside support to act as a restraint on nuclear use. A third party (or parties) has its own incentives to counterbalance powerful nonnuclear weapon states more than weak ones because the former are greater potential threats. External actors that may otherwise want to prevent nuclear use might delay intervention on behalf of a powerful NNWS, willing to allow a conflict to evolve if it weakens a powerful NNWS. That in turn reduces the threat to the third party itself or promises greater influence in the future. By contrast, a weak NNWS presents a much more limited threat to third parties. Precisely because the danger is smaller, a third party interested in arresting nuclear use is more likely to threaten intervention early in a conflict. In addition, a weak NNWS is better positioned to confront an opponent with the prospect that outside intervention will change the nature of the war. A powerful NWS has an incentive to avoid widening the conflict and creating a perilous situation. A weak NWS already faces a perilous situation; the threat of third-party involvement is a less effective tool for a powerful NNWS as a result.

Finally, a nuclear strike against a weak NNWS is likely to be seen as a more egregious violation of nuclear nonuse norms than such a strike against a powerful adversary. It would invite greater international and domestic sanctions. George Quester speculates that the international "shock" over nuclear use "would be much less" following a very destructive conventional war.[96] A powerful NNWS would be in a better position to fight such a conflict. Scott Sagan and Benjamin Valentino find that American public support for nuclear strikes increases rapidly with the danger to US forces in a hypothetical conflict.[97] To be sure, many other factors would influence the reaction to nuclear strikes against a nonnuclear opponent. And a weak NNWS that inflicted large losses against a nuclear opponent would have to fear nuclear strikes (which returns to the importance of managing aims and means). All else equal, though, states that cannot decisively defeat a nuclear-armed opponent can rely more on normative inhibitions.

THE PERILS OF WEAKNESS

While a weak NNWS can leverage a number of strategies to minimize the risks of nuclear strikes, this does not mean that it will rush headlong into war against a nuclear opponent. To begin with, if there is no underlying political conflict, then it does not matter if the NNWS is conventionally weak and able to devise brilliant plans to minimize the risks of nuclear use. There is simply no reason to fight. Similarly, if the NNWS is satisfied with the diplomatic trajectory during the dispute, then it is unlikely to rush to war. For example, Egypt secured American involvement in negotiations with Israel following the October 1973 War. As such, Sadat preferred to avoid fighting as diplomacy led to a series of agreements, in fits and starts, that culminated in the 1979 peace treaty.

A weak NNWS may wish to avoid fighting and concede early in any dispute if it believes that it lacks a conventional strategy or sufficient domestic or international support to attain its political objectives. An NNWS that lacks any plausible chance for success is unlikely to act even if it were confident that nuclear weapons would not be used. As noted, the NNWS will tend to pursue only limited offensives or defensive strategies. This requires that the NNWS be able to manufacture local superiority at the point of attack or face the NWS on or near its territory. If neither condition holds, then war is unlikely. Even with these limitations, my argument highlights that there are more opportunities for a weak NNWS to stand firm in a dispute than for a powerful NNWS. A powerful NNWS, even if it believes it could succeed in a conventional conflict with an NWS, must curtail its aims and means because they pose a greater danger to the NWS, thus raising the benefits of nuclear use.

SUMMARY

A conventionally powerful NNWS is more likely to be able to block NWS conventional operations, more likely to inflict major defeat on the NWS, less likely to be able to signal limited intentions, more likely to deliberately or inadvertently threaten the NWS arsenal, and more likely to generate dynamics that lead to accidental or unauthorized nuclear launch. As such, a powerful NNWS must fear nuclear strikes and is more likely than a weak NNWS to significantly limit its aims and means during any dispute with a nuclear opponent.

Predictions

My argument makes four main predictions. First, wars should be rare when the NNWS is militarily powerful relative to the NWS. A powerful NNWS can still confront a nuclear-armed opponent, but it will face strong pressure to restrain its behavior and avoid actual fighting. Most wars involving a powerful NNWS relative to an NWS opponent will be "selected out" of the system as the powerful NNWS seeks an alternative solution.[98] Second, those wars that do occur in nuclear monopoly should not pose a danger to the survival of the NWS or its nuclear forces, or involve major combat operations on its homeland.

Third, during confrontations, NNWS leaders should discount nuclear use because they believe the costs to the NWS of using nuclear weapons outweigh the benefits. The NNWS cannot know the precise threshold for nuclear use, and aspects unique to each situation matter. As a result, not every case will feature the same discussions as the NNWS probes the limits of the nuclear shadow. But there should be evidence that the NNWS assessed strategic factors that influence the costs and benefits of nuclear use. In terms of benefits, discussions are likely to focus on the dangers that the NNWS actions pose for the nuclear opponent. If the NNWS is very weak and fighting entirely defensively, there may be little discussion at all. Yet this is not solely the product of capabilities; even a weak NNWS must worry if its forces begin inflicting serious harm on the nuclear opponent, because this raises the benefits of a nuclear strike. Additionally, if costs of nuclear use are very low, then even modest benefits might be sufficient to create incentives for nuclear strikes. In terms of costs, the NNWS can focus on how nuclear use would be counterproductive for the nuclear state. Some costs are intrinsic to the situation. For example, Iraqi leaders believed that US nuclear strikes that damaged oil wells would harm US interests. States not blessed by geography cannot rely on such a constraint. Other costs are subject to NNWS manipulation. Importantly, if the NNWS fears that the benefits of nuclear strikes will outweigh the costs, its leadership should identify additional strategies to pursue to reduce benefits or raise costs. In some cases, the NNWS will have to do very little. In other cases, it will struggle to bring benefits below costs and have to constrain its behavior accordingly.

Finally, NNWS behavior should coincide with this planning. That is, the NNWS will act within the red lines that its leadership identifies. The NNWS need not pursue every means to raise the costs or decrease the benefits of nuclear use. But there should be evidence that it takes the nuclear balance into consideration and behaves in a manner it believes will not invite a nuclear strike.

Assessing the Argument

I rely on cross-case and within-case analysis to assess my argument. Specifically, I examine whether there is general congruence between power asymmetries and war in nuclear monopoly. I also examine process evidence to determine if NNWS leaders factored nuclear weapons into their decision making, the rationale they identified as to why nuclear use was unlikely, and if their behavior matched that planning.[99] By themselves, the case studies and cross-case comparisons have a number of limitations. By including both I am able to assess more observable implications, increasing the confidence in the overall findings. In the rest of this section I discuss each approach.

WITHIN-CASE ANALYSIS

The case studies combine congruence methods with historical process tracing. In terms of congruence, I determine if the wars observed were fought when the NWS possessed a large conventional military advantage.

I focus on military power at the outset, because the core logic of the argument centers on whether the NNWS poses a large military danger in the short term that requires nuclear weapons to offset. Even if the NWS has more latent power, such as a larger overall economy or greater energy, iron, and steel production, that advantage may not have time to manifest itself before the NNWS is able to defeat the NWS's conventional forces.

I use quantitative and qualitative measures for military power. I rely on military spending and levels of economic development as the main quantitative indicators.[100] For qualitative indicators, I examine how participants at the time, and how historical assessments, characterized the military balance. In cases where multiple conflicts occurred I include performance from past confrontations to inform this assessment. Thus, Egyptian performance in the 1967 Six Day War cannot be used to code the military balance for that war but can be used to inform the assessments of the balance prior to the 1969 and 1973 wars. Where possible, I also assess the ability of the NWS and the NNWS to perform complex operations and tactics.[101]

The case studies also employ historical process tracing. Historical analysis is used to inform the coding of military capabilities and provide general background for the cases. Process tracing then also examines the steps to see if the key actors behave and talk in a manner consistent with the argument's underlying logic. This also allows examination of possible confounding factors that may be influencing decision making or factors that can mask the influence of nuclear weapons in the conflict.[102] I rely on internal meetings, military orders, and actual behavior during each conflict. Importantly, the planning *and* conduct must be consistent. For instance, if the NNWS leaders plan for a major offensive that threatens the survival of the nuclear-armed opponent but are only able to execute a limited offensive, this challenges my argument. Nor is my argument supported if the NNWS leadership plans for a limited offensive but expands the scope of operations as opportunities emerge, without taking other measures to minimize the risks of nuclear use.

Process evidence is particularly important in establishing the causal import of my argument. All explanations for conflict in nuclear monopoly explicitly or implicitly rest on the NNWS discounting the likelihood of nuclear use. The key issue is why states would discount the likelihood of nuclear use. For instance, Narang claims that nuclear weapon states with catalytic or assured retaliation force postures are less likely to deter conventional assaults because adversaries will not fear force postures aimed primarily at drawing in third parties or deterring nuclear strikes.[103] Most normative arguments only investigate the role that nuclear nonuse norms play in causing an NNWS to believe nuclear weapons will not be used.[104] My argument does not claim these explanations are incorrect; I directly incorporate several of their insights. Process evidence can establish that these alternative explanations are insufficient by themselves, however.

CASE SELECTION

I examine four disputes in detail: the Soviet Union versus the United States (1945–1949), the People's Republic of China versus the United States (1949–1964), Iraq versus the United States (1979–2003), and Egypt versus Israel (1967–1979). These cases provide several sources of leverage for my argument. First, three of the cases involve an NNWS confronting a nuclear-armed opponent with a small number of nuclear weapons. One might expect state leaders to take large nuclear arsenals more seriously. If NNWS leaders still take nuclear weapons into consideration even when the NWS possesses limited destructive power, it is reasonable to conclude they would do so when the nuclear opponent could draw on a larger number of weapons as well.

Second, the nuclear weapon states in these four cases are both democracies. Theory and intuition suggest that nuclear nonuse norms are more likely to constrain democracies than autocracies. This is not to argue that autocracies do not adopt or recognize various norms, merely that they are less likely to do so than their democratic counterparts. Selecting democracies therefore biases the cases in favor of finding evidence that norms alone influenced NNWS decision making.

Third, the cases are diverse. This allows me to determine if the argument's key features were present in each case while other factors change. If different leaders in different time periods facing arsenals of varying size, sophistication, and force postures all identified strategic factors that inhibited nuclear use, this suggests the importance of those dynamics. This approach has several drawbacks, but these can be compensated for by other parts of the analysis.[105]

Fourth, the Egyptian-Israeli case appears as a major outlier for my argument. After all, Egypt consistently had at least as large a military as Israel and a much larger overall population. Egypt could also rely on the support, albeit tepid at times, of Arab allies and the Soviet Union. A careful inspection of this case is therefore imperative. As I show in chapter 3, though, Israeli conventional capabilities consistently outstripped those of its Egyptian rival. The case is in fact consistent with my argument.

Finally, in each case the NNWS could avoid a major conflict. That is, these are not cases where the NWS simply attacked its nonnuclear-armed opponent. A direct assault against a weaker opponent fought on NNWS territory that led the NNWS to fight would be consistent with my argument. The NNWS would be fighting defensively, pose little danger to the NWS, and the location of the operation would create challenges to nuclear use. But those are easy cases and not particularly surprising. More interesting are cases where the NNWS confronted the nuclear-armed opponent or had the opportunity to give in to demands without risking its regime or territory.

CROSS-CASE ANALYSIS

The cross-case analysis seeks to supplement the within-case analysis by examining the generalizability of two key predictions. It cannot confirm or refute the basic argument on its own, but shows it can plausibly account for additional cases. First, I compare the conventional balance in wars in nuclear monopoly to the conventional balance in wars without nuclear-armed states. I show that wars in nuclear monopoly are fought when conventional capabilities are more unbalanced than they are in wars between two or more nonnuclear-armed states.

Second, the cross-case analysis demonstrates that wars in nuclear monopoly pose limited danger to the NWS. My argument predicts that in nuclear monopoly, the NNWS will not pose certain dangers to the nuclear-armed state. There is not an obvious comparison in wars with only conventional states—it is not clear which side should limit its behavior—but we know that in some wars involving only conventionally armed states, one or both sides have faced major threats to their territory and regime.[106] This provides an implicit background comparison: if we never or very rarely observe nuclear-armed states facing this type of danger, then one can infer, albeit with limited confidence, that nuclear weapons play a role in that outcome.[107]

This chapter developed a framework to account for conflict in nuclear monopoly. It began by outlining the benefits and costs of nuclear use in nuclear monopoly for the NWS. This established the strategic environment that the NNWS confronts. NNWS leadership can act so long as it believes that the costs of nuclear use for its nuclear-armed opponent outweigh the benefits of nuclear use relative to conventional military alternatives. The more militarily capable the NNWS is relative to the NWS, the more the former must limit its behavior. As a result, wars in nuclear monopoly will tend to occur when the NWS has a large conventional military advantage. In all confrontations, the NNWS will highlight strategic factors that inhibit nuclear use and, when necessary, seek to reduce the benefits and raise the costs of nuclear use for the NWS.

Iraq versus the United States

On August 2, 1990, Iraq launched a massive surprise attack on Kuwait. Within forty-eight hours, Iraq effectively controlled the country. Saddam Hussein and his lieutenants undertook this action despite the expectation that the United States would oppose the invasion and respond in some way. Iraq subsequently resisted US efforts to compel Iraqi withdrawal from Kuwait. Iraqi documents captured after the 2003 US invasion make it clear that the Iraqi leadership took the US nuclear arsenal very seriously. Why, then, did Iraq invade Kuwait knowing it would invite some form of American response, and subsequently resist American demands? This is particularly puzzling because Iraq's own nuclear program was progressing rapidly. Had Saddam Hussein waited a few more years he might have possessed his own, albeit limited, nuclear deterrent.[1]

Iraqi leadership believed that as long as the conflicts were kept limited, the United States would be unlikely to use nuclear weapons for fear of incurring strategic costs that would outweigh the benefits it could expect from nuclear use. From the perspective of the Iraqi leadership, the domestic and international situation was bleak and growing worse in 1990. Iraq attacked Kuwait in an effort to redress these problems and then settled into a defensive posture to await the American response. Even though Iraq was a relatively weak actor, Iraqi leaders considered the possibility that the United States might use nuclear weapons if Iraq inflicted large losses on US forces and the Americans were unwilling to seek a negotiated settlement. Consistent with my argument, Iraqi leaders recognized that in such an eventuality the benefits of using nuclear weapons might increase. The Iraqis sought external support but, finding it lacking, focused on the potential costs that reduced the incentives for the US to use nuclear weapons, such as the destruction of valuable targets, particularly oil, and Iraqi use of chemical weapons against American regional allies. Iraqi leaders also hedged by preparing for a possible nuclear strike in the event they misjudged the threshold for nuclear strikes. In 2003, Iraq was willing to concede to most American demands but ultimately chose to fight when it was clear that the United States would settle for nothing less than regime change. Faced with the destruction of the regime, Iraqi resistance is less puzzling. I therefore focus on the 1990–1991 case, only briefly outlining the background to the 2003 war.

This chapter draws heavily on private conversations within the Iraqi government, from documents captured by the United States after the 2003 invasion. In addition to relying on published collections of these documents, I also examined several hundred pages held at the Conflict Records Research Center in Washington, DC. These sources provide an invaluable insight into the inner workings of a dictatorial regime. They also demonstrate quite clearly that the Iraqi leadership factored US nuclear capabilities into their decision making, particularly in the lead-up to and prosecution of the 1991 Gulf War. I supplement these sources with American interviews with key Iraqi officials from the 1980s through the 2000s. For instance, I include unclassified interviews the FBI conducted with Saddam Hussein in 2004. Finally, as in the other chapters, I also rely on secondary accounts and American documents to explain additional aspects of the case.

The rest of this chapter presents the argument in three sections. First, I review the nuclear and conventional military balance. Second, I discuss the background for Iraqi behavior during the period of American nuclear monopoly beginning in 1979 when Saddam Hussein was officially Iraqi president, focusing most heavily on events in 1989–1991. Finally, I examine Iraqi behavior and views on the American nuclear arsenal, ending with a summary of key points from the chapter.

The Military Balance

The United States had an atomic monopoly against Iraq throughout Saddam Hussein's tenure as Iraq's leader. In addition, the US conventional military advantage was very large, and Iraq had no way to strike the US homeland.

THE NUCLEAR BALANCE

Though the George H. W. Bush administration drastically reduced the number of deployed nuclear weapons during its term (see table 2.1), the United States maintained an obvious and overwhelming nuclear capability. The US possessed nuclear platforms capable of striking any part of Iraq. Iraq had no defense against such capabilities.

Table 2.1 US nuclear weapons, 1979–2003

Year	Total nuclear warheads	Strategic nuclear warheads	Estimated total yield (megatons)
1979	24,138	11,088	5,696.34
1980	24,104	10,768	5,618.86
1981	23,208	10,464	5,382.91
1982	22,886	10,291	5,358.89
1983	23,305	10,610	5,232.47
1984	23,459	11,308	5,192.20
1985	23,368	11,590	5,217.48
1986	23,317	12,314	5,414.54
1987	23,575	13,685	4,882.14
1988	23,205	13,080	4,789.77
1989	22,217	12,780	4,743.34
1990	21,392	12,304	4,518.91
1991	19,008	9,300	3,795.94
1992	13,708	8,280	3,167.88
1993	11,511	7,528	2,647.31
1994	10,979	7,688	2,375.30
1995	10,904	7,248	2,300.00
1996	11,011	6,862	2,301.50
1997	10,903	6,286	1,935.88
1998	10,732	6,236	1,937.13
1999	10,685	6,298	2,016.05
2000	10,577	6,298	1,982.17
2001	10,526	5,380	1,982.17
2002	10,457	5,092	1,752.32
2003	10,027	4,848	1,698.32

Sources: Department of State, "Fact Sheet: Transparency in the U.S. Nuclear Weapons Stockpile," April 29, 2014, https://2009-2017.state.gov/documents/organization/225555.pdf; "Estimated U.S. and Soviet/Russian Nuclear Stockpiles, 1945–94," Bulletin of the Atomic Scientists 50, no. 6 (1994): 58–59; Polmar and Norris, U.S. Nuclear Arsenal, 258–59.

Note: I estimated yields for 1995–2003 based on warhead counts and yields from the Nuclear Notebook series published by the Bulletin of the Atomic Scientists. For variable yield warheads I used the highest yield.

THE CONVENTIONAL BALANCE

The United States possessed a very large conventional advantage against Iraq. The US was far more economically developed than Iraq. In 1989, US per capita GDP was at a nearly 6:1 advantage and would grow to greater than 10:1 in the next decade (figure 2.1). The overall American economic advantage was even larger, as American GDP was always at least fifty times greater than Iraqi GDP. The US had a larger overall military than Iraq as well (figure 2.2). That advantage grew after the Iraqi defeat in 1991. Not surprisingly, the US economic edge meant that US spending per service member was much higher than Iraqi spending. True, not all US troops were deployed or were able to be deployed in the region, whereas Iraqi troops were concentrated in Iraq (and in Kuwait briefly in 1990–1991). More importantly, though, Iraq had no power projection capability that would allow it to strike the United States or even American interests and allies outside the region. In 1990, the Iraqi navy was estimated to have five thousand sailors serving primarily on five frigates and thirty-eight coastal and patrol ships that included six corvettes and eight Osa-class missile boats.[2] By contrast, the US could, and did on multiple occasions, deploy armies numbering in the hundreds of thousands in the area. Its naval and air forces also allowed the US to strike Iraq from platforms and bases hundreds and

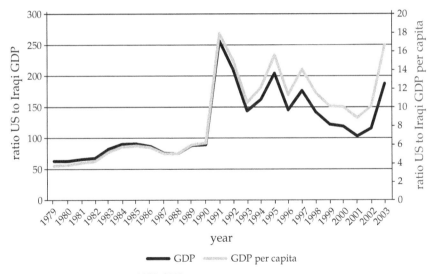

Figure 2.1 Economic ratios, 1979–2003

Source: Gleditsch Expanded GDP data version 6.0 (September 2014), http://ksgleditsch.com/exptradegdp. html.

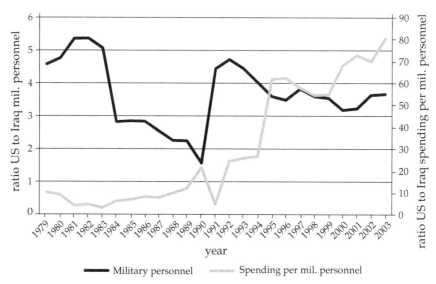

Figure 2.2 Military ratios, 1979–2003

Source: Correlates of War, National Material Capabilities, version 5.0, http://www.correlatesofwar.org/data-sets/national-material-capabilities.

Note: Iraqi military expenditures estimated for 2002–2003 using 2001 data.

even thousands of miles away from Iraqi territory. In short, the US could strike Iraqi territory at will; Iraq had no equivalent capability.

The US qualitative advantage was equally decisive. On the eve of the Gulf War, the average age of US weapons was twelve years ahead of Iraqi equipment, a historically large gap.[3] The US military was a professional organization capable of implementing effective force employment techniques. The Iraqi military had gained experience during the Iran-Iraq War. Much of that skill was wasted, though, as Saddam began reinstituting coup-prevention practices after the war that strengthened his control of the regime and country at the price of battlefield effectiveness.[4] Indicative of the US advantage, the debate within the United States prior to the 1991 Gulf War was not about whether the US could defeat the Iraqi military conventionally or if Iraq posed a threat to the American homeland. US victory in any conflict was overdetermined. Rather, the debate centered on how costly victory would be for the Americans.[5] Thereafter the situation only worsened for Iraq.[6]

The Americans were largely content to rely on their conventional advantage and did not seriously integrate nuclear options into their planning even prior to the 1991 Gulf War when the Iraqi military was more formidable than in 2002–2003. My argument focuses on NNWS decision making and does not attempt to explain the decision making in the NWS. I do not seek to test my argument against US nuclear policy. The point is simply that the limited US discussion of nuclear weapons underscores the US conventional advantage and lack of military necessity for nuclear strikes. This is not to say there was no nuclear-related discussion. In January 1991 Secretary of State James Baker issued a veiled warning to Iraq that chemical weapon use might invite nuclear retaliation.[7] In addition, Secretary of Defense Richard Cheney asked Pentagon planners, "How many tactical nukes are we going to have to use to take out an Iraqi Republican Guard division?" Those inquiries were prompted, as Cheney later put it, by a desire to know if the US got "into a situation and we have to follow through on our threat, what's that going to look like?"[8] Analysts reportedly replied that seventeen nuclear weapons would be necessary for each division. Overall, though, interest in nuclear options was low. Colin Powell, then chairman of the Joint Chiefs of Staff, recalled that he brushed off calls for nuclear planning: "Let's not even think about nukes. You know we're not going to let that genie loose."[9] Former US national security adviser Brent Scowcroft wrote that during a meeting of senior officials "no one advanced the notion of using nuclear weapons, and the President rejected it even in retaliation for chemical or biological attacks."[10] This was not a closely guarded secret. For instance, the *Los Angeles Times* wrote on October 2, 1990, that US military officials stated that the "United States has placed no nuclear weapons in Saudi Arabia or surrounding countries and has no plans to use them even in response to an Iraqi attack using chemical or biological weapons."[11]

Dispute Overview

The core concern of Saddam Hussein was maintaining his regime. Saddam had gradually accumulated power during the 1970s, culminating in his ascension to the presidency on July 16, 1979, following the resignation (willingly or not) of Ahmad Hassan al-Bakr.[12] As Phil Haun writes, the Iraqi dictator's "dominant and perpetual concern was for his political and personal survival."[13] True, Iraqi leaders at times harbored broader regional ambitions. Saddam sought to place Iraq, at least at the rhetorical level, at the center of a new pan-Arabism following the Egyptian-Israeli peace treaty in 1979.[14] Iraq also occasionally joined efforts to confront nuclear-armed Israel before and after the 1968 Ba'athist takeover. That support was always limited, and Iraq was a small player as others states, usually Egypt, were at the center of those confrontations. Moreover, Saddam explicitly argued that without nuclear weapons a major confrontation with Israel would be too dangerous. In such a war, Saddam mused, "Israel is going to say, 'We will hit you with the atomic bomb.' So should the Arabs stop or not? If they do not have the atom, they will stop."[15] As Hal Brands and David Palkki note, Saddam "believed that an Iraqi bomb would neutralize Israeli nuclear threats, force the Jewish state to fight at the conventional level, and thereby allow Iraq and its Arab allies to prosecute a prolonged war that would displace Israel from the territories occupied in 1967."[16]

Throughout the 1980s Iraq avoided confrontations with the United States. Iraq's deadly war with Iran provided Saddam little room for maneuver elsewhere. Iraqi leaders continued to harbor doubts about US intentions, though. Those fears were reinforced by the Iran-Contra scandal involving US weapons sales to Iran, which Saddam worried portended a long-term danger. But Iraq also relied on several forms of US support during the war and did not perceive an immediate threat.[17] That situation changed at the end of the 1980s.

Iraq invaded Kuwait in 1990, expecting that the United States would oppose the operation. True, Iraqi leaders may not have predicted the full scope of the US ground campaign, but they did consider military action a strong possibility. In short, the Iraqis were not deterred for fear of US retaliation. As Dianne Pfundstein Chamberlain concludes, "Saddam anticipated an American response to the annexation. That is, he knew that the United States had a lot of raw military capability and was likely to use it against him, but he chose to invade Kuwait anyway."[18] Tariq Aziz, the Iraqi foreign minister and longtime Saddam confidant, later stated that "we had no illusions that the Americans will not retaliate against being in Kuwait because they knew that this was a conflict between the two of us—Iraq and the United States."[19] After conquering Kuwait, Iraq then resisted US compellent demands to withdraw, choosing instead to fight a war.

Two factors pushed Iraq to action. First, Iraq's economic situation deteriorated following the Iran-Iraq War, with little hope for improvement. Despite a slight improvement at the end of the war, the trend quickly reversed itself. Iraqi per capita GDP was lower in 1990 than in 1980.[20] To complicate matters, Iraq owed at least $80 billion to its neighbors. The Iraqi government dedicated 22 percent of its budget to service this debt by 1989. Saudi Arabia was willing to restructure the terms. Kuwait, however, elected to use the issue as leverage to settle long-standing disputes.[21] A decline in world oil prices was also cutting deeply into Iraqi revenue. Though global oil prices had recovered somewhat at the end of the decade, they were well below prices from the end of the 1970s (figure 2.3). Saddam maintained in 2004 that "at the end of the [Iran-Iraq] war as Iraq began the rebuilding process, the price of oil was approximately $7 a barrel. . . . Iraq could not possibly rebuild its infrastructure and economy with oil prices at this level. Kuwait was especially at fault regarding these low oil prices."[22] The poor condition of Iraqi infrastructure left the regime unable to increase oil production to offset the lower prices.

Second, there was fear that foreign collusion spearheaded by the United States sought to destabilize the regime. Iraqi leadership became convinced that the United States was urging Kuwait to deliberately undermine Iraqi stability.[23] In May 1990 the Iraqi General Military Intelligence Directorate

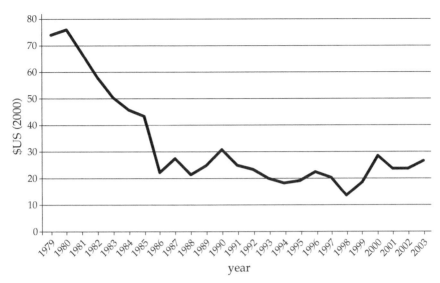

Figure 2.3 Oil prices per barrel, 1979–2003

Source: Quality of Governance Standard Data (January 2018), Ross Oil Prices, https://qog.pol.gu.se/data/datadownloads/qogstandarddata.

(GMID) reported that both "the United States of America and Britain are trying to create a political climate suitable for directing a hostile strike against the country."[24] This reflected Saddam's thinking, as he reportedly told the GMID deputy director in March that "America is coordinating with Saudi Arabia and the [United Arab Emirates] and Kuwait in a conspiracy against us. They are trying to reduce the price of oil to affect our military industries and our scientific research, to force us to reduce the size of our armed forces."[25] As Aziz explained several years later, "We started to realize that there is a conspiracy against Iraq, a deliberate conspiracy against Iraq, by Kuwait, organized, devised by the United States."[26] US-Kuwaiti military cooperation reinforced Iraqi paranoia. Saddam recalled that the "visit of US General [Norman] Schwarzkopf to Kuwait also provided further confirmation" of nefarious American intentions.[27] The US ambassador to Iraq April Glaspie reported in March 1991 that the Iraqis were "quite convinced that the United States . . . was targeting Iraq. They complained about it all the time. . . . Day after day, the Iraqi media since February [1990]—literally every day—was full of these accusations. And I think it was genuinely believed by Saddam Hussein."[28]

The worsening economic condition and perception of increasing US hostility caused Iraq to bring the issue to a head. Without action on its part, Baghdad feared, external forces would continue their efforts and lead to the collapse of the regime. Aziz recalled that "when we came to that conclusion [that there was a conspiracy] then we started thinking of how to react against the future aggressors on Iraq."[29] Failing to act would result in the collapse of the regime or force Iraq to fight in the future under worse circumstances. Saddam likened Iraq's situation to "an army standing before a landmine, when they stop, the artillery will finish them. [T]o overcome the landmines, they must pass it as quickly as possible and not stand before it. It is the same thing with the International [community], if we were to stop, we could be exposed to the death of our regime."[30] In 2003 he told FBI interviewers that Iraq invaded Kuwait in 1990 to "defend by attacking."[31] Taha Ramadan reiterated this line of thinking in a Revolutionary Command Council (RCC) meeting after the Iraqi invasion of Kuwait.

> Imagine if we had waited two years, and the Gulf oil policy had continued as it is. Iraq is $50 billion in debt and the price of oil does not meet 50% of our even minimal needs. . . . The Western states and America decided to stop exporting technology to us after April 1990, and America stopped agricultural facilities [subsidized exports to Iraq] in March 1990. . . . How were we going to maintain the loyalty of the people and their support for the leader if they saw the inability of the leadership to provide a minimal standard of living in this rich country? . . . If death is definitely coming to this people and this revolution, let it come while we are standing.[32]

These were genuine and widely shared concerns. To be sure, many internal reports and statements were influenced by what the authors thought Saddam would want to hear. There was nevertheless real debate on a number of issues in the RCC; yet most members subscribed to the basic thesis that the United States was a growing source of danger. While there was hope for a positive relationship at times, Iraqi leaders had developed a widely held narrative that the US had worked to undermine the Ba'ath regime in the past. Moreover, the Iraqis' complaints had a basis in real events, even if their conclusions were ultimately flawed. Iraq's economy was suffering, Kuwait was proving obstinate, and the United States was gradually—though still with only a light footprint at the time—increasing its military presence in the region and its ties to various Gulf states.[33] Given the tendency for individuals, including those in the United States, to at times take basic data and draw elaborate, and false, conspiratorial conclusions, it should not be particularly surprising that Iraqi leaders, accustomed to distrust, did so as well.[34]

Iraq subsequently undertook several policy initiatives. In July, Saddam demanded Kuwait pay $2.4 billion for a disputed oil field, $12 billion for depressing oil prices, forgive Iraq's $10 billion debt, and agree to a long-term lease of Bubiyan Island.[35] Kuwait refused, triggering the subsequent invasion in the early morning hours of August 2, 1990. Saddam tasked the elite Republican Guard with the operation. They did not disappoint. In under forty-eight hours Iraq effectively controlled the country.

As noted, Iraqi leaders expected the United States would react in some way. They did not believe they had received a "green light" from Ambassador Glaspie in a July 25 meeting. The Iraqi version of the meeting released to Western media quotes Glaspie as stating that the United States had "no opinion on the Arab-Arab conflicts, like your border disagreement with Kuwait."[36] The American record, by contrast, notes that the "border question" referenced the specific location of the border, with Kuwait allegedly claiming an additional twenty kilometers. The issue was not control of all or even a large part of Kuwait. Furthermore, Glaspie "made clear that we can never excuse settlement of disputes by other than peaceful means."[37] Three days later, Deputy Secretary of State Lawrence Eagleburger instructed Glaspie to inform Saddam that President Bush believed "that differences are best resolved by peaceful means and not by threats involving military force or conflict."[38]

Several additional pieces of evidence point to the conclusion that Saddam suspected some type of US opposition. First, there has been no record found (at least so far) of Saddam or his lieutenants discussing the Glaspie meeting prior to the invasion.[39] Such an absence of discussion would be odd if the meeting had figured prominently in Iraqi decision making. Nevertheless, an absence of evidence is hardly conclusive; it simply may not have been recorded. Second, and more directly, on the same day as the Glaspie meeting, the Iraqi GMID reported that "the United States declared that it would intervene to help Kuwait if there was any serious threat."[40] Indeed, the whole premise of the Iraqi concern was that the United States was aiding and emboldening Kuwait. It would have made little sense, then, for Iraq to believe that the United States would abandon Kuwait. Tariq Aziz admitted as much in 1996, stating that Glaspie "didn't tell us anything strange. She didn't tell us in the sense that we concluded that the Americans will not retaliate. That was nonsense you see. It was nonsense to think that the Americans would not attack us."[41] Third, Saddam most likely agreed with the GMID and Aziz's assessment. As he told Glaspie on July 25, he understood that the United States "can send planes and rockets and hurt Iraq deeply." At some point, though, the danger to Iraq would compel action.[42] After the invasion, Saddam told the Yemeni president that Iraq had taken into consideration the possibility of American naval and air strikes and later told his advisers that the United States might institute "a complete boycott" and "strike us in the air, land, and sea—everywhere."[43]

Though the United States had not issued a specific deterrent threat, then, the more general American deterrent had failed.[44] After the Iraqi invasion, the US quickly began deploying forces to the region to deter any further Iraqi aggression while simultaneously compelling Iraq to leave Kuwait. The US also mobilized a worldwide coalition of states to meet those ends. Over the next few months various United Nations resolutions ratcheted up pressure on Iraq, culminating in UN Security Council Resolution 678 on November 29, 1990. That resolution authorized the growing US-led coalition to "use all necessary means" to force Iraqi withdrawal if Iraqi forces did not leave Kuwait by January 15, 1991.[45]

Direct American compellent efforts initially failed. Saddam and his lieutenants believed that even if they withdrew from Kuwait, the American military threat would remain. As Saddam remarked to Soviet presidential adviser Yevgeny Primakov on October 6, even if Iraq agreed to withdraw from Kuwait, "you cannot bring an end to the American siege of Iraq." Any flexibility on Iraq's part would be an invitation to continued "bargaining and blackmailing."[46] Part of the Iraqi obstinacy stemmed from the fact that the US lacked sufficient conventional ground forces in the region early in the crisis to physically evict Iraqi troops from Kuwait.[47] Moreover, Iraq launched several diplomatic offensives with the hope that they might undermine the burgeoning US-led coalition and lead to some settlement, which I discuss in more detail in the next section. Yet by January it was clear that the diplomatic effort had failed and the United States had sufficient forces to launch an assault. The Iraqi fears remained focused on the continuing danger the US posed even if Iraqi forces withdrew. "We have no guarantees if we withdraw," Saddam told Yemeni officials on January 14, 1991. "Why should we surrender at the last moment?"[48] Withdrawal would not improve the economic situation or end the American threat. On the other hand, as Haun notes, "Standing up to the United States . . . would enhance his [Saddam's] standing within Iraq and the Arab world and might present him with a political victory, even if it resulted in a military defeat."[49]

Iraq was initially willing to endure air strikes, but by mid-February 1991 its resolve was cracking. On February 15, Baghdad announced publicly for the first time a willingness to withdraw from Kuwait, but the Iraqi leadership attached a number of conditions unacceptable to the United States. Yet those conditions evaporated with time. Tariq Aziz traveled to Moscow to meet with President Mikhail Gorbachev on February 18.[50] On February 22, Aziz agreed that Iraq would "withdraw all of its troops immediately and unconditionally from Kuwait."[51] Having stood up against US airstrikes for nearly a month, Saddam had grown less concerned about a retreat causing domestic problems. Moreover, even if the United States remained in the region, Iraq's army now faced the prospect of elimination inside Kuwait. Confronted with the danger of losing an important tool to maintain internal order and defend against external threats, the Iraqi leader was willing to leave Kuwait.[52] Saddam continued to express misgivings about a rapid withdrawal, but seemed to endorse the agreement. "It is better to withdraw the troops yourself, instead of the enemy doing it for you!" he told his lieutenants on February 23.[53] Gorbachev relayed the Iraqi decision to President Bush that same day. "In Baghdad, an official statement has been issued that agrees to full and unconditional withdrawal from Kuwait as specified in the U.N. Resolution and that it will happen from Kuwait City in 4 days. That is to say we have a white flag from Saddam Hussein."[54]

On February 22, though, President Bush had demanded that Iraq complete withdrawal in forty-eight hours, beginning at noon on February 23. Two factors were critical in the American decision.[55] First, the United States was unwilling to allow Iraq to withdraw with its army intact. If Saddam was not decisively defeated, the thinking went, Iraq could simply start new hostilities at any time. This would necessitate a large and open-ended American presence in the region. Second, Saddam's earlier decision to destroy Kuwaiti oil production to disrupt coalition air operations convinced the Americans of Iraqi duplicity. In response to coalition incursions on February 21 and 22, the commanders of the Iraqi III and IV Corps implemented part of the oil-as-weapon plan.[56] President Bush argued that "if there ever was a reason not to have a delay or wonder if they are acting in good faith, this report [of Iraqi destruction of the Kuwaiti oil fields and production system] is one. It has been presented to me as authoritative and it is very disturbing. I don't know how this man [Saddam Hussein] can continue to talk peace through the Soviets, and still be taking these kinds of actions."[57]

The US demand created a new danger for Iraqi leadership. Forty-eight hours would not be enough time to evacuate Iraqi heavy equipment from Kuwait. Postwar estimates concluded that Iraq would have had to abandon half its tanks, armored personnel carriers, and artillery. This, in turn, would have dramatically weakened Saddam's ability to fend off any subsequent attack by the United States or other regional actors as well as threaten the regime's control of the country. In other words, Saddam was willing to withdraw his army to protect the regime, but the American terms seemed to negate that option. Saddam therefore reaffirmed his willingness to accept the Soviet terms while rejecting the Bush ultimatum.[58]

The coalition ground attack, after what the Iraqi leadership believed was Iraq's offer for unconditional withdrawal, confirmed to them their reading of American intentions. "We now know the conspiracy is not only to free Kuwait, but also to occupy Iraq, remove the regime and destroy everything we have worked for," Taha Muhyi al-Din Ma'ruf stated during a meeting with Saddam on February 24.[59] In a separate meeting that same day, Saddam agreed, stating that the "Americans' objective is to [destroy] Iraq in its entirety, including its willpower."[60] After the war, Saddam declared that the United States had failed in its goal of destroying the Iraqi regime. This formed part of the basis for his claims that Iraq had won the war.[61]

The relationship from 1991 to 2003 was filled with tension and low-level disputes. Iraqi actions during this period were primarily limited probes, and after 1998 the depth of Iraqi weakness contributed to even more restrained behavior. Iraqi leaders opposed Operation Provide Comfort in

April 1991, an American humanitarian effort backed with ground forces and aircraft enforcing a no-fly zone in northern Iraq to aid the Iraqi Kurds—though at that point there was little Iraq could do.[62] Baghdad subsequently worked with local Kurdish factions at times, routing the American-backed Iraqi National Congress in northern Iraq in September 1996.[63] Iraq protested the imposition of a no-fly zone over southern Iraq in August 1992 but could do little more. The US-led efforts did not prevent Iraq from exercising control over the Shi'a-dominated South, reducing Ba'athist motivation to act. Iraqi leaders frequently frustrated efforts by the UN Special Commission for the Disarmament of Iraq (UNSCOM) and the International Atomic Energy Agency. The former was tasked with overseeing the identification and elimination of Iraqi chemical and biological weapons, while the latter focused on the nuclear program.[64] In November 1997 Iraq expelled UNSCOM inspectors. The ensuing crisis did not subside until February 23, when UN Secretary-General Kofi Annan and Tariq Aziz signed a memorandum of understanding for access to specific Iraqi sites. Iraq again interfered with inspections in late 1998 following UNSCOM requests for "implementation of a more aggressive weapons inspection program."[65] The challenge to American-backed inspections led to Operation Desert Fox, a series of air and missile strikes against Iraqi targets. Only later did it become apparent that these strikes nearly caused the regime to collapse.[66]

Tensions flared again following the September 11, 2001, terrorist attacks by al-Qaeda against the United States. Though Iraq was not responsible for the attacks, the George W. Bush administration almost instantly began planning for an operation against Iraq. Iraq agreed in September 2002 to allow inspectors into the country "to remove any doubts that Iraq still possesse[d] weapons of mass destruction."[67] Saddam was willing to concede to American demands for access and admit that he no longer possessed weapons of mass destruction (WMD). He was not willing to step down, however. For their part, the Americans were ill-disposed to believe the Iraqi leaders' newfound openness. A decade of obfuscation and lack of reliable intelligence after Operation Desert Fox contributed to American skepticism. While key figures in the Bush administration did believe Iraq had some form of a WMD program, attacking Iraq was by that point a key part of the administration's broader grand strategy.[68] On March 17, 2003, Bush delivered the final ultimatum: "Saddam Hussein and his sons must leave Iraq within 48 hours. Their refusal to do so will result in military conflict commenced at a time of our choosing."[69] Saddam elected to resist, gambling that the United States might only use air strikes or, at most, occupy the southern portion of Iraq rather than incur the full costs of regime change and occupation. This offered Saddam some small chance of remaining in power rather than ceding to US demands for regime change that guaranteed his removal and (likely) his death.

The Role of Nuclear Weapons

Iraqi behavior throughout this period conforms with my argument. The underlying political dispute, Iraqi conventional military limitations, and geography explain much of Iraq's confrontation with the United States throughout the 1979–2003 period. At the same time, precisely because Iraq posed such little danger to the United States, war was possible. Moreover, as I detail below, Iraq did factor the US nuclear arsenal into its decision making at several critical points. Iraqi leaders displayed an understanding that as the damage they inflicted on US forces increased so would the potential benefits of nuclear strikes. So long as the benefits of nuclear use remained low, the Iraqi leadership gambled that various costs would be sufficient to prevent the Americans from using their nuclear arsenal.

I focus on the 1990–1991 Gulf War in this section. During the post–Gulf War crises in the 1990s Iraq never undertook any major military action against the United States. In 2003, Iraq fought entirely on the defensive. In that case, moreover, the stated purpose of the United States to liberate the Iraqi people meant that it would have made little sense to use nuclear weapons in areas that would harm the population to be liberated; nuclear use would have been counterproductive to the political goal. Iraqi weakness in 2003, after a decade of sanctions, also made nuclear weapons militarily unnecessary. In short, the benefits of nuclear use were obviously low, and the costs—in destroying parts of the country the United States hoped to liberate—were obviously high.

IRAQI BEHAVIOR

In 1990 Iraq pursued a policy that posed no danger to the US homeland or nuclear arsenal. Iraq would launch a limited offensive to take Kuwait and then shift to a defensive posture. Iraqi control of Kuwait would not shift the global balance of power. Though there was some concern within the Bush administration that Iraq would attack Saudi Arabia, Iraq could credibly commit to halt its advance because it would have faced much greater difficulty invading and occupying even a portion of Saudi Arabia while holding Kuwait. Iraq planned for the Kuwait invasion using the strictest secrecy measures to avoid inviting an early American and international response. The Iraqi army chief of staff General Nizar al-Khazraji recalled that "the invasion was staged by the Republican Guard forces without my knowledge. It came as a surprise to me . . . [when] I was informed of the situation."[70] Saddam explained the need for stealth to his subordinates on August 2, noting that former Iraqi leader Abd al-Karim Qasim had been too transparent with his intentions to press claims on Kuwait in 1961. This allowed the British to deploy troops to Kuwait and block the Iraqi move. Iraq would not repeat the mistake.[71]

Iraq's actions matched its planning. The invasion was carried out quickly and with few casualties.[72] Saddam summed up the operation on August 7: "All that we wanted as a command was for the military operation to be carried out and then to prepare ourselves for a defensive posture under suitable circumstances. I say our timing was more than suitable. First, the operation went very quickly. Second, control of the situation was comprehensive. Third, we had ample time to prepare a defensive posture."[73] Once the invasion was complete, Iraq moved quickly to legitimize its conquest. It annexed Kuwait on August 8, and then on August 28 declared that Kuwait was Iraq's nineteenth province.[74]

To encourage some form of negotiated settlement, Iraq developed a defensive posture. In his detailed study of Iraqi decision making during the Gulf War, Kevin Woods referred to this as "a 'pufferfish' defense." Saddam reasoned that "you don't have to be bigger than your adversary, just big enough to give your enemy pause."[75] Saddam based this strategy on his perception that the United States was casualty-averse. In February 1990 he stated that "we saw that the United States, as a superpower, departed Lebanon immediately when some Marines were killed."[76] This trait led the United States to be overly dependent on air power, which Saddam privately denigrated. "I mean, what will they do if they engage in a fight?" he asked rhetorically on August 7. "All they can do is bring their airplanes and start bombing: boom, boom, boom, boom, boom, boom. So what? . . . Give me one instance when an airplane has settled any situation. . . . Their bombing will increase the number of refugees."[77] As the American campaign unfolded, Saddam continued to rest his dwindling hopes on American sensitivities. When an aide suggested that inflicting five thousand casualties would result in victory, Saddam interrupted him, saying, "Five hundred. . . . I told my soldiers four [Iraqi soldiers killed] to one [American soldier killed]."[78]

The strategy for the defense of Kuwait followed the basic defensive logic. In the three months following the invasion, Iraq expanded its armed forces and set up defensive positions in Kuwait. As the US buildup in the region continued, Iraq began to reconsider its strategy. To that end, Iraq shifted to a defense-in-depth posture in mid-November. The Republican Guard had already fallen back, ready to act as a reserve force and plug any gaps should coalition forces break through the lines.[79] At the same time, Iraq did not undertake military activities against the coalition during the lead-up to the air campaign. Saddam was determined not to give the coalition an excuse to strike early.

The brief exception to the defensive strategy occurred on January 29, 1991, with an attack against the lightly defended Saudi Arabian town of al-Khafji. Iraq had been unable to inflict any meaningful damage against its adversaries during the first two weeks of coalition air strikes. This frustrated the basic Iraqi goal of inflicting casualties on the Americans. "It is better that we attack the enemy while we still have our capability," the Iraqi chief of staff argued. He added that "the main purpose" of the raid "was to drag the enemy into engagements with ground formations in the most expeditious manner or the fastest way possible."[80] The assault began on the evening of the twenty-ninth, with Iraq forces briefly occupying al-Khafji on the thirtieth before withdrawing. In the end, the Iraqi military suffered major losses, with little apparent gain, though the Iraqi leadership considered the battle a major victory.[81]

Iraq also sought to raise the costs of any American action. This was done largely to forestall any US assault and provide time for a diplomatic solution. Yet if the United States avoided any assault, it would also necessarily avoid a nuclear strike. The more actors that Iraq could turn against the US, moreover, the higher the potential price the US would pay for any nuclear use. In the months immediately after the invasion of Kuwait, Wafiq al-Samarra'i reported that Saddam described his strategy as "holding on to the elephant's trunk"—in other words, waiting and drawing out events.[82] The efforts by the United States to create an "international atmosphere" for hostilities might fail. "We don't have atrocities that will evoke humanity as time passes by. On the other hand and as time passes, the human grasp languishes with regard to hostility," Saddam argued on August 7.[83] Two months later he claimed that "the purpose of prohibiting some foreigners from leaving the country [Iraq] is to increase the obstacles for the wicked enemy's intentions, especially the American officials . . . [and] to gain some time."[84] Taha Ramadan reflected Saddam's thinking that time might play to Iraq's advantage. "Time is not on the side of the Americans or those calling for a war," he noted in October, "because the later they are—the more the coalition disbands—and international opinion is now leaning towards peace."[85] Aziz suggested that the United States would not risk a war shortly before Christmas because "the president who brings corpses to his country at Christmas time will be skinned alive in the US. . . . If a war happens, they know it would not end between November 15 and December 15. It would not end in one month and they know it."[86] Ramadan adhered to his position in late November, optimistically claiming that "now we have supporters. There is a peace movement in Europe and America. . . . There is a crack in the economic sanctions and the people are starting to send stuff [to us]."[87]

Iraq contemplated pressing France and the Soviet Union to delay and perhaps restrain the United States. "As I have shared my opinion with you," Aziz counseled, "deducing that the Soviet Union has no interest in a war of this manner happening and at this large scale."[88] The Soviets were not altruistic, he argued, but might act to prevent hostilities out of sheer self-interest. Izzat al-Duri argued at the same meeting that Iraq should focus on France, stating that "European countries hide behind the French position if they want to compromise and take a more conciliatory stance toward us, or to distance themselves from the American sanctions."[89] Others placed emphasis on France as well. "Of any country in the Security Council outside of the United States or Britain which would be able to prevent the war it would be France," noted Ramadan. He added that "France is able through its contacts to influence two or three other countries [like] Italy, Germany, [or] Spain."[90] In the end, Iraq failed to find sufficient outside support to constrain the United States or intervene on Baghdad's behalf.

Finally, two other Iraqi policies would influence the potential costs and benefits of nuclear use for the nuclear-armed opponent. Iraqi leaders refrained from using chemical or biological weapons for fear it could provoke American escalation, choosing instead to hold their unconventional weapons in reserve in the hopes they might serve as a deterrent. The Iraqi leadership also undertook several costly exercises to minimize the effects of a nuclear strike against their cities. I discuss both of these policies, and their links to the US nuclear arsenal, in the next section.

Much of the Iraqi regime's behavior—its limited offensive moves and search for outside support—is congruent with my framework but would likely have occurred with or without the American nuclear monopoly. As I argued in chapter 1, nuclear monopoly allows weaker states to pursue strategies that invite a response but do not create a major danger to the nuclear-armed state. In other words, nonnuclear factors could drive large parts of Iraqi policy precisely because that policy would not create large enough benefits from nuclear use to offset the costs to the United States of a nuclear strike. Iraqi planning centered on its limited offensive into Kuwait and then a shift to a defensive posture that posed no direct threat to the United States. Iraq's actual behavior during its initial assault on Kuwait and then in its resistance to the United States matched its planning. At the same time, Iraq leaders were cognizant that their strategy rested on inflicting losses on the Americans. As those losses mounted, so too might the benefits of nuclear use. As I show in the next section, Iraqi leaders gambled that the United States would be reluctant to use nuclear weapons given the various costs and benefits of nuclear strikes in this type of conflict.

IRAQI NUCLEAR VIEWS

The evidence indicates that the Iraqi leadership factored the American nuclear arsenal into their decision making in a manner consistent with my argument. This finding is particularly surprising, because no country had used nuclear weapons for forty-five years, and the United States had refrained from nuclear use in the Korean and Vietnam Wars. Yet the Iraqi leadership frequently referenced US nuclear capabilities and undertook costly preparations in response. They hoped that they could fight conventionally, were determined not to use their own unconventional weapons first, and thought that by holding those weapons in reserve they could deter nuclear strikes. If that failed, they hedged by implementing various civil and military measures to minimize the impact of nuclear strikes. The reason they discounted early American nuclear use centered primarily on a strategic logic: that such use would be counterproductive to US interests in the current situation.

Iraqi elites discussed the American nuclear arsenal frequently throughout the crisis. Saddam privately informed the Yemeni president in August 1990 that "we considered that America and Israel . . . may attack us by the atomic bombs. . . . We are ready for that."[91] During a January 1991 confidential meeting with Yasser Arafat, the Iraqi president boasted to his guest that they had carefully considered confronting the United States, including the "case of [America] bombarding Baghdad with atomic bombs."[92]

These Iraqi debates explicitly took American cost-benefit considerations on nuclear use into account. In other words, as the military benefits of nuclear use increased, so too would the likelihood of an American nuclear strike. "I know if the going gets hard, then the Americans or the British will use the atomic weapons against me, and so will Israel," Saddam explained.[93] At an October Revolutionary Command Council meeting, Iraqi leaders considered the likelihood and timing of a US attack. During the meeting, Izzat Ibrahim al-Duri, a member of the RCC and Saddam's inner circle, argued that "we must also expect that the United States could hit us with a nuclear bomb, because the United States . . . cannot imagine our situation, cannot fathom how a little country stands in defiance in front of the United States and dares to challenge it and to win." He then added, "It is possible that if the United States hits us and after six or seven months did not get the result and saw that the war is going to start tearing the [American] people apart, it is possible that it will use nuclear bombs to strike two or three cities."[94] That is, the Americans might escalate to nuclear use if US losses (and thus the benefits of ending those losses) increased and the US had not withdrawn after enduring casualties as the Iraqi leaders hoped.

There was an obvious problem with the Iraqi strategy of inflicting casualties on the Americans to force negotiations, then. If the US did not negotiate, nuclear use would become more likely. The Iraqis never fully resolved this problem. Part of the reason they were willing to run such a risk was their belief, discussed earlier, that inaction could result in the end of their regime. But another reason was the nature of the conflict and costs associated with nuclear use.

The Iraqis had not simply resigned themselves to nuclear strikes. A speech draft for Saddam Hussein dated August 12, 1990, focused on comments by "Samuel Nan" (likely Senator Sam Nunn of Georgia), that the United States would not rule out using "tactical atomic weapons" in response to Iraqi chemical attacks.[95] Though the focus was on tactical nuclear weapons, the document contains insight into Iraqi thinking more broadly on what might constrain US nuclear use.

The document raised three possible reasons the US might not use nuclear weapons. Each centered on the costs of nuclear use for the Americans. The first highlighted a reputational concern consistent with normative nonuse arguments, while the second and third focused on material considerations. First, "international public opinion for today is not the same as it was during the 2nd World War. . . . If America was the one to start using such weapons, they will be dragged down to a lower degree on the ladder of the force centers and international influence." Second, any fighting would "be inside the operation field of one of the biggest oil fields in the world. The pollution would harm the world's economy and ultimately it would cause America an enormous horrifying crisis." Third, "What is more important than these other two factors, is that America knows or at least can realize, that Iraq has weapons that could match their tactical weapons and that Iraq is able to respond to such usage . . . by retaliating against their forces or retaliating against Israel. . . . If Iraq was forced to conduct a self defense against such a massive assault, Iraq will not hesitate to use whatever he has in regards to weapons in order to slam the attack back."[96]

There are a number of reasons to take these arguments seriously. To begin with, the Iraqi leadership spoke of the US interest in petroleum and believed it to be a powerful influence on US policy. They also frequently highlighted the utility of their unconventional weapons. As Benjamin Buch and Scott Sagan report, "Saddam viewed chemical weapons as a final trump card, to be held in reserve to deter American or Israeli use of chemical, biological, or nuclear weapons and to prevent coalition forces from marching on Baghdad."[97] At a December 29, 1990, RCC meeting, Dr. Sa'dun Hammadi counseled that the Iraqi leadership should calm public anxiety by rebroadcasting foreign reports about Iraqi biological weapons to inform "our citizens that we are not fighting the enemy with empty hands but with weapons."[98] Indeed, Iraqi leadership publicly and privately asserted that Iraq would use every weapon in its arsenal in an attempt at deterrence. The targets included Saudi Arabia, Israel, and US forces in the region.[99] To be sure, Saddam recognized that chemical weapons were not equivalent to nuclear weapons.[100] Yet when discussing the American nuclear threat with his military advisers, he noted that "the only things I have are chemical and biological weapons, and I shall have to use them. I have no alternative."[101]

This is not to say that the Iraqis would use the weapons first. While they sought to inflict US casualties, they were hesitant to use every weapon in their arsenal to do so. At a meeting in November 1990, Aziz cautioned that using chemical weapons "would give them [the Americans] an excuse for a nuclear attack."[102] During the second week of January 1991, Saddam stated that Iraq would use chemical weapons "only in case we are obliged and there is a great necessity to put them into action."[103] After the war, Iraqi officials told the United Nations Monitoring, Verification, and Inspection Commission that "these weapons were only to be used in response to a nuclear attack on Baghdad."[104] Richard Cheney, serving as secretary of defense in 1991, later recalled that the Iraqi military intelligence leader said after the war that Iraqi leaders understood that if they used chemical weapons the "allied troops were certain to use nuclear arms and the price will be too dear and too high."[105] While Cheney attributed this to veiled American threats, Aziz's comments occurred before Secretary of State Baker's implicit warning on January 9, 1991, which suggests that Iraqi leaders had already come to this conclusion independently.[106] This is consistent with the argument advanced in this book that states without nuclear arms will probe and set their own red lines when confronting a nuclear-armed opponent.[107]

Iraq's behavior matched its planning. In mid-January 1991 Saddam informed his advisers that Iraq would soon strike Israel with "conventional missiles." He added, "I mean we will use the other warheads, you know, in return for the warheads they use."[108] On January 8, the commander of Iraq's surface-to-surface missiles, Lieutenant General Hazim Abd al-Razzaq al-Ayyubi, received instructions to use biological and chemical weapons "the moment a pertinent order is given, or in the event of a massive strike against Iraq."[109] Kevin Woods found that Saddam "personally made clear to al-Ayyubi that conventional weapons would be the first response option in case of a Coalition attack. In case this last piece of guidance changed, Saddam dedicated a trusted bodyguard to manage a special code word communication system with its own dedicated radio and phone network to ensure communication with the missile commander."[110]

The conceptualization of the chemical arsenal as a deterrent force becomes more apparent when placed alongside Saddam's decision to delegate authority for burning the Kuwaiti oil fields. While there is some evidence that Saddam provided predesignated launch orders for chemical and biological weapons, discussions of this option centered on a response to nuclear strikes. "Despite the purported predelegation of launch authority for missiles with chemical and biological warheads in the event of a nuclear strike on Baghdad," conclude McCarthy and Tucker, "Saddam Hussein probably retained release authority for the tactical use of these weapons during the Gulf War."[111] By contrast, the Iraqi leadership viewed the smoke from burning oil as a valuable battlefield ally, capable of disrupting coalition air operations.[112] It was thus not a strategic deterrent. During a January 13 meeting, an aide sought clarification on the scope of the operation:

> MALE 1: Sir, concerning the oil installations being prepared to be destroyed, there is an order from Your Excellency to blow up these installations in case of a certain degree of danger, or we can wait for an order from Your Excellency. However, Sir, because al-Wafra is near the [Kuwait / Saudi Arabian] borders, Your Excellency has given the local commander the authority to blow it up whenever he believes there is danger. Now, Al-Burgan and the navy remain. Would they be included according to the situation, or—
>
> SADDAM: According to the situation, according to the situation. . . . You could decide this according to the situation in the field of operations—[113]

During the war the oil fields burned; the chemical weapons remained unused.

The Iraqi claim that nuclear weapons had political utility and that their unconventional arsenal could deter nuclear use also matched longer-term thinking and behavior. Throughout the 1980s Iraq had pursued chemical, biological, and nuclear capabilities. In March 1979, Saddam explained that in a hypothetical war with Israel, "we will hear the Americans threatening that if we don't stop our advance, they will throw an atomic bomb at us. Then we can tell them, 'Yes, thank you, we will stop. What do you want?' 'Stop and don't move, not even one meter, otherwise we will throw an atomic bomb on you,' they reply. We state that we have stopped, but we have not given up."[114] In addition, Iraq recognized the value of an unconventional deterrent against nuclear-armed states. "According to our technical, scientific, and military calculations, [Iraq's chemical and biological weapons are] a sufficient deterrent to confront the Israeli nuclear weapon," Saddam said in July 1990.[115]

The Iraqis also instituted costly military and civil defense procedures to hedge against US nuclear use. This would potentially reduce the effects of nuclear use and thereby the benefits to the United States and (marginally) reduce destruction should all else fail. This provides further corroboration that Iraqi discussions on US nuclear capabilities were not simply idle conversation but had a direct effect on Iraqi behavior.

There is some evidence the US nuclear arsenal influenced Iraqi force disposition. The commander of the Republican Guard, Lieutenant General Aayad Futayyih Khalifa al-Rawi, made special note of potential battlefield nuclear use. He recalled that Iraqi leaders "called in the Chemical and Biological Weapons Commander and requested that he give us a plan to defend against a nuclear and biological attack. [A]s it turned out, the American forces had within their arsenal [in Saudi Arabia] Pershing missiles which have nuclear warheads. We studied these missiles and their effects carefully and decided on a wide deployment."[116] The United States had already destroyed most of its Pershing missiles at this point in connection with the 1987 US-Soviet Intermediate Nuclear Forces Treaty, and there is no evidence the US had any nuclear-armed Pershing missiles in the area.[117] The Iraqi focus on dispersing ground forces to reduce nuclear effectiveness was reasonable (if likely unnecessary). Colin Powell recalled that it was difficult to estimate how many tactical nuclear weapons would be necessary to destroy a single Iraqi Republican Guard division because the answer depended on the Iraqi deployment. As Jon Meachem notes, "If the Iraqi troops were thinly spread along a long front, it would require more; if they were more densely massed, it might require fewer."[118]

The Iraqi regime also undertook extensive civil defense preparations to deal with a nuclear attack.[119] For instance, a Ministry of the Interior memo described the purpose of the High Committee for the Evacuation of Baghdad as "preparing an evacuation plan for the city of Baghdad in the event that nuclear weapons are used suddenly." During a series of meetings from October 17 to October 20, 1990, the committee explicitly considered "the impact of a 20-kiloton nuclear bomb on the city of Baghdad."[120] On December 21, there was a large-scale evacuation drill in Saddam City (Sadr City), a suburb of Baghdad.[121]

This planning was not done to enhance Iraqi morale. Indeed, top officials began to worry that the information was damaging the Iraqi will to resist. For instance, at an RCC meeting on December 29, Ali Hassan al-Majid raised the issue of "what is happening in Baghdad with regard to civil defense awareness. There is an explanation about the effects of atomic, nuclear bombs, its efficacy, what does it do, how many people will it kill and how many people will it decimate. All of this awareness is frightening people and instilling fear. . . . We do not have to do that; we only have to provide awareness about preventive measures of such bombs."[122] Izzat al-Duri agreed: "We do not have to explain what the bomb will do; we do not have to explain what the effects of chemical weapons are . . . we can explain only the preventive measures."[123] After criticizing his lieutenants for harming morale, Saddam pushed for a simpler option. "We should decide on the evacuation plan and tell them that every citizen should befriend a rural citizen, just in case the war expands and we are forced to evacuate. We should not explain to the citizen what the atomic bomb will do."[124]

Iraqi elites were not alone in thinking that the United States was capable of nuclear attacks. After one particularly large explosion on January 28, 1991, both the Soviet and the Israeli governments contacted the United States to ask if the Americans had detonated a nuclear weapon. A few days later another large explosion prompted a British soldier to announce on the open radio that "the blokes have just nuked Kuwait."[125] If allies and neutral parties could conceive of the United States using nuclear weapons in the dispute, it is not surprising that Iraqi leaders in a direct adversarial role did the same. Moreover, as noted earlier, US officials as senior as the secretary of defense inquired privately about nuclear options.

Iraqi behavior is congruent with my argument. In an intense political dispute, Iraqi leadership took actions they believed would fall below the threshold of nuclear use. Most of the limitations that Iraq exhibited were due to its own weakness; it could do little more. For Iraq as a weak actor, war with the United States was possible precisely because it would pose such a low danger to the United States. Even then, Iraqi leadership incorporated the US nuclear arsenal into their decision making in 1990–1991. That confrontation is the most important to examine because it involved Iraqi military action that Iraqi leaders believed would invite some form of US response, and US compellent demands did not center on Iraqi regime change. In 1990, Saddam and his lieutenants held their own unconventional weapons in reserve and discounted an American nuclear strike because of the high strategic costs that such a strike would impose on the United States. They also undertook various civil defense measures to minimize losses from nuclear strikes. Fortunately, the Americans had little intention of using nuclear weapons and did not face a need to resort to nuclear use.

Egypt versus Israel

On October 6, 1973, Egyptian military forces launched a massive assault against Israeli positions on the eastern side of the Suez Canal. Simultaneously, Syrian forces attacked the Golan Heights. In both cases the Arab armies performed competently, inflicting some of the worst defeats on the Israeli Defense Forces (IDF) in Israel's history. Only a few years earlier, Egypt had launched a sustained low-level campaign of artillery barrages and commando operations against Israel. Why did Egypt risk such a large-scale assault in 1973, coordinated with another state, against an adversary it knew to possess nuclear weapons? Why was Egypt willing to use military force for over a year from 1969 to 1970?

Egypt had an intense political dispute with Israel centering on the Sinai Peninsula that Israel captured during the 1967 Six Day War. Egyptian leaders settled on force when diplomatic and military trends seemed to make recovering the Sinai less likely. Conversely, when the diplomatic situation improved after 1973, particularly with more direct American involvement, Egypt avoided military action. Egypt's strong interests, rooted in recovering territory, did not cause its leaders to ignore the Israeli nuclear arsenal. They believed that so long as they executed only limited campaigns, the benefits to Israeli of using its nuclear weapons would be low. At the same time, Cairo sought to raise the costs of Israeli nuclear use by developing its own unconventional weapons and relying on the superpowers, in particular the United States, to constrain Israel. Thus while the Israeli nuclear arsenal did not deter a conventional attack, it is not the case that Egyptian leaders ignored the Israeli nuclear arsenal in 1973.[1] In short, the Israeli nuclear arsenal was neither all-imposing nor irrelevant. As I show, there is clear evidence that Egypt took Israeli nuclear weapons into consideration throughout this period. They took actions to offset that advantage and were able to discount the likelihood of Israeli nuclear use given the cost-benefit factors associated with nuclear use. In other words, my argument helps explain why leaders believed that nuclear weapons would not play a large role, which allowed other factors to drive decision making.

This case is also important to examine because it is the one instance in which aggregate material indicators suggest that the nonnuclear weapon state was as conventionally capable as its nuclear-armed opponent, and yet war occurred. These measures therefore seem to contradict my argument, which predicts war is unlikely in such cases. As I show in this chapter, though, Israel's conventional military capability was in fact far superior to that of its Egyptian opponent. The case is therefore consistent with my broader argument.

I focus primarily on the Egyptian-Israeli dispute following the 1967 Six Day War in this chapter. The most thorough accounts of the Israeli nuclear program contend that Israel completed a deliverable nuclear weapon immediately prior to the war.[2] As such, the nuclear arsenal could play only a limited, if any, role in Egyptian decision making. I discuss the 1967 war in the conclusion chapter and appendix B.

The evidence presented in this chapter comes from a variety of sources. The conclusions remain tentative, owing to the lack of direct access to Egyptian documents. I rely heavily on declassified conversations between American and Egyptian officials. This method offers some utility in gauging leader intentions. I also draw from memoirs and later accounts of events from participants, including those from Egypt, the Soviet Union, and the United States. Finally, I rely on a number of secondary works, themselves frequently based on interviews or limited access to documents, to better develop the picture. The evidence is nevertheless less complete than in other chapters. While it is clear that Egyptian leaders factored Israeli nuclear weapons into their decision making, it is difficult at times to link a specific behavior to nuclear issues.

The rest of this chapter unpacks my argument in three main sections. First, I review the basic military balance. Next, I provide the background to the dispute. In the third section of this chapter I discuss Egyptian behavior and views on Israeli nuclear weapons. While the core focus is on Egypt, I briefly address the Syrian offensive in 1973 as well. I conclude with a short summary of the evidence.

The Military Balance

Israel has never publicly acknowledged possessing nuclear weapons. It is therefore necessary to demonstrate that Egyptian leaders understood that Israel possessed nuclear weapons during this period. Next, I discuss the conventional balance. While in some rough indicators of power the two sides appeared equivalent, a more fine-grained analysis demonstrates that Israel had a large conventional advantage throughout the period.

THE NUCLEAR BALANCE

Israel had nuclear monopoly relative to Egypt beginning in 1967. According to Avner Cohen, who has done the most extensive work on the Israeli nuclear arsenal, "On the eve of the [1967 Six Day] war Israel 'improvised' two deliverable nuclear explosive devices."[3] The arsenal expanded from there. Using estimates of plutonium production from the Dimona reactor and various US intelligence reports, analysts have constructed rough estimates for the size of the Israeli nuclear arsenal over time. Based on these sources, Israel likely increased its arsenal at a rate of about two warheads per year during the 1970s (table 3.1). Estimates for warhead yields are more difficult to find. Sources suggest Israel was capable of producing weapons with yields in the range of ten to twenty kilotons during this period. I use these estimates to provide a rough estimate of the total Israeli nuclear yield, also in table 3.1, though these numbers should not be taken as precise.[4]

Table 3.1 Israeli nuclear weapons, 1967–1979

Year	Warheads	Estimated total yield (megatons)
1967	2	0.02–0.04
1968	4	0.04–0.08
1969	6	0.06–0.12
1970	8	0.08–0.16
1971	11	0.11–0.22
1972	13	0.13–0.26
1973	15	0.15–0.30
1974	17	0.17–0.34
1975	20	0.20–0.40
1976	22	0.22–0.44
1977	24	0.24–0.48
1978	26	0.26–0.52
1979	29	0.29–0.58

Sources: Hans M. Kristensen and Robert S. Norris, "Global Nuclear Weapons Inventories, 1945–2013," *Bulletin of the Atomic Scientists* 69, no. 5 (2013): 75–81; Elbridge Colby, Avner Cohen, William McCants, Bradley Morris, and William Rosenau, "The Israeli Nuclear Alert' of 1973: Deterrence and Signaling in Crisis," CNA, April 2013: 22. See also note 4 in this chapter.

Note: Estimated yields based on 10–20 kiloton warhead yield.

Israel's delivery capabilities evolved as well. In 1967 the ability to deliver a nuclear device was limited. Yitzhak Ya'akov, the Israeli Defense Forces colonel in charge of weapons development in 1967, later relayed that Israel contemplated using "Super Frelon" helicopters to explode a nuclear device for demonstrative purposes.[5] Had Israel contemplated a nuclear strike against an adversary, one delivery candidate was the French-made Vautour light bomber, because of its payload and range abilities. The Vautour's estimated range allowed Israel to strike targets deep inside Egypt; Israeli Vautours struck distant Iraqi air bases in the Six Day War.[6] In 1968 the first American-made A4-Skyhawk achieved initial operating capability. Though Israel privately committed to not use American-made aircraft to carry nuclear weapons, analysts viewed the A4 as a likely nuclear delivery platform until the arrival of the American-made F-4E Phantoms. These aircraft were first deployed to strike into Upper Egypt in January 1970. The Israeli-made Jericho I missiles (based on an earlier French design) had an estimated range of 500 kilometers and were deployed by 1972 or 1973. Initial guidance difficulties limited any availability in 1972. During the 1973 October War, though, there were reports that Israel conducted an operational check of its Jericho missiles and that some Israeli leaders, notably the defense minister Moshe Dayan, may have pushed for additional options.[7]

There is substantial evidence that Egyptian leaders were aware of Israeli nuclear weapons. It is not the case, then, that Egyptian leaders behaved provocatively toward Israel because of a mistaken belief that Israel lacked a deliverable nuclear capability. Egyptian presidents Gamal Abdel Nasser and Anwar Sadat both publicly acknowledged the existence of Israeli nuclear weapons.[8] Mohamed Heikal, the influential editor of the newspaper *Al-Ahram* and a confidant of Nasser, later wrote that in 1969 Nasser told Libya's Muammar Gaddafi that Israel likely possessed nuclear weapons.[9] Some suggest that Soviet intelligence had penetrated Israeli defense and intelligence offices in the late 1960s, gained knowledge of Israeli decisions relating to nuclear weapons, and passed that information to its Arab allies.[10] Whether that occurred or not, the Israeli nuclear program was not a well-kept secret. In July 1970, the *New York Times* reported that "for at least two years the United States government has been conducting its Middle East policy on the assumption that Israel either possesses an atomic bomb or has component parts available for quick assembly."[11] During a meeting with President Richard Nixon in 1973, Hafiz Ismail, the Egyptian national security adviser, "pointed out the development of long-range missiles and atomic weapon research going on in Israel."[12] A few days later, in meetings with US national security adviser Henry Kissinger, Dr. Hafiz Ghanim, a member of the Central Committee of the Arab Socialist Union, raised the possibility of limiting Israeli nuclear arms, implying that Israel already possessed a nuclear stockpile.[13] Finally, based on conversations with Syrian officials on the eve of the 1973 October

War, Murhaf Jouejati reports that Egypt's ally "Syria, of course, knew that Israel has a massive nuclear capability."[14]

Egyptian leaders were also aware of advances in Israeli nuclear delivery capabilities. In January 1966, the *New York Times* published an article discussing Israeli intentions to purchase intermediate range ballistic missiles from France. Within Egypt, the move was seen as further evidence of Israel's desire and growing ability to deliver a nuclear weapon.[15] Egyptian leaders also closely followed the Israeli acquisition of nuclear-capable aircraft, including the French Mirage and American-made Skyhawk and Phantom. In May 1973, Ismail raised the issue of nuclear weapons and delivery capabilities with Kissinger, highlighting the "enormous data about political and technical aspects of the employment of atomic weapons [that] are being forwarded to Israel." Kissinger asked Ismail from where he believed Israel was receiving this information. Ismail replied simply, "From the United States."[16]

The concentration of its population along the Nile River made Egypt vulnerable to even a few nuclear weapons. A US State Department report in 1964 highlighted that "of all the countries of the Near East, the UAR [Egypt] is the most vulnerable to nuclear attack. A single, well-placed nuclear device would bring a sheet of water 400 feet high cascading down the narrow Nile valley where the entire Egyptian population is concentrated."[17] Egyptian leaders were aware of the danger.[18] This potential was not a closely guarded secret. "Lower level Israeli officials," Secretary of State Dean Rusk informed President Johnson in May 1965, "speak frankly about Israel's strategy toward the United Arab Republic: a) surface-to-surface missiles targeted on the Nile delta, and b) a capability to bomb and release the waters behind the Aswan High Dam. Destruction of the Aswan Dam would require a nuclear warhead; bombing with high explosives could not be counted on to do the job."[19] Israeli air superiority, most vividly displayed during the deep penetration bombing raids beginning in January 1970, demonstrated a clear ability to execute such a strike.[20]

THE CONVENTIONAL BALANCE

Aggregate material indicators can obscure the Israeli conventional military advantage. The Composite Indicator of National Capabilities (CINC) score, a commonly used measure for power, indicates that Egypt was more powerful than Israel throughout this period.[21] Israel had less than half the measured capabilities of Egypt in every year from 1967 to 1979; in five of the years, Egypt had greater than a 3:1 advantage. According to this measure, then, the NNWS had a large conventional advantage when it fought two wars against the NWS. This challenges my argument, which posits that war in nuclear monopoly is likely to occur only when the NWS has a large conventional advantage.

A closer examination of the military balance, though, reveals that Israel possessed a persistent advantage relative to its regional neighbors, including Egypt. In economic development, a good predictor of military success, the Israeli power advantage was decisive. Israel's per capita gross domestic product (GDP) advantage grew from more than a 7:1 advantage in 1967 to nearly 12:1 by 1973 (figure 3.1). This allowed Israel to extract a great deal more from its society than Egypt and field a more effective military force. Even with Egypt's much larger population, the overall size of the two economies were similar. It was not the case, then, that Egypt could simply overwhelm Israel with a larger total economic base. This allowed Israel's qualitative advantage in economic development to be decisive.

In military power, the balance appears roughly equivalent using indicators for total troops and spending per soldier. Egypt had a lead in the total number of soldiers, though this advantage was a modest one (figure 3.2). Even that advantage may be overstated. Estimates from the International Institute of Strategic Studies (IISS) report that Israel's fully mobilized military actually outnumbered the fully mobilized Egyptian military in ten of the thirteen years from 1967 to 1979. Israel could thus field a military at least as large if not slightly larger than Egypt within forty-eight to seventy-two hours of mobilization.[22] The Egyptian chief of staff Saad El Shazly conceded that "we had no real advantage in front line forces. No less than 58 percent of our vast total were not field troops."[23] Israel possessed a consistent advantage in spending per soldier, hovering around a 2:1 advantage and approaching a 3:1 advantage in 1973.

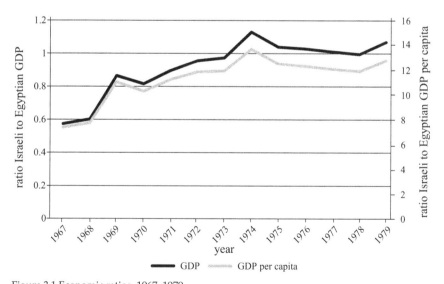

Figure 3.1 Economic ratios, 1967–1979

Source: Gleditsch Expanded GDP data version 6.0 (September 2014), http://ksgleditsch.com/exptradegdp.html.

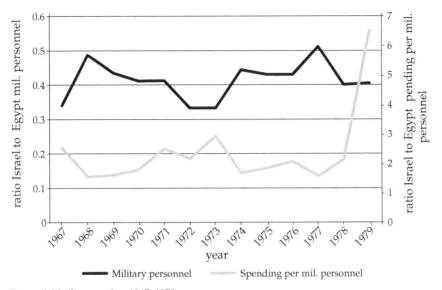

Figure 3.2 Military ratios, 1967–1979

Source: Correlates of War, National Material Capabilities, version 5.0, http://www.correlatesofwar.org/data-sets/national-material-capabilities.

The Israeli advantage is more apparent in a qualitative and fine-grained assessment of the conventional balance. The Egyptian military was not a professional fighting force in 1967. Field Marshal Muhammad Abd al-Hakim Amer, the leader of the Egyptian military at the time, treated the armed forces as his "own personal fiefdom," where personal loyalty was more important than military competence.[24] The army was plagued by poorly organized command structures that had difficulty even communicating with one another in battle. Compounding this problem, low-level officers lacked initiative. The 1967 Six Day War dramatically confirmed Egyptian military ineptitude and set the stage for estimates of the military balance thereafter. "The Egyptian army," writes Kenneth Pollack, "was all but obliterated during the Six Day War."[25]

Israel's advantage was thus very large for several years as Egypt rebuilt its military. Following the debacle in June 1967, Nasser sacked Amer and asserted more direct control over the military. Other high-ranking officers were arrested, tried, and sentenced. All told, Nasser's reforms led to the removal of eight hundred to a thousand officers, fundamentally remaking the officer corps. The command structure was rationalized to eliminate duplicate chains of command, reduce military ranks for various commands, and centralize power. The ratio of officers with a college degree went from less than 2 percent in 1967 to 60 percent by 1973.[26] While necessary for long-run success, the reforms would take time to have their effect. By the end of

1969, Nasser knew that his military still posed little threat to Israel. Egypt was thus much weaker than Israel when it launched the War of Attrition in 1969.

The 1969–1970 War of Attrition took a toll on Egypt's military. The war did give the Egyptian military valuable experience in fighting Israel in sustained combat operations. Yet it necessarily degraded Egyptian fighting forces as they were still struggling to rebuild. Ultimately, the Israeli military eliminated enough of the Egyptian defensive capabilities that the Egyptians were forced to turn over defense to the Soviet Union.[27] Unable to even effectively defend itself, Egypt posed little offensive threat to Israel during the next few years.

The Egyptian military did perform admirably during the 1973 October War. Risa Brooks characterizes the Egyptian offensive operations across the Suez Canal as "one of the most remarkable campaigns in military history."[28] The operation demonstrated marked improvements in the Egyptian military from the experiences of 1967 and 1970, although it must be noted that many regarded the operation so highly precisely because the baseline of expectations for the Egyptian military was so low. The key question for my argument, though, is the extent to which the Egyptian military posed a major threat to Israel.

The answer remains that the Egyptian danger was limited. To begin with, internal Egyptian assessments prior to the 1973 assault confirmed that the Israelis maintained decisive advantages in armor and air power. Any attempt at maneuver warfare in the open Sinai would be disastrous. As such, Egyptian elites recognized that they lacked the power projection capability to threaten pre-1967 Israeli territory, or even to advance deep into the Sinai.[29] This fact was widely recognized beyond Egypt. Indeed, part of the reason why the Egyptian 1973 assault proved surprising was that Israeli intelligence did not expect the Egyptians to start a war they would militarily lose.[30] In addition, Egypt continued to face difficulties implementing effective force employment critical to success on the modern battlefield.[31] This reduced the Egyptian military threat to Israel. Ryan Grauer and Michael Horowitz find that Israel partially implemented the modern system at the operational and tactical level in 1967, while Egypt managed to only partially implement it at the operational level and failed to do so at the tactical level.[32] Moreover, as John Mearsheimer points out, Israel was capable of launching a breakthrough and exploitation at the operational level in 1967, a fact key leaders recognized.[33] In 1973, Grauer and Horowitz conclude, Egypt had failed to adopt the modern system at all at the operational or tactical levels, while Israel had fully adopted its tenets at both levels. To be sure, implementation of the modern system during war cannot be measured prior to the fighting. Yet the consistent Israeli advantage in this regard underscores the qualitative difference, and past performances can inform later assessment. Moreover, effective implementation of the modern system requires heavy investment prior to war, which can be observed by opponents at the time. Egyptian and Israeli performance indicates that Israel was training its military in this way prior to conflict, whereas Egypt was not. This is what one would expect, given the difference in levels of economic development between the two states.

True, Egypt could count on regional support against Israel. These alliances did not add markedly to Egyptian power or offset the Israeli conventional advantage, though. The 1967 war demonstrated that even when facing several adversaries at the same time, Israel enjoyed a decisive military advantage. Israeli pilots also proved themselves capable against Soviet opponents (who were better equipped and trained than their Arab allies) during the 1969–1970 war. Perhaps most importantly, the Arab states were never able to coordinate effectively against Israel, degrading their ability to aggregate capabilities.[34] And while Egypt received aid from the Soviet Union, that was offset by US support to Israel.[35]

For its part, Israel apparently did not integrate nuclear weapons into its military planning. "With Israel's decisive victory against the Arab coalition in the 1967 war," argues Vipin Narang, "Israel's conventional superiority was established as its primary deterrent."[36] The Israeli conventional advantage, increasingly underwritten by the United States, reduced the danger that Egypt and other Arab states could pose and with it the benefits of nuclear use. This allowed the costs to Israel of nuclear use to loom large. I discuss the conduct of the wars in 1969 and 1973 in more detail below. Here it is sufficient to note that the Egyptian threat in 1969–1970 was very limited; there is little evidence that Israel considered nuclear use. In 1973, the scope of the danger to Israel was larger, and Egypt took additional steps to signal its limited intentions. Israel's defense minister Moshe Dayan considered a nuclear threat or demonstration, but Golda Meir and other Israeli leaders ruled out nuclear strikes. As noted earlier, at most Israel ordered a series of operational checks of its Jericho missiles. This was likely done as a signal to the United States that it should speed conventional resupply.[37] Had the danger to Israel increased, then the Israeli leadership might have considered more direct measures against Egypt and Syria.

In sum, Israel possessed a meaningful conventional advantage throughout this period. Israel had a larger advantage in per capita GDP that was not counterbalanced by an Egyptian advantage in overall economic size. The two military forces were roughly similar in size, yet Israeli troops possessed a major qualitative advantage over their Egyptian opponents.

Dispute Overview

The totality of the 1967 defeat shocked the Egyptians. Prior to that, President Nasser had entertained broader ambitions in the region, drawing on

Arab nationalism to exert influence.[38] After the defeat, Nasser's ambitions were significantly curtailed. He initially resigned, only to resume power following public demonstrations clamoring for him to return. His focus then settled on overturning Israel's occupation of the Sinai Peninsula and regaining control of the Suez Canal. The closing of the canal had deprived financially strapped Egypt of critical revenue. According to one estimate, the loss of the Sinai cost Egypt $400–500 million annually.[39] Firing across the canal continued sporadically throughout 1967. In October, Israel struck another blow against the Egyptian economy by destroying oil refineries in Suez City in retaliation for the Egyptian sinking of the Israeli destroyer *Eilat*. Additionally, fully 60 percent of the Egyptians who lived along the Suez had been relocated to the Nile Valley, causing severe economic and social turmoil.[40] Beyond the economic and strategic implications, most Egyptians felt a sense of humiliation and deep animosity toward the Israeli occupation. President Richard Nixon would later recall that when he visited shortly after the war, he encountered "a residue of hatred among their [Israel's] neighbors that I felt could only result in another war."[41]

It did not take long for war to occur. Egypt initiated sustained hostilities against the Israeli positions across the Suez Canal on March 8, 1969. These included a series of artillery barrages and limited commando raids into the Sinai to disrupt Israeli military operations.[42] Two factors converged to convince the Egyptians it was necessary to act. First, the diplomatic impasse in resolving the status of the Sinai seemed to increase. The former US diplomat Richard Parker relates that in June 1968 Ashraf Ghorbal, then chief of the Egyptian Interests Section in Washington, complained that "an entire year had passed since the June War began and that there had been no movement on the withdrawal issue. [UN Security Council] Resolution 242 had passed, [Gunnar] Jarring had been appointed, and there had been no results. How long will this stalemate be permitted to go on?"[43] Parker recalls similar sentiments expressed by the Egyptian foreign minister a few months later: "A year had passed and nothing had happened. Egypt would not acquiesce in the indefinite occupation of its territories."[44] As Nasser explained on January 21, 1969, "We must realize that the enemy will not withdraw unless we force him to withdraw through fighting. Indeed, there can be no hope of any political solution unless the enemy realizes that we are capable of forcing him to withdraw through fighting."[45]

Second, Israel began construction of the Bar-Lev Line, a series of fortifications along the Suez Canal named for the Israeli Defense Forces chief of the general staff, Haim Bar-Lev. Completed on March 15, 1969, the defenses included forts, trenches, sand walls, and artillery and tank posts. It provided a formidable barrier to any future Egyptian assault. Moreover, it signaled that the Israelis were treating the Suez Canal as a permanent border, reinforcing a sense that diplomatic efforts were failing. "As the Bar-Lev Line fast became a reality at the beginning of 1969, Nasser confronted a difficult strategic situation," writes George Gawyrch. "Prospects for any serious diplomatic movement were slim indeed. . . . Egypt could ill afford to allow both the diplomatic and military fronts to remain frozen for an indefinite period."[46] By February 1969 Egypt considered the destruction of those fortifications "vital."[47] On top of the new fortifications, President Johnson announced the sale of advanced F-4 Phantom aircraft to Israel on October 8, 1968.[48] The conventional military balance, already unfavorable to Egypt, seemed to be dramatically worsening.

Throughout the War of Attrition, the United States put forward various initiatives to end hostilities. The most ambitious US effort was the Rogers Plan, named for the US secretary of state, William Rogers. The plan called for an Israeli withdrawal from Egyptian territory in exchange for an Egyptian-Israeli peace treaty and future negotiations on the Palestinian issue. The Egyptians were skeptical; the Israelis flatly rejected the initiative. Soviet rejection of the plan provided the final nail in the coffin for Rogers's initiative.[49] As the war plodded along, the United States responded to new Egyptian peace overtures in May 1970 by increasing contacts and proposing a cease-fire on June 19. Nasser explained to the Soviet leader Leonid Brezhnev that the settlement would give Egypt time to recover and improve its defenses for future diplomatic and, if necessary, military initiatives. "In other words, we exploit that period to reinforce our positions?" Brezhnev asked. "That is true," Nasser replied. "But it would also benefit us politically, and prove that Egypt and the Soviet Union were working for peace."[50] The new cease-fire went into effect in August; Egypt immediately used the time to move antiaircraft units forward in violation of the agreement.[51]

Following Nasser's death on September 28, 1970, Anwar Sadat became Egypt's leader.[52] He also took over its problems. The Egyptian economy remained stagnant, Egypt was dependent upon the Soviet Union for defense, and Israel remained entrenched on the east bank of the Suez Canal. Sadat shared the general commitment to retake the Sinai. He devoted considerable time to that end, making a number of proposals. Through intermediaries he privately urged the Americans to "tell the Israelis to take this Suez Canal proposal very seriously."[53] To Secretary of State Rogers he explained in May 1971 that "I don't want to bother Israel. . . . I'll sign an agreement. . . . I just want my land back."[54] In October 1971, the Egyptian foreign minister Mahmud Riad told the US national security adviser Henry Kissinger in a private meeting that "the position of Sadat was now very difficult; he [Sadat] would agree to any reasonable settlement as long as there was some prospect of getting Egyptian territory back."[55]

The concern for the Sinai went beyond the Egyptian political elite. The ongoing Israeli occupation remained deeply unpopular among the Egyptian public and threatened Sadat's regime. As Donald Neff points out, following the cease-fire ending the 1969–1970 War of Attrition, the "reminders of no war-no peace added to the frustrated, depressing atmosphere gripping Egypt, and to Sadat's problems."[56] The popular mood did not improve with time. For example, in January 1972 university students demonstrated against the regime on campuses and in the streets, calling for military action against Israel. Egyptian leaders subsequently closed the universities and used military force to end the demonstrations. Mothers of arrested students carried signs reading "Send our sons to Sinai, not to Egyptian prisons."[57] When Hafiz Ismail met with President Nixon in February 1973, he took care to point out that "30 months of ceasefire was no reason for congratulations. The ceasefire was becoming a burden and a strain, and that it was necessary either to break it or to establish peace."[58]

The root causes of war in 1973 were thus the same as in 1969: perceptions that diplomatic efforts were proving counterproductive, and Israeli military improvements. On the diplomatic front, the burgeoning US-Soviet rapprochement seemed to relegate the Egyptian-Israeli problem to the back burner. This would deprive Sadat of the superpower pressure on Israel he believed necessary to attain a settlement. Egypt's relationship with the Soviet Union grew more strained as the latter moved toward détente with the United States. The Soviets consistently provided less military hardware than Egypt desired. In addition, the Soviets counseled that Egypt should avoid provocations toward Israel.[59] True, the Soviets provided additional arms in March 1973, but they continued to press Egypt to avoid any military action while providing no new diplomatic initiatives. For the Egyptians, the Soviets seemed unwilling or unable to take the political steps to make progress. The Soviets, Sadat complained, were "being passive and handing over all initiatives to the Americans."[60] Over time, Sadat became convinced that the root cause of Soviet waffling was a desire to avoid a regional conflagration that could strain US-Soviet relations. In May 1972 Murad Ghaleb, Egypt's minister of foreign affairs, told Yugoslavian president Josip Tito that Sadat feared the Soviet Union would reach agreements with the United States that would be "at the expense of the Egyptians" or that would relegate the Middle East to a "question of secondary importance."[61]

The outcomes of two superpower summits in 1972 and 1973 seemingly confirmed this impression. Addressing the Middle East during the May 1972 summit in Moscow, the United States and the Soviet Union reaffirmed support for UN Security Council Resolution 242 adopted in the aftermath of the 1967 war and called for a "military relaxation in that area." The statement was "a violent shock to us," Sadat said. In his view, Egypt "lagged at least twenty steps behind Israel and so 'military relaxation' in this context could mean nothing but giving in to Israel."[62] Sadat subsequently summoned the Soviet ambassador to Egypt, Vladimir Vinogradov, and informed him that "I have decided to dispense with the services of all Soviet military experts and that they must go back to the Soviet Union within one week from today."[63] The Soviets departed shortly thereafter.

After another banal statement by Brezhnev and Nixon in June 1973, Ismail Fahmy informed Sadat that "the superpowers were contributing to the maintenance of the 'no peace, no war' because a permanent settlement in the Middle East had low priority for them. Détente was likely to make this priority even lower, as the two superpowers would now be preoccupied with safeguarding their rapprochement."[64]

Egypt's entreaties to the United States also seemed to elicit no favorable developments. The joint US-Soviet statements suggested that the United States was unwilling to upset relations with the Soviet Union or Israel to aid Egypt. Even the dramatic expulsion of Soviet advisers elicited no progress. Ashraf Ghorbal recalled that the Americans gave Sadat "a note saying 'bravo,' but that's all he got."[65] Frustrated Egyptian officials consistently highlighted the non-change in US policy with the Americans in 1973.[66] Indeed, the immediate American response focused on assuring the Soviets they had not colluded with Egypt to force the withdrawal of Soviet forces.[67] Ismail's meetings with Nixon and Kissinger in February 1973 reinforced Sadat's disappointment. "If we don't take our case in our own hands," Sadat complained, "there will be no movement, especially given Washington's ridiculous ideas evidenced by Hafiz Ismail's trip."[68]

The second factor that influenced Egyptian decision making was the perception that the military situation was reaching a critical juncture. US support to Israel dramatically increased after 1970 (figure 3.3). For instance, US military loans increased from $30 million in 1970 to $300 annually in 1972 and 1973.[69] True, Nixon attempted to use arms transfers to prod Israel to negotiate in the summer of 1971.[70] That occurred behind closed doors, though, and US aid after 1971 was still much higher than it had been before 1970.

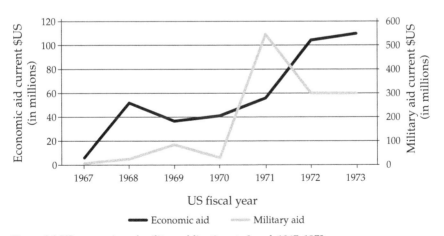

Figure 3.3 US economic and military obligations to Israel, 1967–1973

Source: US Agency for International Development, "Foreign Aid Explorer: The Official Record of U.S. Foreign Aid," Country Summary, https://explorer.usaid.gov/data.html.

The Egyptians frequently pointed to unequivocal US support for Israel as harmful to negotiations. Foreign Minister Riad complained to Kissinger in October 1971 of "the insistence by the United States on maintaining Israeli superiority and therefore depriving Israel of any incentive to come to an agreement."[71] Sixteen months later, Ismail told Nixon that "Egypt did not understand the U.S. policy of balance of force. This policy permitted Israel to hold on to Egyptian land. . . . At one time, the Soviet Union was in Egypt, but the Soviet Union has now left and Egypt saw no further genuine motive for its [US] support of Israel."[72] Adding to Egyptian frustrations, a short time later word leaked of another US-Israeli arms agreement.[73] From the Egyptian point of view, the Americans seemed to have no interest to facilitate a settlement without a disruption of the status quo.

By 1973 the military trajectory was decidedly negative for the Egyptians. "We see the [aircraft] deliveries [to Israel] extending through '74, '75 [as] very revealing," Ismail explained to Kissinger in May. "We see the technological assistance to be given by the U.S. military to the military industry of Israel [as] a very dangerous policy. Because it means that maybe in a couple years' time the U.S. can restrict its deliveries but Israel at that time will be able to maintain its balance of force and then the U.S. will come and say we cannot influence Israeli policy." To drive the point home, he later added that "it is not only a question of a provision of the most complicated, most sophisticated armament which some people say that even American allies don't get; it is also that question of industrial capacity, and our concern [is] that in a couple of years Israel will defy any approach towards peace."[74] In the near future, Israeli conventional capabilities would so dwarf Egyptian forces that military action by Egypt would be completely impossible. That would remove whatever small leverage Egypt had to prod Israel to negotiate.

So the two factors—diplomatic impasse and military change—were converging during 1972 and into 1973. It was at this point that Sadat settled on military action to break the stalemate. "It was impossible," he noted in his memoirs, "for the United States to make a move if we ourselves didn't take military action to break the deadlock."[75] As Sadat put it at the time, "The time has come for a shock. . . . Everyone has fallen asleep over the Mideast crisis. But they will soon wake up to the fact that Americans have left us no other way out."[76] It would not take much. Sadat had long believed that even limited military action could benefit Egypt. "I have to shake up the world and draw its attention to this problem," he explained to senior Soviet officials in March 1971. "I need to gain only ten centimeters of land east of Suez. That is all."[77]

US and Soviet leaders were aware of Egypt's growing desperation. Brezhnev, who had been counseling Egypt to avoid military action, warned Nixon on June 23, 1973, that they "must put this warlike situation to an end. . . . If there is no clarity about the principles we will have difficulty keeping the military situation from flaring up."[78] Nixon parried the Soviet leader, but privately he shared Brezhnev's concerns. In February, Nixon responded to a suggestion that additional delays would not "be disastrous for US interests" by writing, "I totally disagree. This thing is getting ready to blow."[79] The United States nevertheless made little effort. While open to Egyptian overtures, Kissinger stuck to a delaying strategy. Kissinger hoped that this would increase Soviet-Egyptian tensions as well as convince Egypt that it had no choice but to make concessions. In 1973, Kissinger believed that the Egyptians were still hedging on the issue of full peace with Israel and pointed out to Brezhnev that it was "hard to convince Israel why they should give up the territory in exchange for something they already have [a cease-fire], in order to avoid a war they can win."[80]

Egypt launched its offensive on October 6, 1973. The fighting continued for three weeks, ending on October 26. Though Egypt suffered a military defeat, Sadat was successful in generating greater American involvement.

From the Egyptian point of view, the political trajectory on the Sinai Peninsula then began moving in a positive, albeit uneven, direction. As such, Egypt refrained from large-scale military action against Israel. On October 29, 1973—just days after the war—the two sides met at the 101st kilometer of the Cairo-Suez Road. Shortly thereafter they reached an agreement on supplying the trapped Egyptian Third Army, exchanging prisoners of war, and starting disengagement talks.[81] Kissinger, by then secretary of state as well as national security adviser, directly engaged in the negotiations. From 1973 to 1975 the United States put heavy pressure on Israel to offer concessions to Egypt and withdraw in a series of steps from the Sinai Peninsula. On January 18, 1974, Israel agreed to withdraw twenty kilometers east of the Suez Canal. Egypt maintained a foothold to place troops on the eastern bank of the canal, allowing Sadat to claim gains from the war. An international force was also put in place to separate the two sides. The Sinai II agreement followed on September 1, 1975. Israel withdrew farther into the desert, and Egypt allowed "the installation of an American observation station that could be used by Israel."[82] In May 1977 the rightist Likud Party came to power in Israel. Through back channels, the new Israeli prime minister conveyed to Sadat that he was interested in a peace agreement with Egypt. The Americans again became heavily involved with the process, allowing the Egyptians to hope for a favorable diplomatic outcome in the near future.

In 1977 Sadat expressed a willingness to travel to Jerusalem. Israel subsequently extended an invitation, and Sadat addressed the Israeli Knesset. In doing so he essentially recognized Israel. Following his trip to Jerusalem, the Israelis agreed to further political and military negotiations. When negotiations bogged down, the new US president, Jimmy Carter, invited leaders from both sides to meet at Camp David. The two sides began talks on September 5, 1978. The United States remained deeply involved, with

Carter engaging in his own shuttle diplomacy over the next year, placing pressure on both sides to reach an agreement. The diplomatic efforts reached fruition with the March 27, 1979, signing of the Egyptian-Israeli Peace Treaty.

The Role of Nuclear Weapons

The underlying political dispute and Egyptian concern with diplomatic and military developments pushed Egypt to confrontation with Israel. The shape that those confrontations took is consistent with my argument on the role that nuclear weapons play in disputes under the shadow of nuclear monopoly. In the 1969–1970 War of Attrition, Egypt pursued a (very) limited war strategy. In 1973, Egypt launched a limited offensive that was more expansive than in 1969–1970. As such, it took additional steps to minimize the risks of nuclear use. Throughout both periods, Egypt pursued various policies to raise the costs of escalation for Israel. It would be a mistake to argue that Egyptian behavior was solely the product of the Israeli nuclear monopoly. Nevertheless, Egyptian leaders clearly took the Israeli nuclear arsenal into consideration. Egyptian behavior highlights the paradox of conventional military weakness when facing a nuclear-armed adversary. On the one hand, weak states can fight precisely because they lack the capabilities to pose a major danger to the nuclear weapon state. On the other hand, that same conventional weakness makes it difficult to achieve success.

EGYPTIAN BEHAVIOR

Egypt had no intention of displacing Israeli forces in 1969–1970. Though Nasser occasionally spoke of attempts to reconquer the Sinai by 1970, no such plans were in place.[83] Kenneth Pollack notes that the plan that did emerge was to "harass and attack the Israelis along the canal, [with] low-intensity strikes but on a constant basis."[84] Egypt had two goals. First, it hoped to put some pressure on Israel to show that controlling the Sinai did not guarantee security. Second, Nasser wanted to more directly engage the United States and the Soviet Union in pushing for a diplomatic settlement. Indeed, intermittent artillery barrages in late 1968 were "Nasser's way of signaling to the Israelis and the Americans that lack of political progress would lead to further escalation quite soon."[85] As those proved ineffective, Egypt moved to the more sustained use of force to accomplish the same goal. Egyptian leaders were prepared to suffer greater losses than the Israelis, but they were not ready for the conflict to escalate into a larger war.[86]

In short, Egyptian plans would not create a major danger to Israel. The target along the canal was in an isolated area. Moreover, the lack of any effort for a major crossing provided a natural stopping point for the fighting that could not threaten to move deeper toward Israel. Egypt would not be threatening Israel's homeland, its nuclear arsenal, or the destruction of a significant portion of the IDF.

Egyptian behavior during the War of Attrition matched this planning. In March 1969, Egypt began intensive artillery barrages and undertook small-scale commando raids into the Sinai. As the conflict continued, Egypt took heavy losses but did not escalate the level of violence. Force attrition necessitated that the Egyptians rely even more on the Soviet Union, with Nasser traveling to the Soviet Union in December 1969 and again the next month to secure more active Soviet involvement in Egyptian air defense. Israeli deep penetration raids against the Egyptian heartland beginning in January 1970 added urgency to these Egyptian requests.[87] Though the Egyptian motive for increased Soviet support was the deteriorating military situation, the general Soviet involvement would also raise the costs to Israel for any nuclear strike. Following greater Soviet involvement, the war reverted to limited strikes by both sides until the cease-fire in August 1970.

Egypt planned for a limited offensive in 1973. Though the attack across the Suez Canal would be massive, it centered on simply crossing the canal and then digging in for the inevitable Israeli counterattack.[88] During a meeting with the Egyptian Armed Forces Supreme Council on October 24, 1972, the military pressed Sadat on the ultimate goal for the operation. "Is the object the liberation of the occupied territories or is it merely a resumption of military activities so as to give you a better chance of a political solution?" Sadat replied: "Breaking the ceasefire."[89] Sadat had long noted that he needed to take only "ten centimeters" of land across the canal in order to make progress. The "plan was set for a comprehensive 'local' war in which only conventional arms would be used," Egypt's General Mohammed el-Gamasy wrote in his memoirs.[90] True, Sadat told President Hafez al-Assad of Syria that Egypt would go farther and seize the strategic Giddi and Mitla passes and from there move to retake the entire Sinai. Privately, though, Sadat ordered the military to focus on taking six to ten miles on the east side of the canal. Further plans were a ruse to maintain Syrian support.[91] Improved civil-military relations and training gave Sadat the confidence his military would execute the orders for a limited, rather than an expansive, attack.[92]

Egyptian behavior matched the underlying planning. On October 6–7 the Egyptians moved ninety thousand soldiers and 850 tanks across the canal under the cover of an artillery barrage and surface-to-air missiles.[93] Egyptian commando teams operated in the Israeli rear to disrupt reinforcements. The main body of troops then moved to eliminate the Bar-Lev line and set up defensive positions. Egyptian forces beat back hasty Israeli counterattacks on the sixth and eighth, inflicting heavy losses on Israeli armor and air forces. The Egyptians advanced steadily, hoping to reach their goal of a six- to nine-mile penetration. Sadat and Ismail Ali, the commander in chief and war minister, refused to press the attack forward to the Giddi and Mitla passes deeper in the Sinai for several days, despite pressure from Egyptian generals.

The scale of the Egyptian assault could potentially have created a danger to Israel, which would have raised the benefits for nuclear strikes early in the conflict. While Egypt never planned to advance deep into the Sinai, Israel could not be expected to know that at the start of hostilities. Moreover, Israel would need to fully mobilize its society and resources to prosecute the war.

Egyptian leaders offset these dangers by seeking outside support and communicating the limited nature of their assault to the Israelis. Early in the war Sadat used back channels to communicate to Kissinger, and through him to Israel, that Egypt "did not intend to deepen the engagements or widen the confrontation."[94] While the message raised other issues, Ismail later asserted that none were new except "the commitment not 'to intensify the engagements or widen the confrontation.'" He added that "where we had committed ourselves not to deepen the engagements . . . our aim was to safeguard our dense population centers and our vital economic interests."[95] Kissinger took the Egyptian pledge seriously. At a meeting of the Washington Special Action Group [WSAG] that evening, he argued that his "judgement is that he [Sadat] *will* cross the Suez and just sit there. I don't think he will penetrate further."[96] Kissinger subsequently replied to Sadat that "the United States will use its maximum influence to prevent any [Israeli] attack on [Egyptian] civilian targets. Strong representations to that effect have been made to the Israeli Government."[97] Any limitations on conventional retaliation would also apply to nuclear retaliation. Thus the US served two purposes. It could constrain Israel, raising the costs of major conventional and nuclear retaliation. The US would also communicate that Egypt did not seek to inflict a massive defeat on Israel, removing a benefit of major conventional or nuclear retaliation.

In addition to encouraging Israeli restraint, the Americans and Soviets sought to end the fighting. Kissinger initially attempted to organize a cease-fire that returned forces to the pre-October 6 lines. To entice the Egyptians, he offered high-level US involvement in working toward a "just peace."[98] Syria was also pressing the Soviets for an early cease-fire.[99] As a result, the Soviets presented plans to Egypt that called for a cease-fire in place. Sadat seemed to have achieved his goals: there was greater superpower involvement, and Egypt had demonstrated combat prowess, challenging Israeli "invincibility." Yet Sadat rejected the cease-fire appeals as well as efforts to involve the United Nations.[100] Moreover, within a few days he would order Egyptian forces to advance farther into the Sinai.

Why did Sadat reject the offer and subsequently order Egyptian forces to advance? Answering this question is important to establish that Egypt's strategy was limited. Several factors influenced Sadat's decision to reject the initial cease-fire proposals. Most importantly, the initial proposals might not allow Egypt to reacquire the Sinai. Sadat's primary goal was to fully involve the United States to put pressure on Israel to withdraw. A return to the status quo ante with only a promise of US support seemed to trade away Egyptian gains for very little. Even the Soviet proposal for a cease-fire in place with only vague future promises would not guarantee US involvement. As Sadat explained to Soviet ambassador Vinogradov, "The United States had to be advised to use its influence on Israel to give up her policy."[101] As Yoram Meital points out, Sadat realized well before the war that the "longer the Egyptian forces succeeded in holding a strip of land east of the Suez Canal, the greater the chance for intervention on the part of the great powers as well as by the Arab states."[102]

Second, initial success created incentives to attain the best possible outcome. The Egyptians were surprised at how successful their crossing of the Suez Canal had been. Egyptian planners had estimated 10,000 to 30,000 casualties; the actual number was 208.[103] The Egyptians were not alone in their surprise; the success shocked the Israelis, Soviets, and Americans as well. Kissinger had predicted that Israel would win quickly once it mobilized its forces. When the Israeli ambassador informed him that Israel had lost four hundred tanks to Egypt and one hundred to Syria, Kissinger exclaimed: "500 tanks! How many do you have? We should get [White House chief of staff General Alexander] Haig here. . . . Explain to me, how could 400 tanks be lost to the Egyptians?"[104] A longer war that inflicted higher losses on Israel would have the added benefit of driving home the point that Israel could not avoid negotiations forever out of a belief that the Arab forces were militarily helpless. Prior to the war, Saudi Arabia had encouraged Egypt to hold out to gain more time to gather Arab support, which would increase pressure on the Americans.[105]

Those factors did not necessitate that Egypt advance deeper into the Sinai, though. The primary impetus for the advance was mounting Israeli pressure on Syria. Israel had concentrated its initial effort against the Syrians. With Syrian forces on the verge of collapse, Assad pressed Sadat to allow Egyptian armies to advance in accordance with prewar arrangements.[106] The goal was therefore not decisive Israeli defeat, but to prevent the collapse of the Syrian position. Importantly, the Soviet ambassador Vinogradov told Sadat that the Soviet high command had given its approval for such an operation.[107] With Soviet backing, the Egyptians made the limited assault to take the passes. Egyptian generals voiced their opposition, knowing that any advance would move beyond Egyptian air defenses and open holes in their lines. When Chief of Staff Shazli protested the order, his superior Ismail Ali said the attack had to go forward. "It is a political decision," he explained.[108] The result was unsurprising: the Egyptian advance was beaten back with heavy loss. The Israeli Defense Forces advanced rapidly. By October 16, Israeli advance units had crossed the Suez Canal into Egypt, and an Israeli crossing in force took place on October 18.[109]

The collapsing military situation at that point pushed Sadat to accept a cease-fire in place.[110] He approved Kissinger's visit to Moscow and agreed to accept the joint US-Soviet proposal. Israel, itself now having attained a decisive military victory, accepted the cease-fire reluctantly and completed encircling the Egyptian Third Army prior to halting its advance. The Israeli actions infuriated Sadat, but there was little Egypt could do at that point. Despite the military defeat, Sadat succeeded politically. Egypt maintained forces on the eastern side of the canal, and secured greater US involvement in the dispute. The stage was set for six years of negotiation, which would lead to the Egyptian-Israeli peace treaty and restoration of Egypt's control of the Sinai.

EGYPTIAN NUCLEAR VIEWS

Israel's nuclear progress caused considerable concern within Egypt. For example, Sadat, then president of the Egyptian National Assembly, told Dean Rusk in 1966 that regarding an Israeli nuclear weapon, Egypt "felt equal concern and would be forced [to] launch [a] preventive war if Israel acquired [a nuclear] bomb."[111] Though Egypt did not launch that preventive war, unease over the Israeli nuclear arsenal remained and influenced Egyptian policy. Efforts were made to raise the costs of any Israeli nuclear use, and there was a general belief that as long as Egypt posed only a minor threat, the benefits of nuclear use for Israel would be low.

Egyptian leaders believed that the limited danger to Israel would reduce the risks of a nuclear strike. It is not the case that Israeli nuclear capabilities did not enter into Egyptian planning, but rather that, consistent with my argument, the nature of Egyptian plans and capabilities meant that the danger to Israel would be low and with it the likelihood of nuclear use. Highlighting the underlying thinking, one Egyptian military official recalled that in "1973, we knew that Israel had nuclear weapons, missiles with armed nuclear warheads. So there was some gambling that Israel would not go nuclear unless we crossed their borders. That was not in our plan, or even in our capacity."[112] Similarly, General Gamasy and Egyptian government spokesman Tahseen Basheer both expressed the belief that as long as Egypt did not threaten Israel's pre-1967 borders, nuclear use was unlikely.[113] Kenneth Pollack stated that "a number of Egyptian generals, including Gamasy," made the case that in 1973 the Egyptian military was "never going past the bridgeheads. There was not a chance the Israelis were going to use nuclear weapons."[114] Such beliefs could have been expected during the 1969–1970 confrontation when Egypt was both weaker and the fighting more limited.

Egyptian thinking also tracked with American assessments at the time. "We must at least contemplate the possibility that, faced with a massive Arab attack, Israel might launch a pre-emptive nuclear strike," argued the assistant secretary of defense for international security affairs Paul Warnke.[115] At the height of the October War, a National Security Council memorandum noted that "the Israelis will probably use an atomic bomb before they concede the 1967 borders."[116] In 1991, William Quandt, a member of the NSC at the time of the war, wrote that Israel might make "a nuclear threat . . . if Egyptian troops broke through at the passes [that is, deeper in the Sinai and thus closer to Israel proper]. None of this had to be spelled out in so many words by the Israelis."[117] If Israel's closest ally after 1967 believed Israel might use nuclear weapons in certain situations, it would be surprising if Israeli adversaries did not take nuclear weapons into consideration.

To reiterate, my claim is not that Israeli nuclear weapons forced Egypt to pursue limited military options. Egypt lacked the conventional capabilities to do much more than it did. That is precisely the point. Egypt could pursue its limited aims with the hope that nuclear use would be unlikely. Even then, in language similar to the theoretical framework introduced in chapter 1, any attack would be a "gamble." To further reduce the benefits of a nuclear strike for Israel, the Egyptians communicated their limited intentions to the Israelis through the Americans. Egyptian leaders also identified additional factors that would raise the costs for nuclear use and pursued several policies to reinforce those factors where possible.

Chief among those was the belief held in both Cairo and Damascus that the Soviet Union and United States would constrain Israeli nuclear use.[118] Officials in Damascus at the time did not believe Israeli nuclear strikes likely "because the Soviet Union and the United States would not have permitted such an event to happen."[119] Nasser reportedly told a disappointed Gadaffi in 1969 that it was impossible to destroy Israel because "neither the Russians nor the Americans would permit a situation that might lead to nuclear war."[120] Donald Neff writes that in 1972–1973, the Egyptian general staff concluded that the "superpowers would not allow a complete victory by either side."[121] Moreover, Egyptian leaders conveyed a belief the United States had strong influence over Israel throughout this period. During the 1973 war, Egypt relied on the United States both to communicate limited Egyptian aims and constrain Israel. The decision to convey Egypt's limited intentions was thus consistent with the belief that the United States could exercise a restraining influence on Israeli nuclear use, except in cases of a threat to Israeli survival.[122]

The Egyptian expectation of external constraint against Israeli nuclear use was reasonable. There is some evidence that the Soviets provided guarantees against an Israeli nuclear strike. The *New York Times* reported in February 1966 that during the December visit of Soviet deputy defense minister

Andrei Gretchko to Cairo, the Soviets "promised to give President Gamal Abdel Nasser a guarantee of nuclear protection if Israel developed or obtained such weapons."[123] Nasser allegedly told *Al-Ahram* editor Mohamed Heikal that the Soviet Union would supply Egypt with a nuclear umbrella if Israel threatened nuclear use, and Heikal claimed in 1973 that the Soviet Union had previously "guaranteed" the Aswan High Dam against Israeli nuclear attacks.[124] There are reasons to doubt the Soviets offered a nuclear security guarantee, but that does not preclude conventional security guarantees if Israel was to escalate to nuclear use.[125] Indeed, US officials took seriously the possibility of Soviet action. "Should Israel brandish nuclear weapons, the Soviets would counter it and it would be very dangerous for Israel," Kissinger explained to US senators following the October War.[126]

Soviet support was not simply rhetorical. In addition to supplying Egypt with weapons and training, the Soviet Union intervened directly, albeit in a limited manner, in 1970 following Israeli deep-penetration attacks and raised the prospect of joint intervention with the United States during the October War to prevent the destruction of the Egyptian Third Army.[127] It was not unreasonable, then, to conclude that the Soviets would act in the event of nuclear use against one of its clients, even if the bulk of its advisers had left in 1972. In sum, the Soviets likely did attempt to assuage Egyptian fears, US officials in both the Johnson and Nixon administrations considered it likely the Soviets would move to counter any overt Israeli nuclear actions, and the Soviet Union intervened when Israel struck Egyptian targets in 1970. Israeli leaders would have to take the Soviet reaction into account. If faced with its own destruction, Israel may have judged the benefits of nuclear use sufficient to set the potential costs aside; but as long as Egypt could not pose a major threat, such costs would loom larger.

More puzzling is Egyptian reliance on the United States. The United States had influence over Israel, but why would the United States use that on Egypt's behalf? Extended deterrence guarantees are considered difficult to make credible in the best of circumstances.[128] The United States was not even an Egyptian ally. Indeed, Maria Post Rublee rightly points out that Egyptian leaders would likely discount the depth of any US commitment because Egypt "has not received any formal security guarantee from the United States and knows that Washington would side with Tel Aviv over Cairo."[129] Egyptian leaders never lost an opportunity to complain about unreserved American support for Israel.

There were nevertheless grounds for the Egyptian belief that the United States would act to constrain Israeli nuclear use. To begin with, the centerpiece of Sadat's strategy in 1973 was to force the Americans to engage. Sadat expected US involvement. On nuclear weapons more specifically, the Egyptians were aware of the general US nonproliferation policy. This was hardly a secret, as the United States openly pushed states to sign the

Nuclear Nonproliferation Treaty.[130] US officials flatly told Egypt that they opposed the introduction of nuclear weapons into the Middle East. In a 1966 meeting with Sadat, Secretary of State Rusk "stressed [the] unalterable US commitment [to] oppose [the] proliferation [of] nuclear weapons," adding that the introduction of "nuclear weapons into [the] Near East arms race would cause [the] US [to] react very harshly. . . . Israel [is] under no illusions about [the] US stand on nuclear weapons proliferation."[131] As Rublee demonstrates, part of the Egyptians' reason for abandoning their own nuclear program was the understanding that US policy was firmly against nuclear proliferation.[132]

The United States eventually did accept an Israeli nuclear weapon capability, of course. Yet indicative of ongoing American concern with proliferation in the region, President Nixon and Prime Minister Meir made arrangements, the precise details of which remain unknown, by which Israel would exercise nuclear restraint in return for US conventional support and an end to US pressure on Israel to abandon its nuclear program. Subsequent "documents suggest that Meir pledged to maintain nuclear restraint—no test, no declaration, no visibility."[133] Use of nuclear weapons against Egypt would obviously create "visibility" and make a declaration superfluous. That could lead to further nuclear proliferation in the Middle East or the direct introduction of Soviet nuclear weapons in the region.

In addition to proliferation concerns, the United States feared Israeli nuclear use would directly harm American security and influence. US and Soviet leaders both hoped to keep conflicts in the area limited for fear that escalation might draw the two superpowers into direct confrontation.[134] Assistant Secretary of Defense Warnke outlined a fearful scenario in 1968 in which Israeli nuclear use prompted Soviet retaliation. In that event, the United States faced "totally unacceptable alternatives. The first of these, a nuclear strike by the United States, is almost unthinkable. If directed against the Soviet Union, it would lead inexorably to all-out nuclear war. If directed against an Arab state, it would virtually compel Soviet retaliation against U.S. territory, particularly in view of the fact that Israel would have been the first to resort to nuclear arms."[135] Such concerns were not overly alarmist. After all, the mere suggestion by the Soviets on October 24, 1973, that they might intervene to prevent Israeli destruction of the Egyptian Third Army prompted the United States to move various forces and raise its alert status to Defense Condition (DefCon) III.[136] Even if Soviet units did not intervene directly in the fighting, an expansion of any Egyptian-Israeli conflict to nuclear use that inflicted a major defeat on Arab forces would provide the Soviets an opportunity to gain influence in the region. That would undermine the long-term US foreign policy goal to reduce the Soviet role in the Middle East.[137]

Throughout this period, Egyptian leaders also worked to delegitimize the Israeli nuclear program and pursued chemical weapons to raise the costs of any Israeli nuclear strike. "Egypt worked in two tracks," one former Egyptian military official explained. "We tried to get rid of Israel's nuclear weapons through diplomatic efforts, and we sought military alternatives such as strong conventional forces, surface-to-surface missiles, and chemical weapons options."[138] Egypt signed the Nonproliferation Treaty on the first day it opened for signature in the hope that this would increase US pressure against the Israeli nuclear program and as a way to signal that Israel's nuclear program placed it outside the international community.[139]

Egypt also sought to leverage biological and chemical weapons to raise the costs of any Israeli nuclear use. Though there are reasons to doubt the extent of the Egyptian biological weapons program, in 1970 Sadat stated that "Egypt has biological weapons stored in refrigerators and could use them against Israel's crowded population."[140] Egypt remains outside the Chemical Weapons Convention, refusing to join until Israel signs the Nuclear Nonproliferation Treaty.[141] As in the 1991 Iraq case, Egyptian elites recognized that chemical weapons were not equivalent to nuclear weapons. Yet as Rublee notes, the Egyptian chemical capability "may have helped assuage both security concerns and psychological needs: Egypt would not be left without any defense against a WMD attack and in fact could launch one of its own."[142]

Though the focus in this chapter has been on Egyptian decision making, it is worth briefly addressing Syrian behavior during the October 1973 War. The Syrian plan was limited as well, largely centered on retaking the Golan Heights. As Kenneth Pollack notes, Syrian forces "were to concentrate on seizing the small number of points of entry onto the Golan from Israel, sealing the plateau to prevent a counterattack by reserve units assembling in Galilee and trapping the Israeli forces defending the Golan."[143] When asked about the possibility of Israeli nuclear strikes, Murhaf Jouejati related that Syrian leaders made two calculations. The first, noted above, was the Soviet and American restraining influence on Israel. The second was that "part of the reason why the Syrian army stopped on October 7 where it did . . . was to send the signal to Israel that the Syrian attacking force did not have the intention of going any further. . . . So Syrian leaders were sending a signal, 'We're not going to go any further. Don't panic.'"[144] In addition, President Assad planned for and then pressed the Soviet Union to push an early cease-fire. Victor Israelyan relates that Assad explained to the Soviet ambassador on October 4 that "after the initial victories of the Arabs, the Soviet Union should promptly initiate a cease-fire resolution in the United Nations Security Council." The "military phase" would take only one or two days.[145] Much of the motivation for the cease-fire was to consolidate gains and avoid an Israeli conventional counterattack. Had the cease-fire been quickly enacted, though, it would also allay Israeli fears that the Syrian army would rapidly advance into the heart of Israel. Ultimately, Syrian forces enjoyed some initial success but were unable to reach key Jordan River bridges and secure the heights before the Israeli counterattacks.[146]

The basic Egyptian behavior toward Israel is consistent with my argument. An intense political dispute pitted Egypt against Israel. Egypt was markedly weaker than Israel. That conventional military imbalance and the shape that the conflict took provided low benefits for Israel to use nuclear weapons. Egyptian leaders gambled that various costs associated with using nuclear weapons could loom large. They frequently discussed the Israeli nuclear arsenal and pursued various steps to further minimize the already low likelihood of an Israeli nuclear strike. Nuclear weapons did not deter Egyptian action, but neither were they irrelevant to Egyptian considerations.

China versus the United States

On November 25, 1950, military forces of the People's Republic of China (PRC)[1] launched a series of massive attacks against advancing American and South Korean troops. The assault was devastating, routing portions of US forces and compelling a lengthy retreat back down the Korean Peninsula. The Korean War, which had only recently seemed destined for a decisive American victory, settled into a bitter stalemate before negotiations ended the fighting in 1953. Barely a year later in 1954, and then again in 1958, the PRC shelled offshore islands controlled by the Nationalist Chinese exiled on Taiwan (Formosa) after their defeat in the Chinese Civil War. The assaults necessarily involved the United States, the main patron of the Nationalists. All three Chinese actions occurred in spite of the American atomic monopoly. Why did the PRC risk such a devastating assault just as the American nuclear capabilities were becoming more substantial in 1950? Why did the PRC then escalate tensions twice more in such a short period if it became more cognizant of the destructive power and danger of nuclear weapons?[2]

I argue that China pursued several strategies to minimize the likelihood of an American nuclear strike. In each confrontation the Chinese perceived a growing danger to what they considered vital interests. Nevertheless, China did not rush into war in 1950. Mao Zedong, leader of the PRC, took several steps, most notably pursuing Soviet support, to help reduce the risks of fighting the United States. Additionally, the fighting itself posed little danger to the United States outside the Korean Peninsula. Though publicly the Chinese sought to downplay the dangers of nuclear strikes to discourage American attempts at nuclear blackmail, in private they took the American nuclear arsenal very seriously. In both Taiwan Straits crises, the Chinese took several steps to avoid fighting the United States.

This chapter relies on several types of sources. To begin with, it incorporates secondary sources, many based on declassified Chinese documents, as well as memoirs and statements by participants. I note if there is widespread disagreement or multiple compelling interpretations for events. I also directly incorporate Chinese and Soviet-bloc documents translated to English. Many of these are available at the Cold War International History Project (CWIHP) and can be accessed online. These allow me to reconstruct, at times day by day, the events surrounding Chinese decision making as well as interrogate the role that nuclear weapons played. There are a number of cases where nuclear weapons can be shown to have had a direct influence on specific Chinese decisions during their confrontations with the United States. There remain limits to the conclusions that one can draw, and, as in the other cases, it is important to note that many factors beyond nuclear weapons influenced Chinese decision making. Finally, I supplement these sources with declassified American documents, particularly when assessing the military balance.

I expand on this argument in the rest of the chapter. I first outline the nuclear and conventional military balance. Next, I review the background for the three disputes investigated: the 1950 Korean War, the 1954 Taiwan Straits Crisis, and the 1958 Taiwan Straits Crisis. The third section examines Chinese behavior and strategies to raise the costs and lower the benefits for the Americans to execute a nuclear strike.

The Military Balance

The United States fielded a more destructive nuclear force in 1950 than several nuclear-armed states possess in 2019. The PRC was a conventionally weak opponent relative to the United States. Its military and economic capabilities allowed it to do little more than pursue ground operations within mainland China or the immediate vicinity.

THE NUCLEAR BALANCE

Nuclear monopoly existed between the United States and the People's Republic from the official birth of the PRC on October 1, 1949, to China's first nuclear test on October 16, 1964. The Chinese were obviously aware of the American atomic capability given the US use of nuclear weapons against Japan and subsequent US policy. The American nuclear arsenal was small, however, with a limited delivery capability from 1945 to 1949.[3]

Beginning in 1950, the US nuclear arsenal grew rapidly. As table 4.1 shows, the number of US strategic nuclear warheads, not counting the introduction of tactical nuclear warheads, grew from approximately three hundred in 1950 to more than forty-six hundred by 1964. The introduction of thermonuclear weapons into the US arsenal in 1954 is apparent by the jump in total yield. In 1955 the first lightweight hydrogen bomb, the B15, entered service, with a yield of 3.4 megatons.[4]

US delivery capabilities were rapidly improving as well. The B-29 and B-50 (essentially a modified B-29) were phased out in the early 1950s, replaced by

Table 4.1 US nuclear weapons, 1949–1964

Year	Total nuclear warheads	Strategic nuclear warheads	Total yield (megatons)
1949	170	170	4.19
1950	299	299	9.53
1951	438	438	35.25
1952	841	660	49.95
1953	1,169	878	72.80
1954	1,703	1,418	339.01
1955	2,422	1,755	2,879.99
1956	3,692	2,123	9,188.65
1957	5,543	2,460	17,545.86
1958	7,345	2,610	17,303.54
1959	12,298	2,496	19,054.62
1960	18,638	3,127	20,491.17
1961	22,229	3,153	10,947.71
1962	25,540	3,451	12,825.02
1963	28,133	4,050	15,977.17
1964	29,463	4,654	16,943.97

Sources: Department of State, "Fact Sheet: Transparency in the U.S. Nuclear Weapons Stockpile," April 29, 2014, https://2009-2017.state.gov/documents/organization/225555.pdf; "Estimated U.S. and Soviet/Russian Nuclear Stockpiles, 1945–94," *Bulletin of the Atomic Scientists* 50, no. 6 (1994): 58–59.

the B-36, B-47, and, beginning in 1955, the B-52.[5] Increases in range and airborne refueling allowed American aircraft to strike targets throughout China's populated and industrial areas. American intercontinental ballistic missiles (ICBMs) and submarine launched ballistic missiles (SLBMs) began entering service in 1959 and 1960, respectively. Though range and deployment locations meant not all missiles could strike Chinese targets, the number of platforms threatening China nevertheless increased. Finally, on June 20, 1953, President Eisenhower began transferring operational nuclear weapons to direct military control. This reversed Truman-era policies that had kept nuclear weapons largely separated from the military.[6]

THE CONVENTIONAL BALANCE

The conventional balance was highly asymmetric in favor of the United States throughout the period of American atomic monopoly. Figure 4.1 shows that the United States always had at least a 10:1 advantage in per capita GDP. In most years the advantage was 15:1 or more. This allowed the United States to extract a great deal more from its society and field a larger

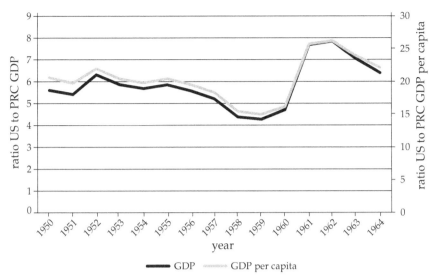

Figure 4.1 Economic ratios, 1950–1964

Source: Gleditsch Expanded GDP data version 6.0 (September 2014), http://ksgleditsch.com/ exptradegdp.html.

quantity and better quality of weapons, as well as sustain advanced forces in battle. The overall ratio of US to Chinese GDP was less extreme because of China's large population, but always greater than 4:1 and in most years 5:1 or more. In the early 1950s China was recovering from devastation wrought by years of warfare against Japan and its own civil war. Massive amounts of infrastructure were destroyed, agricultural land abandoned, and industrial centers shuttered. More than forty million people were unemployed in 1950, and famine was widespread.[7]

US officials were cognizant of the power imbalance. In 1948, the director of the policy planning staff at the State Department, George Kennan, wrote that the area that China occupied had such little power potential that "in any war in the foreseeable future China could at best be a weak ally or at worst an inconsequential enemy."[8] After the Korean War, US observers concluded that China had made impressive gains, but numerous obstacles meant that it was "unlikely that they can soon achieve a modern economy or major economic capabilities."[9] Similarly, one 1960 National Intelligence Estimate found that "Communist China has made impressive gains in industrial and military strength." Nevertheless, China would "continue to face major economic problems for many years to come."[10]

Rough indicators for the military balance also show an American advantage. This too was somewhat tempered by China's larger population, which in 1950 was 570 million people, compared to 150 million in the United States.

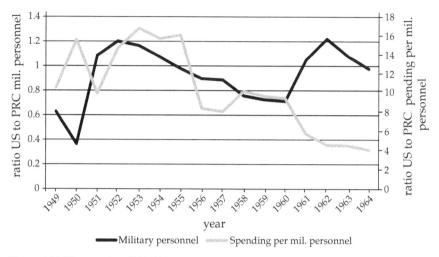

Figure 4.2 Military ratios, 1949–1964

Source: Correlates of War, National Material Capabilities, version 5.0, http://www.correlatesofwar.org/data-sets/national-material-capabilities.

This allowed China to field a larger military force than the United States, a point driven home to American leaders on the battlefields of Korea. Though even in this key area one notes that the Chinese advantage over Americans in raw numbers of soldiers, sailors, and airmen was never greater than 3:1, and in several years the United States actually fielded a larger military. The US advantage becomes more apparent when comparing levels of military spending per soldier. As figure 4.2 shows, that ratio often exceeded 10:1 in favor of the United States and was greater than 8:1 throughout the 1950s.

More detailed assessments of the military balance reinforce the picture created by the rough indicators on military size and spending. PRC manpower and terrain provided a major advantage against any attempts at invasion or major offensive actions against the PRC homeland. Yet the PRC had little power projection capability, no ability to strike the US homeland, and no ability to quickly conquer territory that would decisively alter the balance of power.[11] Finally, both sides had the ability to implement modern force employment techniques of differential concentration and defense in depth at the operational level, with cover, concealment, dispersion, and suppressive fire at the tactical level. This is not to say both sides did so in every engagement or always would have in potential conflicts, but that the PRC did not have an advantage in this regard. When both sides are capable of implementing this modern system of force employment, imbalances in material and technological capability prove decisive.[12]

The People's Liberation Army (PLA) units had limited firepower capabilities. For military equipment, the Chinese relied heavily on what they could capture and Soviet support.[13] In October 1950, Mao informed Stalin that China could field large numbers of ground troops "thanks to available reserves, but as to technological equipment of Chinese troops they totally count on the assistance of the Soviet Union."[14] Mao may have exaggerated somewhat to gain additional Soviet aid, but not by much.[15] On the eve of the Korean War, Marshal Lin Biao argued that an American division possessed ten to twenty times the firepower of its Chinese counterpart.[16] Despite initial surprise and manpower advantages, the PLA was consistently unable to annihilate American combat formations.[17] As Zhang concludes, during the Korean War the Chinese military, "although a gigantic force of some 5 million men, lacked naval and air arms. Its soldiers were irregulars, its equipment was heterogeneous and largely obsolete . . . [and] its command and control structure was rudimentary."[18]

Chinese capabilities increased after the Korean War but continued to decisively lag the Americans. In his detailed study of the PLA, Xiaobing Li notes that "after the Korean War, Chinese generals were convinced that the Chinese military was a regional force, not a global one."[19] For instance, Marshal Nie Rongzhen recalled that during the 1950s the "conventional weapons we could produce at the time were far behind, in capabilities and qualities, those of the technologically advanced countries."[20] Throughout the 1950s, the Chinese sought to reverse what Mao called the "backward conditions" of the military, relying heavily on Soviet support.[21]

The Chinese had little ability to project power over water. Attempted amphibious assaults in 1949 against the Nationalist islands of Jinmen and Dengbu ended in disaster.[22] The Chinese military subsequently increased its amphibious capabilities and overcame the Nationalists, taking several islands immediately off the mainland coast. China primarily fielded small gunboats and torpedo boats, frequently relying on commandeered civilian vessels for troop transport. These would be ineffective against American naval capabilities.[23] The PLA Air Force (PLAAF) had only formed in 1949 and so was extremely limited at the outset of the Korean War. Though its capabilities increased after the war, the PLAAF lacked effective bombing capabilities and had difficulty projecting power beyond the PRC's shore.[24]

American assessments were similar to those of the Chinese. The Central Intelligence Agency surmised in early November 1950 that "the Chinese Communists could probably make available as many as 350,000 troops . . . for sustained ground operations in Korea and could provide limited air support and some armor." Chinese forces would thus be capable of "halting further UN advance northward" or "forcing UN withdrawal to defensive positions further south."[25] At best, though, the Chinese could force a stalemate. There was no danger to the United States unless the conflict escalated to a general war involving the Soviet Union. After the war the United States viewed China as a capable but minor adversary with minimal power projection ability. The National Security Council noted in November 1953 that on "the basis of the Korean experience, and of our intelligence as to the level and quality of Chinese Communist forces not committed in the Korean theater, it may be estimated that the Chinese Communists, with continued assistance from the USSR, have a considerable capability for defending mainland China against amphibious or ground assault; modest defensive and offensive air capabilities; limited amphibious capabilities; and negligible naval capabilities."[26] Later National Intelligence Estimates noted Chinese military improvements but concluded that China remained "dependent on the USSR for most major items of military equipment."[27]

Dispute Overview

Mao declared the formation of the PRC on October 1, 1949. The first task, common to most states, was to minimize threats to PRC territory. This focus was reinforced by the Chinese memory of the hundred years (or century) of humiliation, from the mid-nineteenth to mid-twentieth centuries as foreign powers effectively negated Chinese sovereignty over large parts of the country.[28] Thus, in September 1949 Mao stressed to the Chinese People's Political Consultative Conference that "no imperialist will be allowed to invade our territory again."[29]

The second task centered on consolidating control of Han Chinese areas outside the PRC. These included Hong Kong, Macao, and Taiwan. All three areas have been so significant that Chinese leadership terms disputes over their status "domestic affairs (*neizheng*), not interstate conflicts."[30] For example, Zhou Enlai argued in April 1955 that the "relationship between China and the Jiang Jieshi [Chiang Kai-shek] clique [on Taiwan] is an internal issue. The relationship between China and the United States is an international issue."[31] Taiwan attracted the most attention. As Zhang Baijia and Jia Qingguo write, Chinese leaders have long regarded reunification with Taiwan as a "core national interest[;] it is highly unlikely that any Chinese leader has ever entertained the idea of sacrificing Taiwan for other interests."[32] Indeed, upon its formation the PRC set the "liberation of Taiwan" as one of its key strategic goals.[33] "The fact that Taiwan belongs to China can never be altered no matter what obstructionist tactics American imperialism may adopt," Zhou stated on June 28, 1950.[34]

The PRC initially sought to avoid a major confrontation with the United States. True, the Communists looked to complete their victory by conquering Taiwan. US leaders were willing to accept that outcome at that point, though.[35] Chinese suspicions of US intentions and ideological affinity led Mao to "lean" toward the Soviet Union, signing the Sino-Soviet Treaty in February 1950. The Chinese Communist Party (CCP) nevertheless made several public and private overtures to engage the United States. "If the United States (and Great Britain) cut off relations with the GMD [Nationalists], we could consider the issue of establishing diplomatic relations with them," argued Mao.[36] Though negotiations came to little, China was reluctant to risk a confrontation.[37] When North Korea raised the possibility of invading South Korea on May 13, 1950, Mao sought clarification that the Soviets had, in fact, assented. The new leader feared such a move would provoke the United States. Mao ultimately bowed to the wishes of his new ally, despite misgivings.[38]

The Democratic People's Republic of Korea (DPRK) launched its assault on South Korea on June 25, 1950. President Harry Truman quickly decided to act, securing UN Security Council approval on June 27 to assist South Korea to repel the attack owing to the absence of the Soviet delegation. The United States also placed the Seventh Fleet between Taiwan and the mainland. Though the US argued this would neutralize the Nationalists, it blocked Chinese efforts to take the island and contributed to Chinese hostility.[39]

The PRC leadership quickly considered the possibility of involvement and took steps to minimize the danger. As PLA commanders agreed during a July meeting, it was better "to repair the house before it rains."[40] The principal policy result was the movement of troops to the Korean border.[41] Mao contemplated some form of military involvement as early as mid-July. Yet he did not push this policy aggressively, and the Chinese leadership continued to focus on the danger of a US victory when considering intervention.[42] Throughout the summer, as Shen Zhihua points out, "with the [North] Korean People's Army still advancing south, and with no prospect of the U.S. military crossing the 38th parallel, the question of possibly deploying Chinese forces still seemed remote."[43] As late as August 19, Mao declared that "if the US continues its operations in South Korea with its current-level forces, soon the KPA [Korean People's Army] will drive them out of the Korean Peninsula."[44] The movement of forces would be a hedge against uncertainties and allow China to appear a loyal ally, all while taking on very little risk at that time.

The situation changed rapidly in September. American and UN forces routed DPRK troops following the amphibious landing at Inchon. The success provided a tantalizing opportunity to the Americans to roll back communism in Asia. On September 27, Truman authorized General Douglas MacArthur to cross the prewar border between North and South. South Korean (Republic of Korea, ROK) forces crossed on September 30, followed by MacArthur's October 1 ultimatum calling for North Korea's unconditional surrender. American troops crossed the border six days later on October 7 and steadily advanced northward.[45]

As early as July, the PRC leadership had set an American advance into North Korea as an explicit condition for intervention. Zhou informed the Soviet ambassador Nikolai Roshchin that the Chinese army would engage the Americans in the guise of volunteers if the Americans moved north of the thirty-eighth parallel.[46] "If the U.S. imperialists won the war, they would become more arrogant and would threaten us. We should not fail to assist the Koreans," Mao argued during an August 4 meeting with Central Committee members.[47] Similarly, the director of the political departments in the Chinese People's Volunteer Force, Du Ping, recalled that at a meeting of the Northeast Military Region commanders on August 13, "all attending commanders believed that if imperialist America occupied all of Korea, it would retrace imperialist Japan's old path to invade our Northeast and North China. . . . Where would we then have to resist?"[48]

The American decision thus created a growing sense of danger to the Chinese homeland. If the United States occupied North Korea, the end result would almost certainly be US troops permanently deployed in a hostile country directly adjacent to China. Mao outlined the basic logic in a draft telegram for Stalin on October 2, arguing that if "we allow the United States to occupy all of Korea, the revolutionary strength of Korea will suffer a fundamental defeat, and the American invaders will run more rampant, with negative effects for the entire Far East."[49] Mao summarized the security concerns again on October 13, telling Roshchin that "if the U.S. troops advance up to the border of China, then Korea will become a dark spot for us [the Chinese] and the Northeast will be faced with constant menace."[50] Moreover, northeast China contained the main industrial strength of the country, as well as the main supply lines to the Soviet Union.[51] As Paul Godwin concludes, "Should Beijing come to Pyongyang's aid, China would be confronting the most powerful state in the industrial world. Mao nevertheless feared more a unified Korea on China's borders under U.S. control."[52]

Mao's view was widely shared. For example, after an agonizing night contemplating intervention, Marshal Peng Dehuai, who would command Chinese "volunteers" in Korea, argued during a Politburo meeting on October 5 that "sending the troops to aid Korea is necessary. . . . If the American military places itself along the Yalu River and in Taiwan, it could find an excuse anytime it wants to launch an invasion."[53] Peng's statement was unlikely to have been made simply to earn Mao's approval. "Given Peng's reputation for forthrightness and frankness," Andrew Scobell argues, "if the general had concluded that intervention was wrong, he would undoubtedly have stated his opinion, as he did on other occasions much to his detriment."[54] China could not "sit back with folded hands and let the Americans come up to their border," Marshal Nie informed Indian diplomat K. M. Panikkar over dinner on September 25. "We know what we are in for, but at all costs American aggression has to be stopped."[55] The Chinese concern was sufficiently clear that American intelligence accurately captured it. "The Chinese Communists probably genuinely fear an invasion of Manchuria despite the clear-cut definition of UN objectives," CIA director Walter Bedell Smith wrote to Truman on November 1.[56]

On the night of October 19, Chinese forces began crossing the Yalu into North Korea.[57] As I discuss in more detail below, the PRC leadership was not eager for a fight. At a key Politburo meeting on October 2, many top officials were skeptical of intervention.[58] Ultimately, Mao's arguments were sufficient to sway hesitant officials.

Chinese forces again challenged the United States in 1954–1955 by shelling territory controlled by American-backed Taiwan (the Republic of China, or ROC). Chinese officials had watched nervously following the end of the Korean War as US-Taiwanese ties deepened. Particularly alarming was discussion of a US-ROC defense treaty. In the wake of divisions in Germany, Korea, and Vietnam, this seemed to portend a permanent division between Taiwan and the mainland.[59] "In order to *break up* the collaboration between the United States and Chiang Kai-shek, and keep them from joining together militarily and politically," Mao told Zhou in July 1954, "we must announce to our country and to the world the slogan of liberating Taiwan."[60] Earlier that month, Mao had argued in the Politburo that "we should destroy the chances of the United States to conclude the treaty with Taiwan. We should think of ways to achieve this objective, including enhancing our propaganda. . . . Our objective is to put pressure on the United States so that [it] will not conclude the treaty with Taiwan."[61] The PRC thus initially responded to the situation with public warnings against any attempts to alter Taiwan's status.[62]

The failure to arrest the deteriorating situation led to more confrontational measures. The PRC accelerated preparations to seize several of the Dachen islands, some two hundred miles north of Taiwan and close to the mainland. Peng Dehuai, then defense minister, explicitly linked the military action to the threat from US-ROC treaty negotiations. The offensive would "attack the American-Chiang mutual defense plot," he argued.[63] On September 3, 1954, PLA artillery began the first of seventy barrages over the next two months against Jinmen Island.

The situation nevertheless deteriorated further from the Chinese perspective. American and ROC officials continued negotiations, signing the defense agreement in December. Zhou labeled the move "open aggression" and warned the United States it would have to accept the consequences.[64] Mao concurred, stating that the treaty "is not by any means a defense treaty. . . . It is a treaty of total aggression."[65] The bombardment of Dachen subsequently intensified to "make it clear that the Chinese Government and people firmly stand against the [US-Taiwan] treaty of aggression."[66] In addition to signaling hostility, the CCP leadership sought to determine the precise physical territory that the treaty covered. Su Yu, the chief of the general staff, issued an operation order on November 30 stating that the "East China Military Region should attack and seize Yijiangshan Island on or around December 20 to force the scope of the so-called 'defense treaty' that America and Chiang are about to sign to exclude our coastal islands that the enemy occupies."[67] The offensive was delayed for nearly a month, but on January 18, 1955, PRC forces seized Yijiangshan Island. The assault killed 567 ROC soldiers and captured another 519. The United States evacuated ROC forces from nearby islands, which the PRC then occupied. China continued its advance, so that by the end of February it controlled the Dachens, Beiji, Nanji, and a series of smaller islands.[68] With the scope of the American commitment now probed, the US-ROC treaty a reality, and American military threats increasing, the PRC sought to defuse tensions. The crisis effectively ended on April 23, 1955, when Zhou expressed a desire for negotiations with the US government during a meeting with Asian and African leaders in Bandung, Indonesia.[69]

Two years of relative quiet followed until August 23, 1958, when Chinese forces began shelling Jinmen and Mazu. Artillery barrages continued for two months, killing and wounding nearly twenty-five hundred ROC personnel. The crisis subsided when Zhou resumed negotiations with the Americans in September. On October 25 the PRC announced that it would shell Jinmen only on odd-numbered days. By then it had abandoned plans to seize Jinmen and Mazu as part of the liberation of Taiwan. Shelling continued through 1961, when the Chinese stopped using live ammunition and instead switched to propaganda leaflets. The shelling stopped entirely in 1979.[70]

Several factors pushed Mao to act. He may have been seeking to increase his stature in the international Communist movement by challenging the United States during the latter's intervention in Lebanon. Yet Chinese preparations for military action began well before the Lebanon issue came up, and China commenced shelling after the crisis was resolved.[71] There is evidence that Mao believed a crisis against an external enemy could mobilize domestic support for his development programs.[72] As he put it on September 5, "A tense situation can mobilize the population, can particularly mobilize the backward people, can mobilize the people in the middle, and can therefore promote the Great Leap Forward in economic construction."[73]

A critical factor once again proved to be perceptions that Taiwan was sliding toward permanent separation from the mainland. As M. Taylor Fravel argues, "as the situation deteriorated across the Taiwan Strait in late 1957, China's leaders began to contemplate military action."[74] Sino-American negotiations had stalled in December 1957, US military deployments appeared to increase, including the deployment of nuclear weapons to Taiwan in 1958, and the ROC ramped up statements proclaiming an intention to take back the mainland.[75] US policy, Zhou warned in February 1958, threatened to make two Chinas a reality.[76]

The Chinese goal centered on arresting the movement toward an independent Taiwan. PRC leaders understood their action would antagonize the United States. According to Wu Lengxi, then editor of the *People's Daily* who would later become deputy director of the Central Committee's Propaganda Department, Mao's goal was "to punish the Americans" for their Taiwan policy.[77] Before the start of the bombardment, Mao wrote to Peng Dehuai to "prepare to shell Jinmen now, dealing with Jiang [Chiang Kai-shek] directly and the Americans indirectly."[78] After shelling began, Zhou and Mao made it clear to the Soviet foreign minister Andrei Gromyko that, in Zhang's words, "China's bombardment was intended mainly to 'punish the KMT [ROC]' and 'pressure the United States not to pursue a 'two-Chinas' policy.'"[79] As Mao explained to the Politburo Standing Committee on August 23, "Our demand is that American armed forces withdraw from Taiwan, and Jiang's troops withdraw from Jinmen and Mazu. . . . We did not put the Americans in the wrong; they did it by themselves—they have stationed several thousand troops on Taiwan, plus two air force bases there."[80]

The US response included the dispatch of additional forces to the region, clarification of its commitment to Jinmen and Mazu, and escorting ROC resupply efforts to the islands. The Eisenhower administration did not rule out nuclear use, but against a low-level challenge and a conventionally weak adversary the administration saw little benefit and numerous costs in the early use of nuclear weapons.[81] Mao sought to assure his colleagues (as well as nervous Soviet officials) that the Americans would be hesitant to use force. But he refrained from escalation.

The PRC moved to defuse the crisis once the bombardment seemed to only further the prospects of a permanent division with Taiwan. When negotiations began on September 15, the PRC rejected an American cease-fire proposal. A cease-fire would only strengthen the ROC position, making separation more likely. PRC leaders countered again and again that they would reduce tensions if the Americans withdrew all forces from Taiwan and the Straits. Secretary of State John Foster Dulles then expanded the cease-fire option on September 30, hinting the Americans would be willing to remove ROC forces from Jinmen and Mazu. Though this seemed to meet part of the PRC objectives, Zhou warned that Dulles's proposal in reality would "seize this opportunity to create two Chinas. . . . In one word, Dulles' policy was designed to exchange Jinmen and Mazu for Taiwan and Penghu."[82]

A firmer division was the very thing the PRC hoped to prevent. "Honestly, we do want to take over Jinmen and Mazu," Mao argued on September 30. "But this is not just about Jiang; this is especially about U.S. policy, which needs to be taken into consideration."[83] Mao now fell back on his "noose" concept. It was an acceptable outcome for Jinmen and Mazu to remain in America-backed ROC hands. "Whenever necessary, we may shell them," Mao explained a few days later. "Whenever we are in need of tension, we may tighten this noose, and whenever we want to relax the tension, we may loosen the noose."[84]

The Role of Nuclear Weapons

The Chinese pursued several different avenues to minimize the risks of a nuclear strike. In every case Chinese military action was directed to an area that had a natural stopping point, and the PRC took various steps to hedge against a nuclear strike. In 1954 and 1958 they were careful to limit the scope of their actions. My argument predicts a conventionally weak NNWS may escalate to war if it believes it is in its interest. During the Korean War the Chinese posed no threat to the American homeland, to the US military outside the Korean peninsula, or to the US nuclear arsenal. At the same time, the Chinese sought to inflict serious losses on US forces operating in Korea. They therefore pursued additional means to raise the costs of any American escalation. Specifically, Mao was hesitant to intervene without assurances of Soviet support. In the first section I outline the general Chinese behavior, before turning in the second section to more explicitly link nuclear weapons to this behavior.

CHINESE BEHAVIOR

Despite their general belief that intervention in the Korean War was necessary for security reasons, the Chinese leadership agonized over the final decision to fight. In an effort to deter the Americans, the PRC issued several warnings that an advance to the Yalu risked war. Zhou explained to Soviet officials on September 18 that the Western countries were concerned about Chinese and Soviet intervention. "We should take advantage of the fear of the Western countries and take actions to demonstrate our intentions," he argued. "From this perspective, China's transfer of troops from the south to the northeast was enough to upset the British and American governments."[85] On October 2, Zhou asked the Indian ambassador to warn the Americans that China would enter the war if US forces crossed the thirty-eighth parallel.[86] The Americans did not halt their advance.

Having accepted the necessity of war in Korea, China initially sought to avoid directly confronting US forces. Mao told Zhou on October 13 that the Chinese People's Volunteers (CPV) would "concentrate on fighting the [South Korean] puppet army" while avoiding American troops. "If we can eliminate several divisions of the puppet army in the first phase, the Korean situation will take a turn in our favor."[87] Indeed, there was some hope that no fighting at all would occur, and that the Chinese would simply present the Americans with a fait accompli that would deter any further American advance. As Mao explained, if the CPV intervened quickly north of American positions, then "the U.S. and its puppet troops, concerned [by the intervention of China], would stop their advance northward and thus we would be able to protect the areas north of the Pyongyang-Wonsan front . . . from being occupied by the enemy."[88] Mao and Peng's plans in late October after the CPV crossed into North Korea continued to focus on avoiding combat with the United States, instead focusing on wiping out "three or even four [ROK] puppet divisions with a surprise attack." If such an attack was successful, the thinking went, American forces would have to reconsider their advance.[89] The Chinese would then set up a defensive perimeter in the northern part of North Korea to build up their forces, gain greater Soviet air support, and launch a larger counteroffensive if necessary. The first campaign (October 25 to November 8) went largely to script. However, it did not halt the American advance, and there was no new diplomatic effort. The CPV then disengaged in an effort to lure the Americans farther north for a massive counterattack.[90]

The second campaign (beginning November 25) planned to, and did, inflict a large number of casualties on US military forces. Despite its scope, the Chinese strategy would not threaten US forces outside Korea, the US homeland, its regime, or its nuclear arsenal. The strategy focused on defeating US forces currently operating in Korea, capturing South Korean territory, and then switching to a defensive posture. The United States would again be presented with a choice to escalate further or halt the fighting. The Central Military Commission highlighted the coercive nature of Mao's strategy on December 4, stating that "we will mainly aim at eliminating the enemy [strength] and first of all wipe out the ROK forces. [With this action] we will be in a stronger position to compel [the] United States imperialists to withdraw from Korea."[91] Mao hoped the UN would allow elections for the Korean people to select a single government under UN and Chinese and Soviet supervision. This was not simply a rationalization brought on by stalemate; at that point CPV forces were still rapidly advancing, and US formations had yet to stabilize. The limited nature of the advance was credible because China had no way to project power beyond the continent to harm US interests elsewhere in the Pacific, to say nothing of the US homeland.

The Chinese also took steps to avoid making a broader declaration of war against the United States, further limiting the danger posed to the Americans. Mao accepted advice to term Chinese forces "volunteers" to highlight the "unofficial nature" of the PRC's involvement.[92] Peng explained to his subordinates prior to intervention that "at present [we] do not want to fight a major war. Nor do we intend to declare war on America, but only to assist the Koreans' revolutionary war under the name of People's Volunteers."[93] The Chinese would not seek to escalate the war by confronting Americans or American allies elsewhere. Hostilities would be limited to the Korean Peninsula. After the conflict settled into a stalemate, the PRC took various steps to prevent further escalation. For example, the Chinese air force, in a reciprocal action to US forces not engaging north of the Yalu River, refused to allow air strikes south of the thirty-eighth parallel.[94]

The Chinese would still be inflicting large casualties on the Americans, despite the limited overall danger to the United States. As such, the

Chinese also sought ways to increase the costs of escalation for the United States. In particular, the Chinese sought a Soviet commitment of air forces.

The problem was that the Soviets were hesitant to offer such support. As the situation in Korea deteriorated for the North Koreans, the Soviets increased pressure on China to intervene. Stalin cabled Mao on October 1 urging intervention. On October 7 he again reminded Mao that the Sino-Soviet alliance would likely deter any American expansion of the war. For added encouragement, Stalin suggested a windows logic, arguing that a war now would be better than in several years when Japan and South Korea would be stronger.[95] Yet the Soviets were unwilling to become directly involved. They initially offered air support and material resources to the PRC, but had begun backing away from those commitments as early as August. Then in early September Stalin withdrew the 151st Air Division, which, notes Donggil Kim, meant that, "in effect, Soviet air cover for Northeast China was removed."[96]

With Soviet support wavering, China balked at the prospect of fighting. On October 2, Mao seemed ready to enter the fight—he even drafted, but did not send, a telegram to Stalin to that effect—but faced intense opposition within his own government. "We originally planned to move several volunteer divisions to North Korea," Mao informed the Soviet ambassador. "However, having thought this over thoroughly, we now consider that such actions may entail extremely serious consequences."[97] After several days of debate, on October 5, the Chinese Politburo adopted a resolution to send troops to North Korea, conditional, as Kim highlights, "on Soviet assistance."[98] On October 7, the leader of the Soviet military mission in North Korea reported on Sino-Korean discussions, relaying that Mao told the North Koreans that "we [China] will do whatever we can, but we can't send troops. . . . Although the Chinese army is large, they don't have modern weapons, aviation, and a navy."[99] On October 8, North Korean leader Kim Il Sung briefly celebrated an apparent PRC decision to intervene.[100] The situation remained fluid, though. China was still uncommitted. In a fight with the Americans, Mao explained to Roshchin on October 6, China would "completely depend on Soviet assistance."[101] That assistance appeared doubtful.

To clarify the Soviet position and secure support, Mao dispatched Zhou and Lin Biao to meet with Stalin. During their meetings, Stalin backed away from his commitment to provide Soviet air support. On October 11, Zhou and Stalin jointly signed a telegram to Mao that said Chinese forces "should not cross the Korean border, so as to avoid falling into a disadvantageous situation."[102] While the meeting was taking place, Mao authorized his military commanders to execute plans to move all four armies into North Korea.[103] Upon hearing the news from Moscow, Mao abruptly reversed himself. On October 12, he informed Peng that the "order of 9 October will not be implemented for the time being; all units of the 13th Army [Group] are hereby required to stay where they are to undergo more training, not to begin operations." He also ordered his top commanders back to Beijing for consultations.[104] Reflecting the view that Beijing would not intervene, on October 13 Stalin counseled a despondent Kim Il Sung to abandon the peninsula and set up a regime in exile.[105]

China's leaders reversed themselves once again on October 13, deciding at the Politburo meeting that day that China would intervene after all. As noted, Mao reiterated the basic strategic necessity for intervention, warning that the Americans would pose a "constant menace" if they advanced to the Chinese border.[106] In addition, Mao convinced skeptics that even though the Soviets could not be counted on to supply air forces to fight over Korea, Stalin remained committed to providing air protection for China itself.[107] Mao then telegrammed Zhou and made clear, notes Shen, that the "Chinese troops would not attack American armies before the arrival of Soviet air volunteers and weaponry."[108] On October 14, Molotov and Stalin reiterated to Zhou that Soviet air forces would protect Chinese territory but not enter Korea for at least two months.[109] On October 17 Mao once more briefly held up intervention but, satisfied by Zhou that the Soviets would provide air defense, gave the final green light to go forward.[110]

The Soviets then increased their support. After initial CPV engagements, the Soviet chief military adviser in North Korea, M. V. Zakharov, told Zhou on October 29 that the Soviet Air Force would take "charge of air defense at Andong" next to the Yalu River, as well as engage in limited operations in North Korea. By November, Soviet pilots began operating over the Yalu.[111] At the end of October, Mao and his generals were no longer discussing just annihilating South Korean forces but also "the American 24th Division, [and a] unit of the First American Cavalry Division."[112] As the CPV pushed US troops back that winter, Chinese leaders remained in daily contact with Moscow.[113]

During and after the Korean War, the Chinese also undertook various hedging policies. On the battlefield, Mao and Zhou approved a February 1952 recommendation by Nie Rongzhen to dispatch nuclear specialists to Korea to help Chinese troops prepare "for possible nuclear strikes."[114] In 1953 the CPV constructed fortifications including "in the frontline battlefield, Anti-Atom shelters . . . built deep in the middle of the mountains."[115] Strategically, in late 1950 China shifted raw materials and industrial machinery away from coastal areas and into the interior.[116] Zhang highlights that to "prepare for a general nuclear attack, Beijing stressed the importance of a national defence system. The Central Military Commission had already decided on the construction of national defence works in August 1952."[117] Robert Pape notes that "U.S. intelligence reported air-raid drills and the building of air-raid shelters and anti-aircraft facilities in Shanghai, Beijing, Shenyang, Guangdong, Hubei, and other places. Also reported were evacuations of population, heavy industrial equipment, and other supplies from Shenyang, Guangzhou, Beijing, Shanghai, and cities along the Manchuria-Korea border."[118] And in early 1955 China made the decision to construct a nuclear capability of its own to deter nuclear strikes or attempts at atomic blackmail.[119]

In 1954 and 1958 China limited its behavior in a number of ways. First, in both cases the PRC targeted isolated areas—islands—that could clearly signal limited intentions. The islands were also located very near to the Chinese mainland. At its closest point, Jinmen is less than two miles off China's coast, but approximately 140 miles from Taiwan.[120] The initial targets in 1954–1955 were farthest from American forces, with the intent of keeping the conflict limited. The Chinese were able to fight several engagements with ROC forces in early 1954.[121] "Chinese leaders also took diplomatic measures to demonstrate that the PLA's actions would be limited to islands very near the mainland coast," notes Niu Jun.[122] If the Americans forced the ROC to abandon the islands, it did not markedly worsen their position elsewhere. Indeed, US officials during both crises noted that the military utility of the islands was limited. The key concern was the psychological implications of withdrawal that might negatively affect the ROC.[123]

In both cases the PRC sought to avoid directly attacking US military forces. "We shall never be the first to open fire on U.S. troops, and [we] will only maintain a defensive position there so that we should avoid direct conflict to the best of our ability," Mao stated in June 1954 in support of decisions not to engage US forces.[124] "At present," the Central Committee concluded on July 24, "the direct target of our military struggle is Chiang Kai-shek and his cohorts in Taiwan. The United States should not be treated as our direct target; we should confine the conflicts with the United States to the diplomatic arena only."[125]

The Chinese maintained this position as they began military operations. In December, Mao delayed an assault after the United States began a series of naval maneuvers in the area. The seizure of Yijiangshan the next month was done in part to probe US intentions. China continued to place emphasis on avoiding any direct engagement with US forces. General Nie Fengzhi, commander of Chinese air forces in the campaign, spoke personally with his pilots to make clear they were not to engage American aircraft. The PLAAF was prohibited from striking Dachen when American ships were in the area and not allowed to engage US forces, even when they violated PRC airspace, unless directly attacked. When Chinese leadership believed that US naval movements indicated a willingness to defend the Dachen Islands, Mao ordered the assault halted. As it became apparent that the United States was evacuating ROC forces from Dachen, the Central Military Commission refused requests to strike, for fear it would involve the Americans. Mao personally made clear on at least two occasions during their island campaigns that the PLA should "let the enemy evacuate safely."[126]

PRC caution was apparent during the 1958 crisis as well. The Chinese hoped that as long as they limited the means employed to compel the

Nationalists to evacuate Jinmen, they could minimize the risks involved. During the crisis, Zhou told the Soviet foreign minister that "the PRC has taken into consideration the possibility of the outbreak in this region of a local war of the United States against the PRC, and it [China] is now ready to take all the hard blows, including atomic bombs, and the destruction of [its] cities."[127] Despite such boasts, the PRC once again sought to avoid major hostilities with the Americans. At a Central Military Commission combat operations meeting on July 17, Peng Dehuai ordered the PLA to avoid contact with American forces, though Chinese leaders realized they might inadvertently kill Americans in large-scale shelling.[128] Nervous about the operation, Mao endured a sleepless night before the initial scheduled assault and ordered the attack postponed. The shelling did not commence until August 23. American targets were to be avoided, and PLA aircraft were told not to go beyond Jinmen and Mazu, to minimize the chance of confronting American planes.[129] On August 25 Mao explained the need for caution. "The problem was not the 95,000 Nationalist troops stationed there—this was easy to handle. The problem was how to assess the attitude of the American government. Washington had signed a mutual defense treaty with Taiwan. The treaty, however, did not clearly indicate whether the U.S. defense perimeter included Jinmen and Mazu."[130] After learning in early September that US ships were escorting ROC vessels, Mao's instructions were clear: "attack the KMT [ROC] ships only. Don't attack the U.S. ships. If the U.S. ships open fire, don't return fire without an order." The Chinese commander in the region, Ye Fei, asked for clarification three times. Mao remained firm.[131] As discussed above, after the American cease-fire offer that threatened to deepen Taiwan's division from the mainland, Mao decided against escalating the crisis. Instead, Jinmen remained in Chiang's hands with a face-saving noose logic developed.

CHINESE NUCLEAR VIEWS

Chinese behavior was not only consistent with reducing the benefits and raising the costs of nuclear use for the United States. There was also a link between Chinese thinking on nuclear weapons and their actions. During the Korean War, Chinese leaders highlighted potential reasons to discount nuclear weapons that focused on the minimal benefits or high costs that nuclear use would entail for the United States. Chinese generals asserted in August 1950 that "an [American] atomic bomb used on the battlefield would inflict damage not only on the enemy's side but also on friendly forces."[132] The generals then turned to a cost argument, highlighting that "the people of the world opposed the use of nuclear weapons; the United States would have to think twice before dropping them."[133] In a public document, the PRC argued that another American use of nuclear weapons against Asia would offend morality. "The peoples of Asia and around the world will rise against" America. The "prospect of losing moral grounds and consequently political support" might restrain US nuclear use.[134] Nie Rongzhen reported to Zhou in early 1952—after two years of fighting—that "the US might want to test its tactical atomic weapons in Korea . . . [but] the enemy won't use the weapon on a large scale." Military leaders in Beijing argued that "the United States is under great pressure of world opinion and is also deterred by possible Soviet nuclear retaliation from doing this in the Far East."[135]

Even with these considerations, the PRC was concerned over the nuclear issue. As noted in the previous section, Nie Rongzhen suggested better preparing Chinese forces in Korea for possible nuclear strikes. In addition, the PRC leadership agonized over the initial decision to intervene. Nuclear weapons factored into that debate. For instance, during a Central Military Commission meeting on October 6, 1950, Shen and Li reported that Marshal Lin Biao cautioned against intervention because the United States might "attack China with atomic bombs and a large-scale air offensive."[136] And the Chinese took various steps to hedge against the possibility of American nuclear strikes.

Raising the costs for nuclear use by enlisting Soviet support also proved critical. To be sure, securing Soviet air support was done in part to satisfy conventional needs for CPV forces facing a superior American opponent. There was a strategic aspect at play as well, though. Evidence for this comes from two sources. First, Mao wrote to Zhou on October 13, during the height of the campaign to secure Soviet support, that only "if the Soviet Union is able within two to two-and-a-half months to provide air assistance to our Volunteers in Korea, and also to mobilize air cover over Beijing, Tianjin, Shanghai, Ningbo, and Qingdao, can we then be free of the fear of comprehensive bombing."[137] Late on October 6 Mao made the point directly to the Soviet ambassador, stating that in his opinion Soviet air cover was necessary for the "largest industrial centers: Shanghai, Tianjin, Beijing, Mukden (Anshan, Fushun). [He] believes that the Americans can, first of all, destroy from the air the Chinese industrial base, disorganize economic life and mess up communications."[138]

Second, as noted in the previous section, the PRC ultimately decided to intervene without Soviet air support in Korea but with Mao's assurances that the Soviets would provide air support for Chinese territory. This would make little sense if the Chinese leadership was solely interested in Soviet air support for its operational or tactical utility. It does, however, follow if a major Chinese concern was American nuclear strikes against Chinese cities. Thus, Soviet air power in the defense of the mainland could provide strategic defense if American air attacks commenced. Such support would hopefully deter the United States from initiating broad air-atomic attacks in the first place for fear of provoking a broader war with the Soviet Union. The assertion by a Chinese editorial in 1950, echoed by military leaders two years later, that it was "the United States who should be afraid of using atomic bombs against us, because its densely concentrated industries are more vulnerable to serious damage by Soviet nuclear retaliation," was likely not just propaganda but reflected underlying thinking by the CCP.[139] Near the end of the war Zhou highlighted the role that the Soviet Union played in increasing the costs of nuclear escalation for the Americans. "Right after he took the presidency, Eisenhower fired empty cannons to scare people. He talked about . . . nuclear intimidation, and . . . invasion of China's mainland. . . . [The] two could not be accepted by America's allies lest these cause a world war."[140] Zhou was correct in noting that some American allies opposed nuclear use for fear it would lead to major hostilities with the Soviet Union. Particularly early in the conflict, Western leaders worried about their strength relative to the Soviets.[141] The cost of widening the war would reduce the incentives for nuclear use.

US nuclear forbearance during the Korean War did not lead the Chinese leadership to dismiss the possibility of future nuclear strikes or nuclear blackmail. Chinese military leaders agreed after the war that they must prepare to "fight a general war on the assumption that it will break out any time soon and it will be on a grand scale and nuclear."[142] In addition, despite severe resource constraints, China began pursuit of its own nuclear deterrent in 1955.

The Chinese directly addressed US nuclear capabilities during the 1954–1955 Taiwan crisis. Zhou noted in April 1955 that the Eisenhower administration was "openly boasting of nuclear missiles as conventional weapons and preparing for nuclear war." The Chinese press reported on stories highlighting that "the Seventh fleet was equipped with tactical nuclear bombs and any action to attack Taiwan would have to go through [the Americans] first."[143] President Eisenhower and Secretary Dulles increased rhetoric regarding the possibility of nuclear use, including in the Taiwan Strait, if necessary. Shortly thereafter, the PRC sought to defuse the situation. The timing of events, while hardly definitive, is suggestive that the nuclear threat played a role in defusing the crisis.[144] As Todd Sechser and Matthew Fuhrmann point out, China did not abandon its determination to control Taiwan or accept a US presence in the area in response to such threats.[145] More broadly, though, the Chinese were aware of the American nuclear monopoly and engaged in only limited behavior they believed would not invite major retaliation. Thus any nuclear threats made in 1955 did not introduce the nuclear issue into the situation; the Chinese were already factoring nuclear weapons into their decision making. Examining the crisis, Shu Guang Zhang concludes that "Chinese forces would have tried to take Jinmen, Mazu, and the other offshore islands if Beijing leaders had not been concerned about the nuclear threat."[146]

There is direct evidence the American nuclear monopoly influenced Chinese leaders in 1958. Wu Lengxi recalled that in late October "Chairman Mao said that we only had 'hand grenades' right now, but no atomic bombs. 'Hand grenades' could be successful for us to use in beating Jiang's troops on Jin[men]-Ma[zu], but not a good idea to use in fighting against Americans, who had nuclear weapons. Later, when everybody had nuclear weapons, very likely nobody would use them."[147] Wu's recollection is likely authentic; his references to Mao's statements on other occasions track with available documents from the period.[148] Mark Ryan, David Finkelstein, and Michael McDevitt note that the noose policy Mao ultimately adopted seemed "a fig leaf designed to obscure the fact that any serious PLA attempt to retake the offshore islands of Jinmen and Mazu may well have triggered a sizable U.S. retaliation, including nuclear strikes."[149]

Chinese leadership, and Mao in particular, frequently downplayed the utility of nuclear weapons. A skeptic could conclude that any nuclear discussions were minor ones and that the broader Chinese view toward nuclear weapons was dismissive. For example, during an interview with Anna Louis Strong, an American correspondent, Mao famously remarked that the "atomic bomb is a paper tiger which the US reactionaries use to scare people."[150] To sway reluctant members of the CCP prior to the Korean War, Mao asserted that the United States "may bomb [us] with the atomic bomb, but we will respond with our hand-grenades. We will then catch your [America's] weakness to tie you up and finally defeat you."[151] In a 1955 meeting with the Finnish envoy to China, Mao argued that "the Chinese people are not to be cowed by U.S. atomic blackmail. . . . The United States cannot annihilate the Chinese nation with its small stack of atom bombs. Even if the US atom bombs were so powerful that, when dropped on China, they would make a hole right through the earth, or even blow it up, that would hardly mean anything to the universe as a whole, though it might be a major event for the solar system."[152] Chinese propaganda reinforced these points. The Ministry of Foreign Affairs released a document in December 1950 highlighting that "we should smash the myth of the atomic bomb" and listing the bomb's limited physical effects.[153] Press reports in the spring of 1955 reiterated that the Chinese people "are not afraid of atomic bombs but we don't want a nuclear war."[154]

The evidence does not support the claim that the Chinese simply did not fear nuclear weapons. Chinese leadership understood the power of nuclear weapons. They worried that possession of a nuclear arsenal would embolden actors and be used to intimidate nonnuclear-armed states. In September 1953 Marshal Peng Dehui told the Central People's Government Council that the PRC must pay more attention to the "new weapon's 'omnipotence' which US imperialists have applied in bluffing, threatening, and scaring people."[155] The determination to avoid blackmail and deter nuclear strikes was an important factor motivating the Chinese atomic program, again highlighting the fear within the CCP leadership.[156] "Imperialists assess that we only have a few things and then they come to bully us," Mao argued in 1954. "They say, 'how many atomic bombs do you have?'"[157] During an enlarged Politburo meeting in 1956 Mao proclaimed that "in today's world, if we don't want to be bullied by others, we should have atomic weapons by all means."[158] Foreign Minister Chen Yi expressed a similar sentiment, arguing that "I cannot be very firm at the negotiating tables without that bomb."[159]

As long as China did not have nuclear weapons, though, it made sense to act as if the weapons did not convey much leverage. Chinese statements dismissing nuclear weapons were aimed at convincing the United States it could not gain from nuclear threats. George Quester outlined the basic logic, arguing that "to discourage nuclear attacks" NNWS leaders would "deny any military significance for atomic weapons," and to "discourage intimidation, the pain-inflicting or terroristic effects of nuclear weapons must also be minimized."[160] After the Cold War, John Lewis Gaddis highlighted that both "Stalin and Mao quickly sensed that the way to defuse this [nuclear] danger was to deprecate it, to treat it as a 'paper tiger' whose capacity to frighten people depended solely upon their willingness to be frightened."[161] Similarly, Fravel and Medeiros argue that Mao disparaged nuclear weapons "to persuade the Chinese public not to be intimidated by the highly destructive weapons possessed by China's opponents."[162] Minimizing the utility of nuclear weapons thus played an important role in bolstering public morale and deterring American confidence that the US could compel China to alter its behavior.

More generally, Mao counseled that it made little sense to become paralyzed in fear of American nuclear weapons. In September 1958 he argued to the Supreme State Council that if "the imperialists definitely want to fight a war and attack us first, using atomic bombs, it does not matter whether you fear fighting a war or not." Fear or no fear, the enemy might still attack with atomic bombs. "If that were the case," he asked, "what should be our attitude? Is it better to fear or not to fear? It is extremely dangerous [for us] to fear this and fear that every day."[163] Constant fear would lead to paralysis with no gain; it was necessary then to remain steadfast in the face of danger in order to move forward. The Chinese did not want a major war, Mao frequently stated. "Nevertheless," he argued the prior May, "there is also the possibility of war." There were "war maniacs" in the world, after all.[164] It made sense then to not engage in fatalist thinking; that would only facilitate American nuclear blackmail.

Mao also distinguished between short- and long-term events. In the long term, imperialists were "paper tigers" who would succumb to the forces of history. American nuclear weapons could not arrest that trend, even if China suffered greatly in a nuclear strike. Why fear nuclear weapons, or paper tigers more generally, at all then? As Mao asked rhetorically shortly after the 1958 Taiwan crisis, "Some people say that, since it is a paper tiger, why don't we attack Taiwan?"[165] The issue was that paper tigers had teeth; even if they were destined to fail in the long run, they could do great damage in the near term. Mao's argument that "we are afraid of atomic weapons and at the same time we are not afraid of them" was therefore not a contradiction.[166] Or, as he put it more generally on another occasion, "The temporary appearance is real, but in the long run it is made of paper. We have always maintained that we must give it serious attention tactically but regard it with contempt strategically." In the long run, "strategically," nuclear weapons could not alter history. Yet "tactically," in the short term, they were very dangerous.[167] Thus Mao could argue that nuclear weapons were paper tigers but simultaneously that a "war of atomic and hydrogen bombs is of course terrible since many people will die. That is why we oppose a war." In other words, it made little sense to invite a devastating confrontation, particularly because long-term historical forces were on the side of the Communists. Better to be cautious. Though even then there could be no guarantee. "Everything in the world," he noted in September 1958, "needs a safety factor."[168] It was always prudent to hedge and prepare for the worst.

If nuclear monopoly was a constant throughout this period and a consistent influence on Chinese decision making, what explains variation in Chinese behavior? Specifically, why were the Chinese so much more cautious in 1954 and 1958 than in 1950? To begin with, other factors aside from nuclear weapons mattered. As I note in chapter 1, nuclear weapons are not the only factor that influences NNWS decision making. The PRC's ability to act clearly mattered. CPV ground forces could strike the exposed US divisions as they marched northward in Korea. By contrast, the Chinese had no real naval capability that could overcome the US Seventh Fleet. Nuclear monopoly in conventionally asymmetric relationships favoring the NWS permits aggressive actions by the NNWS, but it does not compel the NNWS to engage in a war in which it has no conventional strategy to attain its objective. Still, in 1954 and 1958 the PRC could have elected to target American forces more directly with artillery and aircraft in an attempt to compel US concessions. It chose not to. Thus conventional inability to act, while an important factor, cannot be the whole explanation for Chinese restraint in 1954 and 1958 relative to 1950.

Several factors likely influenced Chinese decision making. These include new credibility for the American nuclear arsenal, the immediacy of the American threat, and changes in outside support. My argument does not incorporate these factors systematically. The purpose of the framework developed in chapter 1 was to simplify by focusing on the costs and benefits of nuclear strikes given NNWS strategies and the conventional military balance. While these explanations do not confirm the theory, then, they are consistent with its general emphasis on specific strategic factors that influence the likelihood of nuclear use.

First, the capability of the US nuclear arsenal and statements hinting at nuclear use increased from 1950 to 1958. This may have made the US nuclear deterrent more credible over time and thus have a greater effect. Though as I showed above, the PRC was already factoring nuclear weapons into its decision making and engaging in behavior to minimize the risks of a nuclear strike in 1950. Moreover, even if Mao was not fully cognizant of the destructive nature of nuclear weapons in 1950, other Chinese officials were. Mao's top lieutenants, including Zhou Enlai, Chen Yi, and Nie Rongzhen, "kept pushing Mao to pay more attention to nuclear-weapon programmes."[169] Mao's views were primary, but there was debate on foreign policy issues.

Second, the PRC leadership may have perceived the danger as more immediate in 1950 than in 1954 or 1958. In 1950, American combat forces were actively advancing toward a key Chinese strategic and industrial region, and China feared US leaders had aggressive intentions.[170] In 1954 and 1958 there was no overt military action being taken by the United States. China was willing to live with a separate Taiwan as long as there was a possibility it would eventually be unified with the PRC. As Mao put it at the end of the 1958 crisis, "not taking Jinmen-Mazu would have little impact on our construction of a socialist country. Jiang's troops on Jinmen-Mazu alone could not cause too much damage."[171] In Korea the issue was intervening in an existing war against an advancing military that could pose a large threat. With Taiwan, the issue was starting hostilities without any imminent military threat.

Finally, Chinese views on the value of Soviet support declined markedly during the 1950s. The Sino-Soviet treaty increased PRC confidence in the Soviet Union, although the CCP maintained misgivings.[172] The Soviets were tough negotiators but generally fulfilled their initial promises. Despite tense negotiations and some Chinese disappointment, the Soviet Union did dispatch air forces at the outset of the Korean War. Thus the PRC leadership had reasons to view Soviet support as credible.

The Chinese became more skeptical of Soviet backing during and after the Korean War.[173] Decline in Soviet support, considered so critical when debating intervention, contributed to China's decision to end the fighting. Stalin's death on March 5, 1953, resulted in the new Soviet leadership pushing for an end to the Korean War. As Soviet support waned, the Chinese, many eager to end the costly fighting, began making concessions in negotiations with the Americans. The Soviets then withdrew their pilots in May 1953. When talks resumed in June the Chinese quickly accepted UN terms. As Pape notes, with "the withdrawal of Soviet pilots . . . China's capacity for defense against nuclear air strikes was substantially reduced."[174] There is little evidence to support Dulles's and Eisenhower's later claims that new nuclear threats compelled China to quit the war. That does not mean, though, that the American nuclear capability was absent from Chinese consideration as Soviet support dissipated. The US nuclear ability had been a constant; what changed was the nature of external support.

In some ways, 1954–1955 seemed the high point for the Sino-Soviet alliance. Soviet advisers and support poured into China. During the 1954 crisis, Mao telegrammed Nikita Khrushchev that "the great alliance between China and the Soviet Union increasingly reveals its extraordinarily great role in promoting the common prosperity of the two countries' security and defending the peace in the Far East."[175] Yet as Xiaobing Li notes, during "the 1954–55 Taiwan Strait Crisis, Moscow complained about China's aggressive actions and expressed its unwillingness to use its atomic weapons if the United States retaliated over the PLA's invasion of Taiwan." Beijing worried about "decreasing protection from the Soviet Union's nuclear umbrella." The Soviets were hesitant to encourage action that risked a major confrontation over what to them was a minor issue.[176] Mao also undoubtedly remembered that the Soviet Union under Stalin had refused to support an attack on Taiwan in 1949.[177] Khrushchev turned down a Chinese request for Soviet support for China's nuclear research in 1954, telling China that "it is too expensive to develop your own nuclear weapons."[178] Though the Soviets would eventually agree to some support, Matthew Kroenig points out that in "the early 1950s, when Sino-Soviet ties were at their strongest, Moscow continually rebuffed Beijing's requests for nuclear assistance."[179] Alongside American nuclear threats, questions about the scope of the Soviet nuclear umbrella contributed to the Chinese decision in January 1955 to initiate their own nuclear weapons program.

Tensions steadily increased prior to the 1958 crisis. In January of that year, the Soviets proposed jointly constructing and operating a long-wave radio station on Chinese territory.[180] The Chinese replied that they would accept Soviet technology but would be solely responsible for paying for and operating the project. The PRC would share intelligence, but under no circumstances would they allow the Soviets to establish a military base in China. The Soviet leadership, somewhat tone deaf on Chinese sensitivities, continued to press for a truly joint enterprise. Then in July they upped the ante by proposing a joint submarine force in East Asia. Mao flatly rejected the proposal. On July 22 Mao berated the Soviet ambassador, highlighting a litany of past Soviet offensives. "You may accuse me of being a nationalist or another Tito, but my counterargument is that you have extended Russian nationalism to China's coast."[181] Soviet policy heightened Mao's fear of Soviet domination and growing desire to no longer play 'little brother.' Inviting Soviet support for the Jinmen operation was out of the question. That might mean lower costs for US escalation, but it was a price that had to be paid, given the competing priorities. In any event, in January 1958 Mao reportedly argued that the Soviet nuclear umbrella was "unreliable."[182]

China did not even bother to seek Soviet support prior to the 1958 shelling of Jinmen. The Chinese staff did inform the Soviet Ministry of Defense that they were undertaking some preparations regarding Taiwan. During a tense meeting in 1959, then, Mao reminded Khrushchev that they had "informed you about our intentions regarding Taiwan a month ahead, before we began shelling the off-shore islands." Khrushchev responded that the Chinese had "reported to us not about your policy on this issue, but about some separate measures."[183] Khrushchev had a right to be upset.

When he had visited Mao from July 31 to August 3, 1958, to alleviate the growing Sino-Soviet tensions, Mao did not mention the coming operation.[184] Had Mao seriously sought Soviet support, he surely would have raised the issue directly with the Soviet leader less than a month before the attack. If Mao had been considering asking for support, Khrushchev dashed any hopes during the meeting. The Soviet leader expressed concern that new tensions in the area could lead to a dangerous situation and suggested that China accept the status quo. The implication was that China would face the United States alone in the event of a conflict over Taiwan.[185]

Subsequent Soviet support during the 1958 crisis was a bit of political theater. Alarmed by the American reaction to the shelling of the offshore islands, Khrushchev asked the Soviet ambassador to ascertain Chinese intentions and dispatched Gromyko to Beijing for consultations. Mao and Zhou assured the Soviets that the PRC was carefully managing the confrontation and had no intention of escalating the dispute. Only after receiving such assurances did the Soviets issue statements supporting the PRC. "Khrushchev's response," writes Gaddis, "was wholly in character. He waited until Zhou, with Mao's approval, had loosened the 'noose' by calling for a resumption of talks with the United States; then he issued a blunt warning to the Americans. . . . It was his [1956] Suez [Crisis] ploy all over again: an attempt to look tough by claiming credit for an outcome already determined."[186] Indeed, in October 1959 Khrushchev seemingly confirmed the Soviet hesitancy, telling Mao that "between us, in a confidential way, we say that we will not fight over Taiwan, but for outside consumption, so to say, we state the contrary, that in case of an aggravation of the situation because of Taiwan the USSR will defend the PRC."[187]

Chinese behavior is consistent with my argument. In each case when China confronted the United States, the Chinese acted in a way that created limited dangers for the United States. While much of the limitations were due to their own low conventional military abilities, these would necessarily reduce the threat to the Americans and thus create low benefits for nuclear use. The PRC also took various steps to hedge in the event of nuclear use, such as preparing troops for nuclear strikes, relocating some industry, and exploring civil defense procedures. In the most forceful action, the attack in Korea in 1950, the Chinese leadership sought external support. This would raise the costs to the Americans for any nuclear escalation. There is also good process evidence that the Chinese leadership consistently took nuclear weapons into account when making these decisions. Given the stakes involved, the leaders believed they had no choice but to act. Even then, they pursued various means to raise the costs and lower the benefits of nuclear use for the Americans.

The Soviet Union versus the United States

On June 24, 1948, the Soviet Union severed all land connections between Berlin and the Western-occupied regions of Germany. The Soviet action constituted the first direct confrontation with the United States involving the two superpowers' military forces in the nascent Cold War. Soviet behavior is puzzling because the Soviet atomic program was rapidly progressing. While an exact date for completion was uncertain, the Soviets could have waited until they acquired their own nuclear capability to offset the US atomic monopoly. According to the basic deterrence logic, the Soviets should have waited to directly challenge the United States until they could retaliate in kind. Why did the American nuclear monopoly fail to block Soviet action? Were American nuclear weapons simply irrelevant? Finally, why did this case not escalate to war?

I argue that the Soviet Union proceeded cautiously throughout the period of American atomic monopoly. That restraint continued during the Berlin crisis and is attributable in part to US nuclear monopoly. The Soviets avoided a direct challenge to the United States outside their immediate sphere of influence prior to 1948. From the Soviet perspective, the worsening security situation in Germany in 1948 necessitated action. The subsequent Berlin blockade was designed to exert considerable pressure on the Americans. As a conventionally capable nonnuclear power, though, the Soviets imposed tight constraints on their actions for fear of fighting a war with the United States that would turn nuclear. As a result, no war occurred despite the Soviet ability to inflict a rapid military defeat on the United States in a key area of the world for both countries. This case is thus important to examine alongside the other cases in this book because it provides an example of a conflict not escalating to war. Consistent with the framework developed in chapter 1, Soviet leaders took steps to reduce the benefits of nuclear use for the Americans by reducing the danger to the United States during the crisis and taking steps to hedge against an American nuclear attack. For example, the Soviets first probed the US position and pressed the United States in a geographically isolated area. They also undertook few major military preparations for a broader conflict. When the Americans succeeded in circumventing the blockade, the Soviet Union accepted defeat rather than escalate the conflict. The Soviets explicitly took the US nuclear arsenal into consideration throughout this period. Publicly, Soviet leaders worked to downplay the danger of nuclear weapons to demonstrate resolve in an effort to discourage American policies. Privately, though, the Soviet leadership feared a US nuclear strike if war occurred.

While Soviet behavior was largely consistent with my argument, the case has several limitations. First and foremost, Soviet leaders clearly took the US nuclear arsenal into account during this period, but there is little direct evidence that they explicitly factored in a potential US nuclear response during their decision making for the Berlin Crisis itself. This case therefore relies on general Soviet views of the US nuclear arsenal and the congruence of Soviet behavior with my argument's basic expectations. Second, and related, there are limited primary sources available from the Soviet side for this case. In this chapter, I therefore rely on declassified American documents and secondary sources that draw on Russian sources. Declassified private conversations between Soviet and American leaders help provide insight into Soviet motives and interests. These sources must be carefully interrogated, because Soviet leaders may have had incentives to convey specific messages to their American counterparts. Nevertheless, other scholars have usefully employed this method to assess a state's decision making when direct documents from that state were absent.[1]

The rest of this chapter proceeds in three sections and a summary. First, I review the military balance between the United States and the Soviet Union. I show that the United States had a modest nuclear arsenal and that the Soviet Union had sizeable conventional military capabilities relative to the United States. Next, I provide a basic overview for the Soviet-American dispute. In the third section I demonstrate that Soviet behavior during the Berlin Crisis was congruent with my argument and that the Soviet leadership feared the American nuclear monopoly.

The Military Balance

This section reviews the military balance between the United States and Soviet Union during the period of American atomic monopoly, from July 1945 to August 1949. Though the focus in this book is on nonnuclear weapon state views, I include a discussion of the nuclear aspects of US military planning for two reasons. First, this reinforces the argument that the conventional military balance did not favor the United States. Second,

Soviet espionage almost certainly made their leaders aware of the general contours of these plans.

THE NUCLEAR BALANCE

The American nuclear arsenal and delivery capabilities were limited from 1945 to 1949. Table 5.1 lists the total number of American nuclear weapons and yield in megatonnage. The yields during this period were low relative to what would come after the United States tested a thermo-nuclear, or hydrogen, bomb, on November 1, 1952.

The United States faced difficulties delivering nuclear weapons against Soviet targets as well. The B-29 Superfortress was the only platform that could deliver nuclear weapons from 1945 into 1948. Not all B-29s were con-figured to carry nuclear weapons, though. From 1946 until mid-1948 the United States had only approximately thirty to thirty-five bombers that could deliver nuclear weapons, in the 509th Bomb Group based in Roswell, New Mexico. Range limitations meant that the aircraft had to be stationed abroad in order to hit targets in the Soviet Union. In 1948 it took a thirty-nine-person Air Force crew nearly two days to assemble a single weapon. In mid-1948 these assembly teams could make only two bombs ready per day.[2] Upon taking command of Strategic Air Command in late 1948, General Curtis LeMay ordered a simulated attack. Edward Kaplan notes that no crew managed to hit the target successfully, and that "of 303 runs . . . the circular error probable was 10,100 feet, outside the effective radius of a Hiroshima-sized weapon."[3] B-50 and B-36 bombers began entering service in June 1948. The B-36 had a range of seventy-two hundred miles, allowing for it to "fly an Arctic route to reach the Soviet Union from bases in the United States without in-flight refueling."[4] The effect of the new arrivals was limited by lack of operational experience and small num-bers, though. Compounding these problems was the lack of detailed tar-geting information and US fighter escorts for the bombers.[5]

Table 5.1 US nuclear weapons, 1945–1949

Year	Total nuclear warheads	Strategic nuclear warheads	Total yield (megatons)
1945	2	2	0.04
1946	9	9	0.18
1947	13	13	0.26
1948	50	50	1.25
1949	170	170	4.19

Source: "Estimated U.S. and Soviet/Russian Nuclear Stockpiles, 1945–94," Bulletin of the Atomic Scientists 50, no. 6 (1994): 59.

THE CONVENTIONAL BALANCE

The conventional balance between the United States and the Soviet Union was roughly even during this period. The American advantage was largest in economic capabilities. Initially, the Americans enjoyed a large 5:1 advantage in per capita gross domestic product (GDP). The ratio rapidly decreased as the Soviet Union recovered from World War II's devastation (figure 5.1). A similar story is apparent when examining the overall economies. By 1949, the US advantage was less than 3:1. The Soviet potential for growth was not lost on US observers. For example, in 1944 Admiral William Leahy commented on the "recent phenomenal development of heretofore latent Russian military and economic strength . . . which has yet to reach the full scope attainable with Russian resources." In April 1945, the Office of Strategic Services, forerunner to the Central Intelligence Agency, concluded that "Russia's natural resources and manpower are so great that within a relatively few years she can be much more powerful than either Germany or Japan has ever been."[6] The comparison to Germany was telling, as it had taken Soviet power combined with American power to defeat Germany in World War II. In other words, the United States could expect an even greater struggle if conflict with the Soviet Union occurred.

Soviet and American military forces were comparable, using rough indicators for troops and military spending. Figure 5.2 shows that the Soviet

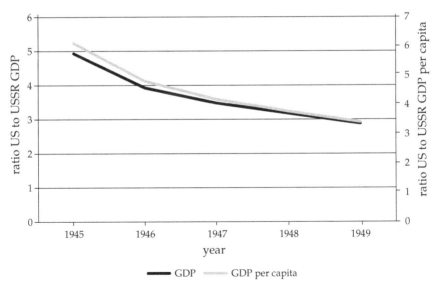

Figure 5.1 Economic ratios, 1945–1949

Source: Angus Maddison Project 2010 database, https://www.rug.nl/ggdc/historicaldevelopment/maddison/releases/maddison-database-2010.

Note: Data for Soviet GDP per capita for 1945 estimated using 1946 population.

Union enjoyed a consistent advantage in total military personnel. In 1948, the Soviets had a 2:1 superiority against the United States. The Red Army consisted of an estimated 175 divisions that could rapidly expand to 320 divisions thirty days after mobilization.[7] The United States spent slightly more per soldier than the Soviet Union, but by 1947 that ratio had dropped considerably. In short, the Soviets had a large military, and its soldiers received funding similar to that of US forces on a person for person basis. To be sure, the forces were not fully comparable. The Soviets lacked a strategic air force and blue-water navy, while the Americans were deficient in ground troops. The similarity in spending is actually more surprising as a result, because naval and air forces are more capital intensive than land forces.[8]

In Europe the Soviets enjoyed a decisive military advantage. The British prime minister Winston Churchill worried that the American troop drawdown following World War II left the Soviets in a preponderant position on the Continent. As he pointed out in 1945, "Anyone can see that in a very short space of time our [Allied] armed power on the Continent will have vanished except for moderate forces to hold down Germany. . . . What will be the position in a year or two, when the British and American Armies have melted and the French have a handful of divisions . . . and when Russia may choose to keep two or three hundred [divisions] on active service."[9] By 1948 the United States had only 114,550 army and air force

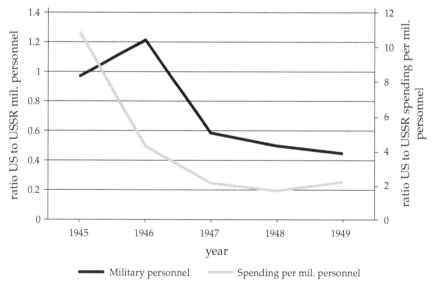

Figure 5.2 Military ratios, 1945–1949

Source: Correlates of War, National Material Capabilities, version 5.0, http://www.correlatesofwar.org/data-sets/national-material-capabilities.

personnel in Germany, with the main combat formations consisting of just two division equivalents engaged in occupation duty.[10] To supplement this in an emergency the Americans could call on ten divisions spread around the globe. The British estimated that in March 1949 Western forces, including American troops, could muster only ten divisions, plus some assorted brigades, to counter any Soviet attack. The Soviets had approximately 30–35 divisions in Eastern Europe outside the Soviet Union, with another 135–140 inside the Soviet Union itself. To that total the Soviets could add 90–100 less capable divisions from their East European satellites.[11]

Soviet ground forces were of comparable or superior quality to their American counterparts, though Soviet naval and air forces were qualitatively inferior. The Soviet military had defeated the vaunted Wehrmacht only a few years earlier in some of the toughest fighting of the war. In August 1945 Soviet troops swept aside Japanese troops located on the Eurasian continent. During the course of World War II, the Red Army had mastered operational and tactical practices for modern warfare.[12] The experience gained during the war left the Soviets a capable military force.

Soviet divisions also became better equipped after the war. As Karber and Combs write, "The peacetime Soviet military structure of 175 divisions kept and made use of much of the armament that had formerly supplied a 500-division wartime force."[13] In 1948, US intelligence estimated that Soviet mechanized and rifle divisions possessed two-thirds and one-half the combat power of American armored and infantry divisions, respectively.[14] Peacetime strength for most Soviet divisions was short of 100 percent, but that could be quickly expanded, potentially in as little as five days.[15] "Even a brief comparison of these opposing strengths leads to the conclusion that Soviet conventional forces in Germany, and in Europe as a whole, were considerably superior in terms of overall strength, firepower, combat potential, and combat capabilities to opposing Western forces stationed in the region during the Berlin blockade," writes Victor Gobarev.[16]

The quantitative and qualitative realities in Europe led American military planners to estimate that the Red Army could quickly conquer much of Western Europe. National Security Council document 20/4, approved by President Truman in November 1948 and the key document outlining general American policy at the time, argued that "present intelligence estimates attribute to Soviet armed forces the capability of over-running in about six months all of Continental Europe and the Near East as far as Cairo. . . . Meanwhile, Great Britain could be subjected to severe air and missile bombardment."[17] Other analyses put the timeframe for Soviet conquest in as little as two months.[18] To be sure, some estimates exaggerated Soviet capabilities and downplayed difficulties that the Red Army would face in any offensive operation. Yet even if American intelligence did overestimate Soviet capabilities prior to 1948, it was not by enough to change the underlying dynamic that Western conventional military forces were insufficient to defend Europe.[19] Few senior American officials thought the Soviets would deliberately begin a war. Rather, they worried that war might occur through accident or miscalculation by one side or the other.[20] If war came, however, US leaders recognized they faced a formidable adversary.

American planners assumed that in any war American forces would initially retreat prior to launching a counteroffensive. It was taken for granted and then made explicit that any counterattack would include a nuclear component. That is, given the conventional military balance—the existing Soviet capabilities, and the ability of the Soviet Union to sustain an industrialized war, particularly if it could incorporate the industrial production potential of Western Europe—the United States war plans necessarily relied on nuclear use. As Steven Ross argues, "The JCS [Joint Chiefs of Staff] felt they had no choice but to rely heavily on atomic weapons."[21] Allied troops would withdraw from the Continent to Great Britain and the Cairo-Suez areas, possibly holding the Italian and Iberian peninsulas.[22] By the summer of 1946, planners assumed that "the principal initial effort against the USSR had to consist of an air offensive effort, probably deploying atomic weapons," notes Ross.[23] Thereafter it was generally supposed that following the initial Anglo-American withdrawal, the United States would engage in an atomic campaign to degrade Soviet military and industrial capabilities. Given the state of US nuclear forces, the campaign would be slow, despite the desire of some officials for a rapid air offensive. The United States would in essence be replaying World War II, with nuclear weapons substituting for conventional ordnance delivered by fleets of bombers. The atomic campaign by itself would not be enough to defeat the Soviet Union. As the air atomic campaign progressed, the United States would rely on its vast industrial and manpower reserves to mobilize a ground force capable of either threatening Russia directly or retaking Europe and occupying key points.

Presidential policy came to endorse nuclear use. Harry Truman held out hope in the early postwar period that some form of international control of nuclear weapons might emerge and remained cautious about using nuclear weapons again. Truman kept the nuclear arsenal outside military control in peacetime. Indeed, few in government or the military knew the total number of nuclear weapons the United States possessed.[24] Despite the lack of guidance, when Secretary of the Army Kenneth Royall noted that there was doubt atomic weapons might be available in a conflict, the State Department replied that "we know of no opinion in the Government which would warrant the Defense Establishment in ceasing to plan on the use of the bomb."[25] Truman provided more formal guidance when he approved NSC 30 on September 16, 1948. In the oft-quoted conclusion, the decision was made that the United States "must be ready to utilize promptly and effectively all appropriate means available, including atomic weapons."[26] Defense Secretary James Forrestal recalled that "the President said he prayed that he would never have to make such a decision [to use nuclear weapons again], but that if it became necessary, no one need have a misgiving but that he would do so."[27]

One might object to assessing the US-Soviet conventional military balance as even, because several rough indicators place the US decisively ahead, and the Soviet Union could not significantly threaten the US homeland during this period. This objection ignores the ability of the Soviet Union to seize vital regions that could seriously threaten US security in the long term. The United States had, after all, recently fought a massive war in large part to keep totalitarian regimes from attaining hegemony in Europe and Asia.[28] American officials in the postwar world identified Western Europe, Japan, and the Middle East as critical regions because of their industrial potential and/or resource endowments.[29] US planners were not particularly worried that the Soviet Union could seize Japan, but were greatly alarmed at the Soviet ability to seize all of Europe as well as key parts of Asia and the Middle East. NSC 20/4 argued that "Russian seizure of these areas would ultimately enhance the Soviet war potential," resulting in "an eventual concentration of hostile power which would pose an unacceptable threat to the security of the United States."[30] Most alarming was the prospect of Soviet direct or indirect control of Germany. Secretary of State George Marshall argued that the United States could not "permit [the] reestablishment of German economic and political unity under conditions which are likely to bring about effective domination of all of Germany by [the] Soviets. It would regard such an eventuality as the greatest threat to [the] security of all Western Nations, including [the] US."[31] The nature of economic production at the time was conducive to occupying powers exploiting industrial production and resources for gain.[32] Soviet control of Europe would thus force the United States to massively increase defense spending, harm the US economy, and put the Soviets in a position to defeat the United States. Even short of actual defeat, many feared that in such a world the United States would be forced to become a garrison state, its free institutions under strain. In sum, the Soviet Union was a major conventional threat, against which military and civilian leaders believed nuclear weapons offered significant military benefits.

Dispute Overview

Initial postwar Soviet policy centered on expanding its influence and consolidating its World War II gains. Yet the Soviets continually avoided direct confrontation with the United States. At various points the Soviets pushed for a role in administering Italy and its former colonies. The Americans refused, but the Soviets did little, accepting the American position and signing a peace treaty with Italy in February 1947.[33] The Soviet Union also briefly sought an occupation zone in Japan. "Russian public opinion would be gravely offended if the Russian troops had no occupation area in any part of the territory of Japan proper," Stalin wrote to Truman on August 16.[34] Truman, willing to risk offending Russian public opinion, refused. On August 27 the Soviet military determined that in "order to avoid creating conflicts and misunderstandings with the allies, it is categorically forbidden to send any kind of ship or plane whatever in the direction of [the northernmost Japanese island of] Hokkaido."[35] The United States rejected Soviet requests for a governing role in Japan, and the Soviet leadership let the matter rest. From 1945 to 1947 Stalin kept a tight lid on French and Italian Communists. "Stalin chose not to encourage revolution in Europe or Asia," explains David Holloway. "To have done so would have created a risk of war with the Western allies."[36] Rather, the Soviet dictator encouraged local Communists to work within coalition governments.[37]

Arguably the first set of crises pitting the Soviet Union against the United States occurred in the Eastern Mediterranean and Middle East. In each case, though, Soviet probes were limited and quickly reversed. Soviet troops initially remained in Iran after the agreed-upon withdrawal date of March 2, 1946. The Iranians sought US support and took the issue to the new United Nations. The Soviets removed all their troops by May. Later, when the Iranian regime reneged on an oil agreement the Soviets did not reintroduce troops.[38] The Soviets pressed Turkey for control of the Turkish Straits at several points in 1945 and 1946. On August 7, 1946, the Soviet Union issued a diplomatic note requesting revision of the treaty governing the straits and moved modest military forces in the region. The Turkish government, with US and British support, rejected the Soviet proposal.[39] Following a brief back-and-forth, the Soviets did not press the matter, and the issue died. Stalin limited support to Greek Communists because he recognized a predominant Western role there. The Soviets counseled the Greek Communists against conflict with the monarch in 1945, did not permit Greek Communists to meet with Stalin and Vyacheslav Molotov during a Moscow visit in 1946, and did not recognize the Greek Communist provisional government in 1947.[40] The March 1947 Truman doctrine extending support to Turkey and Greece therefore caused little alarm in the Soviet Union.[41] For Soviet leaders this merely replaced British with American power in an area in which they had already decided not to overtly challenge the West.

Events involving Germany were of much greater concern. Soviet leaders had long directed their attention toward Germany. While the war was still being fought, Stalin informed Winston Churchill that he "thought that

Germany had every possibility of recovering from this war and might start on a new war within a comparatively short time. He was afraid of German nationalism."[42] As Geoffrey Roberts concludes, it "cannot be overemphasized that for Stalin the resolution of the German question—the problem of how to contain or tame German power and aggression in Europe—was the key to Soviet postwar security."[43] Soviet policy evolved over time, but the core focus on creating either a weak Germany or one amenable to Soviet influence remained constant. In June 1945 Stalin instructed the East German Communist Party (KPD) to work for a united Germany "via a united KPD [and] united central committee . . . a united workers party in the centre."[44] In 1946 he pushed for the merger of the East German Communist and Socialist parties to increase Communist, and with it Soviet, influence. Stalin might have been willing to give up the Soviet position in the eastern zone of Germany, but only in exchange for a Germany completely detached from the West. That would leave an isolated Germany vulnerable to Soviet influence in the future.[45]

Stalin's views were widely shared. Maxim Litvinov, often recognized as a pro-Western voice in Soviet affairs, argued for dismembering Germany into seven units.[46] Ivan Maiskii made the case to Molotov in a memorandum that Germany should be militarily weakened.[47] The German issue remained critical to the Soviet Union throughout the rest of the Cold War, figuring prominently even in US-Soviet negotiations in 1989–1991.[48] The consistency of Soviet concern was not lost on the Americans, who recognized that the Soviet Union had an intense interest in Eastern Europe and Germany. For instance, George Kennan argued in PPS/13 in 1947 that the Russians would oppose a united, independent Germany because it would "exercise a highly disruptive influence on communist power in Eastern Europe. Rather than risk that, the Russians would probably prefer a continuance of the present status, under which they are at least sure of being able to neutralize the political potential of eastern Germany."[49]

The Soviets therefore paid close attention to American policy that might harm Soviet interests in Germany. Though American policies were largely defensive to counter growing Soviet power, those policies nevertheless constituted a problem for the Soviets.[50] The first major challenge was the European Recovery Program (ERP), or Marshall Plan, that threatened to pull Germany to the West. The US secretary of state George Marshall announced the policy to revive and bind Western European countries to undercut Soviet influence in June 1947.[51] US leaders recognized that for the Marshall Plan to succeed it must include German participation. Germany remained the economic engine for Europe. To attain German participation, it was necessary to provide the Germans with some political autonomy to govern their own affairs. Some form of German state had to be created. Toward this end, the Americans and British sought to merge their (previously merged) occupation zones with the French zone. Beginning in February 1948 the three countries met in London to establish what would become a West German government. The meeting culminated in the agreement on June 1, 1948, of the London Conference recommendations.[52] The Western powers would create a German state with modest external controls directly integrated with Western Europe economically, and perhaps eventually politically and militarily, in order to restrain West German freedom of maneuver. On June 18, 1948, the American military governor in Germany, General Lucius Clay, informed the Soviet Union that a new currency would soon be introduced into the Western zones.[53]

For Soviet leaders these policies were a step too far. The Soviet position would only grow worse as Germany recovered and integrated itself into a West European bloc. The Soviets initially considered allowing their East European satellites to participate in the Marshall Plan. They quickly reversed themselves, judging participation as a threat to Soviet influence. For instance, in June 1947 Nikolai Novikov, the Soviet ambassador to the United States, cabled the Kremlin that "the outlines of a Western European bloc directed against us [the USSR] are patently visible. The State Department is now working furiously on this plan."[54] More ominously, the plan threatened to pull a large part of Germany away from the Soviet Union. "This is a matter not of propaganda or political blackmail but a real threat of the political and economic division of Germany and the inclusion of western Germany with all its resources in a western bloc created by the United States," warned Soviet Foreign Ministry official Andrei Smirnov on October 3, 1947.[55] Molotov explained the Soviet about-face on allowing their East European satellites to participate on July 8, arguing that "under the guise of formulating a plan for the reconstruction of Europe, the initiators of the conference in fact desire to establish a Western bloc with the participation of Western Germany."[56] The alarm increased throughout 1948 as the Marshall Plan became law and German statehood progressed. Smirnov warned on March 6, 1948, just days before the Senate voted to pass the ERP, that the "Western Powers are transforming Germany into their stronghold and will include it in the formation of a politico-military bloc directed against the Soviet Union and the countries of the new democracy."[57]

As the situation in Germany deteriorated from Moscow's point of view, Soviet behavior became more confrontational. In the fall of 1947 Stalin instructed Communist parties in France and Italy to end their cooperative policies and work to frustrate the Marshall Plan.[58] In March 1948 US diplomat Robert Murphy noted that the "Soviet delegation now seizes upon every question on the agenda and every statement by any other delegation no matter how simple, how friendly or how innocent, to launch violent propaganda attacks on the other three delegations."[59] Later that month the Soviet Union's Marshal Vasily Sokolovsky "walked out of the allied control council, with the result that it ceased to function."[60]

Soviet intransigence went beyond diplomatic wrangling and Communist subterfuge, though, distinguishing it from earlier behavior. Following the failure of the four-party London Council of Foreign Ministers meeting in the fall of 1947, the Soviets began harassing Western land and air transports to and from Berlin. In March 1948, Soviet authorities reduced the number of passenger and troop trains moving between Berlin and the Western zones in what was later termed a "baby blockade." Murphy cabled that the Soviets "undoubtedly will continue with [the] series of strictures and annoyances which it has inaugurated affecting our continued presence in Berlin."[61] The Soviets believed their harassment was effective. "Our control and restrictive measures have dealt a strong blow at the prestige of the Americans and British in Germany," the Soviet Military Administration in Germany informed Moscow. "The German population believes that the Anglo-Americans have retreated before the Russians and that this testifies to the Russians' strength."[62]

The currency reform provided the catalyst for the blockade. After learning of it on June 18, Marshal Sokolovsky replied two days later that the American-led initiative was illegal, constituted the division of Germany, and would necessitate a Soviet response.[63] On June 19, the Soviet Union suspended road traffic between the Western occupied zones and Berlin. Five days later, the Soviets severed all rail and river transportation. Berlin was effectively blockaded by land, reachable from the West only by air.[64]

Soviet officials made clear that their concerns went beyond the new currency to the broader issue of a West German state. In private conversations they highlighted the "danger of war" and asked "whether [the] US did not consider that it was skating on very thin ice in respect of its recent actions in Germany."[65] At a meeting of the four military governors on July 3, Sokolovsky "made no special reference to the currency situation." Rather, he highlighted the relation of "the Berlin situation to the London Conference as a whole. He made it quite clear that he was not prepared to answer any question on the resumption of traffic unless the results of the London Conference were also to be discussed."[66] Stalin reiterated the basic Soviet position during a meeting with the US, British, and French ambassadors on August 3. The Soviet leader rebuffed overtures to end the blockade in exchange for negotiations over the currency issue. The whole German problem was urgent, he insisted. Stalin "understood that a sort of parliamentary council was to be formed soon, and that this would set up a German government." He added ominously that if "this went ahead, the Soviet government would be faced with a *fait accompli* and there would be nothing left to discuss."[67] Though Stalin hinted at negotiating space on the London decisions, the Americans remained skeptical.[68] Molotov vindicated that skepticism three days later, opening a meeting with the Western ambassadors by critiquing the failure to postpone the formation of a West

German government. The Soviet foreign minister insisted postponement was necessary for a satisfactory solution.[69]

The Soviet goal, then, was to pressure the United States to attain a favorable political outcome on an issue they believed deeply affected their security. If the United States sought to stay in Berlin, the Soviets hoped the Americans would be forced to negotiate on the German problem as a whole in order to maintain their position. If instead the US refused to negotiate, the blockade could make the American position in Berlin untenable. In that event, the US would have to abandon Berlin, allowing the Soviets to consolidate their position in Eastern Germany and stabilize their empire. A Western withdrawal might also discredit the United States, frustrating US efforts in Western Europe.[70]

Inaction was simply not an option. As early as March 12, Smirnov wrote that the Soviets needed "to take measures which would not merely restrict separate actions by the USA, Britain and France in Germany but would actively disrupt their plans to put together a Western bloc including Germany."[71] On the eve of the blockade Molotov bluntly explained that "if we were to lose in Germany we would have lost the [last] war."[72] Nikita Khrushchev later wrote that the Western initiatives in Germany "represented a direct threat to our national security, a challenge to the impregnability of our borders. . . . Stalin imposed the blockade as an act of survival."[73] In their detailed analysis, Vladislav Zubok and Constantine Pleshakov conclude that "under these circumstances, a division of Germany into East and West would constitute for Stalin a major geopolitical defeat that would be particularly damaging in view of the continued American atomic monopoly. For Stalin, accepting this defeat would be worse than risking a confrontation with the only country to possess the Bomb."[74]

The Role of Nuclear Weapons

The American nuclear monopoly did not prevent the Soviet Union from confronting the United States in June 1948. The Soviet Union was careful throughout the crisis, though. In this section I first demonstrate that Soviet behavior was congruent with my argument. Specifically, Soviet leaders limited their aims and means throughout the crisis, which reduced the danger to the Americans. As a conventionally powerful NNWS, the Soviet Union ultimately accepted a political defeat rather than escalate to war. The Soviet Union also took some steps to hedge against nuclear use. There were limited options for the Soviet Union to raise the costs to the United States because there was no third party that the Soviets could turn to that could constrain the Americans. The Soviets did, though, seek to appeal to public opinion to delegitimize nuclear weapons. The second section examines Soviet decision making. I show that Soviet leaders consistently took the

American nuclear arsenal into account. At times they explicitly linked their behavior to fear of American nuclear strikes.

Soviet Behavior

The Soviets reduced the danger to the United States, and with it the military benefits of nuclear use, in several ways before and during the Berlin Crisis. First, the Soviets did not immediately institute a full blockade. Throughout the spring of 1948 they engaged in low-level harassment of Western access to Berlin. This allowed Soviet leaders to gauge American reactions to interference.

Second, the Soviet Union pressed the United States over a discrete issue. Berlin's isolation deep inside the Soviet occupation zone provided an opportunity to exert limited pressure against the United States. Berlin provided a logical stopping point. If the Soviets absorbed Berlin, it did not directly threaten any of the other Western occupation zones in Germany or the rest of Western Europe. Soviet assertions that they did not seek a broader confrontation therefore had an inherent credibility. The Soviets could take action to frustrate US policy without having to cross Western territory. It would be the Americans that would have to make the first move. As Zubok notes, Stalin "felt confident in his ability to adjust his use of force around West Berlin to avoid provoking a war and to make the Western powers look responsible for the crisis."[75]

Third, there was no preparation for an immediate military campaign. True, the Soviets deployed some military forces at the outset of the crisis and steadily increased troop strength in Eastern Europe in the next several years. However, there was an "absence of any evidence of Soviet preparations for a military emergency."[76] After reviewing Russian archives, Victor Gobarev concludes that the Soviet military force in Germany was "not ready to attack Western Allied forces on short notice because it had not been assigned such a task."[77] US intelligence and political officials, for their part, took note of the lack of preparation and adopted a restrained view of Soviet force deployments and capabilities.[78]

Fourth, the Soviet blockade was far less aggressive than it could have been, given Soviet capabilities. To begin with, the Soviets avoided seriously interfering with the airlift. The decision to keep the air corridors open reflected the Soviet desire, as Vojtech Mastny puts it, "to avoid a possible military clash there—which it would have itself had to initiate if it had wanted to use its fighters to make the blockade fully effective."[79] Trachtenberg adds that throughout the crisis "Soviet policy was not nearly as confrontational as many western officials had feared. The airlift, for example, was successful because the Soviets chose not to interfere with it. Even nonviolent measures, especially the jamming of radars, would have gone a long way toward compromising its effectiveness. But the Soviets continued to work with western officials at the Berlin Air Safety Center, managing the air routes into the city, and thus bizarrely 'doing something to help the airlift which was undermining their blockade.'"[80]

Occasional Soviet threats failed to materialize. For instance, the commander of the American airlift, General William Tunner, recalled the Soviets announced on one occasion that they would fly in formation over Berlin and East Germany, including the air corridor. "The threatened formation never developed." Indeed, Tunner characterized most Soviet actions as "silly and childish stunts."[81] Though there was a collision between a Soviet and British transport prior to the blockade on April 5, 1948, Daniel Altman notes that it "was the sole collision of this sort during the crisis."[82] Few instances of Soviet target practice with live ammunition occurred close to Western aircraft. "Frequent Soviet warnings of aerial gunnery practice and formation flying in the air corridors did not materialize in threatening form," General Clay later wrote.[83] The Soviets did sometimes use searchlights to interfere with Western pilots' vision at night, but the tactic was easily overcome and never caused a crash.[84]

In addition, the Soviets imposed only a partial blockade. They restricted Western access to the city but did not close off the Western sectors of Berlin from supplies coming in from the Soviet occupation zone. Legitimate and black market trade flourished as a result. Even after a crackdown on such trade in late 1948, the Soviet Union continued to permit the legal trade of food, coal, and other goods.[85] The Office of the Director of Intelligence noted in October 1948 that "the vast majority of the needs of the population and industry in the Western sectors are still met through East-West trade, which is only slightly less necessary to the Soviet sector than to the western parts of the city."[86] William Stivers notes that "if Moscow were at last to seal the city off, the airlift would fail; and should America still insist on holding Berlin, more forceful means would be required, heightening the risk of war."[87] True, the Soviet decision to allow trade stemmed from a number of factors that included economic considerations and an inability to completely seal off the zone. Yet the Soviets could have done much more. They chose not to.

Finally, the Soviets ultimately accepted a political defeat rather than escalate. At the outset of the crisis, time seemed to be on the Soviet side. Officials on both sides doubted the ability of an airlift to supply the city.[88] As early as August 1948, when the future of the airlift was still very much in doubt, though, it was clear the Soviets sought to manage tensions. "Stalin and Molotov were undoubtedly anxious for [a] settlement," Smith reported after one meeting with the two Soviet leaders. "Both [were] literally dripping with sweet reasonableness and [a] desire not to embarrass."[89] As time wore on and the airlift continued, Stalin elected to end rather than escalate the confrontation. In exchange for lifting the blockade, the Western powers agreed to attend a new Council of Foreign Ministers meeting to discuss various German issues.[90] The ministerial meeting reaffirmed the end of the blockade, and the Soviets recognized an "obligation to take measures necessary to ensure the normal functioning and utilisation of rail, water and road transport for such movement of persons and goods, and such communications by post, telephone and telegraph" between the occupation zones.[91] This was a major political victory for the United States. Prior to the blockade, the United States and its allies had struggled to find a justification for their right to access the city.[92] The ministers' meeting resulted in the Soviets confirming the Western transit and communication rights. The Soviets also failed to alter US policy on the formation of a new West German state.

Both before and during the Berlin Crisis the Soviets took additional steps to reduce the benefits or raise the costs of nuclear strikes. These include various civil defense measures put in place by the Soviet Union, as well as the intense Soviet effort to develop their own nuclear device. In terms of raising costs, the Soviet Union undertook various diplomatic initiatives during this period to ban nuclear weapons and organize public opinion against nuclear use. As I discuss in the next section, these were done explicitly to counter the American nuclear monopoly.[93]

SOVIET NUCLEAR VIEWS

Soviet leaders understood the destructive potential of nuclear weapons. They worried that the United States would use nuclear weapons in any war with the Soviet Union. Soviet leaders downplayed the significance of nuclear weapons at the time to demonstrate resolve, not because they discounted the danger. This is not to claim that Soviet decision making was solely the product of the US nuclear arsenal. Moreover, Soviet leaders, like their American counterparts, did not expect their opponent to deliberately launch a war anytime soon. Yet there is good evidence that the US nuclear capability contributed to the Soviet desire to restrain its behavior and avoid even a limited war with the United States.

Soviet leaders quickly grasped the importance of nuclear weapons and the danger the American atomic monopoly posed. Despite Stalin's publicly dismissive attitude, discussed in more detail below, he asserted that the atomic bomb was a "powerful thing, pow-er-ful."[94] As early as October 1942 Stalin is said to have berated scientists who suggested asking President Franklin Roosevelt about the American atomic program for being "politically naïve if you think that they would share information about the weapons that will dominate the world in the future."[95] During the war, the Soviets created an impressive intelligence apparatus to gain information on Anglo-American nuclear efforts.[96] The pressure of total war with Germany and high costs of a long-shot program prevented the Soviet Union from devoting many resources to the nuclear program during the war. Yet Stalin quickly ordered a crash program to develop a nuclear weapon as soon as the fighting stopped. To attest to the intensity of Soviet leaders' interest, the state poured resources into the program despite the struggling Soviet economy. "Hiroshima has shaken the whole world. The balance has been broken," Stalin told his scientists. "Build the bomb—it will remove the great danger from us."[97] After the Soviet atomic test in August 1949, Stalin remarked that if "we had been late with the atomic bomb by a year or year and a half, then we perhaps would have gotten it 'tested' against ourselves."[98]

Stalin was not alone in his assessments. "Soviet nuclear scientists agreed with Stalin that the American atomic monopoly was a terrible danger for Soviet security," concludes Vladislav Zubok. Stalin "was firmly convinced—along with most of his ministers and scientists—that only a similar force could deter the United States from using its atomic weapons again."[99] Alexander Werth, the *Sunday Times* correspondent in Moscow at the time, wrote that news of Hiroshima "had an acutely depressing effect on everybody. It was clearly realized that this was a New Fact in the world's power politics, that the bomb constituted a threat to Russia, and some Russian pessimists I talked to that day dismally remarked that Russia's desperately hard victory over Germany was now 'as good as wasted.'"[100] In 1946 Major General G. I. Pokrovskii outlined the benefits nuclear weapons conveyed: "Atomic aviation bombs will be effective in destroying deep underground installations, large dams and hydroelectric plants, heavy naval vessels . . . and the most important transport junctions."[101]

Soviet intelligence determined that the United States would likely use nuclear weapons in the event of war. While it is unclear the extent to which Stalin and other top officials knew the precise details of American war plans, Raymond Garthoff notes that "Soviet intelligence also obtained highly sensitive secret US and UK assessments of possible military measures to meet a potential Soviet threat, including contingency war plans involving employment of atomic weapons."[102] Official histories of Russian intelligence contain references to September 1945 US plans "in which the USSR was already seen not as an ally but as enemy number one, against which war should be conducted with the employment of atomic weapons."[103] In Novikov's September 1946 telegram to Moscow, heavily influenced by Molotov and often seen as a parallel to George Kennan's "Long Telegram," the Soviets warned that within the United States there were discussions about "a war against the Soviet Union, even a direct call for this war with a threat to use the atomic bomb."[104] Mastny concludes that American war plans "were unlikely to remain hidden from the Russian enemy, whose intelligence supplied accurate enough information about America's fighting potential, including the number of atomic bombs in its arsenal."[105] In any event, US officials at times spoke quite openly about intentions to strike Soviet cities with nuclear weapons. One such incident in 1948 elicited a formal protest from the Soviet embassy. Referencing remarks by the commander of the Strategic Air Command, General George Kenney, published in *Newsweek*, the Soviets complained on June 9 (prior to the Berlin blockade) that the article "set forth a plan to use American air forces, air bases and atomic bombs against the Soviet Union, particularly for the destruction of Soviet cities such as Moscow, Leningrad, Kiev, Kharkov, Odessa, and others."[106]

The Soviet Union pursued plans to defend against and minimize dangers of a nuclear attack. At the beginning of the Berlin Crisis on June 30, 1948, the Soviet Politburo approved new antiaircraft defense forces, focusing on Moscow in particular. Gobarev concludes that the discussion and decision was likely "prompted by Soviet misgivings regarding a possible US Air Force nuclear attack in the event the ongoing Berlin crisis escalated further."[107] This occurred, it should be noted, before American B-29s arrived in Great Britain.[108] More generally, Holloway argues that "defense against atomic attack was a central focus of Stalin's military policy."[109] Soviet military plans in late 1946 and early 1947 included missions to "repel an enemy air attack, including one with the possible use of atomic weapons."[110] The Soviet military upgraded its interceptor aircraft, early warning radars, increased the quantity and quality of antiaircraft guns, and began research and development in antiair missiles all in an effort to deny American airpower access.[111] To be sure, some of these initiatives would have occurred regardless. They were given added urgency by the US nuclear threat. The Soviet Union also explored options to attack American air bases in Eurasia that could be used to deliver nuclear ordnance.

Soviet concerns existed despite the limited nature of the American nuclear arsenal. The US arsenal was small, difficult to deliver, and fission weapons had limited (relative to what would come) destructive power. This did not lead Stalin and other Soviet leaders to dismiss the American nuclear monopoly. True, the limited American nuclear arsenal contributed to Stalin's confidence that the United States would not suddenly attack the Soviet Union, because nuclear weapons alone could not win the war.[112] As Stalin explained in 1949, "America is less ready to attack than the USSR [is] to repulse an attack."[113] This is different from, and should not be conflated with, claiming that Stalin did not carefully consider the American nuclear arsenal when pursuing policies that might lead to war. In other words, there was reason for optimism that the Americans would not launch a sudden attack. That did not cause the Soviet leadership to believe they had little to fear if war broke out for other reasons. Stalin's personal representative to China from May 1948 to January 1950 recalled that "Stalin assessed the correlation of forces in the world soberly enough and strove to avoid any complications that might lead to a new world war."[114] The fact that an American atomic blitz prior to 1949 would not be more destructive than the

1941 German invasion was not particularly good news. The Soviets had no desire to experience that level of destruction again.

There is evidence that even a few atomic bombs created a large amount of concern among Soviet leaders. The American nuclear monopoly, combined with the vast US mobilization potential and the difficulty the Soviets would have in striking the United States, generated a formidable challenge. For example, Andrei Gromyko recalls that upon learning of the atomic bomb, "our General Staff had their heads in their hands. . . . [They] seriously considered that the USA, as soon as it had to its credit 10–15 atomic bombs, could in a possible war with the USSR deploy them against the major cities and industrial centers. The Kremlin and General Staff were nervous."[115] In 1950 Stalin expressed concern that even "a few" atomic bombs could destroy Moscow.[116] With no way for the Soviets to interrupt American production, moreover, the United States could continuously replenish its nuclear arsenal during the course of a conflict.

Soviet concerns thus centered on the basic American ability and apparent willingness to deliver nuclear weapons if war occurred. The general nature of the problem helps to explain the Soviet nonresponse to the one, admittedly weak, US attempt at nuclear signaling during the Berlin Crisis. On July 15 the United States announced it would deploy sixty B-29s to Britain. Two groups were subsequently deployed and arrived by the end of the month.[117] The B-29s dispatched were not nuclear capable, no nuclear weapons were deployed, and there was little American effort, overt or otherwise, to use the deployment to pressure the Soviets. The Soviets were likely aware of the emptiness of the American gesture, which partially accounts for Soviet indifference.[118] Beyond that, though, the Soviets had already considered US nuclear strikes. They believed that in a war the United States would likely use nuclear weapons. The B-29 deployment provided no new information. The Americans were still unlikely to launch a nuclear strike unless the situation deteriorated, and they were still likely to use nuclear weapons if the crisis did escalate to war. In that event, the Soviets could probably not prevent American aircraft from reaching Great Britain. Soviet behavior also posed no threat to the American bombers. There was no real change in the military situation. Throughout the crisis, even before the B-29 deployment, the Soviets carefully managed their behavior. Soviet leaders had set their own red lines and adhered to them before and after the arrival of the American aircraft.

Soviet leaders publicly downplayed the importance of the bomb throughout the period of American nuclear monopoly. Outwardly, the Soviets maintained that nuclear weapons had little influence on the balance of power. For instance, in a widely publicized interview in September 1946, Stalin, in language similar to Mao's, claimed that "atomic bombs are meant to frighten those with weak nerves, but they cannot decide the outcome of a war, since atomic bombs are quite insufficient for that."[119] The next month, at a speech before the UN General Assembly, Molotov belittled attempts to rely on an atomic monopoly.[120]

The Soviet Union took this hard line to demonstrate resolve in an effort to deter American attempts at nuclear compellence. It was not the case that Soviet leaders sought to downplay the nuclear threat in public because they dismissed the US nuclear arsenal in private. Rather, they sought to weaken American confidence in the utility of nuclear weapons. The Soviet leadership feared American efforts at atomic blackmail. Immediately after Truman informed Stalin of the successful nuclear test, the Soviet dictator told Lavrentiy Beria that "Truman is trying to exert pressure, to dominate. His attitude is particularly aggressive toward the Soviet Union. Of course, the factor of the atomic bomb [is] working for Truman."[121] Molotov recalled that the "bombs dropped on Japan were not aimed at Japan but rather at the Soviet Union. They said, bear in mind you don't have an atomic bomb and we do, and this is what the consequences will be like if you make a wrong move!"[122] Soviet intelligence and veterans of the atomic program recalled that "the Soviet government interpreted [the atomic bombing of Japan] as atomic blackmail against the USSR, as a threat to unleash a new, even more terrible and devastating war."[123] The Soviets thus explicitly linked their firm stance to the American nuclear monopoly. "A policy of blackmail and intimidation is unacceptable to us," Stalin argued. "We therefore gave no grounds for thinking that anything could intimidate us."[124] And at the September 1945 Council of Foreign Ministers meeting in London, Molotov deliberately took a hard line to show that the Soviet Union would not be intimidated by nuclear weapons. He argued that his 1946 UN address was motivated by a desire to "set a tone, to reply in a way that would make our people feel more or less confident."[125]

Soviet efforts to delegitimize nuclear weapons aimed to further undercut the American nuclear arsenal. "Beginning in 1946," writes Michael Gordin, "Andre Zhdanov, Stalin's second in command, orchestrated a public-relations campaign with a dual function: to embarrass the United States so they would not use their atomic advantage, and to assure their own client states that the absence of a Soviet deterrent was not a liability."[126] These instrumental efforts to delegitimize the bomb, it was hoped, could cause US leaders to be more cautious in using nuclear weapons for fear of domestic and international public backlash. In other words, these initiatives would raise the costs of nuclear use for the Americans.

The US atomic monopoly subtly influenced Soviet behavior. This argument is at odds with claims that the American nuclear monopoly encouraged Stalin to run risks.[127] This conflates obstinacy with a willingness to escalate confrontations. True, the Soviets probed the American position and directly confronted the Americans in Berlin. The Soviets were certainly ruthless in their occupation zone, and their intransigence during negotiations was a major contributor to the outbreak of the Cold War. But the Soviets avoided escalating their disputes. The Soviets had a number of reasons for behaving cautiously beyond the atomic bomb. Yet it is not the case that the bomb played little, if any, role in Soviet decision making (aside from their decision to acquire one of their own) during the period.[128] Rather, Soviet behavior was most consistent with David Holloway's conclusion that the American atomic monopoly "probably made the Soviet Union more restrained in its use of force, for fear of precipitating war. It also made the Soviet Union less cooperative and willing to compromise, for fear of seeming weak."[129]

Soviet actions were largely consistent with my argument. As a conventionally powerful NNWS relative to its opponent, the Soviet Union behaved with restraint during the Berlin Crisis. While there is not "smoking gun" evidence that the American nuclear arsenal led to specific Soviet policies during the crisis, there is good process evidence that the Soviet leadership considered nuclear weapons an important element of state power and believed the United States would use nuclear weapons during a war. During the Berlin Crisis the Soviets took steps to minimize the danger to the United States. This would reduce the benefits of using nuclear weapons, diminishing the likelihood of nuclear strikes. The Soviets also sought to take advantage of public opinion to raise the costs of nuclear use for the United States. The specific US force posture does not appear to have encouraged Soviet belligerence. The United States had a paltry arsenal that was not at that time deeply integrated with its military.[130] Nevertheless, Soviet leaders were concerned with the American nuclear arsenal. During their most direct confrontation from June 1948 to May 1949, the Soviet Union posed a much smaller danger than they could have to the United States, ultimately conceding rather than escalating.

Conclusion

The world has lived with nuclear weapons for more than seventy years. There is still much that we do not know about nuclear politics and strategy, though. For some, nuclear weapons are the absolute weapon and cast a large shadow over international politics. This claim errs by ascribing too large a role to nuclear weapons. The frequency with which nonnuclear weapon states challenge and resist nuclear-armed states demonstrates the limits of the nuclear shadow. For others, the effects of force structure, norms, and extended deterrence offer evidence that nuclear weapons play a marginal role in many (most) situations. While these factors help explain conflict in nuclear monopoly, many such arguments go too far by assigning little if any role to nuclear weapons. Nuclear weapons cast a definite but limited shadow in nuclear monopoly. The shadow shifts in scope and shape based on a number of factors, yet it looms in the background of any dispute.

The framework developed in chapter 1 received support from four detailed case studies. The analysis allowed for an examination of the strategies and processes by which conflict in nuclear monopoly occurred. In this chapter I briefly explore two key sources of danger that the nonnuclear weapon state (NNWS) can pose to the nuclear weapon state (NWS) across additional cases. I find support for my argument that the danger to the NWS will be low. I first demonstrate that wars in nuclear monopoly are more likely to be fought when there are large power imbalances in favor of the NWS. This observation holds even when comparing wars in nuclear monopoly to wars between nonnuclear weapon states. Next, I examine all wars in nuclear monopoly to show that during the actual fighting there is typically little danger to the NWS.

I conclude with broader implications for nuclear politics. In the introductory chapter, I argued that conflict in nuclear monopoly posed a puzzle for many traditional deterrence and compellence explanations. Moreover, much of what we know about nuclear weapons and conflict focuses on situations when both sides have nuclear weapons. This book joins a small but growing literature on conflict in nuclear monopoly. It incorporates insights on the costs of nuclear use, force structures, and nuclear nonuse norms to help understand the patterns of conflict when only one side has nuclear weapons.[1] I return to these theoretical and policy issues here.

Power and War in Nuclear Monopoly

My argument expects war in nuclear monopoly to be unlikely when the nonnuclear weapon state is powerful relative to its nuclear-armed opponent. The reason is that the benefits of nuclear use are larger for the NWS against a conventionally capable NNWS than a conventionally weak nonnuclear opponent. This is not to claim that it is great to be weak in international politics. A weak NNWS faces all sorts of challenges and may avoid war if it believes it lacks a conventional strategy for success. The NNWS has the option, though, of fighting if it finds such a strategy. A powerful NNWS must worry much more intently that nuclear weapons will be used in any war and thus is less likely to escalate a dispute. Such wars are essentially "selected out," leaving only those wars between powerful nuclear-weapon states and weak NNWS opponents. This dynamic should be absent when two or more nonnuclear weapon states confront one another. Indeed, in those cases wars between conventionally similar opponents are likely to be fairly common because both sides can reasonably believe that they would win.

This leads to the basic observable implication assessed in this section: wars in nuclear monopoly are more likely to be fought when there are large power imbalances in favor of the NWS, and the typical power imbalance between opponents will be larger than when no participant to a political dispute has nuclear weapons. In the rest of this section I first briefly discuss the data. I then show that the historical record generally supports my argument.

POWER AND WAR

The case study chapters relied on multiple indicators for power. In this chapter I use two of those indicators: per capita GDP and military spending per soldier. Both are widely available across cases and capture core parts of my argument. Military spending per soldier accounts for the possibility that a state with a larger military may nevertheless be overmatched by a smaller but better trained and equipped opponent.[2] Moreover, some forces critical to power projection, such as naval and air forces, are more capital intensive than large numbers of ground troops. The lower the offensive capabilities of the NNWS, the less danger it poses to the nuclear-armed opponent.[3] I use economic development as an additional indicator of military power for the post–World War II period. As Michael Beckley demonstrates, economic development is one of the best predictors of military effectiveness.[4] Most basically, "economic development improves a state's ability to produce high-quality military equipment and skillful military personnel."[5] Moreover, developed economies can maintain advanced equipment and modern force employment techniques.[6] Less developed states may be able to purchase weapon platforms from abroad, but they will be ineffective at integrating those with supporting infrastructure or operating them on the battlefield. I follow Beckley and use per capita gross domestic product to measure economic development.[7]

I include the widely used Composite Indicator of National Capabilities (CINC) for comparison and transparency but do not rely on it. First, CINC conflates long-term and immediate military power by including measures such as total population, iron and steel production, and energy consumption, alongside military personnel and military spending.[8] My argument centers on whether the NNWS poses a large immediate danger that requires nuclear weapons to offset. Even if the NWS has more latent power, that advantage may not have time to manifest itself before the NNWS is able to defeat the NWS's conventional forces. Second, CINC is problematic in the post–World War II period. It overvalues certain indicators, such as domestic steel production, that do not take into account changing sources of conventional power or qualitative advantages.[9] For instance, CINC codes the Soviet Union as surpassing the United States in 1971 and holding a superior position until 1988. Yet this was precisely the period during which the Soviet Union fell hopelessly behind the United States economically and militarily.[10]

I use the ratio of NWS to NNWS capabilities in each category to assess relative power. When neither state has nuclear weapons, I use the ratio of the more powerful state's capabilities to the less powerful state's capabilities. It is important to note the subtle difference in ratios. In nuclear monopoly it is possible for the ratio to be less than 1 if the NWS is less powerful conventionally than the NNWS. By contrast, the lowest value that the ratio can take when neither side has nuclear weapons is 1, indicating perfectly balanced capabilities.

I code nuclear monopoly when only one side has nuclear weapons and the other side does not. When neither state has a nuclear weapon, I code the pair as nonnuclear.[11] I use the Correlates of War (COW) list of wars, which defines war as hostilities between states involving a minimum of one thousand battlefield deaths per year.[12] A number of conflicts coded as war seem to be borderline cases (see table C.1, below), but including all wars identified by external coding criteria increases confidence that I did not simply select conflicts that would accord with my argument. Indeed, excluding many of the borderline cases (such as South Africa versus Cuba in 1987 or the Soviet Union versus Hungary in 1956) would strengthen my argument. In wars with multiple participants I compare the power ratios for each NWS-NNWS pairing. I use pairs of states—dyads—because that is the standard in quantitative conflict studies, and it is difficult to aggregate measures such as per capita GDP across several actors fighting on the same side. Several wars in nuclear monopoly—such as the Korean, Vietnam, and Gulf Wars—involve large US-led coalitions that include states without nuclear weapons on both sides. Including all these dyads as examples of NNWS-NNWS interactions would be problematic, because many of the NNWS participants would not have fought in the absence of US leadership. Moreover, the additional states fought on the side of the nuclear power, further enhancing NWS capabilities against the nonnuclear opponent. I therefore count only two nonnuclear weapon states at war when no participant had nuclear weapons or when both sides were major independent participants in a larger conflict in nuclear monopoly, such as North and South Korea in the Korean War.[13] Appendix A provides additional discussion of the coding.

ANALYSIS

The data conform to my argument's expectations. Table C.1 lists all wars in nuclear monopoly. The NWS almost always had a large power asymmetry in its favor. In several wars the NWS was part of a multistate coalition that further shifted the power imbalance in its favor. Chinese capabilities relative to Vietnam were similar in 1979 and 1987, but in both cases the sheer preponderance of material capabilities allowed the NWS to overcome this gap.

Table C.1 Wars in nuclear monopoly

Year	War	Nuclear state(s)	Nonnuclear state(s)	GDP per capita ratio	Military spending per soldier ratio	CINC ratio
1950	Korean War	United States	China	20.6	15.6	2.4
			North Korea	10.8	missing data	106.5
1956	Suez War	United Kingdom	Egypt	16.8	2.3	9.4
1956	Soviet vs. Hungary	Soviet Union	Hungary	1.2	5.3	33.9
1965	Vietnam War	United States	Vietnam (North)	19.9	13.3	50.5
1967	Six Day War*	Israel	Egypt	7.4	2.5	0.2

Year	War	Nuclear state(s)	Nonnuclear state(s)	GDP per capita ratio	Military spending per soldier ratio	CINC ratio
			Iraq	1.0	2.4	0.7
			Jordan	1.8	3.9	2.1
			Syria	2.0	5.5	1.1
1969	War of Attrition	Israel	Egypt	11.0	1.6	0.3
1973	October War	Israel	Egypt	11.9	2.9	0.4
			Iraq	3.0	3.8	1.2
			Jordan	5.5	11.6	3.8
			Saudi Arabia	0.1	1.4	1.2
			Syria	3.2	7.1	1.8
1979	China-Vietnam I	China	Vietnam	1.3	missing data	13.4
1982	Falklands War	United Kingdom	Argentina	5.0	3.0	3.5
1982	Lebanon	Israel	Syria	7.2	4.7	1.1
1987	Angola**	South Africa	Angola	1.9	2.9	7.1
			Cuba	1.5	5.8	2.5
1987	China-Vietnam II	China	Vietnam	2.0	0.8	8.6
1991	Gulf War	France	Iraq	12.7	2.5	2.6
		United Kingdom		12.1	4.9	3.1
		United States		17.9	4.6	16.4
1999	Kosovo	United States	Serbia	6.2	12.4	69.9
2001	Afghanistan	United Kingdom	Afghanistan	43.8	151.1	17.6
		United States		56.7	216.4	116.4
2003	Iraq	United Kingdom	Iraq	12.7	57.7	2.9
		United States		16.7	80.5	22.9

Note: * Israel likely produced a nuclear weapon during or immediately prior to the war.
** May 2018 Correlates of War, Interstate War Dataset lists a discrete start date for this phase of the war over Angola.

Sources: Zeev Maoz, Paul L. Johnson, Jasper Kaplan, Fiona Ogunkoya, and Aaron Shreve, "The Dyadic Militarized Interstate Disputes (MIDs) Dataset Version 3.0: Logic, Characteristics, and Comparisons to Alternative Datasets," Journal of Conflict Resolution 63, no. 3 (March 2019): 811–35; National Material Capabilities, Version 5.0; Kristian Skrede Gleditsch, Expanded Trade and GDP Data, Version 6.

The major outlier is Israel. It frequently fought wars by itself against multistate coalitions. It is also the only NWS in the data to face an opponent with a higher GDP per capita: Saudi Arabia in 1973. Yet in that case Saudi Arabia was only minimally involved in the actual fighting; it did not enter the war for several days after the war began.[14] The CINC ratio of capabilities, again with the notable exception of Israel, also favors the NWS by large margins. I addressed the Israeli qualitative superiority in chapter 3, arguing that in actuality Israel had a sizable military advantage.

While the list of wars is informative, it lacks a comparison to fights involving only nonnuclear weapon states. I next compare the various power ratios between two states in wars in nuclear monopoly to wars between nonnuclear armed states. I use the median rather than average ratio to ensure that outliers—such as the United States versus Afghanistan—do not drive the results. Figure C.1 shows the ratio for, first, all warring dyads in nuclear monopoly (*Monopoly*); second, excluding the Suez, Hungary, Kosovo, and Iraq 2003 wars, where the NWS demand centered on pre-dispute territorial or regime change (*Monopoly—demand*); and third, dyads in wars in which the COW dataset codes the NNWS as the initiator of the overall war (*Monopoly—initiation*). It then displays the power ratio for NNWS-NNWS warring dyads (*Nonnuclear*).

The results show that wars in nuclear monopoly tend to be fought with a larger power asymmetry—favoring the NWS in monopoly—than NNWS wars. When using GDP per capita the ratio is three to five times greater in nuclear monopoly than between nonnuclear weapon states. Military spending per soldier allows a comparison with wars fought prior to the

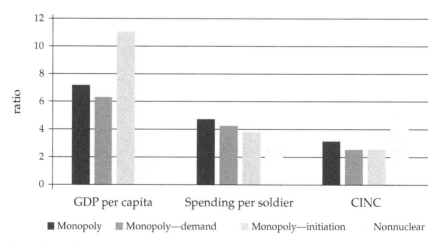

Figure C.1 Median capability ratios by nuclear balance, GDP per capita data, 1950–2010; spending and CINC, 1816–2010

nuclear era. The results are similar; the median ratio is nearly twice as large in nuclear monopoly than nonnuclear relationships. The gap narrows when including only NNWS initiators, but there is still a noticeable difference. The small number of cases when applying the initiator condition—there are only nine dyads fighting wars in nuclear monopoly using GDP per capita and only eight using the spending per soldier measure—cautions against making strong inferences. The CINC score is the exception, though this is driven by Israel. Excluding Israel, the median ratio in nuclear monopoly is generally higher than dyads in wars that had no nuclear-armed states.[15]

Finally, I examine the percentage of disputes in different balances of power that escalate to war. Many nuclear weapon states are also conventionally powerful. There are notable exceptions, but if there are few disputes between actors with similar capabilities, there would be few opportunities for war. The fact that so many weak nonnuclear weapon states still end up in fights against nuclear opponents suggests that they are willing to discount nuclear arsenals and so does not necessarily contradict my argument, but it would qualify the results. I operationalize political disputes by examining militarized interstate disputes (MIDs): "united historical cases of conflict in which the threat, display or use of military force short of war by one member state is explicitly directed towards the government, official representatives, official forces, property, or territory of another state."[16]

I divided all disputes and wars into two sets of balanced and unbalanced categories. There is little guidance for the cutoff between balanced and unbalanced pairings in international politics. I first considered cases where the NWS was up to three times as powerful relative to its nonnuclear opponent to be a NNWS advantage or roughly balanced pairing. I coded ratios where the NWS is three times as powerful or greater as unbalanced. The 3:1 threshold has primarily been used (and critiqued) to identify imbalances at the operational and tactical levels, but it has also been used at the strategic level.[17] I also used a 2:1 threshold, so that an NWS twice as powerful as its opponent is considered to have a large advantage.

In nuclear monopoly, the percentage of disputes that escalate to war is generally higher when the NWS has a large advantage. The basic relationship between power and war therefore holds when accounting for the greater number of asymmetric disputes in nuclear monopoly. As figure C.2 shows, as per capita GDP becomes more favorable to the NWS, the percentage of disputes that become wars increases substantially. This is true for both a 3:1 and 2:1 threshold for NWS advantage. By contrast, in disputes between two nonnuclear armed states, a slightly smaller percentage escalate to wars when per capita GDP is unbalanced. The relationship for the spending-per-soldier metric offers mixed support for my argument. There is only a small increase in the percentage of wars when

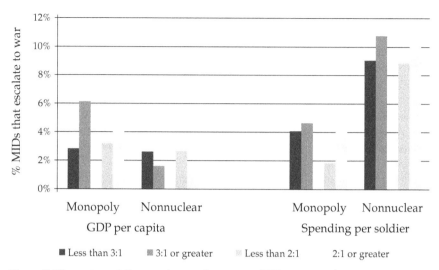

Figure C.2 Percentage of disputes that escalate to war, GDP per capita data, 1950–2010; spending and CINC, 1816–2010

the NWS has at least a 3:1 advantage compared to when it does not. Indeed, there is a slightly larger shift using this measure in nonnuclear relationships.[18] When shifting to a 2:1 advantage, the results show a major change in the direction my argument predicts. The percentage of disputes that become wars when the NWS has a large advantage is nearly triple the percentage of disputes that do so when the NWS does not. The basic reason for this is that there are a number of wars where the NWS enjoys only slightly less than a 3:1 advantage. At the same time, there are very few wars, but a sizable number of disputes, where the NWS approaches a 2:1 or less advantage. There is little change for wars between nonnuclear weapon states.

In sum, across a wide variety of measures, evidence suggests that war in nuclear monopoly tends to be fought when the NWS has a large conventional military advantage. The median power imbalance is larger in nuclear monopoly than in wars involving only nonnuclear weapon states. Israel is an outlier, though it enjoyed a strong qualitative advantage over its opponents that aggregate material indicators can mask. With one exception, a larger percentage of disputes become wars in nuclear monopoly when the NWS has a large advantage. There is also a noticeable difference with NNWS wars, where the influence of power was more modest. Each metric has limitations, the results do not control for a variety of factors, and some qualify the strength of the overall arguments. Nevertheless, the general consistency of the findings increases confidence that the logic accounts for additional cases.

War Conduct in Nuclear Monopoly

This section reviews the conduct of the wars in nuclear monopoly. Chapters 2, 3, and 4 discussed five wars involving the United States (Korea, Gulf War, Iraq 2003) or Israel (War of Attrition, October War). This chapter considers those along with eleven others: the 1956 Sinai War; the 1956 Soviet-Hungary War; the 1965 Vietnam War; the 1967 Six Day War; the 1979 and 1987 China–Vietnam wars; the 1982 Falklands War; the 1982 war over Lebanon; the 1987 war over Angola; the 1999 Kosovo War; and the 2001 Afghanistan War. Appendix B contains a discussion for each of the eleven additional wars. In this section I summarize the main results. In doing so, I establish a basic congruence between nuclear monopoly and the conduct of wars. Unlike in the case study chapters, however, I do not investigate the NNWS internal decision making to ascertain the degree to which the nonnuclear weapon states discussed nuclear weapons.[19]

My argument predicts that the conduct of military operations during wars in nuclear monopoly will generate little danger to the NWS. As long as the danger to the NWS is low, the benefits of nuclear use will also be low. This allows any costs associated with nuclear use to loom large. My claim is not that the NNWS will necessarily alter its behavior; in many cases it lacks the capabilities to deploy more threatening forces or pursue more ambitious objectives. That is precisely the point, though. A state that cannot do more will pose little danger to the NWS; wars that pose more danger should be unlikely to occur in the first place.

I look for several indicators that there is limited danger to the NWS during the war. First, the war should pose little threat to the NWS's homeland or nuclear arsenal. As such, the bulk of the fighting will be away from the NWS, on or near NNWS territory. The evidence strongly supports this expectation. I found no evidence in any of the sixteen wars that the NNWS threatened the NWS's survival or nuclear arsenal.[20] In ten of the wars, the fighting took place entirely outside the NWS territory.

In the six cases where part of the fighting did take place on NWS territory, it was isolated and posed little threat of a large invasion. Vietnam launched occasional minor incursions into China during their decade-long fight. Argentina invaded isolated British territory when it took the Falkland Islands, but there was no danger that Argentina would advance farther. Israel endured the most attacks on territory that it controlled.[21] There was some limited fighting on Israeli territory in 1967, largely involving Jordan. In 1970, the Egyptian military conducted raids and artillery attacks on Israeli territory, but there were no major operations. The notable exception was the 1973 October War. I discussed the limited nature of the Egyptian and Syrian offensives in chapter 3.

Second, my argument expects the NNWS to use either a defensive strategy or a limited aims offensive strategy. Again, the conduct of the wars corresponds to these expectations. Argentina used a limited aims offensive, quickly shifting to the defensive and seeking negotiations after capturing the Falklands. The North Vietnamese pursued offensive operations in South Vietnam, but these posed no threat to expand beyond that territory. As noted, the Vietnamese launched minor incursions into China during their fighting, but otherwise relied on a defensive strategy. Egypt relied on artillery barrages in 1970, and Egypt and Syria pursued limited aims offensives in 1973. China's attack in Korea in 1950 is the possible exception. While Chinese leaders initially considered adopting a defensive posture in Korea, they switched to a more expansive attack plan. The Chinese sought external support prior to their assault, though, and could not project power beyond the Korean Peninsula. In every other war the NNWS used defensive or guerrilla strategies. To be sure, these states may have launched offensives on their territory, such as Angola and Cuba against South Africa, but they did not conduct operations on the opponent's territory.

Third, the NNWS should generally impose only modest losses on the NWS. This necessarily involves killing NWS soldiers and destroying equipment, which may lead to a political defeat for the NWS. Importantly, though, the conduct of the war should not threaten the wholesale destruction of the NWS military or leave the NWS defenseless. Battlefield deaths provide one grim indicator for relative losses. In most of the wars, the fighting was very lopsided in favor of the NWS (table C.2). In others, the NNWS fought tenaciously and inflicted significant losses on the NWS. Yet in no case did the NWS losses risk military collapse or present the NWS with the possibility of being unable to defend its regime and territory. This is not to trivialize the losses of either side, and estimating battlefield deaths is a difficult endeavor. The results are nevertheless consistent with the argument's expectations.

Table C.2 Estimated battlefield deaths in nuclear monopoly wars, 1945–2010

Year	War	Nuclear state(s)	Battlefield deaths	Nonnuclear state(s)	Battlefield deaths
1950	Korean War	United States	54,487	China	422,612
				North Korea	316,579
1956	Suez War	United Kingdom	22	Egypt	3,000

Year	War	Nuclear state(s)	Battlefield deaths	Nonnuclear state(s)	Battlefield deaths
1956	Soviet vs. Hungary	Soviet Union	720	Hungary	926
1965	Vietnam War	United States	58,153	Vietnam (North)	700,000
1967	Six Day War	Israel	1,000	Egypt	10,000
				Iraq	30
				Jordan	6,100
				Syria	2,500
1969	War of Attrition	Israel	368	Egypt	5,000
1973	October War	Israel	2,838	Egypt	7,700
				Iraq	278
				Jordan	23
				Saudi Arabia	100
				Syria	3,500
1979	China-Vietnam I	China	13,000	Vietnam	8,000
1982	Falklands War	United Kingdom	255	Argentina	746
1982	Lebanon	Israel	455	Syria	1,200
1987	Angola	South Africa	missing data	Angola	missing data
				Cuba	missing data
1987	China-Vietnam II	China	1,800	Vietnam	2,200
1991	Gulf War	France	2	Iraq	40,000
		United Kingdom	24		
		United States	376		
1999	Kosovo	United States	2	Serbia	5,000
2001	Afghanistan	United Kingdom	0	Afghanistan	4,000
		United States	2		
2003	Iraq	United Kingdom	33	Iraq	7,000
		United States	140		

Sources: Meredith Reid Sarkees and Frank Wayman, *Resort to War: 1816–2007* (Washington, DC: CQ Press, 2010), chap. 3; Stephen L. Weigert, *Angola: A Modern Military History, 1961–2002* (New York: Palgrave Macmillan, 2011), 88; Michael Clodfelter, *Warfare and Armed Conflicts*, 3rd ed. (Jefferson, NC: McFarland, 2008), 604.

Note: Battlefield deaths are for the interstate war portion of conflicts only. Official reports for the Angola War from 1975 to 1989 list Cuba, 2,100 killed; South Africa, 715 killed. Estimates for Angolan killed in the 1987–1988 Mavinga campaign are 4,700.

Implications for Nuclear Politics

States without nuclear weapons have pursued a variety of means when challenging or resisting a nuclear-armed opponent during intense political disputes that seemed to be worsening. The most direct way to reduce conflict in nuclear monopoly, then, is to address the underlying political disputes. Yet when political disputes occurred (and they are likely to continue to occur), nonnuclear weapon states devised strategies around nuclear monopoly. These strategies took advantage of the costs and benefits associated with nuclear use for the nuclear-armed state. The NNWS leaders discounted the likelihood of nuclear use when they perceived the costs of use as outweighing the benefits for their opponent. They tempted fate, pursuing strategies that they believed would fall short of their opponent's red line for nuclear use.

There were several common elements across the cases as the NNWS probed the limits of the nuclear shadow. Islands were often the center of conflicts. China in 1954 and 1958, as well as Argentina, sought to use military force around islands and limit the danger to the NWS. The Soviets put pressure on the isolated position of Berlin—essentially a Western island in a sea of Soviet-occupied territory. Even with the expansive Chinese intervention in 1950, there was a natural stopping point at the end of the Korean Peninsula, beyond which the Chinese could not go. Additionally, the Soviets, Chinese, and Iraqis all undertook various civil defense measures to reduce the damage of a nuclear strike. This could both minimize the benefits of a strike but also served to hedge in case the conflict escalated. Leaders often downplayed the danger of nuclear weapons to minimize any efforts at nuclear coercion.

The NNWS also pursued various means to raise the costs of a nuclear strike. Egyptian and Iraqi leaders at times hoped that chemical or biological weapons could serve as a deterrent by harming the nuclear opponent or its allies. At the same time, they avoided using those weapons first. The Egyptians and Chinese both attained external support they hoped would restrain nuclear escalation. Interestingly, the Egyptian attack in 1973 and Chinese intervention in 1950 were the two largest offensives against a nuclear opponent. It is perhaps not surprising that the leaders in both countries then went to such lengths to ensure outside assistance. Finally, the Soviet, Chinese, and Egyptian leaders all sought to leverage global public opinion against large-scale war in general and nuclear weapons in particular.

More generally, weak nonnuclear weapon states were more likely than powerful nonnuclear weapon states to fight a war against a nuclear-armed opponent. The Soviet Union sought to push the United States during a period of nuclear monopoly. In contrast to weaker actors, though, the Soviets behaved much more cautiously and ultimately conceded rather than fight. Examination of all wars found that wars in nuclear monopoly are in fact fought only when there is a large power imbalance in favor of the nuclear-weapon state. Moreover, those wars in nuclear monopoly that did occur posed little danger to the nuclear weapon state. This reduced the benefits of nuclear use and allowed any costs to loom large.

I conclude with some broader implications for nuclear strategy and politics. To begin with, it became fashionable after the Cold War to argue that the world had entered a "second nuclear age" that replaced the (allegedly simpler) bipolar superpower nuclear standoff.[22] Others have pushed back against this narrative of bifurcating the nuclear era.[23] This book reinforces the latter; there is more continuity in the nuclear era than often appreciated. To the extent that the "first nuclear age" is taken to mean the Cold War era, nuclear strategy and politics were not limited even then to the US-Soviet standoff or bilateral arms control. To be sure, the bulk of the attention focused on the superpower confrontation. This was quite reasonable and expected, given the scope of the arsenals and intensity of the dispute. Yet throughout the nuclear era, states have struggled to manage nuclear proliferation involving new actors, and newly nuclear-armed states have developed force postures and doctrines quite different from those of the superpowers.[24] Similarly, nuclear-armed states found themselves embroiled in conflicts with nonnuclear-armed opponents during and after the Cold War. The United States has never fought a war against a nuclear-armed state (at least at the time of this writing). At the same time, the United States found itself in disputes and at war with numerous nonnuclear opponents throughout the Cold War and beyond.

Scholars have long debated how many nuclear weapons and what delivery capabilities are enough to be a credible threat and influence adversary calculations. These debates have focused exclusively on situations when both sides have nuclear weapons.[25] This book shifts the focus to nuclear monopoly and finds small arsenals can have an effect. Chinese, Egyptian, and Soviet leaders all took the prospect of nuclear use very seriously even when the opponent possessed relatively limited or unsophisticated nuclear arsenals. For their part, Iraqi leaders did not consider the size and sophistication of the US arsenal in their deliberations. Rather, Saddam Hussein and his lieutenants spoke of the destruction of two or three cities and twenty-kiloton yields. To paraphrase Kenneth Waltz, when nuclear weapons are involved, there is less necessity for fine-grained calculations; the possibility of even a few nuclear strikes focuses the mind.[26] Studies that focus exclusively on whether conflict occurred or not and code such outcomes as a nuclear deterrence or compellence failure may therefore erroneously conclude that nuclear weapons do not influence conflict.

Indeed, one of the central findings in this book is the problem of equating deterrence or compellence success with nuclear weapon influence. The presence of conflict or failure does not mean that nuclear weapons had no influence on decision making. Binary outcomes of conflict / no conflict or victory / defeat can certainly inform assessments of the role that nuclear weapons play.[27] Analysts are right to note that nuclear weapons did not deter the Soviets from blockading Berlin, they did not deter the Egyptians or Chinese from launching military assaults, and they did not compel the Iraqis to abandon Kuwait. A fine-grained analysis of decision making among NNWS leaders that goes beyond aggregate outcomes shows that in each case decision makers clearly recognized the danger of nuclear strikes. They were able to pursue strategies that they believed would not invite nuclear retaliation. Moreover, certain types of conflict are less likely to occur. The influence of nuclear weapons is often subtle, shaping the specific policies that NNWS leaders pursue to avoid nuclear strikes even when they decide to confront a nuclear-armed opponent.

Moreover, as noted above, the evidence in this book highlights that there are similar dynamics at play across diverse situations. Regardless of the nuclear force posture adopted, powerful nonnuclear-armed states have avoided war with nuclear-armed opponents. Norms were referenced or used instrumentally by very different leaders operating in diverse domestic environments. In situations of both extended and direct deterrence, NNWS leaders sought to probe the costs and benefits of nuclear use for their nuclear-armed opponents. States without nuclear weapons have also relied on extended deterrence of their own to raise the costs of nuclear use for their opponent. At times these were alliances with a nuclear-armed state, such as China seeking Soviet commitments prior to intervention in the Korean War. But the state need not be an ally or friend. Egypt sought to leverage US influence over Israel to rein in the latter's nuclear program and even restrain Israel during the October War. Iraqi leaders sought (though failed to receive) Soviet and French support to slow the US march to war, and if there was no war there would be no danger of nuclear strikes.

The limits of the nuclear arsenal should be apparent as well. Many fear that nuclear monopoly will allow a nuclear-armed state to dominate its nonnuclear opponents. For instance, Merrill and Peleg argue that "when the compeller enjoys a monopoly over nuclear weapons, he can virtually dictate conditions to the compellee."[28] Former Israeli ambassador to the United States Michael Oren writes that "Iran with military nuclear capabilities will dominate the Persian Gulf and its vast oil deposits, driving oil prices to extortionary highs."[29] In 1995 the *New York Times* reported that American and Israeli officials feared that with "a nuclear arsenal . . . Iran could also try to dominate its neighbors on the Persian Gulf, including Iraq. . . . Such domination, they say, could lead to Iranian control of the flow and price of oil to the West."[30] If nuclear weapons allow states to dictate to nonnuclear opponents, then the benefits of preventive military strikes to arrest proliferation increase substantially.[31]

This book joins other studies that suggest a state with a nuclear weapon cannot simply dominate nonnuclear opponents.[32] In political disputes, an NNWS has a number of strategies available to it to offset an opponent's nuclear advantage. Nonnuclear states have resisted in the past; they will find ways to do so in the future. To be sure, the international community has a general interest in nonproliferation and working to avoid wars involving any nuclear-armed states. Yet calls for military action to rein in nascent nuclear programs may invite more problems than they solve. Nuclear weapons offer some political leverage and influence to nonnuclear-armed states, but they are not a panacea.

Indeed, there are definite limits to overt attempts at nuclear coercion. In the cases examined, the NNWS leadership factored nuclear weapons into their decision making based on the existence of a nuclear capability and general force posture. Efforts during crises or wars to threaten nuclear use often had little effect, because the NNWS had already taken the nuclear issue into consideration. For instance, Secretary of State James Baker's veiled threat in January 1991 may have not mattered much, because the Iraqis had already considered the possibility that chemical weapons could invite nuclear retaliation.[33] Likewise, even had the B-29s dispatched to Britain in 1948 been nuclear capable, they would not have revealed any new information to the Soviet Union. The Soviets believed that the Americans were unlikely to deliberately start a war but very likely to use nuclear weapons during a war. If the Egyptians were aware of the Israeli "operational check" in 1973, potentially through the Soviets, it would not have altered their basic view that as long as the conflict remained limited, the use of nuclear weapons would be unlikely. To the extent the alert alarmed the United States, it would be fulfilling the Egyptian goal of more directly involving the Americans in the dispute.

The analysis nevertheless points to several factors that can influence the political utility nuclear weapons offer their possessors. For instance, during a period of unipolarity, the options for nonnuclear-armed states to turn to other great powers to restrain a nuclear opponent should decrease. This would reduce one cost of nuclear use and therefore increase the likelihood that the benefits of use outweigh the costs, enhancing the utility of nuclear weapons for regional actors. States are unlikely to be able to control polarity, though. A more manipulable policy lever is a state's conventional military. A state may gain greater political utility from its nuclear arsenal if it reduces its conventional capabilities. In those cases, the lack of conventional alternatives expands the military missions that only the nuclear arsenal can accomplish. This enhances the benefits of nuclear weapons and makes it more likely that the benefits will exceed the cost. Despite this potential benefit, it is not likely to be an attractive policy option. Some of the reasons will be familiar to students of American nuclear strategic history. One of the critiques of the Eisenhower administration's massive retaliation policy and underinvestment in conventional arms (from the critics' perspective) was that it left the president with only the option of nuclear use or retreat in a crisis. The flexible-response alternative faced its own shortcomings, of course, and was only partially implemented by the United States.[34] The basic drawback of tying one's own hands remains, however. It does nothing to reduce the costs of nuclear use. Rather, it increases the benefits by removing any alternatives, making it more likely that benefits will outweigh costs. Any additional leverage comes at the expense of being forced to endure the costs of nuclear use or capitulation if a nonnuclear adversary miscalculates and elects to fight. Particularly for countries such as the United States, flexibility is probably more valuable against nonnuclear opponents than any additional leverage from the nuclear arsenal.

There are a number of limitations and challenges to the analysis. These limit the strength and scope of the conclusions in a number of ways. To begin with, I bracketed factors such as polarity, regime type, civil-military relations, and leader personality that may systematically influence conflict in nuclear monopoly. Nor did I consider how nuclear latency—the possession of enrichment and reprocessing facilities that can be used to acquire, sometimes very quickly, a nuclear weapon—might influence conflict in nuclear monopoly.[35] Next, the case studies traced the origins of each dispute, but the basic framework introduced in chapter 1 and tested throughout the book did not evaluate how disputes over diverse issues may lead to variation in NNWS behavior. I also focused exclusively on nuclear monopoly in an effort to isolate its effects. As a result, it is unclear how the insights in this book travel to cases of extreme nuclear asymmetry when both sides possess nuclear weapons, such as the dispute between the United States and North Korea today. On the one hand, it is possible that North Korea may discount the US nuclear arsenal owing to the overwhelming American conventional advantage. On the other hand, the fact that North Korea has even a small number of nuclear weapons and is developing more-capable delivery platforms may mean that the benefits of US nuclear strikes to offset that threat are very high, making nuclear use more likely and inducing additional North Korean caution. Future research can usefully incorporate these additional factors and examine different strategic dynamics to better understand the role of nuclear weapons in international conflict.

At the time of this writing, no nuclear weapons have been used since 1945. This should be cause for celebration, but not for complacency. It is easy to draw the wrong lesson from the many conflicts in nuclear monopoly. One should not conclude that nuclear weapons provide no utility in nuclear monopoly. Nuclear weapon states have not been able to avoid all fights, but in political disputes they have avoided having to fight against major offensives that threaten their survival or against more conventionally capable nonnuclear opponents. These benefits of nuclear possession will continue to pose obstacles to nonproliferation and global zero efforts. Proponents of these agendas must directly address these incentives to continue to make progress.

At the same time, one should not abandon efforts to manage nuclear proliferation and conflict. There have been a number of political disputes and even wars in nuclear monopoly. So far none have resulted in nuclear strikes. That does not mean that there is no danger of nuclear use in similar disputes in the future and that therefore such conflicts are little cause for concern. After all, the only use of nuclear weapons to date has occurred in nuclear monopoly. In nuclear monopoly after 1945, leaders in states without nuclear weapons have generally acted in a restrained manner, sought to leverage the strategic environment to minimize the likelihood of nuclear use, or pursued strategies that posed little danger to the nuclear-armed state. If those conditions change in the future—if a powerful state without nuclear weapons escalates to a war against a nuclear-armed opponent or pursues expansive aims, for instance—then this book cautions that the world could witness the first nuclear strikes since August 1945.

Counting Wars in Nuclear Monopoly

In this appendix I first discuss in more detail how I generated the list of wars and disputes used in the conclusion chapter.[1] Counting conflicts involves a number of decisions that can influence the results. I therefore next present several sensitivity analyses for the conclusion results using alternative lists of conflicts and relative capability thresholds. With one exception, discussed below, the results are robust to alternative specifications. That change in results reinforces my basic argument by highlighting that power asymmetries in the overall war favor the nuclear weapon state (NWS) side. The last section then shows that a powerful nonnuclear weapon state (NNWS) is not more likely to win disputes prior to fighting.

I took the basic list of wars from the May 2018 Correlates of War (COW) Interstate War Dataset available on the COW home page. I follow standard practice and count only the first year of each war. For example, the COW dataset codes the United States at war with China in 1950, 1951, 1952, and 1953. I count only the war onset in 1950 and drop the years 1951–1953. When large US-led coalition wars occurred in nuclear monopoly (Korea, Vietnam, Gulf, Iraq 2003) I excluded warring dyads between nonnuclear weapon states unless they were major independent participants in the war.[2] Including all the other dyads in these coalition wars as examples of NNWS-NNWS interactions would be problematic because many of the states without nuclear weapons would not have fought absent the presence of the United States. Moreover, the additional states fought on the side of the nuclear power(s), further enhancing NWS capabilities against the nonnuclear opponent.

I used the May 2018 dyadic Militarized Interstate Disputes (MIDs) to capture political disputes that might escalate to war in order to generate the percentage of disputes that escalated across different power balances. The MID coding decisions do not affect the basic comparison of median power ratios and war. I again count only the first year of each individual MID but do not drop subsequent years if an MID is ongoing. For instance, the United States and China experienced a militarized dispute beginning in 1949 that continued into 1950 (no. 634). The two nations then had two more disputes in 1950 (nos. 633 and 51). In this case I counted three militarized disputes: one in 1949 (634) and two in 1950 (633 and 51). This captures the intuition that each dispute was a potential opportunity for war, and one in fact became the Korean War. There is thus a subtle difference with many dyadic conflict studies. In those studies, only one MID is counted per year, even if two states experienced numerous disputes in the same year. In cases where a MID began in one year but escalated to war in the next year I use data for the year that the dispute escalated to war. For example, I count both the war and MID for the Gulf War between the United States and Iraq in 1991, even though the MID that became the Gulf War began in 1990. In other words, I do not consider the MID in 1990 to be a separate opportunity for war. This avoids erroneously claiming a dispute did not escalate to war when in fact it eventually did. I do not count any MIDs that occur during an ongoing war because these could not escalate to war since the countries were already at war. Thus I do not count any MIDs between the United States and China in 1951, 1952, or 1953.

I use three alternative lists of wars to assess the robustness of the median power ratios. I find that the basic results from the conclusion chapter do not change. Figure A.1 includes all warring dyads in US-led nuclear monopoly coalition wars. Figure A.2 reports the results using the alternative war dataset generated by Reiter, Stam, and Horowitz, which ends in 2007.[3] It drops the Korean War as a nuclear monopoly war because they code the Soviet Union as a participant. Figure A.3 excludes wars involving Israel and uses only the CINC measure, which was an outlier in the conclusion. In two

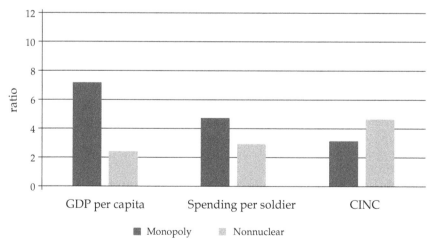

Figure A.1 Median capability ratios by nuclear balance—all warring dyads, GDP per capita data, 1950–2010; spending and CINC, 1816–2010

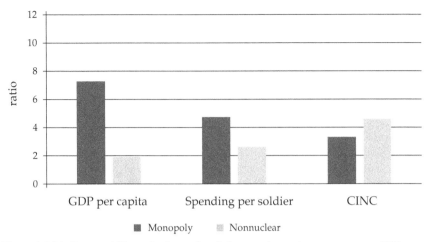

Figure A.2 Median capability ratios by nuclear balance—alternative war measure, GDP per capita data, 1950–2007; spending and CINC 1816–2007

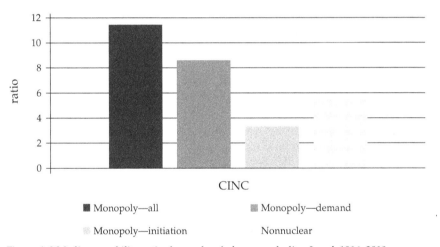

Figure A.3 Median capability ratios by nuclear balance, excluding Israel, 1816–2010

of the three nuclear monopoly lists the median ratio is now larger than in wars between two nonnuclear states.

Next, I include the additional warring dyads in US-led coalition wars in nuclear monopoly (figure A.4) to examine the percentage of MIDs that become wars. The results for the spending measure are similar to those in the conclusion chapter. The pattern for wars between two nonnuclear weapon states does noticeably change for per capita GDP, though. The reason and direction of the change are consistent with my argument's underlying logic and an artifact of using dyads. Specifically, every new

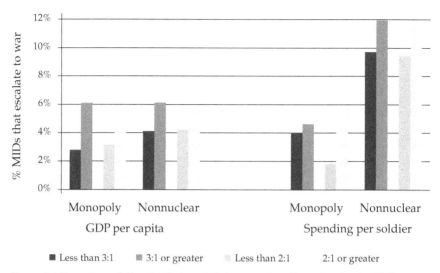

Figure A.4 Percentage of disputes that escalate to war using all warring dyads, GDP per capita data, 1950–2010; spending and CINC, 1816–2010

nonnuclear-versus-nonnuclear dyad with a power imbalance greater than 3:1 occurs when the stronger nonnuclear state is fighting on the side of the United States. In the few cases in nuclear monopoly wars when the nonnuclear state had an advantage over another nonnuclear state on the nuclear state's side, the advantage was less than 3:1. For example, Figure A.4 includes a warring dyad between nonnuclear Britain and nonnuclear North Korea in 1950. Britain had a nearly 8:1 advantage in per capita GDP over North Korea. This shows up as an asymmetric dispute between two nonnuclear weapon states escalating to war. In reality, it is an NNWS fighting alongside an NWS, which results in an even greater NWS advantage against the NNWS. Thus while the other results are robust to alternative coding decisions, in this instance they are sensitive but in a way that reinforces the original coding decision to exclude these dyads in order to best assess the difference between wars in nuclear monopoly and wars involving only nonnuclear weapon states.

Finally, I examine the median capability ratios in disputes that the nonnuclear state wins versus those that it loses. My argument predicts that wars in nuclear monopoly are more likely when the NNWS is weak, because it poses a smaller danger to the NWS that minimizes the risks of nuclear strikes. An alternative explanation might be that this pattern occurs because a powerful NNWS is likely to win a dispute against an NWS prior to war. Therefore, war is unlikely to occur in those situations. Weak nonnuclear states, by contrast, may have no recourse but to fight, because the nuclear opponent will otherwise dismiss their demands. The MIDs dataset

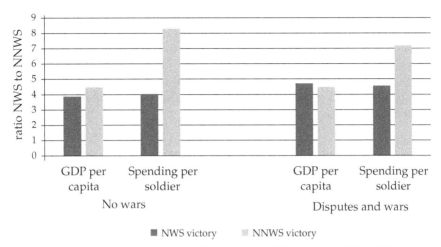

Figure A.5 Median capability ratios and dispute victors, GDP per capita, 1950–2010; spending per soldier, 1946–2010

codes dispute victories, which provides the ability to assess one observable implication for this alternative argument. Specifically, in disputes against nuclear-armed opponents, we should observe the power ratio to be more favorable to nonnuclear weapon states when they win than when they lose. COW codes victory in the last year of a dispute in contrast to the rest of the analysis, which focuses on the first year of a dispute. As a result, the results are not fully comparable, although the vast majority of disputes begin and end in the same year. I follow Maoz et al. and code a state as winning if the dispute ends in its victory or the other side yielding.[4] I code all other outcomes as draws.

Approximately 90 percent of the disputes ended in a draw; neither side did much winning. Not surprisingly, the NWS won twice as many disputes that didn't escalate to war as the NNWS (forty-one to twenty). Surprisingly, though, the median ratio for spending per soldier shows that the NWS had a smaller advantage when it won a dispute compared to when it lost (figure A.5). The median NNWS that won was at an 8:1 disadvantage, while the median NNWS that lost (meaning an NWS victory) was at a 4:1 disadvantage. In other words, when a NNWS did manage to win, the power ratio for the NNWS was actually less favorable than when it lost using this measure. Using per capita GDP, there is little noticeable difference when the NNWS wins versus when it loses. The NNWS is at approximately a 4:1 disadvantage when it loses (NWS victory) and a 4.5:1 disadvantage when it wins (NNWS victory). Including the victor of disputes that escalated to war does not meaningfully alter the findings. These results should be treated with some caution, given the small numbers and difficulties coding victory and defeat. Yet they suggest that powerful nonnuclear weapon states win-ning disputes without having to fight is not the reason for observing the pattern that wars in nuclear monopoly tend to be fought when the NNWS is conventionally weak relative to the NWS. Most disputes end in draws, and while nonnuclear weapon states lose more overall, those that do win are as often, if not more often, weak nonnuclear weapon states rather than powerful ones.

Additional Cases

The Correlates of War database reports sixteen discrete wars in nuclear monopoly. These wars serve as the basis for general discussion of conduct of war in nuclear monopoly in the conclusion chapter. Five of these were addressed in the case study chapters: the Korean War (chapter 4), the War of Attrition and the October War (chapter 3), and the Gulf War and the Iraq War (chapter 2). In this appendix I briefly discuss the remaining wars: the 1956 Sinai War; the 1956 Soviet-Hungary War; the 1965 Vietnam War; the 1967 Six Day War; the 1979 and 1987 wars between China and Vietnam; the 1982 Falkland Islands War; the 1982 war over Lebanon; the 1987 war over Angola; the 1999 Kosovo War; and the 2001 Afghanistan War. I focus on the portions identified as interstate wars. Conflict and instability after the end of organized interstate hostilities between states are beyond the scope of my analysis.

Sinai War (1956)

The 1956 Sinai (or Suez) War pitted Egypt against Israel, France, and nuclear-armed Great Britain. The dispute centered on control of the Suez Canal. Following the coup that deposed Egypt's King Farouk, the new Egyptian government sought to assert its control over the important waterway that cut through its territory. Recognizing its limited options, the British government agreed in October 1954 to remove British troops by 1956. On June 13, 1956, the last British soldiers left the Suez Canal Zone. President Gamal Abdel Nasser nationalized the Suez Canal Company a little over a month later, on July 26. The move, on top of other Egyptian rhetoric, alarmed officials in London. The British prime minister Anthony Eden then conspired with French and Israeli leaders to retake the canal. The plan called for Israeli forces to attack Egypt in the Sinai, strengthening Israeli borders. Britain and France would then demand an end to the fighting and call for both sides to withdraw from the area. Next, they would introduce troops to seize the canal. Israel dutifully attacked on October 29, followed by the planned Anglo-French ultimatum on October 30. When fighting continued, British and French aircraft attacked Egypt, followed by the introduction of ground troops on November 5.[1]

Discussion of nuclear weapons in the war typically center on Soviet nuclear threats. The general consensus is that those threats had little influence on British and French decision making.[2] Rather, US pressure—including economic coercion—compelled the European powers to reverse course and withdraw their forces by the end of December, handing Nasser an important political victory. The British nuclear monopoly relative to Egypt gets little attention. The British had developed a capable bomber force by 1956 that could deliver nuclear weapons, and British bases in the region could have been used as staging areas for nuclear strikes against Egypt.[3]

The British homeland, its nuclear arsenal, and its military faced no danger throughout the war. Without the prospect of military defeat, there were minimal benefits of nuclear use. Any nuclear-related costs—and Britain endured economic and political costs for the conventional military action alone—would therefore loom large. The lack of military danger to Britain from the conduct of the war is evidenced in several ways.[4] To begin with, all the fighting took place outside British territory. Moreover, the Israeli Defense Forces (IDF) conducted the bulk of ground operations and were involved in the most intense fighting. Egyptian military performance was uneven, with some units fighting tenaciously and others quickly abandoning their positions. As a whole, though, Egyptian forces were poorly coordinated across the theater and were unable to execute counterattacks, allowing the IDF to make steady progress. The Egyptian air force posed little threat. Initial British-French attacks destroyed large numbers of Egyptian aircraft on the ground. From October 31 to November 2 the Egyptians lost more than 150 aircraft. Egypt then withdrew forty aircraft to bases out of Anglo-French range, but this removed their ability to engage in the fighting.[5] Anticipating the Anglo-French attack, Nasser ordered the military to fall back from the Sinai on November 1 to meet the new threat. The withdrawal was poorly coordinated, though, and the retreat quickly turned into a rout. As Kenneth Pollack notes, "only one Egyptian battalion returned from the Sinai intact and capable of engaging in combat operations."[6]

The Anglo-French invasion faced little opposition. The Egyptians reasonably concentrated their defense to protect Cairo from an expected British assault. However, the two allies targeted Port Said and Port Faud, massing a British infantry division, airborne brigade, and marine commando brigade alongside a French airborne division, parachute battalion, and mechanized brigade for the assault. The supporting naval force consisted of six aircraft carriers with modern jet aircraft. Out of position, with their air forces immobilized or destroyed, the Egyptian troops were woefully overmatched. For example, the Egyptian force at Port Said consisted of two reinforced bat-talions of reservists and four self-propelled guns.[7] British and French para-troopers seized key objectives on November 5 and easily beat back Egyptian counterattacks. On the sixth, British forces began amphibious landings against little opposition; most Egyptian defenders had fled. Total British and French losses from the operation were 26 killed and 129 wounded.[8]

Soviet Invasion of Hungary (1956)

The conflict began with popular demonstrations in Budapest on October 23.[9] The protesters called for the return of ousted former leader Imre Nagy and demanded a series of economic and political reforms. They also sought the end of any Soviet presence in the country. Fighting erupted between gov-ernment forces and the demonstrators, quickly spreading across most of the country. Rebels, in many cases joined by Hungarian troops, seized key installations such as radio stations, party headquarters, and the Ministry of the Interior. By October 28 the CIA reported that rebel forces were "in con-trol of most of Hungary outside of Budapest."[10] Nagy returned to power on October 24 and initially requested the support of Soviet troops to help restore order. Soviet forces in the country had already been mobilizing as the Soviet leadership debated their response. On October 25 Soviet forces fired on demonstrators outside the Hungarian parliament, killing sixty. The Soviet forces subsequently disengaged from the fighting, awaiting Mos-cow's decision, but mobilization outside Hungary continued. The Nagy government openly identified with the rebels by October 29 and called for the withdrawal of all Soviet forces on October 30. Hungary subsequently announced its intention to withdraw from the Warsaw Pact.

The Soviet leadership decided on October 31 to use the Red Army to restore Soviet influence.[11] While the political effect of Hungary leaving the alliance would have been large for the Soviet Union—Soviet leaders worried that the loss of Hungary would destabilize the Soviet position in Eastern Europe and possibly even lead Hungary to enter the American orbit—the immediate military danger that Hungary posed to the Soviet Union during the fighting was nonexistent.[12] The Soviets invaded on November 4 with a massive force of two hundred thousand troops and some twenty-eight hundred tanks that engaged and overwhelmed Hun-garian freedom fighters and military troops.[13] The entirety of the fighting took place on Hungarian territory, with no danger to the Soviet state. The Hungarian freedom fighters and allied military forces fought with defen-sive and guerrilla tactics; there was no capability of any major offensive against the Soviet Union. While the Hungarian forces fought determinedly, "hurling Molotov cocktails and even themselves at the turrets and treads of the Russian tanks," they were simply outmatched.[14] The Soviets suffered modest losses during the campaign. Precise casualty estimates vary, but the Correlates of War reports 720 Soviet battlefield deaths, compared to 926 Hungarian battlefield deaths.[15] That coding includes the interstate war portion of the conflict and does not include civilian casualties or losses earlier during the initial uprising. Some estimates place those in the thousands.

Vietnam (1965–1973)

In 1919, in the wake of the Great War, a young Vietnamese man named Nguyen Ai Quoc, who would later go by his more famous moniker Ho Chi Minh, traveled to Paris. He had hopes of presenting the US president, Woodrow Wilson, with Vietnamese desires for greater political power and freedoms under French rule, appealing to Wilson's calls for greater self-determination.[16] Less than thirty years later, following another world war, the Vietnamese and the United States found themselves on opposing sides. The United States was initially hesitant to back French efforts to maintain control of Indochina. Yet the US position shifted as the struggle became embroiled in Cold War dynamics. Indeed, by the early 1950s the US was no longer a reluctant French patron but instead a strong proponent of French efforts to counter the growth of communism, and with it fears of Soviet influence, in Vietnam. The French defeat at Dien Bien Phu in 1954 finally led to French withdrawal.[17]

The United States remained involved as Vietnam split into North and South, what would become respectively the Democratic Republic of Vietnam (DRV) and the Republic of Vietnam (ROV).[18] The United States opposed national elections, fearing Ho Chi Minh had effectively seized the nationalist mantle and could out-organize noncommunist opposition. Instead, the US backed the staunch anticommunist Ngo Din Diem's effort to create a viable South Vietnamese state. Throughout the 1950s and into the 1960s, a Communist insurgency, the Viet Cong, supported by the North Vietnamese government in Hanoi, gained strength and controlled sizable parts of the countryside. By the end of 1963 US involvement included sixteen thousand military advisers, though some fought alongside ROV units. Despite US support, Diem failed to build popular support and was overthrown in November 1963. In June 1964 North Vietnamese troops began directly participating in Viet Cong operations, and in September the first North Vietnamese regiment moved down the Ho Chi Minh Trail to South Vietnam.[19] President Lyndon Johnson and his advisers saw little chance of victory but believed that the United States could not afford to walk away. The fear was that abandoning the ROV would call into question US credibility globally. In a series of decisions in 1964 and 1965, then, Johnson dramatically escalated the US presence and combat operations. US ground operations continued until August 1972, and large-scale air operations ended with the termination of the Linebacker II bombing campaign on December 29. After a brief cease-fire, North Vietnam launched an assault on the South. South Vietnam continued to be unable to stand on its own despite the years of US involvement. After Saigon fell in April 1975, Hanoi consolidated control of the newly unified Vietnam.

The United States homeland or interests in regions outside Southeast Asia faced no danger throughout the war. This is not to minimize the American losses suffered. Yet the entirety of the fighting took place in and around Vietnam, thousands of miles from American territory. The Viet Cong relied primarily, though not exclusively, on guerrilla tactics, while the North Vietnamese Army would engage in conventional and mechanized military operations. Importantly, though, they were unable to project power to threaten American interests outside the region. Their stated limited aims to unify the country were therefore credible. While they inflicted losses, they were unable to decisively defeat the US military or cause the US homeland or key positions in Europe and the Pacific to be left defenseless. The sheer number and scope of military engagements make a full review of the combat beyond the scope of this chapter. In brief, North Vietnamese forces inflicted major losses on South Vietnamese forces but struggled to notch any battlefield victories against the United States.[20] The sustained Rolling Thunder bombing campaigns by US forces proved ineffective against guerrilla operations. When North Vietnam adopted more conventional operations, the Linebacker I and II bombing campaigns did help contribute to North Vietnamese flexibility in negotiations that ended the US presence.[21]

Hanoi was ultimately able to achieve a political victory by inflicting losses on the United States that were out of proportion to American interests in the conflict. Years of inconclusive fighting in a country many saw as not vital to US security took its toll. Especially after the Tet Offensive in 1968, opposition to the war grew within the US public and ultimately among the soldiers asked to fight for an unpopular cause with little apparent prospect of success. The US military generally remained effective in combat but began to suffer a decline in morale and discipline.[22] While not discounting American losses, it is clear that the Vietnamese lost more relative to their American opponents. From 1959 to 1975 the United States lost 58,178 killed and over 300,000 wounded (150,000 of which were hospitalized). Estimates are more difficult for the North Vietnamese and Viet Cong. Using conservative figures leads to approximately 730,000 North Vietnamese troops and Viet Cong killed, along with 65,000 North Vietnamese civilians.[23]

Six Day War (1967)

As noted in chapter 3, the inclusion of the Six Day War as a conflict in nuclear monopoly is debatable. The Dimona nuclear reactor came online in

1964, and two years later Israel likely had the ability to produce weapons-grade fissile material. By early 1967, US intelligence estimated that Israel could construct a nuclear weapon in six to eight weeks.[24] Avner Cohen's authoritative work on the Israeli nuclear program concludes that it was not until immediately prior to the war that "Israel 'improvised' two deliverable nuclear explosive devices."[25] Egyptian leaders were aware of Israeli nuclear progress and understood after 1967 that Israel had nuclear capabilities. Yet in May–June 1967 it is doubtful that Egyptian leaders believed Israel possessed a functioning nuclear device.[26] I nevertheless include a more detailed discussion here as a check against excluding a potential relevant case.[27]

The road to the Six Day War began with escalating Israeli-Syrian tensions and subsequent Egyptian troop deployments into the Sinai Peninsula in May 1967.[28] More provocatively, on May 17–18, Nasser requested that UN forces withdraw from the area, and on May 22 he announced that Egypt would close the Tiran Straits to Israeli shipping.[29] On May 17 and May 26, Egyptian aircraft overflew the Dimona reactor, generating alarm within Israel.[30]

Despite these moves, there is little evidence that Nasser or other Arab leaders intended to launch a war against Israel. If conflict came, the Egyptians would fight defensively. Egypt failed to undertake offensive preparations, with the final operational plan calling for a forward defense of the Sinai.[31] Moreover, as noted in chapter 3, the Egyptian military was unreliable because its leader, Field Marshal Muhammad Abd al-Hakim Amer, treated the armed forces as his "own personal fiefdom," where personal loyalty was more important than military competence.[32] Though Egypt had a modest advantage in troop numbers and military platform quality, it lacked a decisive conventional advantage to overcome its other deficiencies. As President Lyndon Johnson told Israel's foreign minister Abba Eben on May 26, "Our best judgment is that no military attack on Israel is imminent, and, moreover, if Israel is attacked, our judgment is that the Israelis would lick them." In case he had not been clear, he added that "you [Israel] will whip the hell out of them."[33] Nasser's motives appeared to center on overturning the post-1956 Suez War status quo, attaining a propaganda victory to offset Egyptian setbacks in Yemen and elsewhere in the region, and deterring further Israeli action against Syria or future action against Egypt.[34] As Nasser told UN Secretary-General U Thant on May 24, Egypt had "achieved its goal by returning to pre-1956 position, with one difference: that they [the Egyptians] were now in a position to defend their country and their rights."[35]

Similarly, Syria and Jordan were in no position to launch major conventional offensives against Israel. Israeli and Jordanian forces were relatively evenly matched in numbers and equipment, even with the bulk of the IDF engaged with the Syrians and Egyptians. Jordan planned for a forward defense of the West Bank. The one limited offensive element in its planning centered on capturing part of Jerusalem in the expectation that Israel would seize large parts of the West Bank elsewhere.[36] "Amman's major objective

during the Six Day War was simply to survive intact," Pollack tersely concludes.[37] The Syrians enjoyed a quantitative superiority along the Golan
Heights, but two decades of political turmoil had taken its toll on the Syrian army. Its troops were poorly equipped, trained, and led. The Syrians
focused primarily on the defense of the Golan. Even after being told (incor-
rectly) that Egyptian forces had routed the IDF, the Syrians launched only
a few uncoordinated air strikes and staged a single limited offensive that
Israeli settlers stopped largely unassisted.[38]

Egyptian planning prior to the war did include the possibility of air
strikes against the Dimona nuclear facility. This appears to contradict my
argument that the NNWS should avoid targeting the NWS's nuclear arsenal. The Egyptian planning, which Cairo was never able to implement, is
not a major challenge to my argument, though. To begin with, Egypt was
not planning to target Israel's nuclear arsenal. Egypt was likely unaware
that Israel had nuclear weapons, or of the precise location of those weapons. Also, my argument focused on the difficulty of eliminating an opponent's nuclear arsenal. This is discrete from a situation when a state believes
the opponent has no nuclear weapons to begin with. In that case, a strike
against the opponent's ability to produce the necessary material can eliminate the future nuclear danger without any risk of immediate nuclear retaliation. Finally, Egypt did not intend to start a war over Dimona, but if war
did occur, then Dimona would be an attractive target.[39]

The Egyptian deployment to the Sinai and ongoing tensions with Syria
created serious problems for Israel. Israeli leaders had previously identified the closing of the Tiran Straits as a "red line" that would necessitate
war, and feared potential attacks against Dimona.[40] More basically, though,
Israel could not afford to maintain mobilization indefinitely to offset Egyptian moves. As Zeev Maoz notes, during the crisis "one-fifth of Israel's labor
force was mobilized. The Israeli economy came to a screeching halt."[41] The
ongoing crisis was creating an intolerable domestic situation for Eshkol,
who resigned the post of defense minister (he retained the prime minister
position) on June 1, with Moshe Dayan selected to take up the post.[42] In
addition, several in the government saw an opportunity to avoid a possible diplomatic defeat and substantially alter the military-political climate
in the region.[43]

Israel launched a series of strikes beginning on June 5 that resulted in a
decisive victory. The conduct of the war accords with my argument: there
was little danger to Israeli territory, regime survival, or its nuclear arsenal
during the fighting. Indeed, Israel dramatically increased its territory, to
take control of the Golan Heights, the West Bank, the Gaza Strip, and the
Sinai Peninsula. The Israeli attack began with Israeli Air Force strikes that
caught Egypt by surprise, essentially eliminating the Egyptian air force on
the ground.[44] Israeli ground forces quickly advanced in the Sinai. While
individual Egyptian units at times fought admirably, they were unable to

respond to the fast-moving Israeli charge. Amer ordered a general retreat on the afternoon of June 6 that quickly turned into a rout.[45] On June 5, Amman ordered a more robust offensive than previously planned in response to erroneous Egyptian claims of military success.[46] That offensive never progressed, though, as Israeli counterattacks on the fifth and sixth occupied the Jordanian forces in the West Bank. At 10 p.m. on June 6, King Hussein ordered the Jordanian military to retreat. Though the king rescinded the order, the Israeli advance and Jordanian confusion created a hopeless situation for Jordan by the morning of June 7.[47] As noted above, the Syrians launched only a single and ineffective ground offensive during the first few days of the war. Combat was limited to an occasional Syrian air raid and artillery exchanges with the IDF. Israel began its major offensive against Syrian positions in the Golan on June 9 after the defeats of Egypt and Jordan. Syrian troops fought determinedly at times but undertook no offensives and indeed failed to even reposition forces or launch counterattacks in service of their broader defensive posture.[48]

China versus Vietnam (1979 and 1987)

The Correlates of War codes two wars between China and Vietnam in nuclear monopoly. The 1979 war was the larger and deadlier fight, after which low-level fighting continued throughout the 1980s. I discuss both wars together because of the continuous hostility during the period. Tensions between Vietnam and China had been increasing throughout the 1970s, brought on by the end of US-Vietnamese fighting and Chinese realignment toward the United States. The Vietnamese role in Southeast Asia was steadily increasing, culminating in the Vietnamese invasion of Cambodia in late 1978. Vietnamese persecution of ethnic Chinese living in Vietnam also increased. Vietnamese assertiveness and growing ties to the Soviet Union alarmed Beijing. The Chinese invasion, dubbed the "Punitive War," sought to inflict military and civilian damage in an effort to deter further Soviet and Vietnamese expansion in the region.[49]

The conduct of the war is congruent with my argument's expectations. The fighting took place almost entirely on Vietnamese rather than Chinese territory. Vietnam was on the defensive throughout the conflict, relying on both conventional and guerrilla means. The military performance of the Chinese People's Liberation Army (PLA) was found wanting in a number of cases. While both sides endured losses, Vietnamese forces likely suffered more. In addition, China inflicted significant damage on Vietnamese infrastructure and civilian assets while suffering no comparable losses. In short, there was never any major danger to China.

The initial Chinese attacks on February 17 caught the Vietnamese by surprise and quickly broke through the Vietnamese front lines. Progress then slowed. In the east, PLA units struggled against determined militia resistance and rugged terrain. They ultimately succeeded in taking their main objectives of Cao Bang and Dong Dang by February 25.[50] In the west, the assault against the provincial capital Lao Cai proceeded methodically against entrenched Vietnamese forces. Superior Chinese numbers allowed the Chinese to capture Lao Cai on February 20–21.[51] The Chinese inflicted substantial losses on Vietnamese militia and People's Army of Vietnam (PAVN) forces, though Chinese units suffered as well. One battalion of the 308th PAVN Division, 3rd Battalion, 460th Regiment, conducted a limited incursion into Yunnan to attack a PLA position in China on February 23. But there was no sustained PAVN offensive into Chinese territory.[52] After the seizure of Lao Cai in Vietnam, the recently arrived PLA 149th Division then moved to seize Sa Pa. Enemy action, rain, and difficult terrain slowed the advance. The Vietnamese countered, with the 316th PAVN Division putting up a determined blocking action in what was some of the most intense fighting of the war. After a week of continuous action, the 149th had lost 420 soldiers, while the PAVN 316th and supporting units lost an estimated 1,398 killed, 620 wounded, and 35 captured.[53]

Chinese forces in the east then moved to take the main target of Lang Son. As Xiaoming Zhang notes, that was the route that "Chinese imperial armies had historically used to invade Vietnam." The city controlled key rail and road networks that could threaten Hanoi less than 140 kilometers away.[54] After pausing to regroup, China launched the offensive on February 27 with seven divisions, totaling roughly eighty thousand troops. The fighting was again intense, but by March 1 PLA forces were shelling Lang Son.[55] The Vietnamese ordered their forces to fall back on March 2, and on March 4 Chinese forces crossed the Ky Kung River to capture the southern portion of the city. Casualties mounted on both sides, but the Vietnamese suffered greater losses. In addition, China had turned Lang Son "into a ruin."[56]

On March 5 Chinese leaders announced they had "achieved the expected objectives" and would "withdraw all troops back to Chinese territory."[57] Beijing had planned for only a short campaign, but the intensity of Vietnamese resistance and PLA struggles likely contributed to China's decision.[58] China's withdrawal announcement did not end the fighting. Over the next two weeks PLA forces engaged in various battles against dispersed Vietnamese forces. As the editorial of the Vietnamese party journal *Nhan Dan* put it on March 7, Vietnam would allow Chinese withdrawal, but that did not mean providing a "red carpet exit."[59] Indeed, PAVN forces managed to rout the PLA's 448th Regiment when the latter engaged in an ill-conceived operation to gain military experience.[60] Beyond the military engagements, the PLA operational commander Xu Shiyou "ordered PLA troops to destroy everything they could along their way home."[61] The damage was extensive. The war ended on March 16 when Chinese forces completed their withdrawal.

Precise estimates of the losses during the monthlong fighting are difficult to come by. The 2010 Sarkees and Wayman *Resort to War* (the basis for the COW dataset) reports 13,000 Chinese and 8,000 Vietnamese battlefield deaths.[62] This makes the 1979 war the only one in the COW dataset in which the NWS suffered greater losses. Other reports list approximately 10,000 battlefield deaths on each side, while Xiaobing Li lists 26,000 Chinese casualties (the Vietnamese number for Chinese killed) and 37,300 Vietnamese troops killed.[63] This does not include civilian losses, which were almost exclusively inflicted on the Vietnamese side. In any event, the losses to China, while not insignificant, did not threaten the destruction of the PLA and were close to Vietnamese military losses.

Military clashes along the Sino-Vietnamese border continued for the next decade. Fighting again took place primarily in Vietnam. China launched a series of limited offensives in 1980 to capture key positions in the Luojiaping Mountains along the border. In 1981 PLA operations concentrated on small areas along both the Guangxi and Yunnan borders. Vietnamese counterattacks failed to dislodge Chinese forces, so that the two sides remained locked in a low-level confrontation with occasional Chinese artillery bombardments in 1982–1983.[64] In April 1984 the PLA launched a series of offensives in the Laoshan area supported by heavy artillery bombardment. Vietnamese counterattacks in June and July ended in failure. For the next several years PLA forces rotated in and out of the area in an effort to provide combat experience to the troops.[65] As Zhang notes, Chinese troops wondered "why they had to fight for hills on the Vietnamese side of the border in 'self-defense.'"[66] Vietnamese sapper commando units conducted occasional raids beyond Chinese lines. From 1979 to 1986 Vietnamese aircraft overflew Chinese airspace on at least twelve occasions, but most such incursions lasted only a few seconds or minutes.[67] For the most part, Vietnamese operations after 1984 were limited to attacks against Chinese encroachments into Vietnamese territory. There was no major offensive launched into Chinese territory, although the border itself was contested.[68] Sarkees and Wayman code the simmering dispute as having escalated to a war from January 5 to February 6, 1987, with eighteen hundred Chinese and twenty-two hundred Vietnamese battlefield deaths.[69] Chinese-Vietnamese relations improved at the end of the decade, in part due to the end of the Cold War, and Chinese troops withdrew and returned to China in 1992.[70]

Falkland Islands (1982)

The United Kingdom fought a nonnuclear-armed opponent once again in April 1982 when Argentina invaded the Falkland (Malvinas) Islands. The fighting was intense at times, and the British fleet faced real danger from

Argentine aircraft. Yet the conduct of the war posed little threat to Great Britain. My argument does not predict that the NNWS will avoid trying to harm the NWS. After all, the NNWS must have some conventional strategy that can outlast or inflict losses so that the NWS will negotiate. In the end, though, the fighting took place far from the core British territory, the Argentines used limited means and did not (because they lacked the ability) go beyond their limited aims, and the British suffered modest losses.[71] The actual conduct of the war, despite the geographic disparity in favor of Argentina, testifies to the British conventional advantages.

The roots of the dispute traced back to the British occupation of the islands in 1833 that ended control of the islands by what would become Argentina.[72] The intensity of the dispute had waxed and waned over the decades. In December 1981 the leaders of the Argentine military junta, President Leopoldo Galtieri, Admiral Jorge Anaya, and Brigadier General Basilio Lami Dozo, decided to invade the islands. A desire to distract from domestic problems drove the decision. As Amy Oakes notes, there is "a considerable degree of scholarly consensus regarding the degree to which the junta was influenced by the rising social unrest when it planned to invade the Falklands."[73]

Though the focus in this appendix is on the conduct of war rather than nuclear views prior to fighting, the nature of the conflict warrants a somewhat lengthier treatment.[74] Importantly, the junta did not initially expect Great Britain to respond with military force at all. If Britain did not fight, this would necessarily rule out the use of British nuclear weapons. As Oakes concludes, the "simple truth is that Argentina's leaders would not have considered an invasion if they thought the United Kingdom was prepared to go to war over the islands."[75] Galtieri later stated that "such a stormy reaction as was observed in the United Kingdom had not been foreseen."[76] Argentine diplomats in London and New York reported to Foreign Minister Nicanor Costa Méndez prior to the war that Britain would likely impose economic sanctions and sever diplomatic relations, but would avoid military action.[77] Several British actions prior to the invasion reinforced this view. Most notable was the British decision to remove its only semipermanent naval presence, the HMS *Endurance*, from the region.[78] Prime Minister Margaret Thatcher's decision to use military force surprised Argentina and even some British and Americans.

The Argentine strategy, doubting a British military response, centered on a bloodless operation to capture the Falklands, present Britain with a fait accompli, and seek negotiations. "Occupy to negotiate" was the basic objective.[79] Initial plans called for withdrawing the bulk of the invasion force and leaving behind a five- to seven-hundred-man garrison to maintain order.[80] As Richard Thornton concludes, as late as March there was no "concept, let alone plan, to defend the Malvinas against a British attempt to recapture the islands."[81]

Perceptions of American neutrality, if not support, also worked to embolden Galtieri and his lieutenants. Relations between the United States and Argentina warmed with the election of Ronald Reagan, buoyed by a shared anticommunism. Some felt Argentina had become a "privileged ally" to the United States.[82] "We expected that the US government would act as a real-go between, a real neutral friend of both parties interested in the full implementation of the UN Charter," Méndez stated. The United States might even lean on Great Britain to avoid any military action as it had done in 1956 during the Suez War.[83] The United States did initially push for a negotiated solution. Ultimately, though, the "special relationship" led the Americans to side openly with the British, dashing Argentine hopes.

The Argentines pursued their planned limited-aims offensive. They could do little more than take the islands, because they lacked significant power-projection capability. Their claims of limited intentions thus had high credibility. Argentine forces seized the islands on April 2 in an operation that resulted in no British deaths. The British estimated Argentina lost five dead and seventeen wounded.[84] With the onset of winter looming, and with it any chance of British military operations, Argentina succeeded in presenting Britain with a fait accompli and sought negotiations.

Once it was clear Britain would not negotiate, the Argentines undertook few defensive preparations. They neglected to extend the runway at Port Stanley to enable the deployment of several types of aircraft, forcing them to fly from the mainland, which reduced combat capability. The Argentine commander, General Mario Menéndez, dispersed his troops in static positions ill-suited to fending off a British attack. Argentina's best units remained deployed along the Chilean border.[85]

The British forces engaged were qualitatively superior to their Argentine counterparts.[86] Argentina had the advantage of fighting much closer to home, though. Buenos Aires sought to inflict sufficient damage on the British task force to deny Britain the ability to retake the islands or, at the least, make the effort to retake the islands too costly. While this would weaken British power projection abilities, it would not leave Britain defenseless. Argentina's task was aided by the limited air support that the British fleet could muster, and British surface vessels were particularly vulnerable to the French-made long-range Exocet missiles. US estimates were cognizant of the challenges that Britain would face and the potential for British losses. Nevertheless, as a US National Security Council briefing report noted on April 28, "Britain has the means—whatever Argentina does—to isolate the islands, disable the airstrip, and attack the defenders, who are likely to run short of supplies in three weeks."[87]

In any event, the conduct of the war ended up inflicting only modest losses on British forces, with Argentina sustaining relatively larger losses. On May 1, the British task force executed an attack against various military targets to convince the Argentines a landing was imminent.

The British engaged four Argentine Mirage III fighter-attack aircraft, destroying two while losing one Harrier aircraft. Britain suffered minor damage to surface ships, although in one case the Argentine planes barely missed the destroyer *Glamorgan* with two-thousand-pound bombs. Later, the British intercepted two Canberra light bombers, destroying one. The response was actually much less than Argentina had intended. Argentina dispatched fifty aircraft from land and their aircraft carrier, the *Vienticinco de Mayo*, to assault the British forces. Yet a third of the aircraft were forced to turn back when they failed to connect with airborne refueling tankers. Thirty planes did manage to reach the Falklands, but only six managed to locate British forces.[88]

The Argentine navy recognized their vulnerability to British submarines and proceeded cautiously. The British located and disabled the Argentine submarine *Santa Fe* on April 25. After briefly moving toward the Falkland Islands, by May 2 Argentine surface ships had turned back toward the mainland.[89] In what became a contentious incident, the submarine HMS *Conqueror* torpedoed the cruiser *Belgrano*. The World War II–era *Belgrano* sank within an hour, killing 321 Argentine sailors.[90] The Argentine navy subsequently refused to venture forth for the duration of the conflict, remaining within twelve miles of the Argentine coast.[91] That policy had the virtue that it minimized Argentine naval losses, which would otherwise have been higher. It also accounts for the discrepancy in the number of surface vessels damaged between the two opponents. Simply put, the Royal Navy was engaged throughout the fight, the Argentine navy was not.

The Argentine air forces proved the most dangerous for the British. The most dramatic success came on May 4. Exploiting a gap in British low-level aircraft defenses, two Super Étendard aircraft each launched one Exocet missile at the British task force. One struck and disabled the destroyer HMS *Sheffield*, which later sank.[92] After British troops began landing, forcing British ships to operate near the islands, Argentine aircraft managed to sink several British ships, including the frigates *Ardent* and *Antelope* (May 21 and 23–24), the logistic landing ship *Galahad* (June 8), the cargo ship *Atlantic Conveyer* (May 25), and the destroyer *Coventry* (May 25).[93] Several more sustained damage. Importantly, though, Argentina failed to hit either British aircraft carrier or troop transports prior to the landings. As D. George Boyce notes, British aircraft armed with Sidewinder AIM-9L missiles "forced the Argentine pilots to deliver their bombs from a low altitude without adequate time for defusing—which resulted in the large number of Argentine bombs which hit their targets but failed to explode."[94]

The air attacks were taking a significant toll on Argentina, though. It is doubtful their air force could have sustained the fight much longer. During the week of May 21 alone, Argentina lost twenty-one planes.[95]

Indicative of the direction the fighting was going, on May 25 US Secretary of State Alexander Haig implored Thatcher "not to try to crush the Argentines."[96] British and Argentine accounts of total aircraft losses differ. The British Ministry of Defense reported they faced 120 fast jet aircraft, along with numerous other aircraft. Argentina claims it deployed eighty-one Mirage IIIs, Vs, and A4 Skyhawks. The British report the destruction of 109 Argentine aircraft of all kinds, including thirty-one Skyhawks and twenty-six Mirage jets. Argentina reports the loss of only thirty-four Mirages and Skyhawks—though even that smaller number would account for more than 40 percent of the force Argentina claims to have deployed.[97] The British lost a total of five Harriers to ground fire, none in air-to-air combat.[98]

Land engagements ended in decisive British victories. The fighting was intense at times—involving aircraft, artillery, and light armor alongside infantry maneuvers—but resulted in few British casualties. On April 25, British soldiers retook South Georgia to the south and east of the Falklands with little resistance. On May 15, a British special forces raiding party surprised one hundred Argentine defenders at Pebble Island, destroying "eleven Pucara turboprop ground support aircraft, an ammunition dump, and other installations before departing."[99] British forces landed at San Carlos, East Falklands, on May 21. Argentine troops did not seriously contest the landings. Indeed, throughout the campaign Argentina failed to mount any counterattacks against the British advance. British mobility and superior firepower overwhelmed the Argentine defenders. The main assault on Port Stanley began on June 12; Argentina surrendered on June 14.[100] "Even without the word 'unconditional,' the surrender was total and comprehensive," writes Freedman.[101]

In this environment—an initial belief that Britain would not oppose the invasion, a limited-aims offensive against an isolated target, and subsequent fighting that posed little danger to British territory or nuclear forces—it would be surprising that the junta discussed the British nuclear arsenal at all. Yet they did just that. Based on interviews with former officials, T. V. Paul reports that Buenos Aires "considered the chances of Britain using its nuclear forces against Argentina, in the event of its losing the conventional battle."[102] This reflects a basic costs-benefits logic. According to one Argentine account, a West German official remarked after the war that it was best for Argentina they had not done more damage to the British fleet. "Queried about this apparent contradiction, he elaborated: 'otherwise, Mrs. Thatcher's government would have resorted to the use of nuclear weapons against the mainland.'"[103] While it is unclear whether that particular exchange occurred, former Ministry of Defense official Michael Quinlan recalls that Thatcher "would have been prepared actually to consider nuclear weapons had the Falklands gone sour on her." In particular, had Britain lost an aircraft carrier, Thatcher told Quinlan, she "would have been willing to face up to the real eventuality of [nuclear] use."[104] It is unlikely Britain ever came close to using nuclear weapons, given the conventional asymmetry and low danger to Britain throughout, but the basic logic in these accounts is consistent with the framework developed in this book: nuclear use is more likely to be considered as the military benefits increase and begin to outweigh the associated costs. In the end, Lawrence Freedman writes in the official British history of the conflict that during his research he "found no references to any consideration of nuclear employment. This was never taken seriously as a realistic possibility." He adds that "while there was never any thought of strategic nuclear use the possibility of tactical nuclear use was less readily dismissed." The British leadership also took pains to transfer nuclear weapons onboard surface naval vessels to the carriers, which had more robust safety measures, and eventually move them back to Great Britain.[105]

In addition, similar to the other cases examined in this book, there is some evidence that the NNWS discounted the likelihood of nuclear use because it believed external actors would constrain the nuclear opponent. As Paul notes, Argentine officials believed that "the US and USSR would have prevented it if the British threatened to use nuclear weapons in a small conventional theater."[106] Argentina could also point to global public opinion against nuclear weapons—heightened during the 1980s amid renewed Cold War tensions and debates about impending American intermediate nuclear force deployments to Europe—as a further restraint against nuclear use.[107] Argentine officials went so far as to raise the issue publicly. "I don't think a country with nuclear arms will use them against a country that doesn't have them," the head of the Argentine National Atomic Energy Commission Castro Madero argued on May 28. Echoing language used by Stalin and Mao to deter nuclear threats, he went on to characterize nuclear discussions as a "psychological action" against Argentina.[108] For their part, the British were aware of potential psychological advantages of conventional and nuclear strikes. During a British cabinet meeting on April 16, Thatcher highlighted that although "there was in reality no intention of attacking the Argentine mainland, there might be some military advantage in the Argentines being afraid of that; the fact that the Vulcans were being given conventional bombing practice in Scotland was in any case likely to become known. . . . Though the Vulcans were associated in the public mind with their long-standing nuclear role, there was of course no question of their carrying nuclear weapons in the present context."[109] Left unexplained was what might lead the "present context" to change.

There is evidence Argentine leaders believed that their own nuclear weapon might offset the British nuclear advantage. As Thornton concludes, for many at the time, "a nuclear weapons capability would permit Argentina to deal with Great Britain over the Falkland Islands dispute from a position of equality, if not strength."[110] To be sure, at most Argentina explored a nuclear device, and Brazil likely loomed larger in Argentine calculations.[111] That did not stop CIA analysts from worrying during the conflict that "the Argentine leadership might somehow calculate that the chances for a favorable outcome would have been greater if Argentina possessed a nuclear weapons capability."[112] Argentina provided reasons for such concerns. As the agency noted later that year, during the war "Buenos Aires asserted publicly that its adherence to nonproliferation rules had placed it at a clear disadvantage. . . . Buenos Aires [claimed it] could not continue to accept a discriminatory situation that denies Argentina the legitimate use of nuclear materials for its national defense." The report concluded that Argentine military leaders probably "believe that if their country had possessed nuclear weapons . . . the British would not have been so quick to send so large an expeditionary force against them."[113] Julio Carasales, a former senior Argentine foreign affairs official, would later acknowledge that the Falklands War "caused some Argentine citizens, for the only time in Argentinean history, to want the country to possess nuclear weapons. . . . The fear that their [British nuclear weapons] mere presence inspired put the Argentinean forces at a disadvantage. More than one Argentinean thus considered that the outcome could have been different, or at least the defeat would not have been so humiliating, if his country had possessed nuclear weapons, even without using them."[114]

A very large danger to Britain could generate sufficient benefits from nuclear use to offset any associated costs. Yet the nature of the participants and conduct of the war meant that the danger to the United Kingdom was low, and Argentina could gamble that Britain would not resort to nuclear strikes. The Falklands were British territory, but they were located nearly eight thousand miles from the British homeland. Their contribution to the British economy or strategic position were minimal, the islanders were not granted full British citizenship, and Britain had been reducing its presence in the South Atlantic for several years.[115] The entire fight took place on and in the immediate vicinity of the islands, which were approximately four hundred miles from Argentina.

War over Lebanon (1982)

On several occasions in the late 1970s and early 1980s Israeli forces attacked individuals associated with the Palestine Liberation Organization (PLO) who were residing in Lebanon. At the same time, Syria had intervened in the Lebanese Civil War in 1976, occupying Eastern Lebanon and attempting to maintain order.[116] This put Syrian and Israeli units in close proximity, and the two occasionally collided, fighting briefly in April 1981, after which Syria deployed some surface-to-air missile units to Lebanon.[117] Limited attacks against the PLO proved insufficient from Israel's perspective, and so Israeli leadership, spearheaded by Defense Minister Ariel Sharon, elected for a larger operation. In particular, Israel sought to eliminate the PLO presence in Beirut. The assault would necessarily bring Israeli Defense Forces (IDF) into contact with the Syrian military, which Israel sought to expel from Lebanon.[118] The immediate catalyst for the war came on June 3 when the Abu Nidal organization, a splinter group of the PLO, gravely wounded Israel's ambassador to the United Kingdom.[119] Israel launched Operation Peace for Galilee on June 6; Israeli forces would remain in Lebanon until May 2000,[120] their operations there directed largely at various non-state actors. In this section I focus on the portion of the fighting against Syria, which constituted a war between two states.

The initial Israeli invasion consisted of two major advances to attack the PLO and engage Syria. The Israeli cabinet was reluctant to authorize military operations against Syrian forces, and so the IDF sought to threaten Syrian forces to provoke a response.[121] During a series of clashes around Ayn Zhaltah on June 8, the Syrians inflicted only minimal damage but managed to delay the IDF. As Kenneth Pollack concludes, that delay "was one of the most important factors in preventing the complete destruction of the Syrian army in Lebanon."[122] That same day, Israeli forces also attacked a Syrian task force at Jazzin. On June 10 the IDF broke through Syrian defenses in the Bekaa Valley and proceeded methodically northward. In addition to the ground fighting, Israel systematically dismantled Syrian air defenses in Lebanon and easily defeated Syrian Air Force (SAF) efforts to contest the skies. Through September the SAF lost eighty-six Soviet-made MiGs to the Israeli Air Force without destroying a single Israeli aircraft.[123] Israel consistently defeated Syrian troops but was unable to completely rout its Syrian opponents, which generally retreated in good order. As a result, Syria remained a factor in Lebanon.[124]

The conduct of the war resulted in little danger to the NWS, consistent with my argument. Syria's President Hafez Asad cautiously observed the Israeli invasion and sought to avoid overtly provoking the Israeli forces. Once fighting began, Syria fought primarily on the defensive, setting ambushes against advancing Israeli units at various places. The fighting took place in Lebanon; Syria did not threaten Israeli positions in the Golan Heights or the Israeli homeland. Syrian aims centered primarily on maintaining the status quo of their position in Lebanon, avoiding a massive military defeat, and guarding against any possible Israeli advance on Damascus itself. Though Syrian forces fought with determination at various points, they inflicted only modest losses on the IDF. Pollack reports the grim relative tally: "the Syrians lost 1,200 dead, 3,000 wounded, and 296 prisoners in addition to 300–350 tanks, 150 APCS [armored personnel carriers], nearly 100 artillery pieces, twelve helicopters, 86 aircraft, and 298 SAM [surface-to-air missile] batteries. Against the Syrians during 6–25 June, the

Israelis suffered 195 killed and 872 wounded in addition to 30 tanks lost (with another 100 damaged) and 175 APCS destroyed and damaged."[125]

War over Angola (1987)

The war over Angola was part of the broader Angolan civil wars. Angolan revolutionaries long contested Portuguese rule. The ongoing conflict contributed to a coup and popular revolution in Portugal that overthrew the fascist dictator António Salazar. Angola then achieved independence in 1975. Several different groups fought for control of the country. The Correlates of War provides one interstate war number but two separate start and end dates, breaking the conflict into two separate interstate wars. This is unusual, but there are a number of other wars that are part of longer ongoing conflicts (e.g., China versus Vietnam and Egypt versus Israel) that are similar. I include the 1987 war here to avoid arbitrarily excluding a case.

The first interstate war began in October 1975 when, as Michael Clodfelter writes, "outside intervention had rapidly turned what was basically a tribal war into an international affair."[126] That phase ended in February 1976 and involved no nuclear-armed states. The Soviet Union backed Cuba and Angola—in particular the Popular Movement for the Liberation of Angola (MPLA)—but limited its involvement to aid and advisers. Internal and unconventional fighting continued, with Angola and Cuba facing a determined guerrilla resistance from the National Union for the Total Independence of Angola (UNITA) operating primarily in southern Angola. This suited the interests of South Africa, which controlled Namibia and sought "to deny a southern Angolan sanctuary to Namibian insurgents and to maintain a buffer against the Angolan regime."[127]

In August 1987 a new Angolan offensive pressed into southern Angola. The offensive was the beginning of the second interstate war, which COW codes starting on August 4, 1987, when South Africa made the decision to undertake a sizable intervention to halt the offensive. The war occurred between, on the one side, Cuba and Angola (with Soviet-supplied equipment and advisers), and on the other, nuclear-armed South Africa. The war ended in June 1988, with a formal cease-fire on August 5 of that year. The Tripartite Agreement signed on December 22 committed the Cubans and South Africans to withdraw from Angola.[128]

South Africa faced little danger throughout the war. Rough indicators of the balance of power understate the South African advantage. For example, South Africa's per capita GDP was only slightly larger than those of Cuba (1.5:1) and Angola (1.9:1). Yet the 1985 *Military Balance* concluded that "South Africa remains the only African country capable of significant force projection operations against her neighbors." Although Angola might be capable of conventional operations against South Africa, even with Soviet and Cuban assistance Angola "is stretched to her limits containing the forces of UNITA and could not also defend against a major South African offensive."[129] As Narang concludes, "South African defense and air forces were both quantitatively and qualitatively superior to their primary regional threats, even with the deployment of Soviet surface-to-air missile batteries in the region."[130] Cuban forces were capable, but they were operating thousands of kilometers from their home and so posed little danger to South African territory.

The fighting itself took place in Angola, far from South African territory. The initial Angolan offensive advanced from the strategic town of Cuito Cuanavale into UNITA territory before being stopped in a series of conventional battles near the Lomba River by smaller South African and UNITA forces. In one particularly lopsided engagement on October 3, South African forces killed over six hundred Angolan troops and destroyed or captured 127 tanks, armored cars, and other vehicles, at a cost of one South African killed and five wounded.[131] The advance then "turned into a headlong retreat over the 120 miles back to the primary launching point at Cuito Cuanavale," writes Chester Crocker, an American diplomat at the time, who would help negotiate an end to the fighting.[132] The South Africans harassed the retreating forces the entire way. On November 15 Cuban leaders decided to reinforce the beleaguered Angolan forces to prevent a deeper UNITA–South African advance. Cuba increased its troop strength in Angola and rushed reinforcements to Cuito Cuanavale.[133] The arrival of Cuban reinforcements stabilized the defenses, though domestic South African political constraints, which prevented Pretoria from committing large numbers of reinforcements, simplified the defensive effort. The battle essentially ended in March, with South African forces shifting to a defensive posture in the area.[134]

As Cuito Cuanavale ended, Cuban forces moved to threaten southwest Angola. Cuba's Fidel Castro hoped that this would put pressure on South Africa and aid the Cuban position in negotiations.[135] As Peter Liberman notes, "Castro warned at the time that South Africa risked 'serious defeat' and hinted at an offensive into Namibia."[136] Despite the bluster, "Cuba never seriously contemplated a decisive military showdown with Pretoria," concludes Stephen Weigert. Moreover, "Castro had secretly agreed with Moscow that Cuban troops would not cross the Angolan/Namibian border."[137] Cuban-Angolan and South African forces instead fought a series of small engagements in Cunene Province. Neither side gained a decisive advantage, and combat effectively ended following bloody air and ground clashes on June 26–27.

South Africa possessed only a rudimentary nuclear capacity. As the chief of the South African Defense Forces from 1985 to 1990, General Jan Geldenhuys, recalled, "Invasions were seen as slight possibilities, adventurous transgressions of borders on such small scale that nuclear capability never came into the picture."[138] South Africa gave little thought to using its nuclear weapons against military or civilian targets. "No offensive tactical application of nuclear weapons was ever foreseen . . . as it was fully recognized that such an act would bring about nuclear retaliation on a massive scale," writes Waldo Stumpf.[139] Rather, Pretoria contemplated using the nuclear weapons in a "catalytic" manner to generate outside involvement, particularly from the United States. Andre Buys, the chair of the strategy group for the state arms procurement and production agency (Armscor) recalled that only if all efforts to elicit support failed, then "the last step would . . . be to threaten to use nuclear weapons on the battlefield in self-defense."[140]

Nuclear weapons played only a minor and indirect role in South African thinking during the Angolan War. South Africa reopened its Kalahari test site in 1987, though the precise date is contested. The activity was limited to Armscor building a hangar above a test shaft, pumping out water, and checking the shaft's readiness.[141] Buys told Liberman in 1999 that the decision was made because "for the first time the government started considering the possibility that we might lose the war militarily." Stage two of South Africa's nuclear strategy—covert signaling or secret acknowledgment of the nuclear arsenal—would "come into operation once we were confronted by a serious and escalating military threat. We got close to that in 1987 . . . in Angola."[142] As one South African counterintelligence officer noted, "we knew satellites would see the whole thing . . . Soviet and Western intelligence were suddenly convinced we were serious about nuclear weapons and the West began to put pressure on the Soviets to get the Cubans to withdraw from Angola."[143] It is debatable if the chain of events worked out this way; as noted, Castro sought to avoid a major conflict but sought some form of battlefield victory to assist in negotiations. In any event, congruent with my argument's predictions, the danger to South Africa was minimal throughout the war against Angola and Cuba.

Kosovo (1999)

The Correlates of War identifies the primary participants in the Kosovo War as the nuclear-armed United States against nonnuclear Yugoslavia (Serbia). Violence erupted in the Yugoslavian province of Kosovo in March 1998 following the killing of twenty-four ethnic Albanians by Serbian police on February 28.[144] Serbian efforts to assert control resulted in the displacement of tens of thousands of people.[145] US mediation efforts stabilized the situation briefly but ultimately collapsed as the Kosovo Liberation Army (KLA) was able to reconstitute itself, leading to Serbian redeployment of its forces.[146] President Slobodan Milošović of Yugoslavia rebuffed US demands to cede Serbian control of Kosovo. In response, NATO launched Operation Allied Force on March 24, 1999. Air strikes continued until June 9, when Serbia agreed to a peace proposal. The combination of mounting costs, Russian pressure, and the reduction in US demands put forth in the G8 (Group of 8) foreign ministers peace proposal led to Serbian acquiescence.[147]

There was no danger to the nuclear weapon state. The fighting was entirely fought in Yugoslavian territory. No NATO ground troops were used, though there is debate whether the threat of a ground invasion contributed to Serbian concessions.[148] Regardless, the campaign was fought entirely with NATO naval and air strikes, which typically operated out of range of effective Serbian counter-fire. The Correlates of War lists two American and five thousand Serbian battlefield deaths.[149] The Serbian goal to maintain rule over Kosovo and not expand the conflict were credible because Serbia could not do more; Serbia struggled to even interfere with NATO operations over its own homeland. As Phil Haun notes, Serbian strategy was limited to inflicting "combat losses on NATO aircraft and aircrew, making it either too costly for NATO to continue air operations or, at a minimum, creating tension among NATO countries that might cause a fissure in the alliance."[150] In sum, the fighting was entirely on NNWS territory, the NNWS had limited and defensive aims, and there were very low losses to the NWS.

Afghanistan (2001)

As of this writing, US combat operations continue inside Afghanistan. The United States (along with Britain and other allies) acted in response to the terrorist attacks by al-Qaeda on September 11, 2001, that destroyed the two towers of the World Trade Center in New York City and part of the Pentagon. The United States initially demanded that the Taliban government of Afghanistan hand over al-Qaeda's leaders, including Osama bin Laden, and shut down al-Qaeda training camps.[151] The Afghan government refused US demands. The interstate war phase of the conflict began on October 7, 2001, with US air strikes and ended on December 22, 2001, with the installation of the interim Afghani government led by Hamid Karzai.[152]

The danger to the United States and the United Kingdom from Afghanistan was minimal. To be sure, al-Qaeda had managed to coordinate an operation that constituted the worst attack on US soil since Pearl Harbor. Yet the interstate war with Afghanistan involved fighting far from the nuclear weapon states. The major US involvement initially was special operations forces and air strikes that assisted Northern Alliance ground forces that opposed the Taliban. Taliban and al-Qaeda fighters were unable to defeat moderately skilled opponents that had American support, though they were able to resist effectively against unskilled opponents.[153] Prior to the attack, concludes Haun, the "probability of U.S. victory against Afghanistan . . . was high and cost of fighting relatively low."[154] During the war "sixteen Americans had died in defeating the Taliban, 15 of them in (predominantly air) accidents or in friendly fire incidents. . . . Taliban losses were uncounted but numerous."[155] In sum, the interstate portion of the war was fought on NNWS territory against an adversary that fought defensively.

Notes

Introduction

1. "U.S. Strategic Bombing Survey: The Effects of the Atomic Bombings of Hiroshima and Nagasaki," June 19, 1946, President's Secretary's File, Truman Papers, https://www.truman library.org/whistlestop/study_collections/bomb/large/documents/pdfs/65.pdf.

2. Bernard Brodie, ed., *The Absolute Weapon: Atomic Power and World Order* (New York: Harcourt Brace, 1946).

3. Robert Jervis, *The Meaning of the Nuclear Revolution: Statecraft and the Prospect of Armageddon* (Ithaca, NY: Cornell University Press, 1989).

4. The Correlates of War data code the NNWS as starting the war or underlying militarized interstate dispute (MID) half the time: Korean War, 1950; Suez War, 1956; Six Day War, 1967; War of Attrition, 1969; October War, 1973; Falklands War, 1982; War over Angola, 1987; Gulf War, 1991. I found 657 MIDs between two states, or dyads, when only one possessed nuclear weapons. Although there are a number of challenges to coding initiation, as I discuss below, using the MID coding, the NNWS initiated approximately 36 percent of disputes. That number increases to 43 percent when including an NNWS that joined on the initiator's side. Using the International Crisis Behavior (ICB) dataset, I found 119 overall crises (many containing multiple dyads) where only one side had nuclear weapons from 1946 to 2015. ICB identified the NNWS as the "triggering entity" in approximately 61 percent of the 87 cases that had a single state actor as the triggering entity. War data are from the Dyadic Inter-state War Data at http://www.correlatesofwar.org/data-sets/COW-war. MID data are from the Dyadic MID data version 3.1, at http://www.correlatesofwar.org/data-sets/MIDs. See Zeev Maoz, Paul L. Johnson, Jasper Kaplan, Fiona Ogunkoya, and Aaron Shreve, "The Dyadic Militarized Interstate Disputes (MIDs) Dataset Version 3.0: Logic, Characteristics, and Comparisons to Alternative Datasets," *Journal of Conflict Resolution* 63, no. 3 (2019): 811–35. ICB data are from the Dyadic-Level Crisis Data and System-level data, Version 12, at https://sites.duke.edu/icbdata/data-collections/.

5. Brodie, *Absolute Weapon*, 85. Brodie relegated the comment to a footnote. For the Schelling quote see Robert Ayson, *Thomas Schelling and the Nuclear Age: Strategy as Social Science* (London: Routledge, 2004), 114.

6. Robert A. Pape, *Bombing to Win: Air Power and Coercion in War* (Ithaca, NY: Cornell University Press, 1996), 38. Pape highlights various constraints on nuclear use but does not develop

them. See also the discussion in John J. Mearsheimer, *The Tragedy of Great Power Politics*, 2nd ed. (2001; New York: W. W. Norton, 2014), 129–30.

7. James J. Wirtz, "Conclusions," in *Complex Deterrence: Strategy in the Global Age*, ed. T. V. Paul, Patrick M. Morgan, and James J. Wirtz (Chicago: University of Chicago Press, 2009), 322. Wirtz adds that this expectation is frequently challenged, calling traditional deterrence arguments into question.

8. Robert Jervis, *The Meaning of the Nuclear Revolution: Statecraft and the Prospect of Armageddon* (Ithaca, NY: Cornell University Press, 1989), chap. 1. See also Kenneth N. Waltz, "Nuclear Myths and Political Realities," *American Political Science Review* 84, no. 3 (September 1990): 731–45.

9. Mark S. Bell and Nicholas L. Miller argue that states frequently expand their interests upon acquiring nuclear weapons. This line of argument again points to the general belief that nuclear weapons convey coercive benefits. See Mark S. Bell and Nicholas L. Miller, "Questioning the Effects of Nuclear Weapons on Conflict," *Journal of Conflict Resolution* 59, no. 1 (February 2015): 74–92, and Mark S. Bell, "Beyond Emboldenment: How Acquiring Nuclear Weapons Can Change Foreign Policy," *International Security* 40, no. 1 (Summer 2015): 87–119.

10. Throughout this book I follow Thomas C. Schelling and use the term "coercion" to include both deterrence and compellence. In both cases a state attempts to influence an opponent's behavior: either to not act (deterrence) or to act (compellence) when the adversary would prefer the opposite. Thomas C. Schelling, *Arms and Influence* (New Haven, CT: Yale University Press, 1966). See also Robert J. Art, "To What Ends Military Power?," *International Security* 4, no. 4 (Spring 1980): 3–35; and Robert J. Art and Kelly M. Greenhill, "Coercion: An Analytical Overview," in *Coercion: The Power to Hurt in International Politics*, ed. Kelly M. Greenhill and Peter Krause (Oxford: Oxford University Press, 2018).

11. Marc Trachtenberg, "The Influence of Nuclear Weapons in the Cuban Missile Crisis," *International Security* 10, no. 1 (Summer 1985): 137–63; Daryl G. Press, *Calculating Credibility: How Leaders Assess Military Threats* (Ithaca, NY: Cornell University Press, 2005); Keir A. Lieber, *War and the Engineers: The Primacy of Politics over Technology* (Ithaca, NY: Cornell University Press, 2005).

12. Kyle Beardsley and Victor Asal, "Winning with the Bomb," *Journal of Conflict Resolution* 53, no. 2 (April 2009): 282, 297.

13. Erik Garzke and Dong-Joon Jo, "Bargaining, Nuclear Proliferation, and Interstate Disputes," *Journal of Conflict Resolution* 53, no. 2 (April 2009): 209–33.

14. Matthew Kroenig, *The Logic of American Nuclear Strategy: Why Strategic Superiority Matters* (Oxford: Oxford University Press, 2018): 123; Matthew Kroenig, "Nuclear Superiority and the Balance of Resolve: Explaining Nuclear Crisis Outcomes," *International Organization* 67, no. 1 (January 2013): 141–71. For a review of studies that find nuclear-armed states are able to successfully compel opponents, see Todd S. Sechser and Matthew Fuhrmann, *Nuclear Weapons and Coercive Diplomacy* (Cambridge: Cambridge University Press, 2017), 7–8, 34–38.

15. Sechser and Fuhrmann, *Nuclear Weapons and Coercive Diplomacy*, 17, 15, 59. See also Todd S. Sechser and Matthew Fuhrmann, "Crisis Bargaining and Nuclear Blackmail," *International Organization* 67, no. 1 (January 2013): 173–95. For general statements that nuclear weapons are useful for deterrence but not compellence see, for example, Waltz, "Nuclear Myths and Political Realities"; Jervis, *Meaning of the Nuclear Revolution*, esp. 29–35; Stephen Van Evera, *Causes of War: Power and the Roots of Conflict* (Ithaca, NY: Cornell University Press, 1999), 246. For evidence that a majority, but by no means all, American IR faculty and former national security policy makers share this view see Paul C. Avey, "MAD and Taboo: Expert Views on Nuclear Weapons," paper presented at the 2018 annual meeting of the American Political Science Association.

16. Matthew Fuhrmann and Todd S. Sechser, "Signaling Alliance Commitments: Hand-Tying and Sunk Costs in Extended Nuclear Deterrence," *American Journal of Political Science* 58, no. 4 (October 2014): 919–35. See also James D. Fearon, "Signaling versus the Balance of Power and Interests: An Empirical Test of a Crisis Bargaining Model," *Journal of Conflict Resolution* 38, no. 2 (1994): 253–57.

17. To be sure, nuclear weapons may generally provide states with deterrent benefits. That nevertheless leaves a large number of important exceptions that require an explanation. Those exceptions are the focus of this book.

18. The strategic-proliferation literature is large and disagrees on the precise conditions under which states will acquire nuclear weapons and the force structure they will ultimately construct. Nevertheless, these explanations share the key intuition that states seek nuclear weapons to enhance their security: to better deter and compel opponents. See, for example, Vipin Narang, *Nuclear Strategy in the Modern Era: Regional Powers and International Conflict* (Princeton, NJ: Princeton University Press, 2014); Nuno P. Monteiro and Alexandre Debs, "The Strategic Logic of Proliferation," *International Security* 39, no. 2 (Fall 2014): 7–51; Gene Gerzhoy, "Alliance Coercion and Nuclear Restraint: How the United States Thwarted West Germany's Nuclear Ambitions," *International Security* 39, no. 4 (Spring 2015): 91–129; Nicholas L. Miller, "Nuclear Dominoes: A Self-Defeating Prophecy?," *Security Studies* 23, no. 1 (January–March 2014): 33–73; Bradley A. Thayer, "The Causes of Nuclear Proliferation and the Utility of the Nuclear Non-proliferation Regime," *Security Studies* 4, no. 3 (July–September 1995): 463–519.

19. M. Taylor Fravel and Evan S. Medeiros, "China's Search for Assured Retaliation: The Evolution of Chinese Nuclear Strategy and Force Structure," *International Security* 35, no. 2 (Fall 2010): 61.

20. For a similar point regarding disputes between two nuclear powers with asymmetric conventional capabilities see Jasen J. Castillo, "Deliberate Escalation: Nuclear Strategies to Deter or to Stop Conventional Attacks," in Greenhill and Krause, *Coercion*, 293. Analysts have applied this basic point to other instances as well, notably US nuclear strategy in the Cold War against the Soviet Union when the latter possessed conventional superiority in Europe, as well as to nuclear-armed states facing overwhelming conventional adversaries today.

21. I thank a reviewer for raising this point.

22. Kroenig, *Logic of American Nuclear Strategy*, 31.

23. Art and Greenhill, "Coercion," 6. In addition to the specific quotes cited in this paragraph see Patrick M. Morgan, *Deterrence Now* (Cambridge: Cambridge University Press, 2003), 2–3; Maria Sperandei, "Bridging Deterrence and Compellence: An Alternative Approach to the Study of Coercive Diplomacy," *International Studies Review* 8, no. 2 (June 2006): esp. 259–61.

24. Marc Trachtenberg, "Waltzing to Armageddon," *National Interest*, Fall 2002, 147.

25. For instance, compare the initiator coding for wars from the Correlates of War Interstate War data with the list by Dan Reiter, Alan Stam, and Michael Horowitz. Specific cases are often contentious; Reiter et al. note that North Vietnam could plausibly be coded as starting the Vietnam War against the United States. Even cases where the NNWS is widely regarded as the initiator can follow very different paths. Both Argentina and Egypt "initiated" wars against a nuclear opponent. Argentina's leaders launched an initially bloodless effort to capture the Falkland Islands, hoping that Britain would not react at all; Egyptian leaders sought to immediately engage Israeli forces in October 1973. Zeev Maoz, Paul L. Johnson, Aaron Shreve, Fiona Ogunkoya, Jasper Kaplan, "Dyadic MID Codebook—Version 3.0," May 24, 2018, 9. Dan Reiter, Allan C. Stam, and Michael C. Horowitz, "A Revised Look at Interstate Wars, 1816–2007: Appendix," October 15, 2014, 18. Miscoding some cases is not problematic if the errors are (1) random and (2) there are a large number of observations. Interstate wars are rare events, and the number of nuclear-armed states few. When dealing with small numbers, changing the coding of even a few data points can easily lead to different results. On these points see Erik Gartzke, "An Apology for Numbers in the Study of National Security . . . if an Apology Is Really Necessary," H-Diplo | ISSF Forum, no. 2 (2014): 82; Vipin Narang, "The Use and Abuse of Large-N Methods in Nuclear Studies," H-Diplo | ISSF Forum, no. 2 (2014): 91–97; Alexander H. Montgomery and Scott D. Sagan, "The Perils of Predicting Proliferation," *Journal of Conflict Resolution* 53, no. 2 (April 2009): esp. 310–13.

26. Richard K. Betts, *Nuclear Blackmail and Nuclear Balance* (Washington, DC: Brookings Institution, 1987), 6, see also 135–41.

27. James D. Fearon, "Domestic Political Audience Costs and the Escalation of International Disputes," *American Political Science Review* 88, no. 3 (September 1994): 578; James D. Fearon,

"Signaling versus the Balance of Power and Interests: An Empirical Test of a Crisis Bargaining Model," *Journal of Conflict Resolution* 38, no. 2 (June 1994): 246–48; Todd S. Sechser, "Goliath's Curse: Coercive Threats and Asymmetric Power," *International Organization* 64 (Fall 2010): 627–60; T. V. Paul, *Asymmetric Conflicts: War Initiation by Weaker Powers* (Cambridge: Cambridge University Press, 1994), 16–17; Phil Haun, *Coercion, Survival, and War: Why Weak States Resist the United States* (Stanford, CA: Stanford University Press, 2015), 33–34.

28. See, for example, Charles L. Glaser and Steve Fetter, "Should the United States Reject MAD? Damage Limitation and U.S. Nuclear Strategy toward China," *International Security* 41, no. 1 (Summer 2016): 49–98; Caitlin Talmadge, "Would China Go Nuclear? Assessing the Risk of Chinese Nuclear Escalation in a Conventional War with the United States," *International Security* 41, no. 4 (Spring 2017): 88–90; Sumit Ganguly, "Nuclear Stability in South Asia," *International Security* 33, no. 2 (Fall 2008): 45–70; S. Paul Kapur, "India and Pakistan's Unstable Peace: Why Nuclear South Asia Is Not Like Cold War Europe," *International Security* 30, no. 2 (Fall 2005): 127–52; Vipin Narang, "Posturing for Peace? Pakistan's Nuclear Postures and South Asian Stability," *International Security* 34, no. 3 (Winter 2009/10): 38–78.

29. See, for example, Jan Ludvik, *Nuclear Asymmetry and Deterrence: Theory, Policy and History* (London: Routledge, 2017); Kroenig, "Nuclear Superiority"; Keir A. Lieber and Daryl G. Press, "The End of MAD? The Nuclear Dimension of U.S. Primacy," *International Security* 30, no. 4 (Spring 2006): 7–44.

30. Jervis, *Meaning of the Nuclear Revolution*, chap. 1; Charles L. Glaser, *Analyzing Strategic Nuclear Policy* (Princeton, NJ: Princeton University Press, 1990); Waltz, "Nuclear Myths and Political Realities."

31. Francis J. Gavin, *Nuclear Statecraft: History and Strategy in America's Atomic Age* (Ithaca, NY: Cornell University Press, 2012), chap. 8.

32. For examples of each position see John Mueller, *Atomic Obsession: Nuclear Alarmism from Hiroshima to Al-Qaeda* (Oxford: Oxford University Press, 2010), 29–54; John Mueller, "The Essential Irrelevance of Nuclear Weapons: Stability in the Postwar World," *International Security* 13, no. 2 (Fall 1988): 55–79; Colin S. Gray and Keith Payne, "Victory Is Possible," *Foreign Policy* 39 (Summer 1980): 14–27; Nina Tannenwald, *The Nuclear Taboo: The United States and the Non-use of Nuclear Weapons since 1945* (Cambridge: Cambridge University Press, 2007), 18–19, 30–38, 45, 370–74; Nina Tannenwald, "Stigmatizing the Bomb: Origins of the Nuclear Taboo," *International Security* 29, no. 4 (Spring 2005): 41.

33. In addition to sources cited in notes 12–14 above see Gavin, *Nuclear Statecraft*; Francis J. Gavin, "Politics, History and the Ivory Tower–Policy Gap in the Nuclear Proliferation Debate," *Journal of Strategic Studies* 35, no. 4 (August 2012): 573–600; Austin Long and Brendan Rittenhouse Green, "Stalking the Secure Second Strike: Intelligence, Counterforce, and Nuclear Strategy," *Journal of Strategic Studies* 38, nos. 1–2 (2015): 38–73; Brendan R. Green and Austin Long, "The MAD Who Wasn't There: Soviet Reactions to the Late Cold War Nuclear Balance," *Security Studies* 26, no. 4 (October–December 2017): 606–41; Keir A. Lieber and Daryl G. Press, "The New Era of Counterforce: Technological Change and the Future of Nuclear Deterrence," *International Security* 41, no. 4 (Spring 2017): 9–49. See also Mearsheimer, *Tragedy of Great Power Politics*, 128–33, 230–32.

34. Kenneth N. Waltz, *Man, the State, and War: A Theoretical Analysis* (New York: Columbia University Press, 1959), 236; Glenn H. Snyder, "The Balance of Power and the Balance of Terror," in *The Balance of Power*, ed. Paul Seabury (San Francisco: Chandler, 1965), 184–201; Robert Rauchhaus, "Evaluating the Nuclear Peace Hypothesis: A Quantitative Approach," *Journal of Conflict Resolution* 53, no. 2 (April 2009): 258–77. For a review see David J. Karl, "Proliferation Optimism and Pessimism Revisited," *Journal of Strategic Studies* 34, no. 4 (August 2011): 619–41. For a critique see Jervis, *Meaning of the Nuclear Revolution*, 19–22.

35. See, for example, Tannenwald, *Nuclear Taboo*; Avner Cohen, "Nuclear Arms in Crisis under Secrecy: Israel and the Lessons of the 1967 and 1973 Wars," in *Planning the Unthinkable: How New Nuclear Powers Will Use Nuclear, Biological, and Chemical Weapons*, ed. Peter R. Lavoy, Scott D. Sagan, and James J. Wirtz (Ithaca, NY: Cornell University Press, 2000), 104–24; George H. Quester, *Nuclear First Strike: Consequence of a Broken Taboo* (Baltimore: Johns Hopkins University Press, 2006); T. V. Paul, *The Tradition of Non-use of Nuclear Weapons* (Stanford, CA: Stanford

University Press, 2009); T. V. Paul, "Taboo or Tradition? The Non-use of Nuclear Weapons in World Politics," *Review of International Studies* 36, no. 4 (October 2010): 853–63.

36. Tannenwald, *Nuclear Taboo*, 3, 372; Paul, *Tradition of Non-use*, chap. 7; T. V. Paul, "Power, Influence, and Nuclear Weapons: A Reassessment," in *The Absolute Weapon Revisited: Nuclear Arms and the Emerging International Order*, ed. T. V. Paul, Richard J. Harknett, and James J. Wirtz (Ann Arbor: University of Michigan Press, 1998), 19–46; Peter Gizewski, "From Winning Weapon to Destroyer of Worlds: The Nuclear Taboo in International Politics," *International Journal* 51, no. 3 (Summer 1996): 397–419; Paul Huth and Bruce Russett, "Deterrence Failure and Crisis Escalation," *International Studies Quarterly* 32, no. 1 (March 1988): 29–45; Robert Farley, "The Long Shadow of the Falklands War, *National Interest*, September 8, 2014, http://nationalinterest.org/feature/the-long-shadow-the-falklands-war-11224?page=show.

37. Paul, *Tradition of Non-use*, 144.

38. Michael S. Gerson, "Conventional Deterrence in the Second Nuclear Age," *Parameters* 39, no. 3 (Autumn 2009): 35.

39. Huth and Russett, "Deterrence Failure and Crisis Escalation," 38, see also 34–35; Bruce Martin Russett, "Extended Deterrence with Nuclear Weapons: How Necessary, How Acceptable?," *Review of Politics* 50, no. 2 (Spring 1988): 290.

40. Tannenwald, *Nuclear Taboo*, 372, see also 3. Tannenwald's discussion of the role of normative and material considerations in accounting for nuclear-armed state decision making is much more nuanced; see esp. 53.

41. McGeorge Bundy, *Danger and Survival: Choices about the Bomb in the First Fifty Years* (New York: Random House, 1988), 588. Bundy did not expand on the tradition concept, but it contained a normative component; see 586–88.

42. Dianne Pfundstein Chamberlain, *Cheap Threats: Why the United States Struggles to Coerce Weak States* (Washington, DC: Georgetown University Press, 2016), 45–47. On American public opinion toward military actions that result in civilian deaths see Scott D. Sagan and Benjamin A. Valentino, "Revisiting Hiroshima in Iran: What Americans Really Think about Using Nuclear Weapons and Killing Noncombatants," *International Security* 42, no. 1 (Summer 2017): 41–79.

43. They thus focus on the regulative rather than the constitutive aspects of the norm.

44. Sechser and Fuhrmann, *Nuclear Weapons and Coercive Diplomacy*, 45–52.

45. Narang, *Nuclear Strategy in the Modern Era*, chaps. 9–10; Vipin Narang, "What Does It Take to Deter? Regional Power Nuclear Postures and International Conflict," *Journal of Conflict Resolution* 57, no. 3 (June 2013): 478–508; Vipin Narang, "Posturing for Peace?"

46. This draws on the basic issue of resolve discussed in "The Argument" section earlier in this chapter. I focus on existing political disputes in which both sides have demonstrated some level of resolve over the issue. A distinct but related claim is that once in a dispute, the weaker side compensates for lack of relative capability with intensity that occasionally allows it to prevail. My argument makes no claim about which side will win the conflict; I focus on the role nuclear weapons play in shaping the scope of the conflict. For discussions and applications to asymmetric conflict see Paul, *Asymmetric Conflict*, 16–18; Haun, *Coercion, Survival, and War*, 12–13, 36; Alexander L. George and Richard Smoke, *Deterrence in American Foreign Policy: Theory and Practice* (New York: Columbia University Press, 1974), 530–31, 550–61; Paul K. Huth, "Deterrence and International Conflict: Empirical Findings and Theoretical Debates," *Annual Review of Political Science* 2 (1999): 34; Glenn H. Snyder and Paul Diesing, *Conflict among Nations: Bargaining, Decision Making, and System Structure in International Crises* (Princeton, NJ: Princeton University Press, 1977), 190, 456, 529. For an excellent overview of how different approaches treat resolve, see Chamberlain, *Cheap Threats*, 7–13.

47. Geoffrey Blainey, *The Causes of War*, 3rd ed. (London: Macmillan, 1988).

48. Dan Reiter, "Exploring the Bargaining Model of War," *Perspectives on Politics* 1, no. 1 (March 2003): 33.

49. For example, Michelle Benson, "Extending the Bounds of Power Transition Theory," *International Interactions* 33, no. 3 (2007): 211–15; William Moul, "Power Parity, Preponderance, and War between Great Powers, 1816–1989," *Journal of Conflict Resolution* 47, no. 4 (2003): 468–89; A. F. K. Organski and Jacek Kugler, *The War Ledger* (Chicago: University of Chicago

Press, 1980). Many studies that include a proxy for relative power as a control variable in their analysis similarly find that increasing power asymmetries make war less likely.

50. David Cortright and Raimo Väyrynen, *Toward Nuclear Zero* (New York: Routledge, 2010), 91; James E. Doyle, "Why Eliminate Nuclear Weapons?," *Survival* 55, no. 1 (2013): 7–34.

1. The Strategic Logic of Nuclear Monopoly

1. This is the basis of nuclear deterrent and compellent threats. In those cases, nuclear weapons are not detonated but are used in the sense that opponents assess the consequences of detonation and alter their behavior accordingly.

2. This draws from Robert A. Pape, *Bombing to Win: Air Power and Coercion in War* (Ithaca, NY: Cornell University Press, 1996), chap. 2; Glenn Snyder, *Deterrence by Punishment and Denial* (Princeton, NJ: Princeton University Center of International Studies, 1959); Robert J. Art, "To What Ends Military Power?," *International Security* 4, no. 4 (Spring 1980): 3–35; Terence Roehrig, *Japan, South Korea, and the United States Nuclear Umbrella: Deterrence after the Cold War* (New York: Columbia University Press, 2017), chap. 1. The authors use slightly different terminology, but the core insights focus on whether one is seeking to inflict costs by harming the civilian population or weakening military capabilities.

3. Wilson D. Miscamble, *The Most Controversial Decision: Truman, the Atomic Bombs, and the Defeat of Japan* (Cambridge: Cambridge University Press, 2011); Barton J. Bernstein, "Eclipsed by Hiroshima and Nagasaki: Early Thinking about Tactical Nuclear Weapons," *International Security* 15, no. 4 (Spring 1991): 149–73; Pape, *Bombing to Win*, 94–96, 104–6. For a dissenting view that the primary intent was to intimidate the Soviet Union see Gar Alperovitz, *Atomic Diplomacy: Hiroshima and Potsdam; The Use of the Atomic Bomb and the American Confrontation with Soviet Power* (New York: Vintage, 1965). Whether the nuclear strikes were the main reason for the Japanese surrender is a separate question from the motivation for the US strikes. On Japanese decision making see Pape, *Bombing to Win*, chap. 4; Ward Wilson, "The Winning Weapon? Rethinking Nuclear Weapons in Light of Hiroshima," *International Security* 31, no. 4 (Spring 2007): 162–79.

4. The classic discussion of nuclear weapons effects is Samuel Glasstone and Philip J. Dolan, eds., *The Effects of Nuclear Weapons*, 3rd ed. (Washington, DC: US Department of Defense, 1977).

5. Lynn Eden, *Whole World on Fire: Organizations, Knowledge, and Nuclear Weapons Devastation* (Ithaca, NY: Cornell University Press, 2004), 25.

6. Eden, 20. On US ICBMs see Hans M. Kristensen and Robert S. Norris, "United States Nuclear Forces, 2017," *Bulletin of the Atomic Scientists* 73, no. 1 (2017): 48–57.

7. "Memorandum from Secretary of State Rusk to President Johnson," May 10, 1965, *Foreign Relations of the United States* (hereafter *FRUS*), *1964–68*, vol. 18, *Arab-Israeli Dispute, 1964–1967*, document 214, https://history.state.gov/historicaldocuments/frus1964-68v18/d214. See also the discussion of nuclear weapons against civilian and military targets in Korea and Vietnam in Nina Tannenwald, "The Nuclear Taboo: The United States and the Normative Basis of Nuclear Non-use," *International Organization* 53, no. 3 (Summer 1999): 433–68.

8. Quoted in Shlomo Aronson, "David Ben-Gurion, Levi Eshkol and the Struggle over Dimona: A Prologue to the Six-Day War and Its (Un)Anticipated Results," *Israel Affairs* 15, no. 2 (April 2009): 117.

9. Alexander B. Downes, *Targeting Civilians in War* (Ithaca, NY: Cornell University Press, 2008), 118.

10. Nina Tannenwald, *The Nuclear Taboo: The United States and the Non-use of Nuclear Weapons since 1945* (Cambridge: Cambridge University Press, 2007), 321–23.

11. Pape, *Bombing to Win*; Edward Kaplan, *To Kill Nations: American Strategy in the Air-Atomic Age and the Rise of Mutually Assured Destruction* (Ithaca, NY: Cornell University Press, 2015), 11–14. In arguably the most successful case of independent air power, US and NATO forces enjoyed complete control of the air against an overmatched and isolated Serbian

opponent. See Daniel R. Lake, "The Limits of Coercive Airpower: NATO's 'Victory' in Kosovo Revisited," *International Security* 34, no. 1 (Summer 2009): 83–112.

12. Dianne Pfundstein Chamberlain, *Cheap Threats: Why the United States Struggles to Coerce Weak States* (Washington, DC: Georgetown University Press, 2016); Michael S. Gerson, "Conventional Deterrence in the Second Nuclear Age," *Parameters* 39, no. 3 (Autumn 2009): 43.

13. On the limits of precision-guided weapons against a capable adversary see Stephen Biddle and Ivan Oelrich, "Future Warfare in the Western Pacific: Chinese Antiaccess / Area Denial, U.S. AirSea Battle, and Command of the Commons in East Asia," *International Security* 41, no. 1 (Summer 2016): 7–48.

14. On the challenges the US air defenses faced against Soviet forces see Richard K. Betts, *Nuclear Blackmail and Nuclear Balance* (Washington, DC: Brookings Institution, 1987), 147–72.

15. Christine M. Leah, *The Consequences of American Nuclear Disarmament: Strategy and Nuclear Weapons* (New York: Palgrave Macmillan, 2017), 4. Limitations in accuracy and yield have restricted the damage that most states throughout history have been able to accomplish with conventional missiles. See, for example, Steve Fetter, George N. Lewis, and Lisbeth Gronlun, "Why Were Scud Casualties So Low?," *Nature* 361 (January 28, 1993): 293–96; Charles L. Glaser and Steve Fetter, "Should the United States Reject MAD? Damage Limitation and U.S. Nuclear Strategy toward China," *International Security* 41, no. 1 (Summer 2016): 66.

16. Kenneth N. Waltz, "Nuclear Myths and Political Realities," *American Political Science Review* 84, no. 3 (September 1990): 734. See also Kenneth N. Waltz, "More May Be Better," in *The Spread of Nuclear Weapons: An Enduring Debate*, by Scott D. Sagan and Kenneth N. Waltz (New York: W. W. Norton, 2013), 33–34.

17. Bernstein, "Eclipsed by Hiroshima and Nagasaki," 151. These discussions were overly ambitious at the time, but such thinking would develop over the course of the nuclear era.

18. Quoted in Bernstein, 166, see also 164–70.

19. Vipin Narang, *Nuclear Strategy in the Modern Era: Regional Powers and International Conflict* (Princeton, NJ: Princeton University Press, 2014), 57, 56, see also chap. 3.

20. Kaplan, *To Kill Nations*, chap. 2; Marc Trachtenberg, *A Constructed Peace: The Making of the European Settlement, 1945–1963* (Princeton, NJ: Princeton University Press, 1999), 89.

21. On the difficulties of cratering runways even with nuclear weapons see Keir A. Lieber and Daryl G. Press, "The End of MAD? The Nuclear Dimension of U.S. Primacy," *International Security* 30, no. 4 (Spring 2006): 42–43.

22. Todd S. Sechser and Matthew Fuhrmann, *Nuclear Weapons and Coercive Diplomacy* (Cambridge: Cambridge University Press, 2017), 48.

23. For example, Lynn Etheridge Davis and Warner R. Schilling, "All You Ever Wanted to Know about MIRV and ICBM Calculations but Were Not Cleared to Ask," *Journal of Conflict Resolution* 17, no. 2 (June 1973): 207–42; Michael J. Salman, Kevin J. Sullivan, and Stephen Van Evera, "Analysis or Propaganda? Measuring American Strategic Nuclear Capability, 1969–88," in *Nuclear Arguments: Understanding the Strategic Nuclear Arms and Arms Control Debates*, ed. Lynn Eden and Steven E. Miller (Ithaca, NY: Cornell University Press, 1989), 172–263; Lieber and Press, "End of MAD?"

24. For example, Keir A. Lieber and Daryl G. Press, "The New Era of Nuclear Weapons, Deterrence, and Conflict," *Strategic Studies Quarterly* 7, no. 1 (Spring 2013): esp. 9–10; Art Pine, "Only A-Bomb Could Destroy Libya Plant, Scientist Says," *Los Angeles Times*, April 24, 1996, http://articles.latimes.com/1996-04-24/news/mn-62181_1_weapons-plant; Alyssa Demus, "Conventional versus Nuclear: Assessing Comparative Deterrent Utilities," American University School of International Service manuscript, August 25, 2012, esp. 14–18, http://www.arcic.army.mil/app_Documents/SLTF/Conventional%20Versus%20Nuclear%20Assessing%20Comparative%20Deterrent%20Utilities.pdf.

25. "Iran Nuclear Sites May Be Beyond Reach of 'Bunker Busters,'" Reuters, January 12, 2012, http://www.reuters.com/article/us-iran-nuclear-strike-idUSTRE80B22020120112; Joby Warrick, "Iran's Underground Nuclear Sites Not Immune to U.S. Bunker-Busters, Experts Say," *Washington Post*, February 29, 2012, https://www.washingtonpost.com/world/national-security/experts-irans-underground-nuclear-sites-not-immune-to-us-bunker-busters/2012/02/24/gIQAzWaghR_story.html?utm_term=.893c93ee5f7c.

26. The Gulf War Air Power Survey reports that "approximately 1,500 coalition strikes altogether were focused against Iraqi ballistic missile capabilities. . . . Roughly another 1,000 'Scud patrol' sorties were planned against mobile Scud launchers but ended up attacking other targets." *Gulf War Air Power Survey*, vol. 2, part 1, *Operations and Effects and Effectiveness* (Washington, DC: Office of Air Force History, 1993), 190n98, see also 189 and vol. 2, part 2, 330–32.

27. Glaser and Fetter, "Should the United States Reject MAD?," 67, see also 66; Caitlin Talmadge, "Would China Go Nuclear? Assessing the Risk of Chinese Nuclear Escalation in a Conventional War with the United States," *International Security* 41, no. 4 (Spring 2017): 87.

28. Austin Long and Brendan Rittenhouse Green, "Stalking the Secure Second Strike: Intelligence, Counterforce, and Nuclear Strategy," *Journal of Strategic Studies* 39, no. 1–2 (2015): 59.

29. Talmadge, "Would China Go Nuclear?," 58. Talmadge was discussing a different situation, but the point applies here.

30. Waltz, "Nuclear Myths and Political Realities," 733.

31. Narang, *Nuclear Strategy in the Modern Era*, 15–16.

32. Elbridge Colby et al., "The Israeli 'Nuclear Alert' of 1973: Deterrence and Signaling in Crisis," *CAN Strategic Studies* (April 2013): https://www.cna.org/CNA_files/PDF/DRM-2013-U-004480-Final.pdf.

33. Narang, *Nuclear Strategy in the Modern Era*, 16.

34. For instance, low destructiveness avoids problems of destroying assets but may prove ineffective and thereby weaken the coercive value of the NWS arsenal.

35. This may be changing; see the discussion on precision-guided munitions.

36. Sechser and Furhmann, *Nuclear Weapons and Coercive Diplomacy*, 47; Todd S. Sechser and Matthew Fuhrmann, "Crisis Bargaining and Nuclear Blackmail," *International Organization* 67, no. 1 (January 2013): 177; Daryl G. Press, Scott D. Sagan, and Benjamin A. Valentino, "Atomic Aversion: Experimental Evidence on Taboos, Traditions, and the Non-use of Nuclear Weapons," *American Political Science Review* 107, no. 1 (February 2013): 191; T. V. Paul, *The Tradition of Non-use of Nuclear Weapons* (Stanford, CA: Stanford University Press, 2009), 23–24; John Mueller, *Atomic Obsession: Nuclear Alarmism from Hiroshima to Al-Qaeda* (Oxford: Oxford University Press, 2010), 14–15, 61–63.

37. Austin Long, "U.S. Strategic Nuclear Targeting Policy: Necessity and Damage Limitation," H-Diplo | ISSF Policy Roundtable 1–4 (December 22, 2016), http://issforum.org/round tables/policy/1-4-nuclear. See also Jeffrey G. Lewis and Scott D. Sagan, "The Nuclear Necessity Principle: Making U.S. Targeting Policy Conform with Ethics and the Laws of War," *Daedalus* 145, no. 4 (Fall 2016): 62–74.

38. Eden, *Whole World on Fire*, 15–36.

39. Pape, *Bombing to Win*, 36; Roehrig, *Japan, South Korea, and the United States Nuclear Umbrella*, 30–31.

40. Mueller, *Atomic Obsession*, 14–15.

41. Roehrig, *Japan, South Korea, and the United States Nuclear Umbrella*, 30.

42. Sechser and Fuhrmann, *Nuclear Weapons and Coercive Diplomacy*, 48–50.

43. Matthew Fuhrmann, "After Armageddon: Pondering the Potential Political Consequences of Third Use," in *Should We Let the Bomb Spread*, ed. Henry D. Sokolski (Washington, DC: Nonproliferation Policy Education Center, 2016), 190. See also Kelly M. Greenhill, *Weapons of Mass Migration: Forced Displacement, Coercion, and Foreign Policy* (Ithaca, NY: Cornell University Press, 2010).

44. On US weakness in 1950–51 relative to 1953–54 and its effect on US policy see Marc Trachtenberg, *History and Strategy* (Princeton, NJ: Princeton University Press, 1991), chap. 3; John Lewis Gaddis, *We Now Know: Rethinking Cold War History* (Oxford: Oxford University Press, 1997), 106; Rosemary J. Foot, "Anglo-American Relations in the Korean Crisis: The British Effort to Avert an Expanded War, December 1950–January 1951," *Diplomatic History* 10, no. 1 (January 1986): 43–57.

45. These are similar to various "soft balancing" mechanisms. See, for example, Robert A. Pape, "Soft Balancing against the United States," *International Security* 30, no. 1 (Summer 2005): 36–37.

46. One notable exception is World War II. US conventional bombing against Japan throughout 1945 killed far more than the two nuclear bombs did. The US atomic bombs were therefore not an escalation in the level of violence. For speculation that American nuclear use prior to 1945 might have caused Japan to expand its level of violence see Geoffrey Blainey, *The Causes of War*, 3rd ed. (London: Macmillan, 1988), 267–68.

47. Kenneth N. Waltz, "Waltz Responds to Sagan," in Sagan and Waltz, *Spread of Nuclear Weapons*, 141; Gaddis, *We Now Know*, 106; Mueller, *Atomic Obsession*, 14–15, 63. For a similar statement see William W. Kaufmann, "Limited Warfare," in *Military Policy and National Security*, ed. William W. Kauffman (Princeton, NJ: Princeton University Press, 1956), 106–7.

48. Keir A. Lieber and Daryl Press, "The New Era of Counterforce: Technological Change and the Future of Nuclear Deterrence," *International Security* 41, no. 4 (Spring 2017): 9–49.

49. Colin L. Powell, *My American Journey* (New York: Random House Large Print, 1995), 738; Tannenwald, *Nuclear Taboo*, 300–301; Jon Meacham, *Destiny and Power: The American Odyssey of George Herbert Walker Bush* (New York: Random House, 2015), 463.

50. Matthew Kroenig, *Exporting the Bomb: Technology Transfer and the Spread of Nuclear Weapons* (Ithaca, NY: Cornell University Press, 2010), 3; Peter D. Feaver, "Optimists, Pessimists, and Theories of Nuclear Proliferation Management: A Debate," *Security Studies* 4, no. 4 (October–December 1995): 771.

51. Francis J. Gavin, "Strategies of Inhibition: U.S. Grand Strategy, the Nuclear Revolution, and Nonproliferation," *International Security* 40, no. 1 (Summer 2015): 9–46; Matthew Kroenig, "Force or Friendship? Explaining Great Power Nonproliferation Policy," *Security Studies* 23, no. 1 (January–March 2014): 1–32.

52. Fuhrmann, "After Armageddon," 195. See also Roehrig, *Japan, South Korea, and the United States Nuclear Umbrella*, 31.

53. Press, Sagan, and Valentino, "Atomic Aversion," 191–92; Sechser and Fuhrmann, *Nuclear Weapons and Coercive Diplomacy*, 50; Tannenwald, *Nuclear Taboo*, 55.

54. On emulation see Kenneth N. Waltz, *Theory of International Politics* (Boston: McGraw-Hill, 1979), 127–28; Barry R. Posen, "Nationalism, the Mass Army, and Military Power," *International Security* 18, no. 2 (Fall 1993): 80–124; Joseph M. Parent and Sebastian Rosato, "Balancing in Neorealism," *International Security* 40, no. 2 (Fall 2015): 51–86.

55. Gaddis, *We Now Know*, 105.

56. Tannenwald, *Nuclear Taboo*; Paul, *Tradition of Non-use of Nuclear Weapons*; T.V. Paul, "Taboo or Tradition? The Non-use of Nuclear Weapons in World Politics," *Review of International Studies* 36, no. 4 (October 2010): 853–63. On the general evolution of norms against harming civilians see Lewis and Sagan, "Nuclear Necessity Principle," 62–72; Pfundstein Chamberlain, *Cheap Threats*, 45–47. The classic modern statement on just war remains Michael Walzer, *Just and Unjust Wars: A Moral Argument with Historical Illustrations*, 3rd ed. (1977; New York: Basic Books, 2000), esp. chap. 17.

57. On limitations see Press, Sagan, and Valentino, "Atomic Aversion"; Scott D. Sagan and Benjamin Valentino, "Revisiting Hiroshima in Iran: What Americans Really Think about Using Nuclear Weapons and Killing Noncombatants," *International Security* 42, no. 1 (Summer 2017): 41–79; Downes, *Targeting Civilians in War*. That US planners take just-war principles of distinction and proportionality into account in targeting see C. Robert Kehler, "Nuclear Weapons and Nuclear Use," *Daedalus* 145, no. 4 (Fall 2016). Though critics contend this is insufficient; see, for example, Lewis and Sagan, "Nuclear Necessity Principle."

58. Paul, *Tradition of Non-use*; Fuhrman and Sechser, *Nuclear Weapons and Coercive Diplomacy*, 48–50; Fuhrmann, "After Armageddon," 192–94.

59. For discussions of technological change and its limitations see Stephen Biddle, *Military Power: Explaining Victory and Defeat in Modern Battle* (Princeton, NJ: Princeton University Press, 2004), esp. chaps. 4, 7, 9; Eliot A. Cohen, "A Revolution in Warfare," *Foreign Affairs* 75, no. 2 (March–April 1996): 37–54; Michael Russell Rip and James M. Hasik, *The Precision Revolution: GPS and the Future of Aerial Warfare* (Annapolis, MD: Naval Institute Press, 2002); Lieber and Press, "New Era of Counterforce"; Lieber and Press, "End of MAD?"; Glaser and Fetter, "Should the United States Reject MAD?," 62–80, 97.

60. Amy F. Woolf, "Conventional Prompt Global Strike and Long-Range Ballistic Missiles: Background and Issues," *Congressional Research Service*, July 7, 2017, https://fas.org/sgp/crs/nuke/R41464.pdf.

61. Dennis M. Gormley, "US Advanced Conventional Systems and Conventional Prompt Global Strike Ambitions: Assessing the Risks, Benefits, and Arms Control Implications," *Nonproliferation Review* 22, no. 2 (2015): 129, see also 133; Gerson, "Conventional Deterrence," 32, 35.

62. Biddle and Oelrich, "Future Warfare in the Western Pacific," 34–38.

63. Kehler, "Nuclear Weapons and Nuclear Use," 52; Lewis and Sagan, "Nuclear Necessity Principle," esp. 70.

64. Nina Tannenwald, "Stigmatizing the Bomb: Origins of the Nuclear Taboo," *International Security* 29, no. 4 (Spring 2005): 43–45; Paul, *Tradition of Non-use*, 185–88; William J. Broad and David E. Sanger, "As U.S. Modernizes Nuclear Weapons, 'Smaller' Leaves Some Uneasy," *New York Times*, January 11, 2016, https://www.nytimes.com/2016/01/12/science/as-us-modernizes-nuclear-weapons-smaller-leaves-some-uneasy.html?_r=0.

65. Nuclear weapons might still be useful at deterring nuclear strikes by other nuclear powers, but this is outside the scope of nuclear monopoly. Of course, if nuclear weapons had no advantage relative to conventional alternatives then it is unclear why a state would need a nuclear weapon to deter a nuclear strike that provided no benefit to the first user.

66. Thomas C. Schelling, *Arms and Influence* (New Haven, CT: Yale University Press, 1966), 135.

67. Kaufmann, "Limited Warfare," 108.

68. As Bernard Brodie speculated, in a war between two nuclear states, "one side or the other would feel that its relative position respecting [the] ability to use the bomb might deteriorate as the war progressed, and that if it failed to use the bomb while it had the chance it might not have the chance later on." Bernard Brodie, ed., *The Absolute Weapon: Atomic Power and World Order* (New York: Harcourt, Brace, 1946), 86. Nuclear weapons pose a particularly dangerous threat to nuclear arsenals because they are the best means to degrade or eliminate nuclear platforms and storage facilities. Michael Salman, Kevin J. Sullivan, and Stephen Van Evera, "Analysis or Propaganda? Measuring American Strategic Nuclear Capability, 1969–88," in *Nuclear Arguments: Understanding the Strategic Nuclear Arms and Arms Control Debates*, ed. Lynn Eden and Steven E. Miller (Ithaca, NY: Cornell University Press, 1989); Lieber and Press, "End of MAD?"; Charles L. Glaser and Steve Fetter, "Counterforce Revisited: Assessing the Nuclear Posture Review's New Missions," *International Security* 30, no. 2 (Fall 2005): 84–126; Glaser and Fetter, "Should the United States Reject MAD?"

69. The fear within the NWS can be mitigated if the NWS has a large and diverse nuclear arsenal and the NNWS has very limited conventional capabilities.

70. Barry R. Posen, *Inadvertent Escalation: Conventional War and Nuclear Risks* (Ithaca, NY: Cornell University Press, 1991), 3.

71. Talmadge, "Would China Go Nuclear?," 58.

72. Keir A. Lieber and Daryl G. Press, "The Nukes We Need: Preserving the American Nuclear Deterrent," *Foreign Affairs* 88, no. 6 (November/December 2009): 48.

73. Lieber and Press, "New Era of Counterforce," 17–18; and Austin Long's contribution to Austin Long, Dinshaw Mistry, and Bruce M. Sugden, "Correspondence: Going Nowhere Fast; Assessing Concerns about Long-Range Conventional Ballistic Missiles," *International Security* 34, no. 4 (Spring 2010): 166–72.

74. Robert E. Osgood, *Limited War Revisited* (Boulder, CO: Westview, 1979), 3. During the Cold War, thinking on limited wars centered on strategies that the United States could pursue to prevent escalation to a major US-Soviet nuclear confrontation. See, for example, Kaufmann, "Limited Warfare"; Spencer D. Bakich, *Success and Failure in Limited War: Information and Strategy in the Korean, Vietnam, Persian Gulf, and Iraq Wars* (Chicago: University of Chicago Press, 2014), 21–24; and the discussion in Steven Peter Rosen, "Vietnam and the American Theory of Limited War," *International Security* 7, no. 2 (Fall 1982): 84–87.

75. Ivan Arrequín-Toft, "How the Weak Win Wars: A Theory of Asymmetric Conflict," *International Security* 26, no. 1 (Summer 2001): 103.

76. I borrow "mechanized" from Pape, *Bombing to Win*, rather than labeling the strategy conventional to avoid confusion with the distinction between conventional and nuclear weapons.

77. Pape, *Bombing to Win*, 30. On defensive operations see Biddle, *Military Power*, 46–48; Mearsheimer, *Conventional Deterrence*, 43–56.

78. On manufacturing superiority and defensive advantage see Mearsheimer, *Conventional Deterrence*, chap. 2; Biddle, *Military Power*, chap. 3.

79. Mearsheimer, *Conventional Deterrence*, 54. See also Paul, *Asymmetric Conflict*, 24–31.

80. Carl Von Clausewitz, *On War*, trans. and ed. Michael Howard and Peter Paret (1976; Princeton, NJ: Princeton University Press, 1984), 81, 80, see also 91–94. Emphasis in original.

81. On Iraqi behavior see chap. 2. On Chinese and Soviet efforts at civil defense measures see chaps. 4–5. The United States explored and briefly implemented the Pentomic Division structure in the 1950s, part of which centered on greater dispersal to enable operation on a nuclear battlefield. A. J. Bacevich, *The Pentomic Era: The US Army between Korea and Vietnam* (Washington, DC: National Defense University Press, 1986). On US, British, and Canadian civil defense and efforts to increase morale see, for example, Tracy C. Davis, *Stages of Emergency: Cold War Nuclear Civil Defense* (Durham, NC: Duke University Press, 2007); Wm. F. Vandercook, "Making the Very Best of the Very Worst: The 'Human Effects of Nuclear Weapons,' Report of 1956," *International Security* 11, no. 1 (Summer 1986): 184–95.

82. Fred Charles Iklé, *Every War Must End* (New York: Columbia University Press, 1991), 40.

83. Michael C. Horowitz and Neil Narang, "Poor Man's Atomic Bomb? Exploring the Relationship between 'Weapons of Mass Destruction,'" *Journal of Conflict Resolution* 58, no. 3 (April 2014): 509–35.

84. In contrast to chemical and biological weapons, nuclear weapons are effective against military forces, there is little or no defense available, and nuclear weapons can visit much greater immediate destruction. As such, facing a nuclear adversary, an NWS would have strong first-strike incentives to eliminate or at least degrade the opponent's nuclear arsenal. Mueller, *Atomic Obsession*, 11–15; Horowitz and Narang, "Poor Man's Atomic Bomb?," esp. 514–16.

85. Waltz, "Nuclear Myths and Political Realities," esp. 738–41; Kenneth N. Waltz, "The Origins of War in Neorealist Theory," *Journal of Interdisciplinary History* 18, no. 4 (Spring 1988): 627; Stephen Van Evera, *Causes of War: Power and the Roots of Conflict* (Ithaca, NY: Cornell University Press, 1999), 244–46; Robert Jervis, *The Meaning of the Nuclear Revolution: Statecraft and the Prospect of Armageddon* (Ithaca, NY: Cornell University Press, 1989), 44–45.

86. Jeffrey W. Knopf, "Recasting the Proliferation Optimism–Pessimism Debate," *Security Studies* 12, no. 1 (Autumn 2002): 59; Matthew Kroenig, *The Logic of American Nuclear Strategy* (Oxford: Oxford University Press, 2018): chap. 2; Jervis, *Meaning of the Nuclear Revolution*, 137; Colin S. Gray and Keith Payne, "Victory Is Possible," *Foreign Policy* 39 (Summer 1980): 25–27; Glaser and Fetter, "Should the United States Reject MAD?," 54–62.

87. Biddle, *Military Power*, 1, 132–33.

88. Narang, *Nuclear Strategy in the Modern Era*.

89. One American concern during the Cold War was that the Soviets would fight "the war in such a way as to delay NATO taking the decision to use nuclear weapons until it was too late for them to influence the outcome of the war." Quoted in Paul Schulte, "Tactical Nuclear Weapons in NATO and Beyond: A Historical and Thematic Examination," in *Tactical Nuclear Weapons and NATO*, ed. Tom Nichols, Douglas Stuart, and Jeffrey D. McCausland (Carlisle, PA: Strategic Studies Institute, 2012), 53. Though these dynamics are very different from nuclear monopoly, the point is that officials have at times worried a conventional conflict could proceed past the point when nuclear weapons would be effective at reversing the situation.

90. Todd S. Sechser, "A Bargaining Theory of Coercion," in *Coercion: The Power to Hurt in International Politics*, ed. Kelly M. Greenhill and Peter Krause (Oxford: Oxford University Press, 2018), 55–76.

91. On costly signaling see James D. Fearon, "Signaling Foreign Policy Interests: Tying Hands versus Sinking Costs," *Journal of Conflict Resolution* 41, no. 1 (February 1997): 68–90.

92. Narang, *Nuclear Strategy in the Modern Era*, 19; Glaser and Fetter, "Should the United States Reject MAD?," 73.

93. Quoted in Scott D. Sagan, *Moving Targets: Nuclear Strategy and National Security* (Princeton, NJ: Princeton University Press, 1989), 16.

94. Steven D. Biddle, "Allies, Airpower, and Modern Warfare: The Afghan Model in Afghanistan and Iraq," *International Security* 30, no. 3 (Winter 2005/06): 161–76.

95. Horowitz and Narang, "Poor Man's Atomic Bomb?," 528, 519–20.

96. George H. Quester, "If the Nuclear Taboo Gets Broken," *Naval War College Review* 58, no. 2 (Spring 2005): 78.

97. Sagan and Valentino, "Revisiting Hiroshima in Iran." Though see Abigail S. Post and Todd S. Sechser, "Norms, Public Opinion, and the Use of Nuclear Weapons," unpublished manuscript.

98. The key exception to this would be if a weak NWS directly attacked a stronger NNWS's homeland. In that case the NWS would likely act in its own defense, resulting in war. Historically there do not appear to have been any such wars. See chaps. 2–5 and appendix B.

99. Alexander L. George and Andrew Bennett, *Case Studies and Theory Development in the Social Sciences* (Cambridge, MA: MIT Press, 2005), esp. chaps. 9–10; David Collier, James Mahoney, and Jason Seawright, "Claiming Too Much: Warnings about Selection Bias," in *Rethinking Social Inquiry: Diverse Tools, Shared Standards*, ed. Henry E. Brady and David Collier (Lanham, MD: Rowman & Littlefield, 2004), 94–98; Stephen Van Evera, *Guide to Methods for Students of Social Science* (Ithaca, NY: Cornell University Press, 1997), 58–67.

100. For details on the data see the individual chapters and appendix A.

101. Biddle, *Military Power*, chap. 3; Ryan Grauer and Michael C. Horowitz, "What Determines Military Victory? Testing the Modern System," *Security Studies* 21, no. 1 (January–March 2012): 83–112; Caitlin Talmadge, *The Dictator's Army: Battlefield Effectiveness in Authoritarian Regimes* (Ithaca, NY: Cornell University Press, 2015).

102. Sebastian Rosato, *Europe United: Power Politics and the Making of the European Community* (Ithaca, NY: Cornell University Press, 2011), 17–18.

103. Narang, *Nuclear Strategy in the Modern Era*.

104. See introduction chapter.

105. This resembles John Stuart Mill's method of agreement. The analyst examines cases where a phenomenon is present (conflict in nuclear monopoly) to determine if the cases share certain underlying characteristics even though they differ in most other aspects. For a discussion see James Mahoney, "Strategies of Causal Assessment in Historical Analysis," in *Comparative Historical Analysis in the Social Sciences*, ed. James Mahoney and Dietrich Rueschemeyer (Cambridge: Cambridge University Press, 2003), 341–47, 351–52.

106. Conventional states fighting other conventional states cannot abstain from threatening nonexistent nuclear forces.

107. This portion of the analysis examines only cases of war. I do not examine cases of nonwar where the NNWS may have planned major operations. Comparison against a background condition can still provide useful information, though. See Van Evera, *Guide to Methods*, 46–47, 58–61.

2. Iraq versus the United States

1. For a counterfactual analysis of the 1991 Gulf War if Iraq had possessed nuclear weapons see Barry R. Posen, "U.S. Security Policy in a Nuclear Armed World Or: What if Iraq Had Had Nuclear Weapons?," *Security Studies* 6, no. 3 (Spring 1997): 1–31.

2. *The Military Balance, 1990–1991*, International Institute of Strategic Studies (1990), 106.

3. Stephen D. Biddle, *Military Power: Explaining Victory and Defeat in Modern Battle* (Princeton, NJ: Princeton University Press, 2004), 135.

4. Caitlin Talmadge, "The Puzzle of Personalist Performance: Iraqi Battlefield Effectiveness in the Iran-Iraq War," *Security Studies* 22, no. 2 (2013): 180–221.

5. Biddle, *Military Power*, 1, 132–33.

6. Joshua Rovner, "Delusion of Defeat: The United States and Iraq, 1990–1998," *Journal of Strategic Studies* 37, no. 4 (2014): 482–507; Phil Haun, *Coercion, Survival, and War: Why Weak States Resist the United States* (Stanford, CA: Stanford University Press, 2015).

7. Kevin M. Woods, David D. Palkki, and Mark E. Stout, *The Saddam Tapes: The Inner Workings of a Tyrant's Regime, 1978–2001* (Cambridge: Cambridge University Press, 2011), 221–22.

8. Quoted in Jon Meacham, *Destiny and Power: The American Odyssey of George Herbert Walker Bush* (New York: Random House, 2015), 463.

9. Quoted in Nina Tannenwald, "The Nuclear Taboo: The United States and the Normative Basis of Nuclear Non-use," *International Organization* 53, no. 3 (Summer 1999): 459.

10. George [H. W.] Bush and Brent Scowcroft, *A World Transformed* (New York: Vintage Books, 1998), 463.

11. "U.S. Forces Have No Nuclear Arms in Gulf States, No Plans to Use Them," *Los Angeles Times*, October 2, 1990, A6, http://articles.latimes.com/1990-10-02/news/mn-1732_1_tactical-nuclear-weapons.

12. F. Gregory Gause, *The International Relations of the Persian Gulf* (Cambridge: Cambridge University Press, 2010), 50–51.

13. Haun, *Coercion, Survival, and War*, 58.

14. For the claim that the Ba'ath regime was less than committed to pan-Arabism see Joseph Sassoon, *Saddam Hussein's Ba'th Party: Inside an Authoritarian Regime* (Cambridge: Cambridge University Press, 2012), 9–10.

15. Quoted in Hal Brands and David Palkki, "Saddam, Israel, and the Bomb: Nuclear Alarmism Justified?," *International Security* 36, no. 1 (Summer 2011): 149.

16. Brands and Palkki, 134–35. This is consistent with my broader argument. In a major war in which Iraq sought to take large portions of Israeli territory through military means and potentially threaten Israel's survival, the benefits of nuclear use would increase to Israel. To offset that would thus require an Iraqi nuclear capability. This is discrete from Egyptian planning in 1973 that sought to take only limited territory and rely on political means to reacquire the Sinai, relying as well on the United States to constrain Israel.

17. Gause, *International Relations*, 70, 78–84; Caitlin Talmadge, *The Dictator's Army: Battlefield Effectiveness in Authoritarian Regimes* (Ithaca, NY: Cornell University Press, 2015): 148; Hal Brands, "Inside the Iraqi State Records: Saddam Hussein, 'Irangate,' and the United States," *Journal of Strategic Studies* 34, no. 1 (February 2011): 95–118; Hal Brands and David Palkki, "'Conspiring Bastards': Saddam Hussein's Strategic View of the United States," *Diplomatic History* 36, no. 3 (June 2012): 641–45.

18. Dianne Pfundstein Chamberlain, *Cheap Threats: Why the United States Struggles to Coerce Weak States* (Washington, DC: Georgetown University Press, 2016), 169. See also Brands and Palkki, "'Conspiring Bastards,'" 657; Amatzi Baram, "Deterrence Lessons from Iraq: Rationality Is Not the Only Key to Containment," *Foreign Affairs* 91, no. 4 (July/August 2012): 82.

19. Public Broadcasting System, *Frontline*, "Oral History: Tariq Aziz," https://www.pbs.org/wgbh/pages/frontline/gulf/oral/aziz/1.html, originally broadcast January 9, 1996.

20. See per capita GDP figures in Gleditsch, version 6.0, http://ksgleditsch.com/exptradegdp.html.

21. Haun, *Coercion, Survival, and War*, 51; Woods, Palkki, and Stout, *Saddam Tapes*, 166–67.

22. Saddam Hussein Talks to the FBI, NSA, Interview Session 9, February 24, 2004, 1, http://www.gwu.edu/~nsarchiv/NSAEBB/NSAEBB279/10.pdf. The general collection is available at https://nsarchive2.gwu.edu/NSAEBB/NSAEBB279/.

23. Brands and Palkki, "'Conspiring Bastards,'" 652–57; F. Gregory Gause III, "Iraq's Decisions to Go to War, 1980 and 1990," *Middle East Journal* 56, no. 1 (Winter 2002): 55–59.

24. Quoted in Brands and Palkki, "'Conspiring Bastards,'" 652.

25. Quoted in Gause, "Iraq's Decisions to Go to War," 56.

26. PBS *Frontline* "Oral History: Tariq Aziz." See also "Saddam and Members of the Ba'ath Party Discuss the Letter That Tariq Aziz Will Send to the Secretary of the Arab League Laying Out Iraq's Grievances toward Kuwait," undated [shortly before July 15, 1990], in Woods, Palkki, and Stout, *Saddam Tapes*, 169–71.

27. Saddam Hussein Talks to the FBI, NSA, Interview Session 9, February 24, 2004, 3, http://www.gwu.edu/~nsarchiv/NSAEBB/NSAEBB279/10.pdf.

28. Quoted in Kevin M. Woods, *The Mother of All Battles: Saddam Hussein's Strategic Plan for the Persian Gulf War* (Annapolis, MD: Naval Institute Press, 2008), 49.

29. PBS *Frontline*, "Oral History: Tariq Aziz."

30. Saddam Hussein quoted in Woods, *Mother of All Battles*, 48.

31. Saddam Hussein Talks to the FBI, NSA, Interview Session 9, February 24, 2004, 5, http://www.gwu.edu/~nsarchiv/NSAEBB/NSAEBB279/10.pdf. Aziz later characterized the war as defensive as well; see PBS *Frontline*, "Oral History: Tariq Aziz."

32. Quoted in Brands and Palkki, "'Conspiring Bastards,'" 655–56. See also Gause, *International Relations*, 95–96.

33. On the US footprint see Joshua R. Rovner and Caitlin Talmadge, "Hegemony, Force Posture, and the Provision of Public Goods: The Once and Future Role of Outside Powers in Securing Persian Gulf Oil," *Security Studies* 23, no. 3 (2014): 568–71.

34. See, for example, Joseph E. Uscinski and Joseph M. Parent, *American Conspiracy Theories* (Oxford: Oxford University Press, 2014).

35. Woods, *Mother of All Battles*, 52.

36. "Confrontation in the Gulf: Excerpts from Iraqi Document on Meeting with U.S. Envoy," September 23, 1990, *New York Times*, http://www.nytimes.com/1990/09/23/world/confrontation-in-the-gulf-excerpts-from-iraqi-document-on-meeting-with-us-envoy.html?pagewanted=all.

37. US Embassy Baghdad to US Secretary of State, "Saddam's Message of Friendship to President Bush," July 25, 1990, 11, 2, *Washington Post*, at http://www.washingtonpost.com/wp-srv/politics/documents/glaspie1-13.pdf?sid=ST2008040203634.

38. "U.S. Messages on July 1990 Meeting of Hussein and American Ambassador," *New York Times*, July 13, 1991, http://www.nytimes.com/1991/07/13/world/us-messages-on-july-1990-meeting-of-hussein-and-american-ambassador.html.

39. Woods, Palkki, and Stout, *Saddam Tapes*, 20; Brands and Palkki, "'Conspiring Bastards,'" 657.

40. Quoted Brands and Palkki, "'Conspiring Bastards,'" 657n135.

41. Aziz's statement was in response to the question: "In April, what was your assessment of what the Americans would do—what was April Glaspie saying?" By "April," the interviewer likely meant Ambassador Glaspie's first name. But it is possible that Aziz was referring to a meeting in April 1990 in which Ambassador Glaspie was present. However, immediately prior to Aziz's comment that Glaspie "didn't tell us anything strange" he was referencing the July 25 meeting, noting that during it a call came from President Mubarak. That call appears in the American minutes of the July 25 meeting. This suggests the comment was in fact in reference to the July 25 meeting. For the Aziz interview and statement see PBS *Frontline*, "Oral History: Tariq Aziz." For the US minutes noting the call from Mubarak see US Embassy Baghdad to US Secretary of State, "Saddam's Message of Friendship to President Bush," July 25, 1990.

42. US Embassy Baghdad to US Secretary of State, "Saddam's Message of Friendship to President Bush," July 25, 1990.

43. Quoted in Brands and Palkki, "'Conspiring Bastards,'" 657; Woods, *Mother of All Battles*, 95.

44. On general versus immediate deterrence see Patrick M. Morgan, *Deterrence Now* (Cambridge: Cambridge University Press, 2003), chap. 3.

45. UN Security Council Resolution 678, November 29, 1990, https://undocs.org/S/RES/678(1990).

46. Quotes in Woods, *Mother of All Battles*, 109. See also SH-PDWN-D-000-533, "Meeting between Saddam Hussein and the Soviet Delegation," October 6 to October 10, 1990, Conflict Records Research Center (CRRC), 18–20. I use the CRRC pagination whenever citing directly from their collection.

47. Haun, *Coercion, Survival, and War*, 53–54.

48. Quoted in Gause, "Iraq's Decisions to Go to War," 60.

49. Haun, *Coercion, Survival, and War*, 58.

50. Robert A. Pape, *Bombing to Win: Air Power and Coercion in War* (Ithaca, NY: Cornell University Press, 1996), 215–16; Gause, *International Relations*, 112–13; Haun, *Coercion, Survival, and War*, 62–63; Serge Schmemann, "Iraqi Aide Arrives for Moscow Talks," *New York Times*, February 18, 1991, https://www.nytimes.com/1991/02/18/world/war-in-the-gulf-soviet-union-iraqi-aide-arrives-for-moscow-talks.html.

51. Quoted in Haun, *Coercion, Survival, and War*, 63; see also Pape, *Bombing to Win*, 216–17.

52. Haun, *Coercion, Survival, and War*, 63–64.

53. "Just before the Ground War Began, Saddam Discussed His Plans to Withdraw Iraqi Forces from Kuwait," February 23, 1991, in Woods, Palkki, and Stout, *Saddam Tapes*, 189–91, esp. 190, and 192n53; Woods, *Mother of All Battles*, 214. On February 22, Secretary of State Baker told President Bush and President François Mitterrand of France that the Soviets informed him that Iraq had agreed to withdraw from Kuwait City in four days, with total withdrawal in twenty-one days. He added that the Soviet ambassador Alexander Bessmertnykh informed him that "the Iraqis have agreed to remove the requirement that economic sanctions be eliminated. . . . There are no linkages. There are no references to other problems in the region. There are no conditions. It is a very big move." George Bush phone call with French President (Mitterrand), February 22, 1991, 4, http://www.margaretthatcher.org/document/D9589C94D7604DAD8528CF714D596751.pdf.

54. George Bush phone call with Gorbachev, February 23, 1991, 1, http://www.margaretthatcher.org/document/9D3A7B1E9D864FC08BF72CB4A4844486.pdf.

55. Haun, *Coercion, Survival, and War*, 64–72; Pape, *Bombing to Win*, 217–18; Gause, *International Relations*, 113.

56. Woods, *Mother of All Battles*, 210. See also the discussion in the "Iraqi Nuclear Views" section later in this chapter.

57. George Bush phone call with French President (Mitterrand), February 22, 1991, 5; see also George Bush phone call to Gorbachev, February 22, 1991, http://www.margaretthatcher.org/document/2983E547B0624D329FDA6653F9FC3506.pdf; and George Bush phone call with Gorbachev, February 23, 1991, 2–3.

58. Haun, *Coercion, Survival, and War*, 65–67.

59. SH-SHTP-A-000-630, "Saddam and His Advisers Discussing the Soviet Union and the State of the Iraqi Military," February 24, 1991, 12, http://crrc.dodlive.mil/files/2013/01/SH-SHTP-A-000-630_TF.pdf. The general site is http://crrc.dodlive.mil/collections/sh/. The February 24 documents are also available in combined form at the New York Times online at https://www.nytimes.com/interactive/projects/documents/transcripts-of-conversations-between-saddam-hussein-and-his-advisors; https://int.nyt.com/data/int-shared/nytdocs/docs/559/559.pdf.

60. SH-SHTP-A-000-931, "Saddam and His Advisers Discussing the US Ground Attack during the 1991 Gulf War," February 24, 1991, 8, http://crrc.dodlive.mil/files/2013/01/SH-SHTP-A-000-931_TF.pdf.

61. Kevin M. Woods and Mark E. Stout, "Saddam's Perceptions and Misperceptions: The Case of 'Desert Storm,'" *Journal of Strategic Studies* 33, no. 1 (February 2010), 5–41; and Woods, *Mother of All Battles*, 304–5.

62. Gause, *International Relations*, 119–20; Thomas E. Ricks, *Fiasco: The American Military Adventure in Iraq* (2006; New York: Penguin Books, 2007), 8–10.

63. Gause, *International Relations*, 123.

64. Gause, *International Relations*, 121–123; "Crisis Summary #422: UNSCOM-I," International Crisis Behavior Dataset (ICB), http://www.icb.umd.edu/dataviewer/?crisno=422.

65. "Crisis Summary #429: UNSCOM II Operation Desert Fox," ICB, http://www.icb.umd.edu/dataviewer/?crisno=429.

66. Ricks, *Fiasco*, 18–22. Desert Fox essentially finished off any lingering nuclear, biological, or chemical weapons programs and ambitions, most of which had already been abandoned in the wake of the Gulf War in the face of inspections and sanctions. Rovner, "Delusion of Defeat," 495, 497–98.

67. Quoted in Haun, *Coercion, Survival, and War*, 75.

68. Hal Brands, *What Good Is Grand Strategy: Power and Purpose in American Statecraft from Harry S. Truman to George W. Bush* (Ithaca, NY: Cornell University Press, 2014), chap. 4.

69. Quoted in Haun, *Coercion, Survival, and War*, 81, also 76–80; and Pfundstein Chamberlain, *Cheap Threats*, 189–90, 201–7.

70. Quoted in Woods, *Mother of All Battles*, 62.

71. Gause, "Iraq's Decisions to Go to War," 62.

72. Kenneth M. Pollack, *Arabs at War: Military Effectiveness, 1948–1991* (Lincoln: University of Nebraska Press, 2002), 235–37.

73. "Saddam Appraises American and International Reactions to the Invasion of Kuwait," August 7, 1990, in Woods, Palkki, and Stout, *Saddam Tapes*, 175.

74. Woods, Palkki, and Stout, *Saddam Tapes*, 172–73, note 11; Woods, *Mother of All Battles*, 313.

75. Woods, *Mother of All Battles*, 125, also 137.

76. Quoted in Woods, 52. See also Pollack, *Arabs at War*, 237.

77. "Saddam Appraises American and International Reactions to the Invasion of Kuwait," August 7, 1990, in Woods, Palkki, and Stout, *Saddam Tapes*, 176.

78. SH-SHTP-A-000-931, "Saddam and His Advisers Discussing the US Ground Attack during the 1991 Gulf War," February 24, 1991, 4.

79. Pollack, *Arabs at War*, 238–41; Woods, *Mother of All Battles*, 137–44.

80. Quoted in Woods, *Mother of All Battles*, 16.

81. On the operation see Woods, chap. 2; Pollack, *Arabs at War*, 243–46; and Woods and Stout, "Saddam's Perceptions and Misperceptions," 20–23.

82. Quoted in Gause, "Iraq's Decisions to Go to War," 60. See also Gause, *International Relations*, 108.

83. "Saddam Appraises American and International Reactions to the Invasion of Kuwait," August 7, 1991, in Woods, Palkki, and Stout, *Saddam Tapes*, 175.

84. Quoted in Woods, *Mother of All Battles*, 107.

85. Quoted in Woods, 115. Woods cites this meeting taking place on November 2, 1990; see notes 91 and 98 on page 123 and the document identifier on page 335. However, a slightly different translation of this passage appears in CRRC SH-SHTP-A-000-670, "Meeting between Saddam Hussein and the Revolutionary Command Council," 25–26, which reports the date of the meeting as October 11, 1990. An excerpt from that document also appears in Woods, Palkki, and Stout, *Saddam Tapes*, 35–37, but the excerpt does not include the passage from Taha Ramadan. The document date there is listed as "circa late October 1990" in the document title but October 11, 1990, in the footnote; see page 35. Some of the information discussed during the meeting would suggest that a date of late October is most appropriate for the meeting, such as reference to statements by Vice President Cheney that were reported on October 25 and 26.

86. "Saddam and His Inner Circle Analyze U.S. Domestic Politics, American Warnings, and the Likelihood of U.S. Military Action against Iraq," late October 1990, in Woods, Palkki, and Stout, *Saddam Tapes*, 37. Note also that this reveals the widespread belief within Iraq that the United States could not win quickly, providing time for Iraq to inflict casualties. See also Woods, *Mother of All Battles*, 114.

87. Quoted in Woods, *Mother of All Battles*, 113.

88. Quoted in Woods, 110. See also SH-SHTP-A-000-670, "Meeting between Saddam Hussein and the Revolutionary Command Council," 13.

89. Quoted in Woods, *Mother of All Battles*, 112.

90. Quoted in Woods, 113.

91. Quoted in Woods, 95.

92. SH-SHTP-D-000-611, "Meeting between Saddam Hussein and Yasser Arafat," circa January 1991, CRRC, 5–6.

93. Quoted in Benjamin Buch and Scott D. Sagan, "Our Red Lines and Theirs," ForeignPolicy.Com, December 13, 2013, http://foreignpolicy.com/2013/12/13/our-red-lines-and-theirs/.

94. Quoted in Woods, *Mother of All Battles*, 159–60. For the full text of the meeting see SH-SHTP-A-000-670, "Meeting between Saddam Hussein and the Revolutionary Command Council," October 11, 1990, CRRC.

95. SH-MISC-D-000-783, "Saddam Hussein Speech Drafts," August 12, 1990, CRRC, 10.

96. SH-MISC-D-000-783, "Saddam Hussein Speech Drafts," August 12, 1990, CRRC, 10–13.

97. Quoted in Buch and Sagan, "Our Red Lines and Theirs."

98. SH-SHTP-A-001-042 "Saddam Hussein and the Revolutionary Command Council Discussing the Iraqi Invasion of Kuwait and the Expected U.S. Attack," December 29, 1990, CRRC, 11, http://crrc.dodlive.mil/files/2013/06/SH-SHTP-A-001-042.pdf. An excerpt from this document is available in Woods, Palkki, and Stout, *Saddam Tapes*, 243–46. Hammadi did not reference nuclear weapons specifically. He was joining a discussion by Izzat al-Duri and Ali Hassan Majid that raised concerns that public preparation and discussion of the effects of potential nuclear strikes were harming Iraqi morale.

99. Woods, *Mother of All Battles*, 151–56; Richard L. Russell, "Iraq's Chemical Weapons Legacy: What Others Might Learn from Saddam," *Middle East Journal* 59, no. 2 (Spring 2005): 199–204; Timothy V. McCarthy and Jonathan B. Tucker, "Saddam's Toxic Arsenal: Chemical and Biological Weapons in the Gulf Wars," in *Planning the Unthinkable: How New Powers Will Use Nuclear, Biological, and Chemical Weapons*, ed. Peter Lavoy, Scott D. Sagan, and James J. Wirtz (Ithaca, NY: Cornell University Press, 2000), 67–68.

100. SH-SHTP-A-000-810, "Meeting between Saddam Hussein and the Delegation of Jordanian Arab Democratic Youth," December 25, 1990, CRRC, 1.

101. Quoted in Buch and Sagan, "Our Red Lines and Theirs."

102. "Saddam and His Inner Circle Discuss Iraq's WMD Capabilities and Deterrent Threats," undated [circa mid-November 1990], in Woods, Palkki, and Stout, *Saddam Tapes*, 239. The discussion included both deterrent threats and actual use of chemical weapons. It is not entirely clear to which Aziz was referring, but if threats invited a nuclear response, then actual use would as well. Moreover, Saddam did publicly state Iraq might use chemical weapons, suggesting Aziz's main concern was actual use. See also Baram, "Deterrence Lessons from Iraq," 85.

103. "Saddam's Personal Involvement in WMD Planning," undated [circa second week of January, 1991], in Charles Duelfer, *Comprehensive Report of the Special Advisor to the DCI on Iraq's WMD*, vol. 1, September 2004, 99, https://www.cia.gov/library/readingroom/docs/DOC_0001156395.pdf.

104. Duelfer, *Comprehensive Report*, 1:33. See also McCarthy and Tucker, "Saddam's Toxic Arsenal," 69.

105. Quoted in Meachem, *Destiny and Power*, 463. See also Scott D. Sagan, "The Commitment Trap: Why the United States Should Not Use Nuclear Threats to Deter Biological and Chemical Weapons Attacks," *International Security* 24, no. 4 (Spring 2000): 95.

106. On Secretary Baker's warning see Woods, Palkki, and Stout, *Saddam Tapes*, 221–22. In addition, Sagan and Buch highlight that in Saddam Hussein's "post-capture interrogation, the Iraqi leader claimed not to know that Baker's threats were even connected with the use of chemical weapons." See Buch and Sagan, "Our Red Lines and Theirs."

107. To the extent American threats were credible, then, this suggests it was because Iraqi leaders already considered that the use of chemical weapons would raise the risks of a nuclear strike.

108. "Saddam and His Advisers Discuss Iraqi Missile Attacks on Targets in Israel and Saudi Arabia," undated [circa January 17 or 18, 1991], in Woods, Palkki, and Stout, *Saddam Tapes*, 251. See also Duelfer, *Comprehensive Report*, 1:33–34.

109. Quoted in Woods, *Mother of All Battles*, 150.

110. Woods, 150, also 155; and "Saddam's Personal Involvement in WMD Planning," second week of January 1991, in Duelfer, *Comprehensive Report*, 1:97–100.

111. McCarthy and Tucker, "Saddam's Toxic Arsenal," 70, also 68–69; Duelfer, *Comprehensive Report*, 1:33, 97–100; Woods, *Mother of All Battles*, 154–56 and 170n114. Some of Saddam's comments can be interpreted as broadening this to include retaliation for chemical or biological strikes against Iraq, for example, "Saddam and His Advisers Discuss Iraqi Missile Attacks on Targets in Israel and Saudi Arabia, undated [circa January 17–18, 1991], 251. There is also some evidence that Saddam delegated launch authority if the United States invaded Baghdad. See Russell, "Iraq's Chemical Weapons Legacy," 201. However, Woods et al. report finding "no evidence in the tapes indicating that Saddam believed American fear of Iraqi chemical or

biological weapon attacks on Israel or the United States deterred an American push toward Baghdad": Woods, Palkki, and Stout, *Saddam Tapes*, 236.

112. SH-SHTP-A-000-931, "Saddam Hussein Meeting with Advisors regarding the American Ground Attack during First Gulf War," February 24, 1991, 12, http://crrc.dodlive.mil/files/2013/01/SH-SHTP-A-000-931_TF.pdf; SH-SHTP-A-000-666, "Saddam Hussein and Iraqi Officials Discussing a US-led Attack on Faylakah Island and the Condition of the Iraqi Army," February 24, 1991, 14, http://crrc.dodlive.mil/files/2013/01/SH-SHTP-A-000-666_TF.pdf; and Woods, *Mother of All Battles*, 132, 136, 179, 210–11.

113. "Iraq Considers How to Counteract the Coalition Air Assault," January 13, 1991, in Woods, Palkki, and Stout, *Saddam Tapes*, 181. For a slightly different translation see Woods, *Mother of All Battles*, 179.

114. "Saddam Predicts the Effects Iraqi Nuclear Weapons Would Have on Conventional Warfare with Israel," March 27, 1979, in Woods, Palkki, and Stout, *Saddam Tapes*, 224.

115. Quoted in Buch and Sagan, "Our Red Lines and Theirs."

116. Quoted in Woods, *Mother of All Battles*, 154. See also Woods, Palkki, and Stout, *Saddam Tapes*, 252–53, note 82; and SH-MISC-D-000-298, "Daily Statements regarding the Iraq War in 1991," entry for February 7, 1991, CRRC, 16.

117. Norman Polmar and Robert S. Norris report that the Pershing II was operational through 1991, with the last missile shipped from West Germany on March 13, 1991. Woods reports the United States destroyed the last Pershing missile in May 1991. Though Iraqi discussion seems to have centered on ground-launched missiles, it is possible that some Iraqi officials were referring to (or confusing the Pershing with) Tomahawk ship-launched cruise missiles. Nonnuclear variants were used during the 1991 Gulf War. The US Navy fired 288 conventional Tomahawks during the conflict from surface vessels and submarines. On these points see Norman Polmar and Robert S. Norris, *The U.S. Nuclear Arsenal: A History of Weapons and Delivery Systems since 1945* (Annapolis, MD: Naval Institute Press, 2009), 176–77, 196–98; and Woods, *Mother of All Battles*, 169–70, note 112.

118. Meacham, *Destiny and Power*, 463.

119. CRRC has over one hundred pages of internal Iraqi documents discussing civil defense plans in the event of a nuclear attack in the collection SH-IDGS-D-001-431, "Correspondence between the Presidential Diwan and several other Iraqi authorities discussing an emergency evacuation plan of different Iraqi cities in the case of a nuclear attack." I identify the specific documents when citing from this collection. See also the brief discussion in Woods, *Mother of All Battles*, 153–54; and Woods, Palkki, and Stout, *Saddam Tapes*, 236.

120. SH-IDGS-D-001-431, "The Evacuation Plan of the City of Baghdad upon the Sudden Use of Nuclear Weapons—Attachment in Ministry of Interior to Baghdad Municipality," circa October 24, 1990, CRRC, source document p. 107.

121. SH-IDGS-D-001-431, "Evaluation of the Evacuation Drill of Saddam City," December 29, 1990, CRRC, 1–2.

122. SH-SHTP-A-001-042, "The Revolutionary Command Council Discusses Civil Defense Measures and Iraqi Morale in the Face of Potential Nuclear Strikes," December 29, 1990, in Woods, Palkki, and Stout, *Saddam Tapes*, 243. All subsequent references to this document rely on the full version of the meeting at http://crrc.dodlive.mil/files/2013/06/SH-SHTP-A-001-042.pdf.

123. SH-SHTP-A-001-042, "The Revolutionary Command Council Discusses Civil Defense Measures and Iraqi Morale in the Face of Potential Nuclear Strikes," December 29, 1990, CRRC, 8

124. SH-SHTP-A-001-042, "The Revolutionary Command Council Discusses Civil Defense Measures and Iraqi Morale in the Face of Potential Nuclear Strikes," December 29, 1990, CRRC, 16. While Saddam's statement is disturbing, it has, admittedly, more thoughtful analogues elsewhere. For instance, Paul Shulte notes that during the 1961 Berlin crisis "President John Kennedy called on his countrymen to learn what to do to protect their families in case of a nuclear attack." Paul Shulte, "Tactical Nuclear Weapons in NATO and Beyond: A Historical and Thematic Examination," in *Tactical Nuclear Weapons and NATO*, ed. Tom Nichols, Douglas Stuart, and Jeffrey D. McCausland (Carlisle, PA: Strategic Studies Institute, 2012), 35. For

general discussions of civil defense preparations see Tracy D. Davis, *Stages of Emergency: Cold War Nuclear Civil Defense* (Durham, NC: Duke University Press, 2007).

125. Scott D. Sagan, "More Will Be Worse," in *The Spread of Nuclear Weapons: An Enduring Debate*, by Scott D. Sagan and Kenneth N. Waltz (New York: W. W. Norton, 2013), 75.

3. Egypt versus Israel

1. Vipin Narang, *Nuclear Strategy in the Modern Era: Regional Nuclear Powers and International Conflict* (Princeton, NJ: Princeton University Press, 2014), 288, 291; Zeev Maoz, "The Mixed Blessing of Israel's Nuclear Policy," *International Security* 28, no. 2 (Fall 2003): 60–61; Yair Evron, "The Relevance and Irrelevance of Nuclear Options in Conventional Wars: The 1973 October War," *Jerusalem Journal of International Relations* 7, nos. 1–2 (1984): 143–76.

2. Avner Cohen, *Israel and the Bomb* (New York: Columbia University Press, 1998), 274; Narang, *Nuclear Strategy*, 183–84, 284–86. Most quantitative datasets code Israel acquiring a nuclear weapon at this time. For example, see Erik Gartzke and Matthew Kroenig, "A Strategic Approach to Nuclear Proliferation," *Journal of Conflict Resolution* 53, no. 2 (April 2009): 151–60.

3. Cohen, *Israel and the Bomb*, 274.

4. Hans M. Kristensen and Robert S. Norris, "Global Nuclear Weapons Inventories, 1945–2013," *Bulletin of the Atomic Scientists* 69, no. 5 (2013): 78; Robert S. Norris and Hans M. Kristensen, "Global Nuclear Weapons Inventories, 1945–2010," *Bulletin of the Atomic Scientists* 66, no. 5 (September/October 2010): 81; Robert S. Norris, William M. Arkin, Hans M. Kristensen, and Joshua Handler, "Israeli Nuclear Forces, 2002," *Bulletin of the Atomic Scientists* 58, no. 2 (September/October 2002): 73–75; Hans M. Kristensen and Robert S. Norris, "Israeli Nuclear Weapons," *Bulletin of the Atomic Scientists* 70, no. 6 (2014): 97–115; Avner Cohen, "How Nuclear Was It? New Testimony on the 1973 Yom Kippur War," October 2013, https://www.armscontrolwonk.com/archive/206909/israel-nuclear-weapons-and-the-1973-yom-kippur-war/#_ftn1; Anthony H. Cordesman, "Israeli Weapons of Mass Destruction," Center for Strategic and International Studies, June 2, 2008, https://csis-prod.s3.amazonaws.com/s3fs-public/legacy_files/files/media/csis/pubs/080603_israel_syria_wmd.pdf; Federation of American Scientists, "WMD around the World: Israel," https://fas.org/nuke/guide/israel/nuke/index.html; Abdullah Toukan and Anthony Cordesman, "Study on a Possible Israeli Strike on Iran's Nuclear Development Facilities," Center for International and Strategic Studies (March 2009), https://csis-prod.s3.amazonaws.com/s3fs-public/legacy_files/files/media/csis/pubs/090316_israelistrikeiran.pdf; Elbridge Colby, Avner Cohen, William McCants, Bradley Morris, and William Rosenau, *The Israeli "Nuclear Alert" of 1973: Deterrence and Signaling in Crisis*, CNA (April 2013), 22, https://www.cna.org/CNA_files/PDF/DRM-2013-U-004480-Final.pdf.

5. Avner Cohen, "The 1967 Six-Day War: New Israeli Perspective, 50 Years Later," Wilson Center, Nuclear Proliferation International History Project, June 3, 2017, https://www.wilsoncenter.org/publication/the-1967-six-day-war.

6. The International Institute of Strategic Studies (IISS) reports that Israel had fifteen Vautour light jet bombers in service in 1967: see IISS, *The Military Balance, 1967*, 40. On Vautour strikes against Iraq see Lon Nordeen, *Fighters over Israel* (New York: Orion Books, 1990), 67–68. The Mirage III aircraft was nuclear capable, although the variant the Israelis possessed was the Mirage IIIC, which was primarily an interceptor. Aronson identifies a subsonic French light bomber as a possible delivery platform, though not stating the Vautour by name. Shlomo Aronson, "Israel's Nuclear Programme, the Six Day War and Its Ramifications," *Israel Affairs* 6, nos. 3–4 (2000): 92. On French use of the Mirage IIIE as a nuclear delivery platform see Robert S. Norris, Andrew S. Burrows, and Richard W. Fieldhouse, *Nuclear Weapons Databook*, vol. 5, *British, French, and Chinese Nuclear Weapons* (Boulder, CO: Westview, 1984), 261–63.

7. Avner Cohen, "Nuclear Arms in Crisis under Secrecy: Israel and the 1967 and 1973 Wars," in *Planning the Unthinkable: How New Powers Will Use Nuclear, Biological, and Chemical Weapons*, eds. Peter Lavoy, Scott D. Sagan, and James J. Wirtz (Ithaca, NY: Cornell University

Press, 2000), 117–19; Seymour M. Hersh, *The Samson Option: Israel's Nuclear Arsenal and American Foreign Policy* (New York: Random House, 1991), 225–26; Colby et al., *Israeli "Nuclear Alert."* On Israeli capabilities see also the IISS *Military Balance* volumes for 1967 through 1973; Nuclear Threat Initiative, "Israel/Missile" November 2012, http://www.nti.org/country-pro files/israel/delivery-systems/; and Norris et al., "Israeli Nuclear Forces, 2002," 73–75. Norris et al. provide an estimated range for the Jericho I of 1,200 km in their table of Israeli Strategic Forces, but note that original Israeli interests centered on a missile with a range of 235–500 km. Other sources report ranges closer to 500 km; see, e.g., SNIE 4-1-74, "Prospects for Further Proliferation of Nuclear Weapons," Central Intelligence Agency, August 23, 1974, 22, National Security Archive (NSA) Electronic Briefing Book (EBB) 240, https://nsarchive2.gwu.edu/NSAEBB/NSAEBB240/snie.pdf; Cordesman, "Israeli Weapons of Mass Destruction"; FAS (Federation of American Scientists), "Jericho 1," https://fas.org/nuke/guide/israel/missile/jericho-1.htm. On Israeli assurances with the Skyhawk see Zach Levey, "The United States' Skyhawk Sale to Israel, 1966: Strategic Exigencies of an Arms Deal," *Diplomatic History* 28, no. 2 (April 2004): 273. For the Phantom see Warnke to Rabin, November 27, 1968, Israel Crosses the Threshold Collection, NSA, EBB 189, http://www.gwu.edu/~nsarchiv/NSAEBB/NSAEBB189/IN-03d.pdf and https://nsarchive2.gwu.edu/NSAEBB/NSAEBB189/index. htm. At times the Israelis hedged their guarantees; see Telegram from Department of State to Embassy in Israel, September 11, 1968, *FRUS 1964–1968*, vol. 20, 490–92, http://history.state.gov/historicaldocuments/frus1964-68v20/d250.

8. Colby et al., *Israeli "Nuclear Alert,"* 10.

9. Mohamed Heikal, *The Road to Ramadan* (New York: Quadrangle, 1975), 76–77; Shlomo Aronson with Oded Brosh, *The Politics and Strategy of Nuclear Weapons in the Middle East: Opacity, Theory, and Reality* (Albany: SUNY Press, 1992), 130–31.

10. Hersh, *Samson Option*, 219–20.

11. Quoted in Cohen, *Israel and the Bomb*, 337.

12. Memorandum of Conversation between President Richard Nixon and Egyptian National Security Affairs Adviser Hafiz Ismail, February 23, 1973, *FRUS 1969–1976*, vol. 25, 76. See also Secret Talks with Hafiz Ismail in New York, February 25, 1973, Digital National Security Archive (hereafter DNSA), Kissinger Transcripts (hereafter KT), item KT00681, 12.

13. Secret Meeting with Hafiz Ismail in New York, February 26, 1973, DNSA, KT, item KT00682, 28. Interestingly, Ismail immediately interrupted Dr. Ghanin and stated, "We are not discussing this." This may reflect Egyptian wariness on sharing with the United States how much Egypt knew of the Israeli nuclear capability. Alternatively, it may reflect Ismail's desire not to discuss the issue in front of such a large group, perhaps preferring to raise the matter off the record and in private with Kissinger.

14. Quoted in Richard B. Parker, ed., *The October War: A Retrospective* (Gainesville: University Press of Florida, 2001), 119.

15. Shlomo Aronson, "David Ben-Gurion, Levi Eshkol and the Struggle over Dimona: A Prologue to the Six-Day War and Its (Un)Anticipated Results," *Israel Affairs* 15, no. 2 (2009): 120–21; Michael Karpin, *The Bomb in the Basement: How Israel Went Nuclear and What That Means for the World* (New York: Simon & Schuster, 2006), 273–74.

16. Secret Conversation with Hafiz Ismail in France, May 20, 1973, DNSA, KT, KT00732, 17. See also Kissinger to Nixon, May 20, 1973, *FRUS 1969–1973*, vol. 25, 189.

17. Quoted in Aronson, "David Ben-Gurion," 118.

18. Dan Sagir, "How the Fear of Israel Nukes Helped Seal the Egypt Peace Deal," *Haaretz*, November 26, 2017, https://www.haaretz.com/israel-news/.premium-how-fear-of-israeli-nukes-helped-seal-the-egypt-peace-deal-1.5626679. On general Egyptian concerns see also Ariel E. Levite and Emily B. Landau, "Arab Perceptions of Israel's Nuclear Posture, 1960–1967," *Israel Studies* 1, no. 1 (1996).

19. Rusk to Johnson, May 10, 1965, *FRUS 1964–1968*, vol. 18, 455, https://history.state.gov/historicaldocuments/frus1964-68v18/d214.

20. Kenneth M. Pollack, *Arabs at War: Military Effectiveness, 1948–1991* (Lincoln: University of Nebraska Press, 2002), 93–94.

21. CINC comprises six measures, including population, urban population, iron and steel production, energy production, military expenditures, and military personnel.

22. IISS, *The Military Balance*, vol. 67, no. 1, to vol. 79, no. 1 (annual editions from 1967 to 1979).

23. Saad El Shazly, *The Crossing of the Suez* (San Francisco: American Mideast Research, 1980), 22.

24. George W. Gawrych, *The Albatross of Decisive Victory: War and Policy between Egypt and Israel in the 1967 and 1973 Arab-Israeli Wars* (Westport, CT: Greenwood, 2000), 12–13; George W. Gawrych, "The Egyptian High Command in the 1973 War," *Armed Forces and Society* 13, no. 4 (Summer 1987): 535–46; Pollack, *Arabs at War*, 58, 82–84; Risa Brooks, "An Autocracy at War: Explaining Egypt's Military Effectiveness, 1967 and 1973," *Security Studies* 15, no. 3 (July–September 2006): 412–19.

25. Pollack, *Arabs at War*, 74.

26. Pollack, 88–90, 104; Gawrych, *Albatross of Decisive Victory*, chap. 3; Gawrych, "Egyptian High Command," 546–54; Brooks, "Autocracy at War," 419.

27. Pollack, *Arabs at War*, 88–98; Zeev Maoz, *Defending the Holy Land: A Critical Analysis of Israel's Security and Foreign Policy* (Ann Arbor: University of Michigan Press, 2006), chap. 4

28. Brooks, "Autocracy at War," 397.

29. Brooks, 427; John J. Mearsheimer, *Conventional Deterrence* (Ithaca, NY: Cornell University Press, 1983), 155–60; Parker, *October War*, 37; Pollack, *Arabs at War*, 99–104.

30. Parker, *October War*, chap. 3; Mohamed Abdel Ghani El-Gamasy, *The October War: Memoirs of Field Marshal El-Gamasy of Egypt*, trans. Gillian Potter, Nadra Morcos, and Rosette Frances (Cairo: American University of Cairo Press, 1993), 222; Mearsheimer, *Conventional Deterrence*, 159–62; Craig Daigle, *Limits of Détente: The United States, the Soviet Union, and the Arab-Israeli Conflict, 1969–1973* (New Haven, CT: Yale University Press, 2012), 195, 281–82; Thomas W. Lippman, *Hero of the Crossing: How Anwar Sadat and the 1973 War Changed the World* (Lincoln: University of Nebraska Press, 2016), 1.

31. Stephen D. Biddle, *Military Power: Explaining Victory and Defeat in Modern Battle* (Princeton, NJ: Princeton University Press, 2004).

32. Ryan Grauer and Michael C. Horowitz, "What Determines Military Victory? Testing the Modern System," *Security Studies* 21, no. 1 (January–March 2012): 83–112. Coding for specific operations is contained in their Stata .dta file, http://www.michaelchorowitz.com/data/.

33. Mearsheimer, *Conventional Deterrence*, 143–44, 150–55. For the similarity of what Mearsheimer labels a blitzkrieg strategy with Biddle's discussion of breakthrough and exploitation, compare Mearsheimer, *Conventional Deterrence*, 35–43, to Biddle, *Military Power*, 40–42. On Egyptian shift from a defense in depth to a forward defense see Pollack, *Arabs at War*, 61.

34. Stephen M. Walt, *The Origins of Alliances* (Ithaca, NY: Cornell University Press, 1987), 51.

35. Narang, *Nuclear Strategy*, 193–97.

36. Narang, 186.

37. On these points see Narang, 186–96, 286–92; Colby et al., *Israeli "Nuclear Alert"*; Cohen, "Nuclear Arms in Crisis," 117–22.

38. Walt, *Origins of Alliances*, chap. 3.

39. Maria Post Rublee, *Nonproliferation Norms: Why States Choose Nuclear Restraint* (Athens: University of Georgia Press, 2009), 118.

40. Maoz, *Defending the Holy Land*, 114–15; Gawrych, *Albatross of Decisive Victory*, 101–2; Richard B. Parker, *The Politics of Miscalculation in the Middle East* (Bloomington: Indiana University Press, 1993), 127.

41. Quoted in Daigle, *Limits of Détente*, 16.

42. Nasser would officially abrogate the cease-fire on April 1, 1969, while Egyptian spokesman noted as early as March 12, 1969, that Egypt would no longer be bound by the cease-fire. See Pollack, *Arabs at War*, 92; Gawrych, *Albatross of Decisive Victory*, 107–8; Parker, *Politics of Miscalculation*, 135; Isabella Ginor, "'Under the Yellow Arab Helmet Gleamed Blue Russian Eyes': Operation Kavkaz and the War of Attrition, 1969–70," *Cold War History* 13, no. 1 (October 2002), 135.

43. Parker, *Politics of Miscalculation*, 128.

44. Parker, 130.

45. Quoted in Gawrych, *Albatross of Decisive Victory*, 107.

46. Gawrych, 106, see also 103–6.

47. Quoted in Yoram Meital, *Egypt's Struggle for Peace: Continuity and Change, 1967–1977* (Gainesville: University Press of Florida, 1997), 63. See also Daigle, *Limits of Détente*, 39.

48. Ginor, "'Under the Yellow Arab Helmet,'" 133.

49. Daigle, *Limits of Détente*, chap. 2; Meital, *Egypt's Struggle for Peace*, 66–67; Parker, *Politics of Miscalculation*, 138–39.

50. Quoted in Daigle, *Limits of Détente*, 119.

51. Daigle, 113–43; Meital, *Egypt's Struggle for Peace*, 70–76.

52. Sadat's appointment as Egypt's president was confirmed by public referendum in October 15, 1970.

53. Diplomatic Relations Initiative between Egypt and Israel, February 8, 1971, DNSA, Kissinger Telephone Conversations, item KA04892. On the proposal and Sadat's intentions see Daigle, *Limits of Détente*, 163; Donald Neff, *Warriors against Israel* (Brattleboro, VT: Amana Books, 1988), 45–46; Meital, *Egypt's Struggle for Peace*, 86–89.

54. Quoted in Daigle, *Limits of Détente*, 171.

55. Discussion of Middle East Settlement with Mahmoud Riad, October 7, 1971, DNSA, KT, item KT00361, 2.

56. Neff, *Warriors against Israel*, 23.

57. Quoted in Meital, *Egypt's Struggle for Peace*, 106. See also Daigle, *Limits of Détente*, 212; Neff, *Warriors against Israel*, 76, 103.

58. Memorandum of Conversation between President Richard Nixon and Egyptian National Security Affairs Adviser Hafiz Ismail, February 23, 1973, *FRUS 1969–1976*, vol. 25, 74.

59. Daigle, *Limits of Détente*, 195, 210–13, 229–35.

60. Quoted in Daigle, 213.

61. Quoted in Daigle, 219; see also 195–201, 212, 216–20, 232–34, 265–68, 286–87; and Victor Israelyan, *Inside the Kremlin during the Yom Kippur War* (University Park: University of Pennsylvania Press, 1995), 16–19.

62. Quoted in Daigle, *Limits of Détente*, 226, see also 195, 232–34; Parker, *October War*, 73; Meital, *Egypt's Struggle for Peace*, 108–10; Neff, *Warriors against Israel*, 85–87.

63. Quoted in Daigle, *Limits of Détente*, 233.

64. Quoted in Daigle, 283.

65. Ashraf Ghorbal remarks in Parker, *October War*, 36, see also 21, 36–37, 48, 53–57, 70–76; Meital, *Egypt's Struggle for Peace*, 110–11; Neff, *Warriors against Israel*, 87–90.

66. Memorandum of Conversation between President Richard Nixon and Egyptian National Security Affairs Adviser Hafiz Ismail, February 23, 1973, *FRUS 1969–1976*, vol. 25, 73–76; Secret Meeting with Hafiz Ismail in New York, February 25, 1973, DNSA, KT, item KT00681, 2; and secret conversation with Hafiz Ismail in France, May 20, 1973, DNSA, KT, item KT00732, 17.

67. Daigle, *Limits of Détente*, 235–36.

68. Quoted in Daigle, 259.

69. See also Jeremy M. Sharp, "U.S. Foreign Aid to Israel," Congressional Research Service, June 10, 2015, 30.

70. Daigle, *Limits of Détente*, 179–91; Neff, *Warriors against Israel*, 68–69.

71. Discussion of Middle East Settlement with Mahmoud Riad, October 7, 1971, DNSA, KT, item KT00361, 1.

72. Memorandum of Conversation between President Richard Nixon and Egyptian National Security Affairs Adviser Hafiz Ismail, February 23, 1973, *FRUS 1969–1976*, vol. 25, 75. Ismail raised the point again with Kissinger two days later; see Secret Meeting with Hafiz Ismail in New York, February 25, 1973, DNSA, KT, item KT00681, 7, 32. Ismail told Secretary Rogers that Egypt hoped "to persuade the U.S. to change its policy in the Middle East to one which would not be based on what Egypt considers total support for Israel." Memorandum of Conversation between US Secretary of State William Rogers and Egyptian National Security Affairs Adviser Hafiz Ismail, February 23, 1973, *FRUS 1969–1976*, vol. 25, 78n3.

73. Daigle, *Limits of Détente*, 259.

74. Secret Conversation with Hafiz Ismail in France, May 20, 1973, DNSA, 10, 17. See also the Egyptian complaint over US arms sales in March in Backchannel Message from the Egyptian Presidential Adviser for National Security Affairs (Ismail) to the President's Assistant for National Security Affairs (Kissinger), March 20, 1973, *FRUS 1969–1976*, vol. 25, 122.

75. Quoted in Daigle, *Limits of Détente*, 259. See also Maoz, *Defending the Holy Land*, 152; Meital, *Egypt's Struggle for Peace*, 111–12.

76. Quoted in Daigle, *Limits of Détente*, 260.

77. Quoted in Israelyan, *Inside the Kremlin*, 72. Sadat recalled making a similar statement to Nasser: "even 10cm on the other side of the canal would change the situation in the western, eastern, and Arab realms equally." Quoted in Meital, *Egypt's Struggle for Peace*, 114.

78. Memorandum of Conversation between President Richard Nixon and General Secretary of the Central Committee Leonid I. Brezhnev, June 23, 1973, *FRUS 1969–1976*, vol. 25, 221.

79. Kissinger to Nixon, February 23, 1973, *FRUS 1969–1976*, vol. 25, 70n3.

80. Quoted in Daigle, *Limits of Détente*, 268. See also Kissinger's statements to Ismail in Secret Meeting with Hafiz Ismail in New York, February 25, 1973, DNSA, KT, item KT00681, 21; and Secret Meeting with Hafiz Ismail in New York, February 26, 1973, DNSA, KT, item KT00682 17. On Kissinger's intention to stall during 1973 see Memorandum of Conversation between Henry Kissinger and Israeli Ambassador to the United States Yitzhak Rabin, February 22, 1973, *FRUS 1969–1976*, vol. 25, 63–65; Memorandum of Conversation between Henry Kissinger and Israeli Ambassador to the United States Simcha Dinitz, March 30, 1973, *FRUS 1969–76*, vol. 25, 125–29, esp. 126–27; State Department Involvement in Middle East Peace Negotiations, February 22, 1973, DNSA, Kissinger Telephone Conversations, item KA09582, esp. 1, 5; and Memorandum of Conversation between Henry Kissinger and Simcha Dinitz, September 10, 1973, *FRUS 1969–1976*, vol. 25, esp. 266–67. For a general discussions of Kissinger's views see Daigle, *Limits of Détente*, 34, 72, 120–22, 236, 243–46, 250–60, 268–69, 281. For a minority view in Washington, in line with Nixon, that the likelihood of conflict in late 1973 was 50–50 because Sadat "seems on the verge of concluding that only limited hostilities against Israel stood any real chance of breaking the negotiating stalemate by forcing the big powers to intervene with an imposed solution" see the Editorial Note discussing the May 31, 1973, State Department Bureau of Intelligence and Research report in *FRUS 1969–1976*, vol. 25, 193–194; and Roger Merrick's remarks in Parker, *October War*, 113–16.

81. For the timeline see Maoz, *Defending the Holy Land*, 420–36.

82. Maoz, 427.

83. Maoz, 116; Gawrych, *Albatross of Decisive Victory*, 107–8.

84. Pollack, *Arabs at War*, 91.

85. Maoz, *Defending the Holy Land*, 117; Parker, *Politics of Miscalculation*, 150.

86. Pollack, *Arabs at War*, 90–98.

87. Parker, *Politics of Miscalculation*, 135–44; Daigle, *Limits of Détente*, chap. 3; Gawrych, *Albatross of Decisive Victory*, 106–18; Pollack, *Arabs at War*, 90–98; Ginor, "'Under the Yellow Arab Helmet'"; Maoz, *Defending the Holy Land*, chap. 4; Dima P. Adamsky, "'Zero-Hour for the Bears': Inquiring into the Soviet Decision to Intervene in the Egyptian-Israeli War of Attrition, 1969–70," *Cold War History* 6, no. 1 (2006): 113–36. Soviet motives for support varied, but there is general agreement Nasser sought greater Soviet involvement in December–January 1969–1970 as Israeli attacks pummeled Egyptian air defenses and then moved to deep-penetration strikes.

88. Mearsheimer, *Conventional Deterrence*, 155–62; Pollack, *Arabs at War*, 98–108.

89. Quoted in Shazly, *Crossing of the Suez*, 179–80. See also Gamasy, *October War*, 149–51.

90. Gamasy, *October War*, 134.

91. Shazly, *Crossing of the Suez*, 36–37; Avraham Sela, "The 1973 Arab War Coalition: Aims, Coherence, and Gains-Distribution," *Israeli Affairs* 6, no. 1 (1999): 55–56; Meital, *Egypt's Struggle for Peace*, 115–16; Daigle, *Limits of Détente*, 285–86.

92. Brooks, "Autocracy at War," 419–27.

93. This paragraph draws on Pollack, *Arabs at War*, 108–17; Neff, *Warriors against Israel*, 141–46, 163–66, 173–85; Gawrych, *Albatross of Decisive Victory*, chap 6.

94. Backchannel Message from the Egyptian Presidential Adviser for National Security Affairs (Ismail) to Secretary of State Kissinger, October 7, 1973 *FRUS 1969–1976*, vol. 25, 347. Heikal contended that Sadat sent a message to Kissinger as early as October 5. I found no such message in the American documents I examined. See Colby et al., *Israeli "Nuclear Alert*," 13n20.

95. Quoted in Gamasy, *October War*, 237–38. Ismail's account of the message closely matches the American record. Gamasy would criticize the message for revealing Egypt's "military intentions" (239–40).

96. Minutes of WSAG Meeting, October 7, 1973, *FRUS 1969–1976*, vol. 25, 355, emphasis in original.

97. Backchannel Message from Secretary of State Kissinger to the Egyptian Presidential Adviser for National Security Affairs (Ismail), undated [October 12, 1973], *FRUS 1969–1976*, vol. 25, 447.

98. Kissinger to Ismail, October 9, 1973, *FRUS 1969–1976*, vol. 25, 407–8; Daigle, *Limits of Détente*, 298–300; Neff, *Warriors against Israel*, 155; Minutes of WSAG Meeting, October 7, 1973, *FRUS 1969–1976*, vol. 25, 357; Kissinger to Ismail, October 8, 1973, *FRUS 1969–1976*, vol. 25, 368–69.

99. Israelyan, *Inside the Kremlin*, 13–15, 43–45.

100. On Sadat's rejection of cease-fire proposals see discussion of Telegram 5360 of October 8, 1973, *FRUS 1969–1976*, vol. 25, 369, notes 3 and 4; Israelyan, *Inside the Kremlin*, 39–51, 81, 105; discussion of Kissinger and Zayyat's conversation of October 7, 1973, *FRUS 1969–1976*, 25, 348n4; and Telcon, Kissinger-Zayyat, October 6, 1973, DNSA, Kissinger Telephone Conversations, item KA11038.

101. Israelyan, *Inside the Kremlin*, 39.

102. Meital, *Egypt's Struggle for Peace*, 114. On the importance of continuing the fight to attain greater US involvement see Daigle, *Limits of Détente*, 300. On Egyptian opposition to the status quo ante see, for example, Telcon, Kissinger-Zayyat, October 6, 1973, DNSA, Kissinger Telephone Conversations, item KA11038, 1–2.

103. Pollack, *Arabs at War*, 111; Neff, *Warriors against Israel*, 146; and Evron, "Relevance and Irrelevance," 161. On the general Egyptian elation at the outcome of the first days of fighting see Israelyan, *Inside the Kremlin*, 45; Maoz, *Defending the Holy Land*, 156. For US views see Minutes of WSAG Meeting, October 7, 1973, *FRUS 1969–1976*, vol. 25, 355; Memorandum of Conversation between Henry Kissinger and Simcha Dinitz, October 9, 1973, *FRUS 1969–1976*, vol. 25, 393.

104. Memorandum of Conversation between Henry Kissinger and Simcha Dinitz, October 9, 1973, *FRUS 1969–1976*, 25, 393.

105. Meital, *Egypt's Struggle for Peace*, 116–17.

106. Neff, *Warriors against Israel*, 213–14; Pollack, *Arabs at War*, 114–16; Meital, *Egypt's Struggle for Peace*, 122; Maoz, *Defending the Holy Land*, 157–58; Gawrych, *Albatross of Decisive Victory*, 202–5; Brooks, "Autocracy at War," 423.

107. Israelyan, *Inside the Kremlin*, 71–72.

108. Quoted in Neff, *Warriors against Israel*, 214. See also Gawrych, *Albatross of Decisive Victory*, 205.

109. Neff, *Warriors against Israel*, 236, 248–50; Gawrych, *Albatross of Decisive Victory*, 215.

110. Gawrych, *Albatross of Decisive Victory*, 224–32.

111. Telegram from the Department of State Embassy in the United Arab Republic, February 28, 1966, *FRUS 1964–1968*, vol. 18, 562–63, https://history.state.gov/historicaldocuments/frus1964-68v18/d277. See also Ariel E. Levite and Emily B. Landau, "Arab Perceptions of Israel's Nuclear Posture, 1960–1967," *Middle Eastern Studies* 1, no. 1 (1996): 34–59.

112. Quoted in Maria Post Rublee, *Nonproliferation Norms: Why States Choose Nuclear Restraint* (Athens: University of Georgia Press, 2009), 117.

113. T. V. Paul, *The Tradition of Non-use of Nuclear Weapons* (Stanford, CA: Stanford University Press, 2009), 147–48, 260n17.

114. Pollack remarks in Parker, *October War*, 118. There is some evidence that after the war Sadat expressed the opinion that deep attacks into the Sinai raised the risks of nuclear strikes,

though he also understood Egypt could not reconquer the Sinai given the conventional balance. For instance, Colby et al. write that in 1977 Sadat told the Israeli defense minister Ezer Weizman that "he had never intended to penetrate deeper into the Sinai because 'he knew what Israel had,'" presumably referring to Israel's nuclear weapons capability. Colby et al., *Israeli "Nuclear Alert*," 10–11. In a colorful anecdote, former Israeli president Shimon Peres told the Israeli media that former deputy prime minister Yigael Yadin "asked Sadat: Why, in the early days of the Yom Kippur War, didn't you proceed toward the Sinai passes? Sadat's answer, according to Peres, was: You have nuclear arms. Haven't you heard?" Dan Sagir, "How the Fear of Israeli Nukes Helped Seal the Egypt Peace Deal," *Haaretz*, November 26, 2017, https://www.haaretz.com/israel-news/.premium-how-fear-of-israeli-nukes-helped-seal-the-egypt-peace-deal-1.5626679.

115. Memorandum from the Assistant Secretary of Defense for International Security Affairs (Warnke) to Secretary of Defense Clifford, October 29, 1968, *FRUS 1964–1968*, vol. 20, 581, https://history.state.gov/historicaldocuments/frus1964-68v20/d295.

116. Memorandum from Helmut Sonnenfeldt [NSC] to Kissinger, October 13, 1973, *FRUS 1969–1976*, vol. 25, 478.

117. Quoted in Colby et al., *Israeli "Nuclear Alert*," 27.

118. Israel's nuclear posture during this period may have encouraged such thinking; see Narang, *Nuclear Strategy*, esp. chaps. 7, 9–10, though I found no evidence Egyptian leaders discussed the nature of Israel's force posture.

119. Dr. Murhaf Jouejati remarks in Parker, *October War*, 119.

120. Heikal, *Road to Ramadan*, 76. See also the April 1969 statement by Fawzi to Kissinger during the War of Attrition that "the UAR [United Arab Republic, i.e., Egypt] knows that the US would not sit back if the UAR committed aggression. 'How could we attack Israel, knowing all this?'" In Meeting with Mahmoud Fawzi on April 10, 1969 [document dated May 29, 1969], DNSA, KT, item KT00023, 2. Though the focus was on attacks against Israel, it reflects the belief that the United States would become involved in any major conflict.

121. Neff, *Warriors against Israel*, 119.

122. For similar interpretations see Gawrych, *Albatross of Decisive Victory*, 181; and Aronson with Brosh, *Politics and Strategy*, 145.

123. Hedrick Smith, "Soviets Said to Offer Cairo Atom Defense," *New York Times*, February 4, 1966, https://timesmachine.nytimes.com/timesmachine/1966/02/04/issue.html. See also Aronson with Brosh, *Politics and Strategy*, 99; Aronson, "The Nuclear Dimension of the Arab-Israeli Conflict," *Jerusalem Journal of International Relations* 7, nos. 1–2 (1984): 112, 124.

124. On nuclear umbrella see Karpin, *Bomb in the Basement*, 274. On Aswan Dam see Aronson with Brosh, *Politics and Strategy*, 135.

125. Rublee, *Nonproliferation Norms*, 136, 251n191. For vague accounts that Soviet naval vessels had orders to use nuclear weapons in specific situations in defense of Syria or Egypt see Isabella Ginor and Gideon Remez, *Foxbats over Dimona: The Soviets' Nuclear Gamble in the Six-Day War* (New Haven, CT: Yale University Press, 2007): 82, 140.

126. Minutes of Bipartisan Leadership Meeting, November 27, 1973, *FRUS 1969–1976*, vol. 25, 993. For similar concerns during the Johnson administration that Israeli nuclear capabilities could provoke the introduction of Soviet nuclear capabilities and support to the area see Letter from President Johnson to Prime Minister Eshkol, May 21, 1965, *FRUS 1954–1968* vol. 18, 463–64, https://history.state.gov/historicaldocuments/frus1964-68v18/d218; Memorandum from the Assistant Secretary of Defense for International Security Affairs (Warnke) to Secretary of Defense Clifford, October 29, 1968, *FRUS 1964–1968*, vol. 20, 581, https://history.state.gov/historicaldocuments/frus1964-68v20/d295; Memorandum of Telephone Conversation between Secretary of State Rusk and Secretary of Defense Clifford, November 1, 1968, *FRUS 1964–1968*, vol. 20, 586, https://history.state.gov/historicaldocuments/frus1964-68v20/d299; Memorandum from the Assistant Secretary of Defense for International Security Affairs (Warnke) to Secretary of Defense Clifford, November 2, 1968, 587, https://history.state.gov/historicaldocuments/frus1964-68v20/d300.

127. There are reasons to question the seriousness of the Soviet intervention proposal; see Parker, *October War*, chap. 5.

128. Terence Roehrig, *Japan, South Korea, and the United States Nuclear Umbrella: Deterrence after the Cold War* (New York: Columbia University Press, 2017), 17.

129. Rublee is addressing Egyptian nuclear forbearance, but the point is applicable in this instance as well. See Rublee, *Nonproliferation Norms*, 137.

130. Francis J. Gavin, "Strategies of Inhibition: U.S. Grand Strategy, the Nuclear Revolution, and Nonproliferation," *International Security* 40, no. 1 (Summer 2015): 9–46.

131. Telegram from the Department of State to the Embassy in the United Arab Republic, February 28, 1966, *FRUS 1964–1968*, vol. 18, 562–63, https://history.state.gov/historicaldocuments/frus1964-68v18/d277. Kissinger would later tell Hafiz Ismail, "We have urged them [the Israelis] to join the Non-Proliferation Treaty, on many occasions and officially." Kissinger was no doubt aware, though, that privately the US had agreed to limit pressure on Israel, as well as of Nixon's somewhat ambivalent attitude toward the NPT more broadly. For Kissinger's statement see Memorandum of Conversation, May 20, 1973, KT00732, 19. On Nixon's views toward the NPT and agreement with Israel see Francis J. Gavin, *Nuclear Statecraft: History and Strategy in America's Atomic Age* (Ithaca, NY: Cornell University Press, 2012), 116–18.

132. Rublee, *Nonproliferation Norms*, chap. 4.

133. Avner Cohen, "Israel Crosses the Threshold Collection," National Security Archive, George Washington University, http://www.gwu.edu/~nsarchiv/NSAEBB/NSAEBB189/index.htm. See also Gavin, *Nuclear Statecraft*, 117; Alan Dowty, "The Enigma of Opacity: Israel's Nuclear Weapons Program as a Field of Study," *Israeli Studies Forum* 20, no. 2 (Winter 2005): 9; Colby et al., *Israeli "Nuclear Alert,"* 45.

134. Daigle, *Limits of Détente*, 8, and chaps. 6–8.

135. Memorandum from the Assistant Secretary of Defense for International Security Affairs (Warnke) to Secretary of Defense Clifford, October 29, 1968, *FRUS 1964–1968*, vol. 20, 581, https://history.state.gov/historicaldocuments/frus1964-68v20/d295.

136. For the Soviet note see Message from Brezhnev to Nixon, October 24, 1973, National Security Archive, "The October War and US Policy," http://www2.gwu.edu/~nsarchiv/NSAEBB/NSAEBB98/index.htm#doc71. On the US reaction to the (as the US record puts it) "real piss-swisher from Brezhnev" see Memorandum for the Record, October 24/25, *FRUS 1969–1976*, vol. 25, 737–42; Minutes of Bipartisan Leadership Meeting, November 27, 1973, *FRUS 1969–1976*, vol. 25, 990. Nixon raised a similar fear in 1970; see Parker, *Politics of Miscalculation*, 134–35.

137. Daigle, *Limits of Détente*, 122–23, 171, 180–88, 344–45.

138. Quoted in Rublee, *Nonproliferation Norms*, 138. See also Gawdat Bahgat, "Nuclear Proliferation: Egypt," *Middle Eastern Studies* 43, no. 3 (May 2007): 409.

139. Rublee, *Nonproliferation Norms*, 115–16.

140. Quoted in Bahgat, "Nuclear Proliferation," 410.

141. Bahgat, 410; Arms Control Association, "Chemical Weapons Convention Signatories and States-Parties," August 2018, https://www.armscontrol.org/factsheets/cwcsig.

142. Rublee, *Nonproliferation Norms*, 138.

143. Pollack, *Arabs at War*, 481.

144. Quoted in Parker, *October War*, 119.

145. Israelyan, *Inside the Kremlin*, 14, see also 13–16, 43–45; and Parker, *October War*, 82, 103, 120.

146. Pollack, *Arabs at War*, esp. 489.

4. China versus the United States

1. Throughout this chapter I use the terms "China," "Chinese," and "People's Republic of China" interchangeably. I recognize that official US policy at the time recognized the regime under Chiang Kai-shek on Taiwan as the legitimate government of China. I refer to Kuomintang (KMT), Nationalist Chinese, and Republic of China interchangeably.

2. For example, Shu Guang Zhang, "Between 'Paper' and 'Real Tigers': Mao's View of Nuclear Weapons," in *Cold War Statesmen Confront the Bomb: Nuclear Diplomacy since 1945*, ed.

John Lewis Gaddis, Philip H. Gordon, Ernest R. May, and Jonathan Rosenberg (Oxford: Oxford University Press, 1999), 194–215.

3. See chapter 5 for additional discussion of the limits of the US nuclear arsenal during this period.

4. Robert S. Norris and Hans M. Kristensen, "U.S. Nuclear Warheads, 1945–2009," *Bulletin of the Atomic Scientists* (July/August 2009): 75; Norman Polmar and Robert S. Norris, *The U.S. Nuclear Arsenal: A History of Weapons and Delivery Systems since 1945* (Annapolis, MD: Naval Institute Press, 2009), 44.

5. Polmar and Norris, *U.S. Nuclear Arsenal*, 89–99.

6. As David Rosenberg notes, "such transfers would continue throughout his administration . . . until by 1961 less than 10 percent of the stockpile remained in civilian control." David Alan Rosenberg, "The Origins of Overkill: Nuclear Weapons and American Strategy, 1945–1960," *International Security* 7, no. 4 (Spring 1983): 27–28.

7. Xiaobing Li, *A History of the Modern Chinese Army* (Lexington: University Press of Kentucky, 2007), 87–88.

8. PPS 39, To Review and Define United States Policy toward China, September 7, 1948, *FRUS 1948*, vol. 8, 147, https://history.state.gov/historicaldocuments/frus1948v08/d122. See also Paul C. Avey, "Confronting Soviet Power: U.S. Policy during the Early Cold War," *International Security* 36, no. 4 (Spring 2012): 184–86.

9. NSC 166/1, U.S. Policy toward Communist China, November 6, 1953, *FRUS 1952–1954*, vol. 14, part 1, 289, https://history.state.gov/historicaldocuments/frus1952-54v14p1/d149.

10. NIE 13–60, Communist China, December 6, 1960, *FRUS 1958–1960*, vol. 19, 739–40, https://history.state.gov/historicaldocuments/frus1958-60v19/d362.

11. This stands in contrast to the Soviet case discussed in the next chapter.

12. Stephen Biddle, *Military Power: Explaining Victory and Defeat in Modern Battle* (Princeton, NJ: Princeton University Press, 2004). Ryan Grauer and Michael Horowitz code two operations during the Korean War in which the United States and/or China participated. They code the United States as implementing the modern system at a high level during the Inchon-Seoul Campaign and a moderate level during the Punchbowl Battles. They code Chinese implementation of the modern system as high during the Punchbowl Battles. See Ryan Grauer and Michael C. Horowitz, "What Determines Military Victory? Testing the Modern System," *Security Studies* 21, no. 1 (January–March 2012): 83–112. Data and coding available in a Stata file at http://www.michaelchoroiwitz.com/data/.

13. Yu Bin, "What China Learned from Its 'Forgotten War,' in Korea," in *Chinese Warfighting: The PLA Experience since 1949*, ed. Mark A. Ryan, David M. Finkelstein, and Michael A. McDevitt (New York: M. E. Sharpe, 2003), 126; "Ciphered Telegram, Mao Zedong to Filippov (Stalin)," November 8, 1950, History and Public Policy Program Digital Archive, Archive of the President of the Russian Federation (APRF), http://digitalarchive.wilsoncenter.org/document/110702.

14. "Telegram from Soviet Ambassador to China N. V. Roshchin to Stalin," October 7, 1950, History and Public Policy Program Digital Archive, Volkogonov Collections, Library of Congress, APRF, trans. for CWIHP by Vladislav Zubok, http://digitalarchive.wilsoncenter.org/document/117314.

15. Yu Bin, "What China Learned," 124–25.

16. Yu Bin, 124. A typical Chinese division was about half the size of an American division. Other estimates note a Chinese army composed of three to four divisions was roughly equivalent to one and a half to two US infantry divisions. Gordon L. Rottman, *Korean War Order of Battle: United States, United Nations, and Communist Ground, Naval, and Air Forces, 1950–1953* (Westport, CT: Praeger, 2002), 16–17, 174–76. The Chinese initially transferred three artillery divisions to the forces for Korea, which would increase to nine artillery divisions after January 1951 and ten by December 1952, along with some armor. Shu Guang Zhang, "Command, Control, and the PLA's Offensive Campaigns in Korea, 1950–1951," in Ryan, Finkelstein, and McDevitt, *Chinese Warfighting*, 120–22; and Li, *History of the Modern Chinese Army*, 105.

17. Yu Bin, "What China Learned," 128–30, 133–37; Li, *History of the Modern Chinese Army*, 93, 98, 111.

18. Zhang, "Command, Control," 112. See also Zhihua Shen and Danhui Li, *After Leaning to One Side: China and Its Allies in the Cold War* (Stanford, CA: Stanford University Press, 2011), 120–21.

19. Li, *History of the Modern Chinese Army*, 112; Zhang, "Between 'Paper' and 'Real Tigers,'" 198–99.

20. Quoted in Avery Goldstein, *Deterrence and Security in the 21st Century: China, Britain, France, and the Enduring Legacy of the Nuclear Revolution* (Stanford, CA: Stanford University Press, 2000): 92n.

21. Mao quoted in Li, *History of the Modern Chinese Army*, 120. On reform efforts and Soviet influence see Li, chap. 4.

22. Li, 129–31; He Di, "The Last Campaign to Unify China: The CCP's Unrealized Plan to Liberate Taiwan, 1949–1950," in Ryan, Finkelstein, and McDevitt, *Chinese Warfighting*, 78; Alexander C. Huang, "The PLA Navy at War, 1949–1999: From Coastal Defense to Distant Operations," in Ryan, Finkelstein, and McDevitt, *Chinese Warfighting*, 250–52.

23. Huang, "PLA Navy at War," 241–69.

24. Xiaoming Zhang, "Air Combat and the People's Republic: The People's Liberation Army Air Force in Action, 1949–1969," in Ryan, Finkelstein, and McDevitt, *Chinese Warfighting*, 270–88, 293–94.

25. NIE-2, Chinese Communist Intervention in Korea, November 8, 1950, *FRUS 1950*, vol. 7, 1103, https://history.state.gov/historicaldocuments/frus1950v07/d789.

26. NSC 166/1, US Policy toward Communist China, November 6, 1953, *FRUS 1952–1954*, vol. 14, part 1, 290, https://history.state.gov/historicaldocuments/frus1952-54v14p1/d149.

27. NIE 13–57, Communist China through 1961, March 19, 1957, *FRUS 1955–1957*, vol. 3, 501, https://history.state.gov/historicaldocuments/frus1955-57v03/d244. See also NIE 13–58, Communist China, May 13, 1958, *FRUS 1958–1960*, vol. 19, 25, https://history.state.gov/historicaldocuments/frus1958-60v19/d13.

28. Wang Jisi and Xu Hui, "Patterns of Sino-American Crises," in *Managing Sino-American Crises: Case Studies and Analysis*, ed. Michael D. Swaine, Zhang Tuosheng, and Danielle F. S. Cohen (Washington, DC: Carnegie Endowment for International Peace, 2006), 139. See also Andrew J. Nathan and Robert S. Ross, *The Great Wall and the Empty Fortress: China's Search for Security* (New York: W. W. Norton, 1997), chap. 2; Michael D. Swaine, "Understanding the Historical Record," in Swaine, Tuosheng, and Cohen, *Managing Sino-American Crises*, 12.

29. Quoted in Shu Guang Zhang, *Deterrence and Strategic Culture: Chinese-American Confrontations, 1949–1958* (Ithaca, NY: Cornell University Press, 1992), 68.

30. M. Taylor Fravel, *Strong Borders, Secure Nation: Cooperation and Conflict in China's Territorial Disputes* (Princeton, NJ: Princeton University Press, 2008), 220, see also 51–52.

31. Quoted in Yafeng Xia, *Negotiating with the Enemy: U.S.-China Talks during the Cold War, 1949–1972* (Bloomington: Indiana University Press, 2006), 83.

32. Zhang Baijia and Jia Qingguo, "Steering Wheel, Shock Absorber, and Diplomatic Probe in Confrontation: Sino-American Ambassadorial Talks Seen from the Chinese Perspective," in *Re-examining the Cold War: U.S.-China Diplomacy, 1954–1973*, ed. Robert S. Ross and Jiang Changbin (Cambridge, MA: Harvard University Press, 2001), 198.

33. Niu Jun, "Chinese Decision Making in Three Military Actions across the Taiwan Strait," in Swaine, Tuosheng, and Cohen, *Managing Sino-American Crises*, 296.

34. Quoted in Gong Li, "Tension across the Taiwan Strait in the 1950s: Chinese Strategy and Tactics," in Ross and Jiang, *Re-examining the Cold War*, 144.

35. Avey, "Confronting Soviet Power," 184–86; Xia, *Negotiating with the Enemy*, 20–21; Thomas J. Christensen, *Useful Adversaries: Grand Strategy, Domestic Mobilization, and Sino-American Conflict, 1947–1958* (Princeton, NJ: Princeton University Press, 1996), 106–9; Nancy Bernkopf Tucker, *Strait Talk: United States–Taiwan Relations and the Crisis with China* (Cambridge, MA: Harvard University Press, 2011), 12–13.

36. Quoted in Xia, *Negotiating with the Enemy*, 23, also 26–34; Christensen, *Useful Adversaries*, 142–43.

37. On the lack of progress see Xia, *Negotiating with the Enemy*, 26–42.

38. Zhihua Shen, *Mao, Stalin, and the Korean War: Trilateral Communist Relations in the 1950s*, trans. Neil Silver (Abingdon, UK: Routledge, 2012), 130–32; James I. Matray, "Korea's War at 60: A Survey of the Literature," *Cold War History* 11, no. 1 (2011): 108; Shen and Li, *After Leaning to One Side*, 57–63; Donggil Kim, "New Insights into Mao's Initial Strategic Consideration towards the Korean War Intervention," *Cold War History* 16, no. 3 (2016): 243–44; "Cable from Roshchin to Stalin, Relaying Mao's Request for Clarification on North Korea Taking Action against South Korea," May 13, 1950, History and Public Policy Program Digital Archive, Russian Presidential Archives, Given by Russian President Boris Yeltsin to South Korean President Kim Young-Sam in Moscow, June 1994, http://digitalarchive.wilsoncenter.org/document/115977.

39. Resolution Adopted by the United Nations Security Council, June 27, 1950, *FRUS 1950*, vol. 3, https://history.state.gov/historicaldocuments/frus1950v07/d130; Melvyn P. Leffer, *A Preponderance of Power: National Security, the Truman Administration, and the Cold War* (Stanford, CA: Stanford University Press, 1992), 361–76; Stephen M. Walt, *Revolution and War* (Ithaca, NY: Cornell University Press, 1996), 319–20; Matray, "Korea's War at 60," 112; Thomas J. Christensen, "Threats, Assurances, and the Last Chance for Peace: The Lessons of Mao's Korean War Telegrams," *International Security* 17, no. 1 (Summer 1992): 136; and Chen Jian, *China's Road to the Korean War: The Making of the Sino-American Confrontation* (New York: Columbia University Press, 1994), 142.

40. Quoted in Zhang, "Command, Control," 91.

41. Zhang, 91–95.

42. Donggil Kim asserts that Mao pushed for intervention on July 12, which, he argues, challenges claims that the US decision to cross the thirty-eighth parallel led to Chinese intervention. His key source is a single meeting that day between Mao and Lee Sang-jo, an envoy for Kim Il Sung. At that meeting Mao argued it was likely the United States would send more troops, and "If North Korea asks, China is ready to send troops." Neither Mao nor China appeared in a rush; Mao only asked for Kim's response by August 10. Aside from preparing some troops, the most direct action China took appeared to be a crackdown beginning on July 23 against domestic opponents potentially emboldened by the American intervention. Donggil Kim, "New Insights," 247–48, and "China's Intervention in the Korean War Revisited," *Diplomatic History* 40, no. 5 (2016): esp. 1005–6. See also "Telegram from Mao Zedong to Filippov," July 22, 1950, History and Public Policy Program Digital Archive, RGASPI, trans. for NKIDP by Gary Goldberg, http://digitalarchive.wilsoncenter.org/document/114904; "Ciphered Telegram, Filippov (Stalin) to Zhou Enlai or Mao Zedong (via Roshchin)," July 13, 1950, History and Public Policy Program Digital Archive, APRF, http://digitalarchive.wilsoncenter.org/document/110692; Shen, *Mao, Stalin, and the Korean War*, 138–42.

43. Shen, *Mao, Stalin, and the Korean War*, 140.

44. Quoted in Kim, "New Insights," 248.

45. Christensen, "Threats, Assurances, " 129–31; Chen Jian, "The Sino-Soviet Alliance and China's Entry into the Korean War," *Cold War International History Project*, Working Paper no. 1 (June 1992), 28–29.

46. Zhihua Shen, "China and the Dispatch of the Soviet Air Force: The Formation of the Chinese-Soviet-Korean Alliance in the Early Stage of the Korean War," *Journal of Strategic Studies* 33, no. 2 (April 2010): 213.

47. Quoted in Chen, "Sino-Soviet Alliance," 26.

48. Du Ping, "Political Mobilization and Control," in *Mao's Generals Remember Korea*, trans. and ed. Xiaobing Li, Allan R. Millet, and Bin Yu (Lawrence: University Press of Kansas, 2001), 62.

49. Telegram to Stalin concerning the Decision to Send Troops into Korea for Combat, October 2, 1950, in Christensen, "Threats, Assurances," 151. On the strategic logic as crucial see, for example, Walt, *Revolution and War*, 320; Chen, "Sino-Soviet Alliance," 25–34; John Lewis Gaddis, *We Now Know: Rethinking Cold War History* (Oxford: Oxford University Press, 1997), 78–82; Andrew Scobell, *China's Use of Military Force: Beyond the Great Wall and the Long March* (Cambridge: Cambridge University Press, 2003), 86–93; Shen and Li, *After Leaning to One Side*, 48–49.

50. "Ciphered Telegram, Roshchin to Filippov (Stalin)," October 13, 1950, History and Public Policy Program Digital Archive, APRF, http://digitalarchive.wilsoncenter.org/document/113743. See also Telegram to Zhou Enlai Concerning [Why] Our Troops Should Enter Korea, October 13, 1950, in Christensen, "Threats, Assurances," 153.

51. Li, *History of the Modern Chinese Army*, 135. See also Zhou's speech explaining the PRC decision to intervene, Speech, Zhou Enlai, at the 18th Meeting of the Standing Committee of the Chinese People's Political Consultative Conference, October 24, 1950, in *Chinese Communist Foreign Policy and the Cold War in Asia: New Documentary Evidence, 1944–1950*, ed. Shu Guang Zhang and Chen Jian (Chicago: Imprint, 1996), esp. 187.

52. Paul H. B. Godwin, "Change and Continuity in Chinese Military Doctrine: 1949–1999," in Ryan, Finkelstein, and McDevitt, *Chinese Warfighting*, 29.

53. Quoted in Li, *History of the Modern Chinese Army*, 85–86. See also Li, 92, and Peng Dehuai's Speech at the Conference of Division-Level Commanders of the Chinese People's Volunteers, October 16, 1950, in Zhang and Chen, *Chinese Communist Foreign Policy*, esp. 176.

54. Scobell, *China's Use of Military Force*, 85.

55. Quoted in Scobell, 86.

56. Smith to Truman, November 1, 1950, *FRUS 1950*, vol. 7, 1026, https://history.state.gov/historicaldocuments/frus1950v07/d731. See also NIE 2, Chinese Communist Intervention in Korea, November 8, 1950, *FRUS 1950*, vol. 7, 1101–6, https://history.state.gov/historicaldocuments/frus1950v07/d789.

57. Zhang, "Command, Control," 97.

58. Li, *History of the Modern Chinese Army*, 82–84.

59. The U.S.-ROC treaty is widely identified as the motivation for Chinese hostilities. See, for example, Fravel, *Strong Borders, Secure Nation*, 234–41; Zhang, *Deterrence and Strategic Culture*, 191–94; Jun, "Chinese Decision Making," 300–303; Thomas J. Christensen, *Worse Than a Monolith: Alliance Politics and Problems of Coercive Diplomacy in Asia* (Princeton, NJ: Princeton University Press, 2011), 136–41; Xia, *Negotiating with the Enemy*, 81. Chang and Di downplay the significance of shelling but agree that it was orchestrated in response to deepening US-Taiwanese relations. Gordon H. Chang and He Di, "The Absence of War in the U.S.-China Confrontation over Quemoy and Matsu in 1954–1955: Contingency, Luck, Deterrence?," *American Historical Review* 98, no. 5 (December 1993): 1507–8.

60. Quoted in Zhang, *Deterrence and Strategic Culture*, 193. Emphasis in original.

61. Quoted in Baijia and Qingguo, "Steering Wheel, Shock Absorber," 179–80.

62. Zhang, *Deterrence and Strategic Culture*, 194; Jun, "Chinese Decision Making," 302; Chang and Di, "Absence of War," 1509; Li, "Tension across the Taiwan Strait," 146–47.

63. Quoted in Fravel, *Strong Borders, Secure Nation*, 238.

64. Quoted in Zhang, *Deterrence and Strategic Culture*, 218.

65. Quoted in Michael M. Sheng, "Mao and China's Relations with the Superpowers in the 1950s: A New Look at the Taiwan Strait Crises and the Sino-Soviet Split," *Modern China* 34, no. 4 (2008): 485.

66. Quoted in Zhang, *Deterrence and Strategic Culture*, 218. See also Xiaobing Li, "PLA Attacks and Amphibious Operations during the Taiwan Strait Crisis of 1954–55 and 1958," in Ryan, Finkelstein, and McDevitt, *Chinese Warfighting*, 152.

67. Quoted in Fravel, *Strong Borders, Secure Nation*, 240. See also Sheng, "Mao and China's Relations with the Superpowers," 484.

68. Fravel, *Strong Borders, Secure Nation*, 233–34; Chang and Di, "Absence of War," 1513–14.

69. Zhang, *Deterrence and Strategic Culture*, 222; Chang and Di, "Absence of War," 1520–22; Xia, *Negotiating with the Enemy*, 82–83; Baijia and Qingguou, "Steering Wheel, Shock Absorber," 180.

70. Fravel, *Strong Borders, Secure Nation*, 241–42; Li, "Tension across the Taiwan Strait," 168–70.

71. For a discussion and debate on this issue see Fravel, *Strong Borders, Secure Nation*, 246–47.

72. For variations of this thesis see Christensen, *Useful Adversaries*, chap. 6; Chen Jian, *Mao's China and the Cold War* (Chapel Hill: University of North Carolina Press, 2001), chap. 7.

73. "Speech, Mao Zedong at the Fifteenth Meeting of the Supreme State Council (excerpt)," September 5, 1958, WCDA, http://digitalarchive.wilsoncenter.org/document/117013.

74. Fravel, *Strong Borders, Secure Nation*, 246.

75. Fravel, 243–45; Xia, *Negotiating with the Enemy*, 96–98; Baijia and Qingguo, "Steering Wheel, Shock Absorber," 187–88; Zhang, *Deterrence and Strategic Culture*, 226–28, 242.

76. Zhang, *Deterrence and Strategic Culture*, 228.

77. Quoted in Fravel, *Strong Borders, Secure Nation*, 248.

78. Quoted in Chen, *Mao's China in the Cold War*, 180.

79. Zhang, *Deterrence and Strategic Culture*, 254–55.

80. Quoted in Chen, *Mao's China in the Cold War*, 182–83.

81. Zhang, *Deterrence and Strategic Culture*, 243–50; Chen, *Mao's China in the Cold War*, 182.

82. "Memoir by Wu Lengxi, 'Inside Story of the Decision Making during the Shelling of Jinmen,'" August 23, 1958, History and Public Policy Program Digital Archive, Zhuanji wenxue (Biographical Literature, Beijing), no. 1, 1994, 7, see also 5–11, http://digitalarchive.wilson center.org/document/117009. See also Fravel, *Strong Borders, Secure Nation*, 249; Chen, *Mao's China and the Cold War*, 192–202.

83. Quoted in Sheng, "Mao and China's Relations with the Superpowers," 493–94. For a slightly different translation see "Memoir by Wu Lengxi," 6.

84. Quoted in Chen, *Mao's China and the Cold War*, 199, also see 195–201; Li, *History of the Modern Chinese Army*, 187–88.

85. Quoted in Shen and Li, *After Leaning to One Side*, 68.

86. Christensen, "Threats, Assurances," 129.

87. Telegram, Mao Zedong to Zhou Enlai, October 13, 1950, in Zhang and Chen, *Chinese Communist Foreign Policy*, 168. For a slightly different translation with the same meaning see Telegram to Zhou Enlai Concerning [Why] Our Troops Should Enter Korea, October 13, 1950, in Christensen, "Threats, Assurances," 153. The focus on ROK rather than US forces was consistent in mid- to late-October: see Telegram Mao Zedong to Zhou Enlai, October 14, 1950, in Zhang and Chen, *Chinese Communist Foreign Policy*, 170; Telegram, Mao Zedong to Peng Dehuai, October 21, 1950, in Zhang and Chen, 180; Telegram Mao Zedong to Peng Dehuai, October 23, 1950, in Zhang and Chen, 183–84. Though Mao did note on October 14 that if small American units were "somehow cut off" the Chinese would fight them as well. See Telegram, Mao Zedong to Zhou Enlai, October 14, 1950, in Zhang and Chen, 171.

88. Quoted in Kim, "China's Intervention," 1022, 1004.

89. Quoted in Zhang, "Command, Control," 98–101.

90. Bin, "What China Learned," 126–28.

91. Zhang, "Command, Control," 103.

92. Quoted in Bin, "What China Learned," 125. See also Li, *History of the Modern Chinese Army*, 86; and Rough Notes on NSC Senior Staff Meeting on Korea, August 25, 1950, *FRUS 1950*, vol. 7, 650, https://history.state.gov/historicaldocuments/frus1950v07/d474.

93. Quoted in Bin, "What China Learned," 125.

94. Zhang, "Air Combat," 277.

95. Shen, "China and the Dispatch of the Soviet Air Force," 222; Kathryn Weathersby, "Should We Fear This? Stalin and the Danger of War with America," *Cold War International History Project*, Working Paper 39 (July 2002), 17–19; and the documents in Kathryn Weathersby, "New Evidence on the Korean War," *CWIHP Bulletin* 6/7 (Winter 1995): 114–17.

96. Kim, "China's Intervention," 1011. On these points see also Shen, "China and the Dispatch of the Soviet Air Force," 219–20, 222–27; Shen, *Mao, Stalin, and the Korean War*, 167–68; William Stueck, *Rethinking the Korean War: A New Diplomatic and Strategic History* (Princeton, NJ: Princeton University Press, 2002), 105; and Chen, *Mao's China and the Cold War*, 55.

97. "Ciphered Telegram from Roshchin in Beijing to Filippov (Stalin)," October 3, 1950 [sent October 2], History and Public Policy Program Digital Archive, APRF, trans. Kathryn Weathersby and Alexandre Mansourov, http://digitalarchive.wilsoncenter.org/document/113732. For the text of the October 2 draft telegram not sent see Christensen, "Threats, Assurances," 151–52. For a discussion of the two messages and Chinese hesitation see Shen, *Mao, Stalin, and the Korean War*, 149–58; Stueck, *Rethinking the Korean War*, 105–6; and Chen, *Mao's China and the Cold War*, 56, 89–90.

98. Kim, "China's Intervention," 1018.

99. "Telegram from Matveev to USSR Council of Ministers," October 7, 1950, History and Public Policy Program Digital Archive, TsAMO RF, trans. for NKIDP by James F. Person, http://digitalarchive.wilsoncenter.org/document/114922. Shen, *Mao, Stalin and the Korean War*, 175; Shen, "China and the Dispatch of the Soviet Air Force," 223.

100. "Telegram from Shtykov to the Soviet Council of Ministers," October 8, 1950, History and Public Policy Program Digital Archive, TsAMO RF, trans. for NKIDP by James F. Person, http://digitalarchive.wilsoncenter.org/document/114924; "Telegram from Matveev to Council of Ministers," October 8, 1950, History and Public Policy Program Digital Archive, TsAMO RF, trans. for NKIDP by James F. Person, http://digitalarchive.wilsoncenter.org/document/114923; Telegram, Mao Zedong to Kim Il Sung, October 8, 1950, in Zhang and Chen, *Chinese Communist Foreign Policy*, 165–66; Alexandre Mansourov, "Stalin, Mao, Kim, and China's Decision to Enter the Korean War, September 16–October 15, 1950: New Evidence from the Russian Archives," *CWIHP Bulletin* 6/7 (1996): 102.

101. Quoted in Shen, "China and the Dispatch of the Soviet Air Force," 223, also 224.

102. Quoted in Shen, *Mao, Stalin, and the Korean War*, 166, also 161–67; and Shen, "China and the Dispatch of the Soviet Air Force," 224; Kim, "China's Intervention," 1018–19; "Cable, Filippov [Stalin] and Zhou Enlai to the Soviet Ambassador, Pass Immediately to Cde. Mao Zedong," October 11, 1950, History and Public Policy Program Digital Archive, APRF, trans. Gary Goldberg, https://digitalarchive.wilsoncenter.org/document/175798. For a contrary view see Mansourov, "Stalin, Mao, Kim," 103.

103. Telegram, Mao Zedong to Peng Dehuai and Others, October 11, 1950, in Zhang and Chen, *Chinese Communist Foreign Policy*, 167.

104. Telegram, Mao Zedong to Peng Dehuai and Others, October 12, 1950, in Zhang and Chen, *Chinese Communist Foreign Policy*, 167–68, and Telegram, CCP Central Committee to Rao Shushi and Chen Yi, October 12, 1950, in Zhang and Chen, 168. On the order of battle and components of the 13th Army Corps (Group) see Order, CCP Central Military Commission on the Formation of the Chinese People's Volunteers, October 8, 1950, in Zhang and Chen, 164–65. This reports the 13th Army Group composed of the 38th, 39th, 40th, 42nd Armies and 1st, 2nd, and 8th Artillery Divisions. Zhang adds the 50th and 60th Armies to the 13th Army Group as well: see Zhang, "Command, Control," 120. On the delay see Shen, "China and the Dispatch of the Soviet Air Force," 226; Chen, *Mao's China and the Cold War*, 58.

105. Gaddis, *We Now Know*, 80; Weathersby, "Should We Fear This?," 19.

106. "Ciphered Telegram, Roshchin to Filippov (Stalin)," October 13, 1950, History and Public Policy Program Digital Archive, APRF, http://digitalarchive.wilsoncenter.org/document/113743.

107. Shen and Li, *After Leaning to One Side*, 43–44; Kim, "China's Intervention," 1021.

108. Shen, "China and the Dispatch of the Soviet Air Force," 227.

109. Shen, *Mao, Stalin, and the Korean War*, 173–74. Kim cites Stalin's October 14 commitment but argues this had little effect on China's decision. See Kim, "China's Intervention," 1023.

110. Chen, *Mao's China and the Cold War*, 58.

111. Quoted in Shen, "China and the Dispatch of the Soviet Air Force," 227–28. See also Shen, *Mao, Stalin, and the Korean War*, 179; Weathersby, "Should We Fear This?," 20.

112. Telegram, Mao Zedong to Peng Dehuai and Deng Hua, October 30, 1950, in Zhang and Chen, *Chinese Communist Foreign Policy*, 199.

113. Chen, *Mao's China and the Cold War*, 59–60.

114. Quoted in Shu Guang Zhang, *Mao's Military Romanticism: China and the Korean War, 1950–1953* (Lawrence: University Press of Kansas, 1995), 237–38. There is also evidence that the CPV headquarters feared US atomic attacks: see Zhang, *Mao's Military Romanticism*, 308n70.

115. Quoted in John Lewis Wilson and Xue Litai, *China Builds the Bomb* (Stanford, CA: Stanford University Press, 1988), 15.

116. Robert A. Pape, *Bombing to Win: Air Power and Coercion in War* (Ithaca, NY: Cornell University Press, 1996), 171.

117. Zhang, "Between 'Paper' and 'Real Tigers,'" 199.

118. Pape, *Bombing to Win*, 171–72. Mao would return to this option later as well; see Godwin, "Change and Continuity," 34.

119. Wilson and Xue, *China Builds the Bomb*, 35–39.

120. Li, *History of the Modern Chinese Army*, 179.

121. Li, 137–41.

122. Jun, "Chinese Decision Making," 310.

123. Zhang, *Deterrence and Strategic Culture*, chaps. 7–8.

124. Quoted in Zhang, *Deterrence and Strategic Culture*, 197. See also Chang and Di, "Absence of War," 1512.

125. Chang and Di, 1510.

126. Quoted in Zhang, *Deterrence and Strategic Culture*, 219, see also 216–22; Fravel, *Strong Borders, Secure Nation*, 240–41; Jun, "Chinese Decision Making," 309–11; Chang and Di, "Absence of War," 1512–14; Li, *History of the Modern Chinese Army*, 140–45; Zhang, "Air Combat," 280–81.

127. Quoted in Sheng, "Mao and China's Relations with the Superpowers," 498.

128. Zhang, *Deterrence and Strategic Culture*, 236–37, 252; Li, "Tension across the Taiwan Strait," 158.

129. Li, *History of the Modern Chinese Army*, 182; Zhang, *Deterrence and Strategic Culture*, 236; Gaddis, *We Now Know*, 251.

130. "Memoir by Wu Lengxi," 3. See also Chen, *Mao's China and the Cold War*, 184.

131. Quoted in Wang Jisis and Xu Hui, "Pattern of Sino-American Crises: A Chinese Perspective," in Swaine, Tuosheng, and Cohen, *Managing Sino-American Crises*, 136. See also Sheng, "Mao and China's Relations with the Superpowers," 492; Zhang, *Deterrence and Strategic Culture*, 252; Xia, *Negotiating with the Enemy*, 98; Li, *History of the Modern Chinese Army*, 185–86.

132. Du Ping, "Political Mobilization and Control," in Li, Millet, and Yu, *Mao's Generals Remember Korea*, 63. See also Chen, *China's Road to the Korean War*, 192. For a general overview at the time see Zhang, "Between 'Paper' and 'Real Tigers,'" 196–98.

133. Du Ping, "Political Mobilization and Control," 63.

134. Quoted in Zhang, "Between 'Paper' and 'Real Tigers,'" 197.

135. Quoted in Zhang, *Mao's Military Romanticism*, 233–34.

136. Shen and Li, *After Leaning to One Side*, 41. See also Scobell, *China's Use of Military Force*, 88.

137. Quoted in Shen, *Mao, Stalin, and the Korean War*, 172. Shu Guang Zhang and Chen Jian translate this passage slightly differently: "If the Soviet air force can, in addition to sending a volunteer air force to support our military operations in Korean in two to two-and-half months, dispatch air force to Beijing, Tianjin, Shenyang, Shanghai, Nanjing, and Qingdao, we then will not need to fear the [American] air attack." See Zhang and Chen, *Chinese Communist Foreign Policy*, 169n.

138. "Telegram from Soviet Ambassador to China N. V. Roshchin to Stalin," October 7, 1950, History and Public Policy Program Digital Archive, Volkogonov Collections, Library of Congress, APRF, trans. for CWIHP by Vladislav Zubok, http://digitalarchive.wilsoncenter.org/document/117314.

139. Quoted in Gaddis, *We Now Know*, 105. See also Zhang, "Between 'Paper' and 'Real Tigers,'" 197; Zhang, *Deterrence and Strategic Culture*, 108; Stueck, *Rethinking the Korean War*, 110; Pape, *Bombing to Win*, 172; Chen, *China's Road to the Korean War*, 193.

140. Quoted in Shen and Li, *After Leaning to One Side*, 109.

141. On the change in Western capabilities and influence on US policy as a result see Marc Trachtenberg, *History and Strategy* (Princeton, NJ: Princeton University Press, 1991), chap. 3.

142. Quoted in Zhang, "Between 'Paper' and 'Real Tigers,'" 199, also 199–211; M. Taylor Fravel and Even Medeiros, "China's Search for Assured Retaliation: The Evolution of Chinese Nuclear Strategy and Force Posture," *International Security* 35, no. 2 (Fall 2010): 57–66.

143. Both quotes from Zhang, *Deterrence and Strategic Culture*, 220.

144. Li, *History of the Modern Chinese Army*, 145–46.

145. Todd S. Sechser and Matthew Fuhrmann, *Nuclear Weapons and Coercive Diplomacy* (Cambridge: Cambridge University Press, 2017), 192–94. They note that nuclear weapons may have had a deterrent effect in this crisis but highlight reasons for skepticism.

146. Zhang, *Deterrence and Strategic Culture*, 224.

147. "Memoir by Wu Lengxi," 11.

148. For instance, see his discussion of Mao's eight points, the noose, and addresses in early September 1958 compared to other texts of Mao's comments on those issues. "Memoir by Wu Lengxi"; "Speech, Mao Zedong at the Fifteenth Meeting of the Supreme State Council (excerpt)," September 5, 1958, History and Public Policy Program Digital Archive, Mao Zedong waijiao wenxuan (Selected Works of Mao Zedong on Diplomacy) (Beijing: Zhongyang wenxian chubanshe, 1994), 341–48, http://digitalarchive.wilsoncenter.org/document/117013; "Speech, Mao Zedong at the Fifteenth Meeting of the Supreme State Council (excerpt)," September 8, 1958, History and Public Policy Program Digital Archive, Mao Zedong waijiao wenxuan (Selected Works of Mao Zedong on Diplomacy) (Beijing: Zhongyang wenxian chubanshe, 1994), 348–52, http://digitalarchive.wilsoncenter.org/document/117015.

149. Ryan, Finkelstein, and McDevitt, introduction in *Chinese Warfighting*, 15.

150. Quoted in Zhang, "Between 'Paper' and 'Real Tigers,'" 196. For additional statements see the quotations in Francis J. Gavin, "Blasts from the Past: Proliferation Lessons from the 1960s," *International Security* 29, no. 3 (Winter 2004/05): 101; Gaddis, *We Now Know*, 249–51; Zhang, "Between 'Paper' and Real Tigers,'" 194–215.

151. Quoted in Zhang, "Between 'Paper' and 'Real Tigers,'" 196.

152. Mao Zedong, "The Chinese People Cannot Be Cowed by the Atom Bomb," January 28, 1955, in *Selected Works of Mao Tse-Tung*, vol. 5 (New York: Pergamon, 1977), 152.

153. Quoted in Zhang, "Between 'Paper' and 'Real Tigers,'" 196. See also Gaddis, *We Now Know*, 104–5; Chen, *China's Road to the Korean War*, 192.

154. Quoted in Zhang, "Between 'Paper' and 'Real Tigers,'" 200.

155. Quoted in Zhang, 198.

156. Fravel and Medeiros, "China's Search," 58–61.

157. Quoted in Fravel and Medeiros, 60.

158. Quoted in Zhang, "Between 'Paper' and 'Real Tigers,'" 205. See also Fravel and Medeiros, "China's Search," 61.

159. Quoted in Li, *History of the Modern Chinese Army*, 170. See also Zhang, "Between 'Paper' and 'Real Tigers,'" 211.

160. George H. Quester, "On the Identification of Real and Pretended Communist Military Doctrine," *Journal of Conflict Resolution* 10, no. 2 (June 1966): 172–73.

161. Gaddis, *We Now Know*, 111. For additional discussion of Soviet efforts at disparaging the American atomic monopoly to forestall blackmail see chapter 5. This logic was not limited to the Communist dictators. For instance, George Kennan made a similar point when addressing American fears of Soviet conventional capabilities. Gaddis, *We Now Know*, 111.

162. Fravel and Medeiros, "China's Search," 60.

163. "Speech, Mao Zedong at the Fifteenth Meeting of the Supreme State Council (excerpt)," September 5, 1958, History and Public Policy Program Digital Archive, Mao Zedong waijiao wenxuan (Selected Works of Mao Zedong on Diplomacy) (Beijing: Zhongyang wenxian chubanshe, 1994), 341–48, http://digitalarchive.wilsoncenter.org/document/117013.

164. The Second Speech, May 17, 1958, Speeches at the Second Session of the Eighth Party Congress (May 8–23, 1958), in *Miscellany of Mao Tse-Tung Thought (1946–1968)*, part 1 (Arlington, VA: Joint Publications Research Service, 1974), 108. The text is also available at https://www.marxists.org/reference/archive/mao/selected-works/volume-8/mswv8_10.htm.

165. Talks with Directors of Various Cooperative Areas (November, December 1958), Speech of November 30, 1958, *Miscellany of Mao Tse-Tung Thought*, part 1, 136. The text is available at https://www.marxists.org/reference/archive/mao/selected-works/volume-8/mswv8_22.htm.

166. Quoted in Zhang, "Between 'Paper' and 'Real Tigers,'" 202.

167. Mao is addressing paper tigers generally here, but the thinking is applicable to nuclear weapons, which he labeled a paper tiger. Talks with Directors of Various Cooperative Areas,

Speech of November 30, 1958, in *Miscellany of Mao Tse-Tung Thought*, 136. See also Mao Zedong, "All Reactionaries Are Paper Tigers," November 18, 1957, in *Selected Works of Mao Tse-Tung*, 5:517–18.

168. "Speech, Mao Zedong at the Fifteenth Meeting of the Supreme State Council (excerpt)," September 5, 1958, History and Public Policy Program Digital Archive, Mao Zedong waijiao wenxuan (Selected Works of Mao Zedong on Diplomacy), 341–48.

169. Zhang, "Between 'Paper' and 'Real Tigers,'" 213.

170. Shen and Li, *After Leaning to One Side*, 48–49.

171. "Memoir by Wu Lengxi," 8.

172. Chen, *Mao's China and the Cold War*, 52–53.

173. Zhang, "Between 'Paper' and 'Real Tigers,'" 215.

174. Pape, *Bombing to Win*, 172; Gaddis, *We Now Know*, 108–10; William I. Hitchcock, "Trump Threatened to Nuke North Korea. Did Ike Do the Same?," *Washington Post*, August 11, 2017, https://www.washingtonpost.com/news/made-by-history/wp/2017/08/11/trump-threatened-to-nuke-north-korea-did-ike-do-the-same/?utm_term=.e2c07fde2da2

175. Quoted in Zhang, *Deterrence and Strategic Culture*, 217. Note also (at 221) the public comments by the chair of Sino-Soviet Friendship Organization, intended to reassure nervous Chinese.

176. Li, *History of the Modern Chinese Army*, 147. See also see Gaddis, *We Now Know*, 249; Christensen, *Worse Than a Monolith*, 141–42.

177. Goldstein, *Deterrence in the 21st Century*, 66.

178. Quoted in Xiaobing Li, "PLA Attacks and Amphibious Operations during the Taiwan Strait Crisis of 1954–55 and 1958," in Ryan, Finkelstein, and McDevitt, *Chinese Warfighting*, 157; and Li, *History of the Modern Chinese Army*, 149–53.

179. Matthew Kroenig, "Force of Friendship? Explaining Great Power Nonproliferation Policy," *Security Studies* 23, no. 1 (2014): 19.

180. Shen and Li, *After Leaning to One Side*, 149.

181. Quoted in Chen, *Mao's China and the Cold War*, 74. See also Shen and Li, *After Leaning to One Side*, 148–53.

182. Quoted in Christensen, *Useful Adversaries*, 208.

183. Memorandum of Conversation of N. S. Khrushchev with Mao Zedong, Beijing, October 2, 1959, *CWIHP Bulletin* 12/13 (Fall/Winter 2001): 264–65.

184. Chen, *Mao's China and the Cold War*, 77; Zhang, *Deterrence and Strategic Culture*, 254; Li, "Tension across the Taiwan Strait," 160–61.

185. Zhang, *Deterrence and Strategic Culture*, 254.

186. Gaddis, *We Now Know*, 252. See also Goldstein, *Deterrence in the 21st Century*, 85–86; Chen, *Mao's China and the Cold War*, 77–78; Li, "Tension across the Taiwan Strait, 160–61. For a contrary view largely based on Khrushchev's memoirs see Mark A. Kramer, "The USSR Foreign Ministry's Appraisal of Sino-Soviet Relations on the Eve of the Split, September 1959," *CWIHP Bulletin* 6/7 (Winter 1995/1996): 174.

187. Memorandum of Conversation of N. S. Khrushchev with Mao Zedong, Beijing, October 2, 1959, *CWIHP Bulletin* 12/13 (Fall/Winter 2001): 264. The document is also available online: "Discussion between N. S. Khrushchev and Mao Zedong," October 2, 1959, History and Public Policy Program Digital Archive, APRF, trans. Vladislav M. Zubok, http://digitalarchive.wilsoncenter.org/document/112088. Jonathan Haslam identifies this statement, with a slightly different translation, as occurring on August 3, 1958. He cites the August 3 conversation from the Volkogonov Papers. Those documents available in the *CWIHP Bulletin* 12/13 and the Wilson Center Digital Archive for the August 3 meeting, drawn from the same papers, make no mention of the issue. It is likely that Haslam is in fact referring to the October 2, 1959, document. Jonathan Haslam, *Russia's Cold War: From the October Revolution to the Fall of the Wall* (New Haven, CT: Yale University Press, 2011), 177. The text of the August 3 meeting in *CWIHP Bulletin* 12/13 is available on pp. 260–62 of that bulletin. The text of the meeting is available at "Fourth Conversation between N. S. Khrushchev and Mao Zedong, Hall of Qinjendiang [Beijing]," August 3, 1958, History and Public Policy Program Digital Archive, APRF, trans. Vladislav M. Zubok, http://digitalarchive.wilsoncenter.org/document/112083.

5. The Soviet Union versus the United States

1. See, for example, Marc Trachtenberg, *A Constructed Peace: The Making of the European Settlement, 1945–1963* (Princeton, NJ: Princeton University Press, 1999).

2. David Alan Rosenberg, "The Origins of Overkill: Nuclear Weapons and American Strategy, 1945–1960," *International Security* 7, no. 4 (Spring 1983): 14–15; Steven T. Ross, *American War Plans, 1945–1950* (New York: Garland, 1988), 12. The number of nuclear-capable aircraft increased over 1948, numbering an estimated 60 by December of that year and 250 by 1950. See Rosenberg, "Origins of Overkill," 19.

3. Edward Kaplan, *To Kill Nations: American Strategy in the Air-Atomic Age and the Rise of Mutually Assured Destruction* (Ithaca, NY: Cornell University Press, 2015), 31.

4. Norman Polmar and Robert S. Norris, *The U.S. Nuclear Arsenal: A History of Weapons and Delivery Systems since 1945* (Annapolis, MD: Naval Institute Press, 2009), 91–97, quote at 92.

5. Ross, *American War Plans*, 13.

6. Quotes from Paul C. Avey, "Confronting Soviet Power: U.S. Policy during the Early Cold War," *International Security* 36, no. 4 (Spring 2012): 159–60.

7. Philip A. Karber and Jerald A. Combs, "The United States, NATO, and the Soviet Threat to Western Europe: Military Estimates and Policy Options, 1945–1963," *Diplomatic History* 22, no. 3 (Summer 1998): 408, 411.

8. Stephen Biddle, *Military Power: Explaining Victory and Defeat in Modern Battle* (Princeton, NJ: Princeton University Press, 2004), 251n50.

9. Quoted in Jonathan Haslam, *Russia's Cold War: From the October Revolution to the Fall of the Wall* (New Haven, CT: Yale University Press, 2011), 55.

10. Hubert Zimmerman, "The Improbable Permanence of a Commitment: America's Troop Presence in Europe during the Cold War," *Journal of Cold War Studies* 11, no. 1 (Winter 2009): 4; Ross, *American War Plans*, 11–12; Karber and Combs, "United States, NATO, and the Soviet Threat," 419.

11. Precise estimates vary, but intelligence estimated 175 total divisions, and Karber and Combs note that 140 were stationed on Soviet soil in 1948, the bulk of the difference likely being deployed in Eastern Europe. In addition, they note that during this period there were 24–25 divisions in East Germany and Poland and 5–6 "located in the remainder of Eastern Europe." See Karber and Combs, "United States, NATO, and the Soviet Threat," 408, 416–19. Holloway writes that in war plans in 1946 the Soviets had 17 ground-force divisions in Germany. Holloway, *Stalin and the Bomb*, 232. See also Ross, *American War Plans*, esp. 86, 104.

12. For example, Grauer and Horowitz code the Soviet Union as failing or minimal implementation of the modern system during the Russo-Finnish War in 1939–1940. Soviet battlefield effectiveness subsequently improved, moving to moderate implementation of the modern system at the tactical and operational level during the winter counteroffensives of 1941–1942. Ryan Grauer and Michael C. Horowitz, "What Determines Military Victory? Testing the Modern System," *Security Studies* 21, no. 1 (January–March 2012): 83–112. On Soviet battlefield effectiveness during 1941 see also Jasen J. Castillo, *Endurance and War: The National Sources of Military Cohesion* (Stanford, CA: Stanford University Press, 2014), chap. 5.

13. Karber and Combs, "United States, NATO, and the Soviet Threat," 409. See also David Holloway, *Stalin and the Bomb: The Soviet Union and Atomic Energy, 1939–1956* (New Haven, CT: Yale University Press, 1994), 231; Victor Gobarev, "Soviet Military Plans and Actions during the First Berlin Crisis, 1948–49," *Journal of Slavic Military Studies* 10, no. 3 (September 1997): 11–13.

14. Ross, *American War Plans*, 104. See also Karber and Combs, "United States, NATO, and the Soviet Threat," 421.

15. Karber and Combs, 407–8.

16. Gobarev, "Soviet Military Plans," 13.

17. NSC 20/4, Report by the National Security Council on U.S. Objectives with Respect to the USSR to Counter Soviet Threats to U.S. Security, November 23, 1948, *FRUS 1948*, vol. 1, part 2, 665, https://history.state.gov/historicaldocuments/frus1948v01p2/d60.

18. Karber and Combs, "United States, NATO, and the Soviet Threat," 411, 414; John Lewis Gaddis, *Strategies of Containment: A Critical Appraisal of American National Security Policy during*

the Cold War (1982; Oxford: Oxford University Press, 2005), 70; Report on Soviet Intentions Prepared by the Joint Intelligence Committee, April 1, 1948, Enclosure in Smith to Marshall, April 1, 1948, *FRUS 1948*, vol. 1, part 2, 552–53, https://history.state.gov/historicaldocuments/frus1948v01p2/d14; Ross, *American War Plans*, chaps. 2–4.

19. Karber and Combs, "United States, NATO, and the Soviet Threat," 411–13. For claims that US and NATO officials deliberately or inadvertently overestimated Soviet capabilities see Matthew A. Evangelista, "Stalin's Postwar Army Reappraised," *International Security* 7, no. 3 (Winter 1982/1983): 110–38; and John S. Duffield, "The Soviet Military Threat to Western Europe: US Estimates in the 1950s and 1960s," *Journal of Strategic Studies* 15, no. 2 (June 1992): 208–27.

20. Melvyn P. Leffler, *A Preponderance of Power: National Security, the Truman Administration, and the Cold War* (Stanford, CA: Stanford University Press, 1992).

21. Ross, *American War Plans*, 17.

22. Early plans cautioned against fighting Soviet ground forces in Western Europe and focused on ground action in the Middle East and the southern Soviet Union, though by late 1948 operational plans began considering ground campaigns to liberate Western Europe. The discussion of war plans in this paragraph draws on Ross, *American War Plans*, chaps. 2–5; Kaplan, *To Kill Nations*, chap. 2; Trachtenberg, *Constructed Peace*, 89–90; Holloway, *Stalin and the Bomb*, 239–40.

23. Ross, *American War Plans*, 32.

24. Rosenberg, "Origins of Overkill," 11–13; Ross, *American War Plans*, 13–14; John Lewis Gaddis, *We Now Know: Rethinking Cold War History* (Oxford: Oxford University Press, 1997), 91.

25. Memorandum Prepared in the Department of State, undated [circa May 1948], *FRUS 1948*, vol. 1, part 2, 571, http://digicoll.library.wisc.edu/cgi-bin/FRUS/FRUS-idx?type=header&id=FRUS.FRUS1948v01p2.

26. NSC 30, United States Policy on Atomic Warfare, September 10, 1948, *FRUS 1948*, vol. 1, part 2, 628: Rosenberg, "Origins of Overkill," 13.

27. Quoted in *FRUS 1948*, vol. 1, part 2, 625n1.

28. John J. Mearsheimer, *The Tragedy of Great Power Politics*, 2nd ed. (2001; New York: W. W. Norton, 2014), 254–56, 259–60.

29. Gaddis, *Strategies of Containment*, chaps. 2–3.

30. NSC 20/4, *FRUS 1948*, vol. 1, part 2, 665, https://history.state.gov/historicaldocuments/frus1948v01p2/d60.

31. Marshall to US Embassy in London, February 20, 1948, *FRUS 1948*, vol. 2, 72, https://history.state.gov/historicaldocuments/frus1948v02/d45.

32. Peter Liberman, *Does Conquest Pay? The Exploitation of Occupied Industrial Societies* (Princeton, NJ: Princeton University Press, 1996), esp. chaps. 3, 7.

33. Geoffrey Roberts, *Stalin's Wars: From World War to Cold War, 1939–1953* (New Haven, CT: Yale University Press, 2006), 175, 297–99, 303–5.

34. Quoted in Roberts, *Stalin's Wars*, 293.

35. Quoted in Haslam, *Russia's Cold War*, 63, also 60, 64; Holloway, *Stalin and the Bomb*, 131, 168; Roberts, *Stalin's Wars*, 271, 279–88, 293, 303.

36. Holloway, *Stalin and the Bomb*, 167.

37. Melvyn P. Leffler, *For the Soul of Mankind: The United States, the Soviet Union, and the Cold War* (New York: Hill & Wang, 2007), 32, 53; Elena Aga-Rossi and Victor Zaslavsky, "The Soviet Union and the Italian Communist Party, 1944–8," in *The Soviet Union and Europe in the Cold War, 1945–1953*, ed. Francesca Gori and Silvio Pons (London: Palgrave Macmillan, 1996), 161–80.

38. Roberts, *Stalin's Wars*, 308–9; Ted Hopf, *Reconstructing the Cold War: The Early Years, 1945–1958* (Oxford: Oxford University Press, 2012): 81–82; Bruce R. Kuniholm, *The Origins of the Cold War in the Near East* (Princeton, NJ: Princeton University Press, 1980), 304–42.

39. Roberts, *Stalin's Wars*, 222–23, 275–76, 310–11; Haslam, *Russia's Cold War*, 47–48.

40. Haslam, 25–26, 80–82, 97–98; Ted Hopf, *Reconstructing the Cold War*, 220–21, 233, 299.

41. Vojtech Mastny, *The Cold War and Soviet Insecurity: The Stalin Years* (Oxford: Oxford University Press, 1996), 26–27; Haslam, *Russia's Cold War*, 82; Roberts, *Stalin's Wars*, 313; Hopf, *Reconstructing the Cold War*, 96.

42. Quoted in Roberts, *Stalin's Wars*, 183.

43. Roberts, 347–48. Stalin was very consistent regarding his fears of Germany and desire to keep it weak. See Roberts, 180–88, 236–40, 243–44, 277; Leffler, *For the Soul of Mankind*, 30–31; Tripartite Dinner Meeting, November 28, 1943, *FRUS Conferences on Cairo and Tehran*, 510, https://history.state.gov/historicaldocuments/frus1943CairoTehran/d362; Bohlen, Supplementary Memorandum, *FRUS Conferences at Cairo and Tehran*, 513; Roosevelt-Stalin Meeting, November 29, 1943, *FRUS Conferences at Cairo and Tehran*, 532, https://history.state.gov/historicaldocuments/frus1943CairoTehran/d363; Tripartite Dinner Meeting, November 29, 1943, *FRUS Conferences at Cairo and Tehran*, 553–54, https://history.state.gov/historicaldocuments/frus1943CairoTehran/d368; Tripartite Political Meeting, December 1, 1943, *FRUS Conferences at Cairo and Tehran*, 602–4, https://history.state.gov/historicaldocuments/frus1943CairoTehran/d379.

44. Quoted in R. C. Raack, "Stalin Plans His Postwar Germany," *Journal of Contemporary History* 28, no. 1 (1993): 62.

45. On evolving Soviet policies see Hopf, *Reconstructing the Cold War*, 111–17; Leffler, *For the Soul of Mankind*, 54–55; Haslam, *Russia's Cold War*, 68–69; Mastny, *Cold War and Soviet Insecurity*, 24–25; Vladislav Zubok, *A Failed Empire: The Soviet Union in the Cold War from Stalin to Gorbachev* (2007; Chapel Hill: University of North Carolina Press, 2009), 64–72; and Roberts, *Stalin's Wars*, 350–59. Trachtenberg argues in *A Constructed Peace* that the Soviets were willing to live with a divided Germany provided the United States limit West German freedom of maneuver. But it was an open question if that would be the end result of US policy, and, as noted below, the Soviets also feared an American-led anti-Soviet bloc.

46. For Litvinov's views see Geoffrey Roberts, "Litvinov's Lost Peace," *Journal of Cold War Studies* 4 no. 2 (Spring 2002): 23–54; Roberts, *Stalin's Wars*, 229–30; Haslam, *Russia's Cold War*, 23, 72–73; Mastny, *Cold War and Soviet Insecurity*, 18–19; Leffler, *For the Soul of Mankind*, 52.

47. Roberts, *Stalin's Wars*, 231–32.

48. Trachtenberg, *Constructed Peace*; Joshua R. Itzkowitz-Shifrinson, "Deal or No Deal? The End of the Cold War and the U.S. Offer to Limit NATO Expansion," *International Security* 40, no. 4 (Spring 2016): 7–44.

49. Report by the Policy Planning Staff, PPS/13, November 6, 1947, *FRUS 1947*, vol. 1, 774, https://history.state.gov/historicaldocuments/frus1947v01/d393.

50. On American policy as a response to Soviet power see Avey, "Confronting Soviet Power."

51. On the general US effort see Trachtenberg, *Constructed Peace*, chaps. 2–4; Michael Cresswell, *A Question of Balance: How France and the United States Created Cold War Europe* (Cambridge, MA: Harvard University Press, 2006), 13–21; James McCallister, *No Exit: America and the German Problem, 1943–1954* (Ithaca, NY: Cornell University Press, 2002), chap. 4; Melvyn P. Leffler, "The United States and the Strategic Dimensions of the Marshall Plan," *Diplomatic History* 12, no. 3 (July 1988): 277–306.

52. Trachtenberg, *Constructed Peace*, 55–79; Leffler, *Preponderance of Power*, 151–57, 198–203; Daniel F. Harrington, *Berlin on the Brink: The Blockade, the Airlift, and the Early Cold War* (Lexington: University Press of Kentucky, 2012), 39–40, 64–65. An earlier communiqué on March 5 outlined the major initiatives, including "West German participation in the Marshall Plan, a federal form of government, and coordination of economic policies of the French zone with those of the [American and British] Bizone." Harrington, *Berlin on the Brink*, 43.

53. Haslam, *Russia's Cold War*, 107.

54. Quoted in Scott D. Parrish, "The Turn toward Confrontation: The Soviet Reaction to the Marshall Plan, 1947," Cold War International History Project, Working Paper 9 (March 1994), 13–14. See also Novikov's comments, 20–21, as well as his warning in September 1946 that American policy was moving in a direction in which the "preconditions would thereby be created for a revival of an imperialist Germany which the US is counting on using on its side in a future war. One cannot fail to see that such a policy has a clearly defined anti-Soviet focus and represents a serious danger to the cause of peace." Telegram from Nikolai Novikov, Soviet Ambassador to the US, to the Soviet Leadership, September 27, 1946, History and Public Policy

Program Digital Archive, AVP SSR, trans. for CWIHP by Gary Goldberg, http://digitalarchive. wilsoncenter.org/document/110808.

55. Quoted in Haslam, *Russia's Cold War*, 106, also 87–89; Roberts, *Stalin's Wars*, 252–53, 301–2, 314–17, 347; Harrington, *Berlin on the Brink*, 39–40; Zubok, *Failed Empire*, 73.

56. Quoted in Parrish, "Turn toward Confrontation," 28.

57. Quoted in Haslam, *Russia's Cold War*, 100–101.

58. Leffler, *For the Soul of Mankind*, 67; Zubok, *Failed Empire*, 73.

59. Murphy to Marshall, March 3, 1948, *FRUS 1948*, vol. 2, 878, https://history.state.gov/ historicaldocuments/frus1948v02/d523. See also Chase to Marshall, April 29, 1948, *FRUS 1948*, vol. 2, 900–902, https://history.state.gov/historicaldocuments/frus1948v02/d540; Murphy to Marshall, May 29, 1948, *FRUS 1948*, vol. 2, 905–6, https://history.state.gov/histori caldocuments/frus1948v02/d545.

60. Haslam, *Russia's Cold War*, 106. See also Michail M. Narinskii, "The Soviet Union and the Berlin Crisis, 1948–9," in Gori and Pons, *Soviet Union and Europe*, 63–64; Harrington, *Berlin on the Brink*, 45.

61. Murphy to Marshall, April 13, 1948, *FRUS 1948*, vol. 2, 892, https://history.state.gov/ historicaldocuments/frus1948v02/d533. For an overview of Soviet harassment policies prior to the June blockade see Harrington, *Berlin on the Brink*, 43–57; Alexander L. George and Richard Smoke, *Deterrence in American Foreign Policy: Theory and Practice* (New York: Columbia University Press, 1974), 119–32.

62. Quoted in Melvyn P. Leffler, *The Struggle for Germany and the Origins of the Cold War*, Alois Mertes Memorial Lecture, no. 6 (Washington, DC: German Historical Institute Occasional Paper no. 16, 1996): 53–54. See also Haslam, *Russia's Cold War*, 106–7.

63. Editorial Note, *FRUS 1948*, vol. 2, 909–10, https://history.state.gov/historicaldocuments/ frus1948v02/d548.

64. Haslam, *Russia's Cold War*, 107; Harrington, *Berlin on the Brink*, 74; Murphy to Marshall, June 19, 1948, *FRUS 1948*, vol. 2, 910–11, https://history.state.gov/historicaldocuments/ frus1948v02/d549.

65. Murphy to Marshall, June 23, 1948, *FRUS 1948*, vol. 2, 915, https://history.state.gov/ historicaldocuments/frus1948v02/d554.

66. Murphy to Marshall, July 4, 1948, *FRUS 1948*, vol. 2, 949, https://history.state.gov/his toricaldocuments/frus1948v02/d574. See also Marshall to Douglas, July 3, 1948, *FRUS 1948*, vol. 2, 946–48, https://history.state.gov/historicaldocuments/frus1948v02/d573; as well as Molotov's comments in Smith to Marshall, July 31, 1948, *FRUS 1948*, vol. 2, 998, https://his tory.state.gov/historicaldocuments/frus1948v02/d593; and the official Soviet response to the American protest of the blockade, Ambassador Panyushkin to Marshall, July 14, 1948, *FRUS 1948*, vol. 2, 962, 964, https://history.state.gov/historicaldocuments/frus1948v02/d579.

67. Smith to Marshall, August 3, 1948, *FRUS 1948*, vol. 2, 1001, https://history.state.gov/ historicaldocuments/frus1948v02/d594. Stalin reiterated several times that the Soviets' "only objection" was the formation of a West German government in the western occupation zones; see 1000–1005.

68. Smith to Marshall, August 3, 1948, *FRUS 1948*, vol. 2, 1005; Marshall to Smith, *FRUS 1948*, vol. 2, 1009, https://history.state.gov/historicaldocuments/frus1948v02/d596. In two separate messages following the meeting, Smith noted that the Soviets were seeking agreement but remained firm on the German government issue. See Smith to Marshall, August 3, 1948, 1006–7, https://history.state.gov/historicaldocuments/frus1948v02/d595, and Smith to Marshall, August 4, 1948, 1010–11, https://history.state.gov/historicaldocuments/frus1948v02/ d597, both *FRUS 1948*, vol. 2. Bohlen, Clay, Douglas, and Marshall all shared this basic assessment; see Memorandum by Bohlen, August 4, 1948, 1013–14, https://history.state.gov/histori caldocuments/frus1948v02/d599; Clay to Bradley and Royall, August 4, 19481012, https:// history.state.gov/historicaldocuments/frus1948v02/d598; Marshall to Smith, August 4, 1948, 1015–16, https://history.state.gov/historicaldocuments/frus1948v02/d600; and the note on the Douglas Telegram, 1013n4, https://history.state.gov/historicaldocuments/frus1948v02/ d598, all *FRUS 1948*, vol. 2.

69. Smith to Marshall, August 6, 1948, *FRUS 1948*, vol. 2, 1018–21, https://history.state. gov/historicaldocuments/frus1948v02/d602. Note too Smith's notes on his August 9 meeting with Molotov in Smith to Marshall, August 9, 1948, 1024–27.

70. Leffler, *Struggle for Germany*, 53–54, 58–59; Zubok, *Failed Empire*, 75; Roberts, *Stalin's Wars*, 354–55; George and Smoke, *Deterrence in American Foreign Policy*, 117–18. See also Murphy to Marshall, June 26, 1948, 919–21, https://history.state.gov/historicaldocuments/frus1948 v02/d559, and Douglas to Marshall, June 26, 1948, 925, https://history.state.gov/historical documents/frus1948v02/d560, both *FRUS 1948*, vol. 2.

71. Quoted in Narinskii, "Soviet Union and the Berlin Crisis," 63.

72. Quoted in Mastny, *Cold War and Soviet Insecurity*, 48.

73. Quoted in Harrington, *Berlin on the Brink*, 45.

74. Vladislav Zubok and Constantine Pleshakov, *Inside the Kremlin's Cold War: From Stalin to Khrushchev* (Cambridge, MA: Harvard University Press, 1996), 51.

75. Zubok, *Failed Empire*, 75. George and Smoke make a similar point, writing that "from the Soviet standpoint the blockade was a *controllable* and *reversible* gambit. Soviet leaders . . . could at any time find a solution to the 'technical difficulties' and open up ground access to West Berlin. Nor need the Soviets persist in the blockade if the Western powers threatened to over-react to it in ways that raised the danger of war." George and Smoke, *Deterrence in American Foreign Policy*, 118.

76. Mastny, *Cold War and Soviet Insecurity*, 49.

77. Gobarev, "Soviet Military Plans," 10, see also 6–7; Vojtech Mastny, "NATO in the Beholder's Eye: Soviet Perceptions and Policies, 1949–56," Cold War International History Project, Working Paper 35 (March 2002), 13.

78. Karber and Combs, "United States, NATO, and the Soviet Threat," 413–16; Daniel W. Altman, "Red Lines and Faits Accomplis in Interstate Coercion and Crisis," PhD diss., Massa-chusetts Institute of Technology, June 2015, 126; Leffler, *Preponderance of Power*, 218–19.

79. Mastny, *Cold War and Soviet Insecurity*, 49. See also Holloway, *Stalin and the Bomb*, 260–61.

80. Trachtenberg, *Constructed Peace*, 87. See also Altman, "Red Lines and Faits Accomplis," 129; Harrington, *Berlin on the Brink*, 246–47, 273.

81. Quoted in Altman, "Red Lines and Faits Accomplis," 123.

82. Altman, 123; Harrington, *Berlin on the Brink*, 54.

83. Quoted in Altman, "Red Lines and Faits Accomplis," 124.

84. Altman, 129.

85. William Stivers, "The Incomplete Blockade: Soviet Zone Supply of West Berlin, 1948–49," *Diplomatic History* 21, no. 4 (Fall 1997): 569–602; Roberts, *Stalin's Wars*, 354–55.

86. Quoted in Stivers, "Incomplete Blockade," 570.

87. Stivers, 600.

88. Harrington, *Berlin on the Brink*, 3–4; Leffler, *Struggle for Germany*, 54, 60. Prior to the blockade Soviet officials concluded that an airlift would be ineffective, and many held this view well into the crisis; see Narinskii, "Soviet Union and the Berlin Crisis," 64–65, 71–72.

89. Smith to Marshall, August 3, 1948, *FRUS 1948*, vol. 2, 1006, https://history.state.gov/ historicaldocuments/frus1948v02/d595.

90. See Editorial Note, *FRUS 1949*, vol. 3, 750–51, https://history.state.gov/historicaldocu ments/frus1949v03/d377.

91. Communiqué of the Sixth Session of the Council of Foreign Ministers, June 20, 1949, *FRUS 1949*, vol. 3, 1064, https://history.state.gov/historicaldocuments/frus1949v03/d522. See also United States Delegation Minutes of the Second Part of the 20th (5th Restricted) Meeting of the Council of Foreign Ministers, June 14, 1949, *FRUS 1949*, vol. 3, esp. 1004–6, https://history.state.gov/historicaldocuments/frus1949v03/d498.

92. Narinskii, "Soviet Union and the Berlin Crisis," 67; Harrington, *Berlin on the Brink*, 7–25, 50.

93. Michael D. Gordin, *Red Cloud at Dawn: Truman, Stalin, and the End of Atomic Monopoly* (New York: Farrar, Straus and Giroux, 2009), 54–60; Vladislav M. Zubok, "Stalin and the Nuclear Age," in *Cold War Statesmen Confront the Bomb*, ed. John Lewis Gaddis, Philip Gordon, Ernest May, and Jonathan Rosenberg (Oxford: Oxford University Press), 51.

94. Quoted in Holloway, *Stalin and the Bomb*, 261.

95. Quoted in Gaddis, *We Now Know*, 93.

96. Zubok, "Stalin and the Nuclear Age," 42–43; Gordin, *Red Cloud at Dawn*, chap. 3.

97. Quoted in Gaddis, *We Now Know*, 96. See also Zubok, "Stalin and the Nuclear Age," 43–49; Holloway, *Stalin and the Bomb*, chaps. 6–10.

98. Quoted in Zubok, "Stalin and the Nuclear Age," 56.

99. Zubok, 45, 60. See also Gordin, *Red Cloud at Dawn*, 143–44.

100. Quoted in Holloway, *Stalin and the Bomb*, 127.

101. Quoted in Holloway, 237.

102. Raymond L. Garthoff, *Soviet Leaders and Intelligence: Assessing the American Adversary during the Cold War* (Washington, DC: Georgetown University Press, 2015), 5.

103. Quoted in Garthoff, 6.

104. "Telegram from Nikolai Novikov, Soviet Ambassador to the US, to the Soviet Leadership," September 27, 1946, History and Public Policy Program Digital Archive, AVP SSSR, trans. for CWIHP by Gary Goldberg, http://digitalarchive.wilsoncenter.org/document/110808. On Stalin and Molotov's influence see Holloway, *Stalin and the Bomb*, 169; John Lewis Gaddis, *The Cold War: A New History* (New York: Penguin, 2005), 29–30.

105. Mastny, "NATO in the Beholder's Eye," 14. See also Zubok, "Stalin and the Nuclear Age," 55, 58. On later plans likely being passed along see Mastny, *Cold War and Soviet Insecurity*, 109–10.

106. The Embassy of the Soviet Union to the Department of State, June 9, 1948, *FRUS 1948*, vol. 4, 887, https://history.state.gov/historicaldocuments/frus1948v04/d594.

107. Gobarev, "Soviet Military Plans," 7.

108. There is little evidence that the Soviet Union—or the Americans, for that matter—took the B-29 deployment as a serious nuclear threat. For a recent discussion see Daniel Altman, "Advancing without Attacking: The Strategic Game around the Use of Force," *Security Studies* 27, no. 1 (January–March 2018).

109. Holloway, *Stalin and the Bomb*, 242.

110. Quoted in Holloway, 231.

111. Holloway, 235–36.

112. Holloway, 153–54, 171, 238, 250–51, 271–72; Gaddis, *We Now Know*, 98–99; Zubok, "Stalin and the Nuclear Age," 54–55.

113. Quoted in Holloway, *Stalin and the Bomb*, 264.

114. Quoted in Holloway, 265.

115. Quoted in Haslam, *Russia's Cold War*, 61–62.

116. Zubok, "Stalin and the Nuclear Age," 58.

117. A third group was already present in Europe, with a squadron in Germany for training. President Truman approved the dispatch to Great Britain on June 28. Richard K. Betts, *Nuclear Blackmail and Nuclear Balance* (Washington, DC: Brookings Institution, 1987), 25; Altman, "Advancing without Attacking," 85–86.

118. Gaddis, *We Now Know*, 91.

119. Quoted in Holloway, *Stalin and the Bomb*, 171.

120. Holloway, 164, see also 156–61; Zubok, "Stalin and the Nuclear Age," 50–52.

121. Quoted in Gaddis, *We Now Know*, 95.

122. Quoted in Gaddis, 96. For a slightly different translation see Holloway, *Stalin and the Bomb*, 164. In the West, Gar Alperovitz would popularize the thesis that the United States dropped the atomic bombs on Japan to intimidate the Soviet Union, though it is unlikely this was a major component in American decision making. For a discussion see Wilson D. Miscamble, *The Most Controversial Decision: Truman, the Atomic Bombs, and the Defeat of Japan* (Cambridge: Cambridge University Press, 2011).

123. Quoted in Zubok, "Stalin and the Nuclear Age," 44–45.

124. Quoted in Gaddis, *We Now Know*, 95. See also David G. Coleman and Joseph M. Siracusa, *Real-World Nuclear Deterrence: The Making of International Strategy* (New York: Praeger, 2006), 9–10. On the general logic of such an approach see George H. Quester, "On the Identification of Real and Pretended Communist Military Doctrine," *Journal of Conflict Resolution* 10, no. 2 (June 1966).

125. Quoted in Gaddis, *We Now Know*, 96; Holloway, *Stalin and the Bomb*, 164; Zubok, "Stalin and the Nuclear Age," 50–52.

126. Gordin, *Red Cloud at Dawn*, 59–60, see also 54–60; Zubok, "Stalin and the Nuclear Age," 51; T. V. Paul, *The Tradition of Non-use of Nuclear Weapons* (Stanford, CA: Stanford University Press, 2009), 93–94; Nina Tannenwald, "Stigmatizing the Bomb: Origins of the Nuclear Taboo," *International Security* 29, no. 4 (Spring 2005): 19–20.

127. For example, Gaddis, *We Now Know*, 92.

128. For example, Zubok, "Stalin and the Nuclear Age," 60.

129. Holloway, *Stalin and the Bomb*, 272.

130. The US arsenal thus lacked most of the hallmarks of Vipin Narang's "asymmetric escalation posture," which he identifies as most likely to deter conventional attacks. Narang's framework is meant to apply to regional nuclear arsenals, though at this point in history the US arsenal resembled such an arsenal. While the US nuclear arsenal failed to prevent the Soviet blockade, I argue that it influenced the shape of Soviet policies. Vipin Narang, *Nuclear Strategy in the Modern Era: Regional Powers and International Conflict* (Princeton, NJ: Princeton University Press, 2014), esp. 19–21.

Conclusion

1. See, respectively, Todd S. Sechser and Matthew Fuhrmman, *Nuclear Weapons and Coercive Diplomacy* (Cambridge: Cambridge University Press, 2017); Vipin Narang, *Nuclear Strategy in the Modern Era: Regional Powers and International Conflict* (Princeton, NJ: Princeton University Press, 2014); T. V. Paul, *The Tradition of Non-use of Nuclear Weapons* (Stanford, CA: Stanford University Press, 2009).

2. I estimated missing values for military expenditure or military personnel by taking the average of the year before and after the missing value. In cases where one of those was missing, I used the same value as the pre- or post-data that was available. In cases where no proximate years were available the value remains missing.

3. I take the data for both military spending and total troop levels from the National Material Capabilities version 5.0 dataset at the Correlates of War, http://www.correlatesofwar.org/data-sets/national-material-capabilities.

4. Michael Beckley, "Economic Development and Military Effectiveness," *Journal of Strategic Studies* 33, no. 1 (February 2010): 43–79.

5. Beckley, 53.

6. On the changes in military production over time see Stephen G. Brooks, *Producing Security: Multinational Corporations, Globalization, and the Changing Calculus of Conflict* (Princeton, NJ: Princeton University Press, 2005). On force employment see Stephen Biddle, *Military Power: Explaining Victory and Defeat in Modern Battle* (Princeton, NJ: Princeton University Press, 2004).

7. Jan Teorell, Stefan Dahlberg, Sören Holmberg, Bo Rothstein, Felix Hartmann, and Richard Svensson, Quality of Government Standard Dataset, version Jan15 (2015), University of Gothenburg: Quality of Government Institute, http://www.qog.pol.gu.se; K. S. Gleditsch, "Expanded Trade and GDP Data," *Journal of Conflict Resolution* 46, no. 5 (2002): 712–24. The Gleditsch data have more comprehensive coverage of countries after 1950 than do alternative datasets such as the Angus Maddison project. See Maddison-Project, http://www.ggdc.net/maddison/maddison-project/home.htm, 2013 version.

8. For a discussion see John J. Mearsheimer, *The Tragedy of Great Power Politics* (2001; New York: W. W. Norton, 2014), chap. 3.

9. On the declining importance of steel see, for example, Mearsheimer, *Tragedy of Great Power Politics*, 67.

10. Stephen G. Brooks and William C. Wohlforth, "Power, Globalization, and the End of the Cold War: Reevaluating a Landmark Case for Ideas," *International Security* 25, no. 3 (Winter 2000/01): 5–53.

11. I exclude cases where both sides had nuclear weapons, because the relevant comparison for nuclear monopoly is to dyads without nuclear weapons. That allows me to isolate the effect

of nuclear monopoly compared to how one might expect the dyad to behave if neither side had nuclear weapons. I take proliferation dates from Erik Gartzke and Matthew Kroenig, *A Strategic Approach to Nuclear Proliferation* 53, no. 2 (April 2009): 151–60. I include Israel in 1967 for coding consistency in this chapter. As discussed, excluding Israel would strengthen my argument. For a discussion of the 1967 war see appendix B.

12. Meredith Reid Sarkees and Frank Wayman, *Resort to War: 1816–2007* (Washington, DC: CQ Press, 2010), 75.

13. I relax this requirement in appendix A. The results for median capability ratios are largely unchanged.

14. COW reports that Saudi Arabia entered the war on October 14 after the Syrian front had stabilized. Iraq and Jordan entered the war on October 12 and 16, respectively. All three exited the war on October 19. The main part of the war involving Egypt and Syria versus Israel began on October 6, with an end date of October 24 for Egypt and October 22 for Syria.

15. See appendix A.

16. Quote from http://cow.dss.ucdavis.edu/data-sets/MIDs. As in the introduction, I exclude ongoing disputes, disputes during wars, and disputes between two nonnuclear weapon states that also involve a nuclear state (e.g., Cuba versus US in the Cuban Missile Crisis). Appendix A shows the results are robust to alternative coding. Glenn Palmer, Vito D'Orazio, Michael Kenwick, and Matthew Lane, "The MID4 Data Set: Procedures, Coding Rules, and Description," *Conflict Management and Peace Science* 32, no. 2 (2015): 222–42; and Zeev Maoz, Paul L. Johnson, Jasper Kaplan, Fiona Ogunkoya, and Aaron Shreve, "The Dyadic Militarized Interstate Disputes (MIDs) Dataset Version 3.0: Logic, Characteristics, and Comparisons to Alternative Datasets," *Journal of Conflict Resolution* 63, no. 3 (2019):811–35.

17. John J. Mearsheimer, "Assessing the Conventional Balance: The 3:1 Rule and Its Critics," *International Security* 13, no. 4 (Spring 1989): 54–89. For extensions see Michael C. Desch, *When the Third World Matters: Latin America and the United States Grand Strategy* (Baltimore: Johns Hopkins University Press, 1993), 198n98; and Sebastian Rosato, *Europe United: Power Politics and the Making of the European Community* (Ithaca, NY: Cornell University Press, 2011), 26–27, 231–40.

18. The percentage of unbalanced wars between nonnuclear weapon states is 1.2 times greater than the percentage of balanced wars (10.8 percent / 9 percent). In nuclear monopoly, the percentage of wars with the NWS having a large advantage is 1.14 times greater than when it does not (4.7 percent to 4.1 percent).

19. I am deliberately selecting on the dependent variable in this section. I do not consider political disputes in nuclear monopoly that did not escalate to war, nor do I compare wars in nuclear monopoly to wars involving only nonnuclear weapon states. This limits the inferences I am able to draw. I seek only to establish that in those wars that we do observe there is limited danger to the nuclear weapon state. At the same time, we know that there are wars of conquest between states that do not possess nuclear weapons, which can provide a useful background condition with which to view these results. On this point see Stephen Van Evera, *Guide to Methods for Students of Political Science* (Ithaca, NY: Cornell University Press, 1997), 46–47, 58–61.

20. See appendix B for a discussion of Egyptian planning regarding Israel's Dimona reactor in 1967.

21. Various British governments had considered ceding control of the islands, and they were not considered part of the core British homeland. See appendix B.

22. Toshi Yoshihara and James R. Holmes, introduction to *Strategy in the Second Nuclear Age: Power, Ambition, and the Ultimate Weapon*, ed. Toshi Yoshihara and James R. Holmes (Washington, DC: Georgetown University Press, 2012), 5; Colin S. Gray, *The Second Nuclear Age* (Boulder, CO: Lynne Rienner, 1999), 5–7; Gregory D. Koblentz, "Strategic Stability in the Second Nuclear Age," *Council on Foreign Relations*, Special Report no. 71 (November 2014), esp. 3–5; Paul Bracken, *The Second Nuclear Age: Strategy, Danger, and the New Power Politics* (New York: St. Martin's Griffin, 2012), 1–11, 106–26; Keith B. Payne, *Deterrence in the Second Nuclear Age* (Lexington: University Press of Kentucky, 1996).

23. Francis J. Gavin, *Nuclear Statecraft: History and Strategy in America's Atomic Age* (Ithaca, NY: Cornell University Press, 2012). Bracken highlights that the "second nuclear age" was

developing during the Cold War and the two eras overlapped, but concludes that "1998 was the turning point. The events in India, Pakistan, Iran, and North Korea were impossible to ignore and crystallized a new way of seeing the world." Bracken, *Second Nuclear Age*, 95–106, quote at 105–6.

24. See, for example, Narang, *Nuclear Strategy in the Modern Era*; Avery Goldstein, *Deterrence and Security in the 21st Century* (Stanford, CA: Stanford University Press, 2000); Nicholas L. Miller, "The Secret Success of Nonproliferation Sanctions," *International Organization* 68, no. 4 (Fall 2014): 913–44; Francis J. Gavin, "Strategies of Inhibition: U.S. Grand Strategy, the Nuclear Revolution, and Nonproliferation," *International Security* 40, no. 1 (Summer 2015): 9–46; Gene Gerzhoy, "Alliance Coercion and Nuclear Restraint: How the United States Thwarted West Germany's Nuclear Ambition," *International Security* 39, no. 4 (Spring 2015): 91–129; Rachel Elizabeth Whitlark, "Nuclear Beliefs: A Leader-Focused Theory of Counter-Proliferation," *Security Studies* 26, no. 4 (2017): 545–74; Alexander Lanoszka, *Atomic Assurance: The Alliance Politics of Nuclear Proliferation* (Ithaca, NY: Cornell University Press, 2018).

25. For a review see Keir A. Lieber and Daryl G. Press, "The Limits of the Nuclear Revolution," unpublished manuscript, chap. 3.

26. Kenneth N. Waltz, "Nuclear Myths and Political Realities," *American Political Science Review* 84, no. 3 (September 1990): 734; Kenneth N. Waltz, "More May Be Better," in *The Spread of Nuclear Weapons: An Enduring Debate*, by Scott D. Sagan and Kenneth N. Waltz (New York: W. W. Norton, 2013), 9.

27. I do this as well when I focus on whether or not war occurred.

28. Quoted in Sechser and Fuhrmann, *Nuclear Weapons and Coercive Diplomacy*, 8.

29. Michael Oren, "Iran's Nuclear Designs Are the Greater Middle East Threat," *Washington Post*, May 24, 2013, https://www.washingtonpost.com/opinions/irans-nuclear-designs-are-the-greater-middle-east-threat/2013/05/24/8fe22228-c490-11e2-914f-a7aba60512a7.

30. Chris Hedges, "Iran May Be Able to Build an Atomic Bomb in 5 Years, U.S. and Israeli Officials Fear," *New York Times*, January 5, 1995, http://www.nytimes.com/1995/01/05/world/iran-may-be-able-build-atomic-bomb-5-years-us-israeli-officials-fear.html?page wanted=all.

31. For a similar point see Sechser and Fuhrmann, *Nuclear Weapons and Coercive Diplomacy*, 5.

32. The nuclear armed state may *try* to leverage its arsenal in this way, but it will likely have limited success.

33. That may also explain why they ignored American warnings regarding Kuwaiti oil wells.

34. Thomas M. Nichols, *No Use: Nuclear Weapons and U.S. National Security* (Philadelphia: University of Pennsylvania Press, 2014), chap. 1; Gavin, *Nuclear Statecraft*, chap. 2; John Lewis Gaddis, *Strategies of Containment: A Critical Appraisal of American National Security Policy during the Cold War* (1982; Oxford: Oxford University Press, 2005), esp. chaps. 5–8; David G. Coleman and Joseph M. Siracusa, *Real-World Nuclear Deterrence: The Making of International Strategy* (Westport, CT: Praeger Security International, 2006), 55–57.

35. Rupal N. Mehta and Rachel Elizabeth Whitlark, "The Benefits and Burdens of Nuclear Latency," *International Studies Quarterly* 61, no. 3 (September 2017): 517–28.

Appendix A

1. All data and replication commands are available at www.paulavey.com.

2. The following dyads remained in these wars: North Korea versus South Korea 1950; China versus South Korea 1950; North Vietnam versus South Vietnam 1965. The updated May 2018 Correlates of War MID and War coding identifies a militarized dispute but not an interstate war between Iraq and Kuwait in 1990. The alternative Reiter, Stam, Horowitz war dataset also does not code the 1990 Iraqi invasion, but does code those two states at war in 1991. I include that dyad as a result.

3. Dan Reiter, Allan C. Stam, and Michael C. Horowitz, "A Revised Look at Interstate Wars, 1816–2007," *Journal of Conflict Resolution* 60, no. 5 (2016): 956–76.

4. Zeev Maoz, Paul L. Johnson, Jasper Kaplan, Fiona Ogunkoya, and Aaron Shreve, "The Dyadic Militarized Interstate Disputes (MIDs) Dataset Version 3.0: Logic, Characteristics, and Comparisons to Alternative Datasets," *Journal of Conflict Resolution* 63, no. 3 (2019): 822–23.

Appendix B

1. Tony Judt, *Postwar: A History of Europe since 1945* (New York: Penguin, 2005), 294–97.

2. Richard K. Betts, *Nuclear Blackmail and Nuclear Balance* (Washington, DC: Brookings Institution Press), 62–65; Todd S. Sechser and Matthew Fuhrmann, *Nuclear Weapons and Coercive Diplomacy* (Cambridge: Cambridge University Press, 2017), 225–26.

3. Mark S. Bell, "Beyond Emboldenment: How Acquiring Nuclear Weapons Can Change Foreign Policy," *International Security* 40, no. 1 (Summer 2015): 101–2, 114–15; Judt, *Postwar*, 296–97.

4. The discussion in this paragraph and the next draws from Kenneth M. Pollack, *Arabs at War: Military Effectiveness, 1948–1991* (Lincoln: University of Nebraska Press, 2002), 27–47.

5. Pollack, 36.

6. Pollack, 38.

7. Pollack, 38.

8. Pollack, 39. Egyptian losses against the British-French-Israeli forces are estimated at one thousand killed, four thousand wounded, and six thousand captured. The Correlates of War (May 2018) estimate twenty-two British battlefield deaths. See conclusion chapter.

9. This paragraph draws on Jonathan Haslam, *Russia's Cold War: From the October Revolution to the Fall of the Wall* (New Haven, CT: Yale University Press, 2011), 168–73; Vladislav Zubok, *A Failed Empire: The Soviet Union in the Cold War from Stalin to Gorbachev* (2007; Chapel Hill: University of North Carolina Press, 2009), 115–19; and Charles Phillips and Alan Axelrod, eds., *Encyclopedia of Wars*, vol. 2 (New York: Facts on File, 2004), 580–81.

10. Quoted in Haslam, *Russia's Cold War*, 172.

11. This reversed an October 30 decision not to intervene. See Zubok, *Failed Empire*, 115–17.

12. On concern with the United States see Haslam, *Russia's Cold War*, 171; Zubok, *Failed Empire*, 117.

13. Phillips and Axelrod, *Encyclopedia of Wars*, 2:581; Meredith Reid Sarkees and Frank Whelon Wayman, *Resort to War: 1816–2007* (Washington, DC: CQ Press, 2010), 106–7.

14. Michael Clodfelter, *Warfare and Armed Conflicts: A Statistical Encyclopedia of Casualty and Other Figures, 1494–2007*, 3rd ed. (Jefferson, NC: McFarland, 2008), 576.

15. The 720 number matches the number of killed (669) and missing in action (51) provided by Clodfelter and Phillips and Axelrod. See Sarkees and Wayman, *Resort to War*, 105; Clodfelter, *Warfare and Armed Conflicts*, 577; and Phillips and Axelrod, *Encyclopedia of Wars*, 2:580.

16. Fredrik Logevall, *Embers of War* (New York: Random House, 2013), 3–4.

17. Logevall, chaps. 5–21; and John M. Schuessler, *Deceit on the Road to War: Presidents, Politics, and American Democracy* (Ithaca, NY: Cornell University Press, 2015), 60–63.

18. On these points see Logevall, *Embers of War*; and Schuessler, *Deceit on the Road to War*, chap. 3; Clodfelter, *Warfare and Armed Conflicts*, 712–17.

19. Schuessler, *Deceit on the Road to War*, 82; Clodfelter, *Warfare and Armed Conflicts*, 715.

20. On Vietnamese victories over South Vietnamese forces see Caitlin Talmadge, *The Dictator's Army: Battlefield Effectiveness in Authoritarian Regimes* (Ithaca, NY: Cornell University Press, 2016), chap. 3. For discussions of US engagements see Jasen Castillo, *Endurance and War: The National Sources of Military Cohesion* (Stanford, CA: Stanford University Press, 2014), 187, 194–202, 207–9; Clodfelter, *Warfare and Armed Conflicts*, 716–38.

21. Robert A. Pape, *Bombing to Win: Air Power and Coercion in War* (Ithaca, NY: Cornell University Press, 1996), chap. 6.

22. Castillo, *Endurance and War*, 202–12.

23. Clodfelter, *Warfare and Armed Conflicts*, 761–62. Using different start and end dates, Sarkees and Wayman, *Resort to War*, 111, report 58,153 US battlefield deaths.

24. Avner Cohen, *Israel and the Bomb* (New York: Columbia University Press, 1998), 232; Vipin Narang, *Nuclear Strategy in the Modern Era: Regional Powers and International Conflict* (Princeton, NJ: Princeton University Press, 2014), 283.

25. Cohen, *Israel and the Bomb*, 274.

26. Narang, *Nuclear Strategy in the Modern Era*, 286.

27. Including the case in fact biases the results against my argument, because aggregate capability indicators discussed in the conclusion chapter code Israel's Arab opponents as having significant capabilities relative to Israel.

28. Pollack, *Arabs at War*, 58.

29. Zeev Maoz, *Defending the Holy Land: A Critical Analysis of Israel's Security and Foreign Policy* (Ann Arbor: University of Michigan Press, 2006), 80–81; Mearsheimer, *Conventional Deterrence* (Ithaca, NY: Cornell University Press, 1983), 143–44; Roland Popp, "Stumbling Decidedly into the Six Day War," *Journal of Cold War Studies* 62, no. 2 (Spring 2006): 285.

30. Avner Cohen, "Cairo, Dimona, and the June 1967 War," *Middle East Journal* 50, no. 2 (Spring 1996): 191 203–6; Narang, *Nuclear Strategy in the Modern Era*, 285–86.

31. Pollack, *Arabs at War*, 58–62. For general reviews that Nasser did not seek to provoke war but took a series of escalatory steps see Ben D. Mor, "Nasser's Decision-Making in the 1967 Middle East Crisis: A Rational-Choice Explanation," *Journal of Peace Research* 28, no. 4 (November 1991): 359–75; Popp, "Stumbling Decidedly," 293–98; Cohen, "Cairo, Dimona, and the June 1967 War," 200; and Richard B. Parker, *The Politics of Miscalculation in the Middle East* (Bloomington: Indiana University Press, 1993), 43, 49, 89–96.

32. George W. Gawrych, *The Albatross of Decisive Victory: War and Policy between Egypt and Israel in the 1967 and 1973 Arab-Israeli Wars* (Westport, CT: Greenwood, 2000), 12–13; Pollack, *Arabs at War*, 58; Risa Brooks, "An Autocracy at War: Explaining Egypt's Military Effectiveness, 1967 and 1973," *Security Studies* 15, no. 3 (July–September 2006): 412, 416.

33. Quoted in Popp, "Stumbling Decidedly," 304. The full conversation is available at Memorandum of Conversation, May 26, 1967, *FRUS 1964–1968*, vol. 19, https://history.state.gov/historicaldocuments/frus1964-68v19/d77.

34. On these points see Cohen, *Israel and the Bomb*, 263–65; Stephen M. Walt, *The Origins of Alliances* (Ithaca, NY: Cornell University Press, 1987), 96–98; Gawrych, *Albatross of Decisive Victory*, 5–6; Narang, *Nuclear Strategy in the Modern Era*, 285.

35. Thant-Nasser UN Memcom, May 24, 1967, in Parker, *Politics of Miscalculation*, 231. See also Anderson to Rusk and Johnson, June 2, 1967, at 236.

36. Pollack, *Arabs at War*, 293–95.

37. Pollack, 295.

38. Pollack, 459–63.

39. On these points see Cohen, *Israel and the Bomb*, 260–66; Narang, *Nuclear Strategy in the Modern Era*, 285; Maoz, *Defending the Holy Land*, 626n16.

40. Maoz, *Defending the Holy Land*, 80–81; Narang, *Nuclear Strategy in the Modern Age*, 284; Cohen, "Cairo, Dimona, and the June 1967 War," 202–5.

41. Maoz, *Defending the Holy Land*, 81.

42. Mearsheimer, *Conventional Deterrence*, 150.

43. For the argument that Israel was aware of its conventional superiority and the crisis created an opportunity for Israel to eliminate potential threats see Popp, "Stumbling Decidedly," 299–308; and Mearsheimer, *Conventional Deterrence*, 150–53.

44. Pollack, *Arabs at War*, 62–63.

45. Pollack, 64–84.

46. Pollack, 297–99.

47. Pollack, 313–15.

48. Pollack, 463–75.

49. M. Taylor Fravel, *Strong Borders, Secure Nation: Cooperation and Conflict in China's Territorial Disputes* (Princeton, NJ: Princeton University Press, 2008): 63; Andrew Scobell, *China's Use of Military Force: Beyond the Great Wall and the Long March* (Cambridge: Cambridge University Press, 2003), 120–25, 135–37; Xiaobing Li, *A History of the Modern Chinese Army* (Lexington: University Press of Kentucky, 2007), 251–53; Henry J. Kenny, *Shadow of the Dragon: Vietnam's*

Continuing Struggle with China and Its Implications for US Foreign Policy (Washington, DC: Brassey's, 2002), 53, 98–100.

50. Xiaoming Zhang, *Deng Xiaoping's Long War: The Military Conflict between China and Vietnam, 1979–1991* (Chapel Hill: University of North Carolina Press, 2015), 94, 99, 108–9; Li, *History of the Chinese Army*, 254.

51. Charles Phillips and Alan Axelrod, eds., *Encyclopedia of Wars*, vol. 3 (New York: Facts on File, 2004), 1061; Li, *History of the Modern Chinese Army*, 255; Zhang, *Deng Xiaoping's Long War*, 100–101.

52. Zhang, *Deng Xiaoping's Long War*, 113n132. Phillips and Axelrod report that Vietnamese forces staged a "counteroffensive into Chinese territory" to which "Chinese defensive forces responded quickly and drove this incursion back, but there was widespread shock over the temerity of the invasion." Phillips and Axelrod, *Encyclopedia of Wars*, 3:1061. It is unclear if Phillips and Axelrod are referring to the 3rd Battalion, 460th Regiment, attack. In any event, Vietnam does not appear to have "invaded" China but rather conducted a limited assault directly across the border with a small force on one occasion to disrupt the Chinese advance.

53. Zhang, *Deng Xiaoping's Long War*, 103–4.

54. Zhang, 95, 104–5.

55. Zhang, 104–6.

56. Zhang, 108, 107; Li, *History of the Modern Chinese Army*, 255.

57. Quoted in Zhang, *Deng Xiaoping's Long War*, 112.

58. As Zhang notes, Beijing "granted operational autonomy to regional commanders but kept the duration and space of the fight under the command of the central leadership in Beijing. Deng Xiaoping was determined to avoid having the invasion turn into a quagmire for China." Zhang, *Deng Xiaoping's Long War*, 71. See also Scobell's account, which highlights concerns that a larger war could lead to escalation with the Soviet Union as well. Scobell, *China's Use of Military Force*, esp. 125–29.

59. Quoted in Zhang, *Deng Xiaoping's Long War*, 113.

60. Zhang, 114–15.

61. Quoted in Zhang, 112. Xu primarily commanded forces in the eastern part of the fighting next to Guangxi; Scobell, *China's Use of Military Force*, 132, 127.

62. Sarkees and Wayman, *Resort to War*. The May 2018 COW dataset reverses the figures to report eight thousand Chinese and thirteen thousand Vietnamese battlefield deaths. This change would strengthen my argument.

63. Clodfelter, *Warfare and Armed Conflicts*, 3rd ed., 669; Li, *History of the Modern Chinese Army*, 258.

64. Zhang, *Deng Xiaoping's Long War*, 142–48; Fravel, *Strong Borders, Secure Nation*, 217.

65. Zhang, *Deng Xiaoping's Long War*, 149–62; Li, *History of the Modern Chinese Army*, 259–60, 263.

66. Zhang, *Deng Xiaoping's Long War*, 164.

67. Zhang, 159–61.

68. Zhang, 162; Fravel, *Strong Borders, Secure Nation*, 217–18; Li, *History of the Modern Chinese Army*, 260.

69. Sarkees and Wayman, *Resort to War*, 141–42. The May 2018 COW dataset has the same start and end dates but reports twenty-two hundred Chinese battlefield deaths with one thousand for Vietnam.

70. Li, *History of the Modern Chinese Army*, 263.

71. The Correlates of War lists 255 British battlefield deaths, with nearly three times as many Argentine battlefield deaths at 746.

72. T. V. Paul, *Asymmetric Conflicts: War Initiation by Weaker Powers* (Cambridge: Cambridge University Press, 1994), 147; Richard C. Thornton, *The Falklands Sting: Reagan, Thatcher, and Argentina's Bomb* (Washington, DC: Brassey's, 1998), 11.

73. Amy Oakes, "Diversionary War and Argentina's Invasion of the Falkland Islands," *Security Studies* 15, no. 3 (July–September 2006): 449, see also 441; Paul, *Asymmetric Conflicts*, 159–65.

74. The case is sometimes cited as evidence that the nuclear nonuse norm is sufficient to explain nonnuclear weapon state belligerency or that nuclear weapons cast little to no shadow

in international politics. For example, see Robert Farley, "The Long Shadow of the Falklands War," *National Interest*, September 8, 2014, http://nationalinterest.org/feature/the-long-shadow-the-falklands-war-11224?page=show; T. V. Paul, *The Tradition of Non-use of Nuclear Weapons* (Stanford, CA: Stanford University Press, 2009), chap. 7; Ward Wilson, "Doubts about Nuclear Deterrence, Part III: Yom Kippur and Falkland Islands," *Arms Control Wonk*, February 6, 2013, https://www.armscontrolwonk.com/archive/206263/ward-wilson-wednesdays-part-3/. My argument, by contrast, is that this is a case where one expects a limited nuclear shadow because of the conventional imbalance and conduct of the war but that one should not generalize beyond similar cases. The benefits of nuclear use for the NWS being low, the NNWS will have greater confidence that any costs associated with nuclear use will be sufficient to constrain the opponent. In other words, a limited nuclear shadow here does not imply a limited nuclear shadow when the NNWS is more conventionally capable or creates larger dangers to the NWS.

75. Oakes, "Diversionary War," 456. See also Thornton, *Falklands Sting*, 106, 113; and Ruben O. Moro, *The History of the South Atlantic Conflict: The War for the Malvinas* (New York: Praeger, 1989), 2–3.

76. Quoted in Oakes, "Diversionary War," 456.

77. Paul, *Asymmetric Conflicts*, 151, also 151–57.

78. Oakes, "Diversionary War," 456n83.

79. Quoted in Paul, *Asymmetric Conflicts*, 152. See also Thornton, *Falklands Sting*, 84–85.

80. Thornton, *Falklands Sting*, 105–6; D. George Boyce, *The Falklands War* (New York: Palgrave Macmillan, 2005), 35.

81. Thornton, *Falklands Sting*, 106. See also Paul, *Asymmetric Conflicts*, 153.

82. Quoted in Paul, *Asymmetric Conflicts*, 158. See also Thornton, *Falklands Sting*, xx, 67–70, 81, 90–91, 122; Boyce, *Falklands War*, 27, 54.

83. Paul, *Asymmetric Conflicts*, 157–59, quote at 157.

84. Bruce W. Watson and Peter M. Dunn, eds., *Military Lessons of the Falkland Islands War: Views from the United States* (Boulder, CO: Westview, 1984), 138; Thornton, *Falklands Sting*, 69; Boyce, *Falklands War*, 39–40.

85. Paul, *Asymmetric Conflicts*, 153.

86. Paul, 146–47.

87. Memorandum for Mr. William P. Clark, National Security Council Meeting Agenda Item—the Falkland Islands Dispute, April 28, 1982, in Jason Saltoun-Ebin and Andrea Chiampan, "The Reagan Files: The Falklands Crisis," August 5, 2011, http://www.thereaganfiles.com/820428-state-paper-for-nsc.pdf. Note too Secretary Haig's comments at the subsequent NSC meeting on April 30: "unless Argentina softens on sovereignty, the British will go ahead and do some damage." Earlier that month, the Joint Chiefs of Staff had highlighted British superiority in naval capabilities but, owing to geographic proximity, Argentine advantages in air capabilities. The Joint Chiefs noted that should Britain dispatch additional nuclear attack submarines it could seek to "engage the Argentine Navy to gain control of the seas off the Argentine coast." Haig comment: Minutes of a National Security Council Meeting, April 30, 1982, *FRUS 1981–1988*, vol. 13, https://history.state.gov/historicaldocuments/frus1981-88v13/d195; Joint Chiefs comment: Background paper for the Chairman, Joint Chiefs of Staff, circa April 15, 1982, https://nsarchive2.gwu.edu/NSAEBB/NSAEBB374/.

88. Thornton, *Falklands Sting*, 184–85. A third Mirage was lost to friendly fire as it returned to base.

89. Thornton, *Falklands Sting*, 171, 186.

90. The official British history reports 321 Argentine deaths. Writing from an Argentine perspective, Ruben Moro lists "368 seamen who went down with the *General Belgrano*." See Lawrence Freedman, *The Official History of the Falklands Campaign*, vol. 2, *War and Diplomacy* (London: Routledge, 2005), 293; Moro, *History of the South Atlantic Conflict*, 141.

91. William J. Ruhe, "Submarine Lessons," in Watson and Dunn, *Military Lessons*, 9; Norman Friedman, "Surface Combatant Lessons," in Watson and Dunn, *Military Lessons*, 21–24.

92. The *Sheffield* would sink on May 10 while being towed outside the combat zone. Boyce, *Falklands War*, 110; Thornton, *Falklands Sting*, 207–8.

93. Dates reflect the day of the main strikes, not necessarily the day the vessel sank. All dates taken from Lawrence S. Germain, appendix, in Watson and Dunn, *Military Lessons*, 150–67.

94. Boyce, *Falklands War*, 92.

95. Thornton, *Falklands Sting*, 233.

96. Quoted in Thornton, 233.

97. Germain, appendix, in Watson and Dunn, *Military Lessons*, 166–67. The International Institute for Strategic Studies reports that Argentina had 240 air force and naval combat aircraft in 1982 and only 125 in 1983. See IISS, *The Military Balance* (London, 1982), 92–93; IISS, *Military Balance* (London, 1983), 99–100.

98. Germain, appendix, in Watson and Dunn, *Military Lessons*, 166. The British lost additional aircraft to accidents.

99. Thornton, *Falklands Sting*, 223; Boyce, *Falklands War*, 120; Germain, appendix, in Watson and Dunn, *Military Lessons*, 147–48, 153–54, 156.

100. For general overviews of the ground campaign see Boyce, *Falklands War*, chaps. 6–7; Freedman, *Official History of the Falklands Campaign*, 2: chaps. 37–42.

101. Freedman, *Official History of the Falklands Campaign*, 2:652. See also Germain, appendix, in Watson and Dunn, *Military Lessons*, 163–64.

102. Paul, *Asymmetric Conflicts*, 152.

103. Moro, *History of the South Atlantic Conflict*, 331.

104. Both quotes in Sechser and Furhmann, *Nuclear Weapons and Coercive Diplomacy*, 168–69.

105. Freedman, *Official History of the Falklands Campaign*, 2:57–61.

106. Paul, *Asymmetric Conflicts*, 152.

107. On the INF debate and renewed antinuclear movements see, for example, Leopoldo Nuti, Frederic Bozo, Marie-Pierre Rey, and Bernd Rother, eds., *The Euromissile Crisis and the End of the Cold War* (Washington, DC: Woodrow Wilson Center, 2015).

108. Quoted in Sechser and Furhmann, *Nuclear Weapons and Coercive Diplomacy*, 169.

109. Minutes of Meeting Held at 10 Downing Street, Defense and Oversea Policy Committee, April 16, 1982, United Kingdom National Archives, CAB 148/211, 33. This meeting is discussed in Sechser and Furhmann, *Nuclear Weapons and Coercive Diplomacy*, 168. Despite Thatcher's statement, there is evidence that the British government did explore possible action against the mainland; see Hannah Kuchler, "Britain Considered Bombing Argentina," *Financial Times*, December 27, 2012, https://www.ft.com/content/fdd00d54-4dcb-11e2-a0fc-00144feab49a.

110. Thornton, *Falklands Sting*, 20, also 81–82, 90, 229.

111. Philip Bleek codes Argentina as exploring a nuclear device from 1978 to 1990: "political authorization to explore (but not pursue) a nuclear weapons option or formal linking of atomic research to defense agencies . . . [or] engaged in proliferation-relevant activity but not with sufficient intensity to merit coding pursuit." See Philip C. Bleek, "Why Do States Proliferate? Quantitative Analysis of the Exploration, Pursuit, and Acquisition of Nuclear Weapons," in *Forecasting Nuclear Proliferation in the 21st Century: The Role of Theory*, vol. 1, ed. William C. Potter and Gaukhar Mukhatzhanova (Stanford, CA: Stanford University Press, 2010), 168–69. On the Argentine nuclear program and role of Brazil see T. V. Paul, *Power versus Prudence: Why Nations Forgo Nuclear Weapons* (Montreal: McGill–Queen's University Press, 2000), esp. 104–5.

112. Warning Meeting—Nuclear Proliferation, Central Intelligence Agency, April 27, 1982, https://www.cia.gov/library/readingroom/docs/CIA-RDP83B01027R000300040028-4.pdf.

113. Argentina's Nuclear Policies in Light of the Falklands Defeat, SNIE 91-2-82, September 8, 1982, Central Intelligence Agency, Digital National Security Archive, U.S. Intelligence on Weapons of Mass Destruction: From World War II to Iraq, item no. WM00268.

114. Julio C. Carasales, "The So-Called Proliferator That Wasn't: The Story of Argentina's Nuclear Policy," *Nonproliferation Review* 6, no. 4 (Fall 1999): 62. See also Paul, *Power versus Prudence*, 105.

115. Paul, *Asymmetric Conflicts*, 148–50; Oakes "Diversionary War," 444, 456n83.

116. Pollack, *Arabs at War*, 514–23.

117. Zeev Maoz, *Defending the Holy Land: A Critical Analysis of Israel's Security and Foreign Policy* (Ann Arbor: University of Michigan Press, 2006), 176.

118. Pollack, *Arabs at War*, 526.

119. Maoz, *Defending the Holy Land*, 189; Clodfelter, *Warfare and Armed Conflicts*, 629.

120. The May 2018 Correlates of War data report the start date of the Israeli-Syrian portion of the war as June 6, 1982, and the termination as June 10, 1982. Sarkees and Wayman, *Resort to War*, date the conflict as April 21 to September 15, 1982. On May 2000 see Maoz, *Defending the Holy Land*, 171.

121. On the internal Israeli political dynamics see Maoz, *Defending the Holy Land*, 174–206, and Pollack, *Arabs at War*, 524–29.

122. Pollack, *Arabs at War*, 531, also 529–31.

123. Pollack, 532–39; Clodfelter, *Warfare and Armed Conflicts*, 630.

124. Syrian combat forces continued to operate in Lebanon until 1990, mostly against Lebanese militias but also occasionally against Israeli forces. See Pollack, *Arabs at War*, 548.

125. Pollack, 540. Clodfelter reports Syrian losses from June 6 to September 3 as 1,350 killed, 4,800 wounded, and 450 tanks. Clodfelter, *Warfare and Armed Conflicts*, 630.

126. Clodfelter, *Warfare and Armed Conflicts*, 603; Peter Polack, *The Last Hot Battle of the Cold War: South Africa vs. Cuba in the Angolan Civil War* (Philadelphia: Casemate, 2013), 17.

127. Peter Liberman, "The Rise and Fall of the South African Bomb," *International Security* 26, no. 2 (Fall 2001): 60.

128. Edward George, *The Cuban Intervention in Angola, 1965–1991: From Che Guevara to Cuito Cuanavale* (London: Frank Cass, 2005): 202–3, 243–46, 249, 254–55; Clodfelter, *Warfare and Armed Conflicts*, 604; Polack, *Last Hot Battle*, 184. COW May 2018 Directed Dyad List of Wars.

129. Quoted in Narang, *Nuclear Strategy in the Modern Era*, 217–18.

130. Narang, 218.

131. George, *Cuban Intervention in Angola*, 206–8.

132. George A. Crocker, *High Noon in Southern Africa: Making Peace in a Rough Neighborhood* (New York: W. W. Norton, 1992), 360. See also the accounts in George, *Cuban Intervention in Angola*, 202–10; Stephen L. Weigert, *Angola: A Modern Military History* (New York: Palgrave Macmillan, 2011): 86–89; and Polack, *Last Hot Battle*.

133. George, *Cuban Intervention in Angola*, 210–2; Polack, *Last Hot Battle*, 135–36; Weigert, *Angola*, 88.

134. George, *Cuban Intervention in Angola*, chap. 10.

135. George, chap. 11; Weigert, *Angola*, 89–91.

136. Liberman, "Rise and Fall of the South African Bomb," 60.

137. Weigert, *Angola*, 89–90.

138. Quoted in Liberman, "Rise and Fall of the South African Bomb," 59.

139. Waldo Stumpf, "South Africa's Nuclear Weapons Program: From Deterrence to Dismantlement," *Arms Control Today* 26, no. 10 (December 1995 / January 1996): 5.

140. Quoted in Liberman, "Rise and Fall of the South African Bomb," 56.

141. Liberman, 57–58. Most sources date the test in 1987, although it is unclear if this was prior to the August South African decision to launch Operation Moduler in response to the Angolan offensive. Other sources date the activity to June–October 1988 or 1986. See Liberman, 58n43; Narang, *Nuclear Strategy in the Modern Era*, 213; David Albright, "South Africa and the Affordable Bomb," *Bulletin of the Atomic Scientists* 50, no. 4 (July/August 1994): 45; Stumpf, "South Africa's Nuclear Weapons Program," 6.

142. Quoted in Liberman, "Rise and Fall of the South African Bomb," 60.

143. Quoted in Narang, *Nuclear Strategy in the Modern Era*, 213.

144. Clodfelter, *Warfare and Armed Conflict*, 582.

145. Phil Haun, *Coercion, Survival, and War: Why Weak States Resist the United States* (Stanford, CA: Stanford University Press, 2015), 115.

146. Haun, 116–17.

147. Haun, 125–32.

148. Andrew L. Stigler, "A Clear Victory for Air Power: NATO's Empty Threat to Invade Kosovo," *International Security* 27, no. 3 (Winter 2002/03): 124–57; Daniel R. Lake, "The Limits

of Coercive Airpower: NATO's 'Victory' in Kosovo Revisited," *International Security* 34, no. 1 (Summer 2009): 83–112; Haun, *Coercion, Survival, and War*, 130–31.

149. Sarkees and Wayman, *Resort to War*. Serbia reported 642 soldiers and 114 police killed from NATO action. See Clodfelter, *Warfare and Armed Conflict*, 583.

150. Haun, *Coercion, Survival, and War*, 126.

151. Haun, 204–5.

152. Sarkees and Wayman, *Resort to War*, 155–56. Reiter, Stam, and Horowitz also code October 7 and December 22 as the start and end date for the international phase of the conflict. The May 2018 updated COW data alter the dates to September 15 and November 15, 2001. It is unclear why this change was made.

153. Stephen D. Biddle, "Allies, Airpower, and Modern Warfare: The Afghan Model in Afghanistan and Iraq," *International Security* 30, no. 3 (Winter 2005/6): 161–76.

154. Haun, *Coercion, Survival, and War*, 35.

155. Clodfelter, *Warfare and Armed Conflicts*, 767. COW estimates four thousand Afghani battlefield deaths.

Index

Note: Page numbers in italics indicate figures; those with a *t* indicate tables.

CPSIA information can be obtained
at www.ICGtesting.com
Printed in the USA
BVHW031941270919
559649BV00002B/24/P